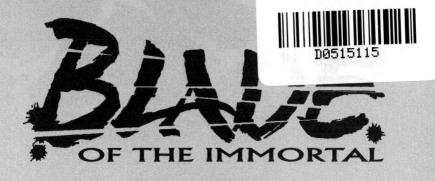

OF THE IMMORTAL

Dreamsong

publisher
Mike Richardson

series editors
Dave Chipps
& Rachel Penn

collection editor
Chris Warner

collection designers
Harald Graham
& Amy Arendts

**English version produced by Studio Proteus
for Dark Horse Comics, Inc.**

This book collects issues twelve through eighteen
of the Dark Horse comic-book series,
Blade of the Immortal.

Published by
Dark Horse Comics, Inc.
10956 SE Main Street
Milwaukie, OR 97222

First edition: February 1999
ISBN: 1-56971-357-X

3 5 7 9 10 8 6 4 2

Printed in Canada

BLADE
OF THE IMMORTAL

art and story
HIROAKI SAMURA

translation
Dana Lewis & Toren Smith

lettering and retouch
Tomoko Saito

Dreamsong

DARK HORSE COMICS®

ABOUT THE TRANSLATION

The Swastika

The main character in *Blade of the Immortal*, Manji, has taken the "crux gammata" as both his name and his personal symbol. This symbol is also known as the *swastika*, a name derived from the Sanskrit *svastika* (meaning "welfare," from su — "well" + asti "he is"). As a symbol of prosperity and good fortune, the swastika was widely used throughout the ancient world (for example, appearing often on Mesopotamian coinage), including North and South America and has been used in Japan as a symbol of Buddhism since ancient times. To be precise, the symbol generally used by Japanese Buddhists is the *sauvastika*, which moves in a counterclockwise direction, and is called the *manji* in Japanese. The arms of the swastika, which point in a clockwise direction, are generally considered a solar symbol. It was this version (the *hakenkreuz*) that was perverted by the Nazis. The *sauvastika* generally stands for night and often for magical practices. It is important that readers understand that the *swastika* has ancient and honorable origins, and it is those that apply to this story, which takes place in the 18th century [ca. 1782-3]. *There is no anti-Semitic or pro-Nazi meaning behind the use of the symbol in this story. Those meanings did not exist until after 1910.*

The Artwork

The creator of *Blade of the Immortal* requested that we make an effort to avoid mirror-imaging his artwork. Normally, all of our manga are first copied in a mirror-image in order to facilitate the left-to-right reading of the pages. However, Mr. Samura decided that he would rather see his pages reversed via the technique of cutting up the panels and re-pasting them in reverse order. While we feel that this often leads to problems in panel-to-panel continuity, we place primary importance on the wishes of the creator. Therefore, most of *Blade of the Immortal* has been produced using the "cut and paste" technique. There are, of course, some sequences where it was impossible to do this, and mirror-imaged panels or pages were used.

The Sound Effects & Dialogue

Since some of Mr. Samura's sound effects are integral parts of the artwork, we decided to leave those in their original Japanese. When it was crucial to the understanding of the panel that the sound effect be in English, however, Mr. Samura chose to redraw the panel. We hope readers will view the un-retouched sound effects as essential portions of Mr. Samura's extraordinary artwork. In addition, Mr. Samura's treatment of dialogue is quite different from that featured in average samurai manga and is considered to be one of the things that has made *Blade* such a hit in Japan. Mr. Samura has mixed a variety of linguistic styles in this fantasy story where some characters speak in the mannered style of old Japan while others speak as if they were street-corner punks from a bad area of modern-day Tokyo. The anachronistic slang used by some of the characters in the English translation reflects the unusual mix of speech patterns from the original, Japanese text.

GLOSSARY

Asakusa and Fukagawa: famous pleasure quarters of old Edo

Bushi: *samurai*

Busu: a poison made by sun-drying the root of the *torikabuto* plant

Dōjō: training centers: here, centers for swordsmanship

Edo: capital of pre-modern Japan: later renamed Tokyo

Haru: "springtime": and in the Edo period, a euphemism for sex

Itto-ryū: the radical sword tradition led by Anotsu

Kaga: a remote feudal domain on the Japan Sea coast southwest of Edo

Kenshi: a swordsman, not necessarily born into the *samurai* caste

Kohan: a gold piece

Koshu-do: the Koshu byway: one of the main routes from Edo to the western provinces

Mon: a small coin

Monzen-naka-cho: a down-scale pleasure quarter in old Edo

Mutenichi-ryū: the sword tradition taught by Rin's father

Nagauta: a musical style of pre-modern Japan, often songs of tragic love from the *Kabuki* theater

O-tento-sama: God, providence (lit. "the sun")

Ryo: a gold piece (*ryo* and *kohan* have similar values)

Sensei: a teacher, a master: here, Rin's painter friend

Yotaka: "nighthawk": a streetwalker, the lowest rank of Edo prostitute

DREAMSONG
Part 1

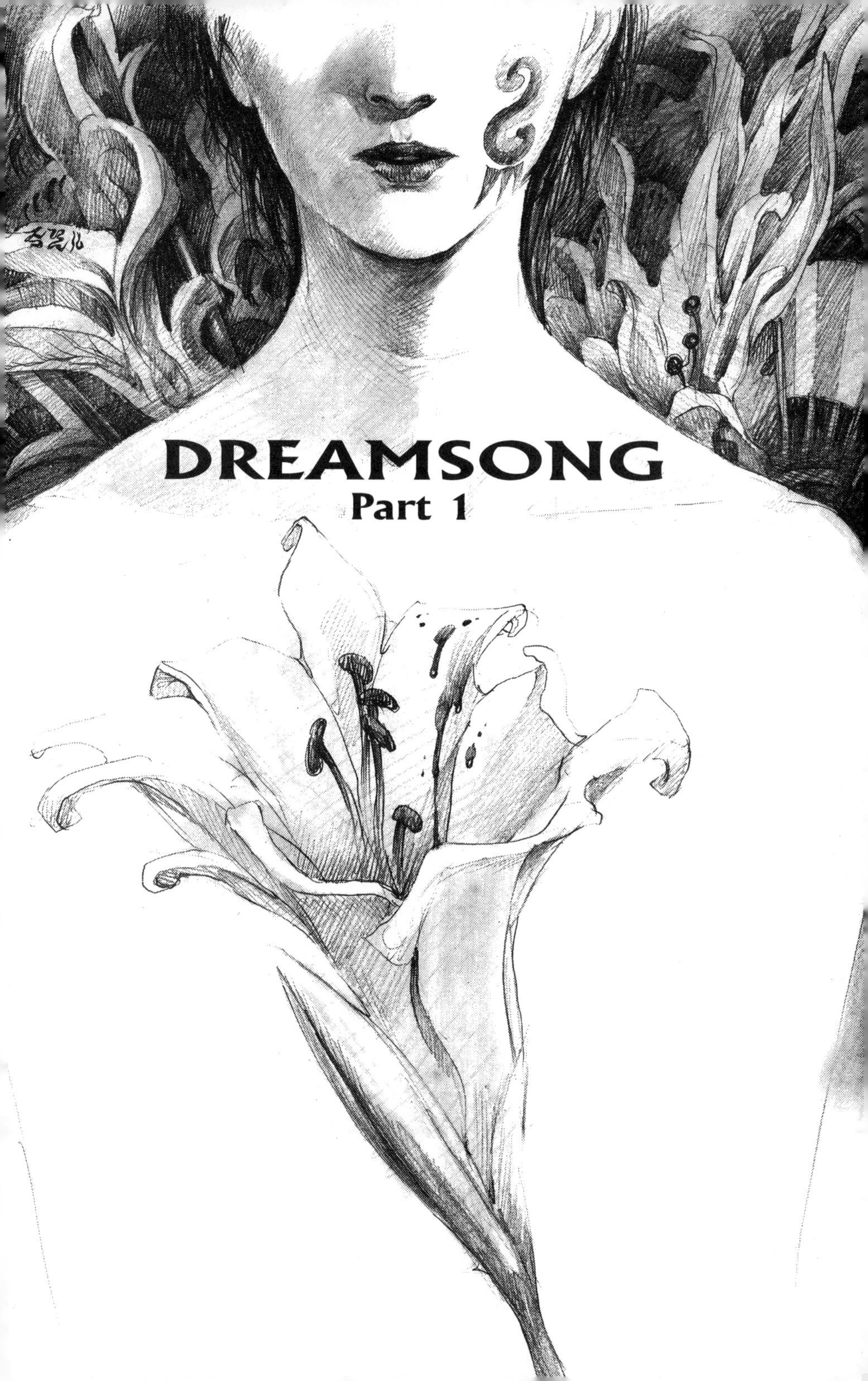

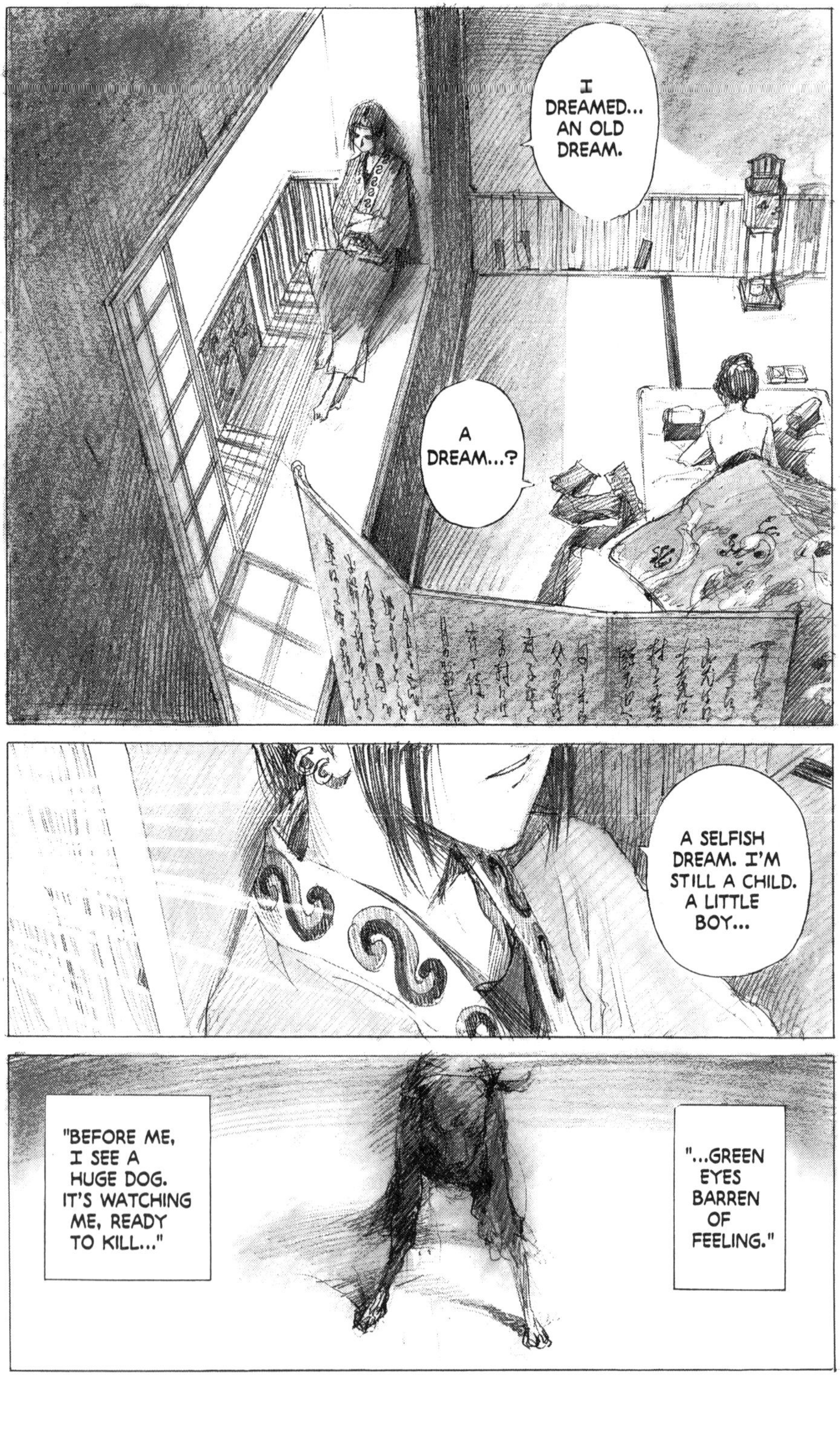
I DREAMED... AN OLD DREAM.
A DREAM...?
A SELFISH DREAM. I'M STILL A CHILD. A LITTLE BOY...
"BEFORE ME, I SEE A HUGE DOG. IT'S WATCHING ME, READY TO KILL..."
"...GREEN EYES BARREN OF FEELING."

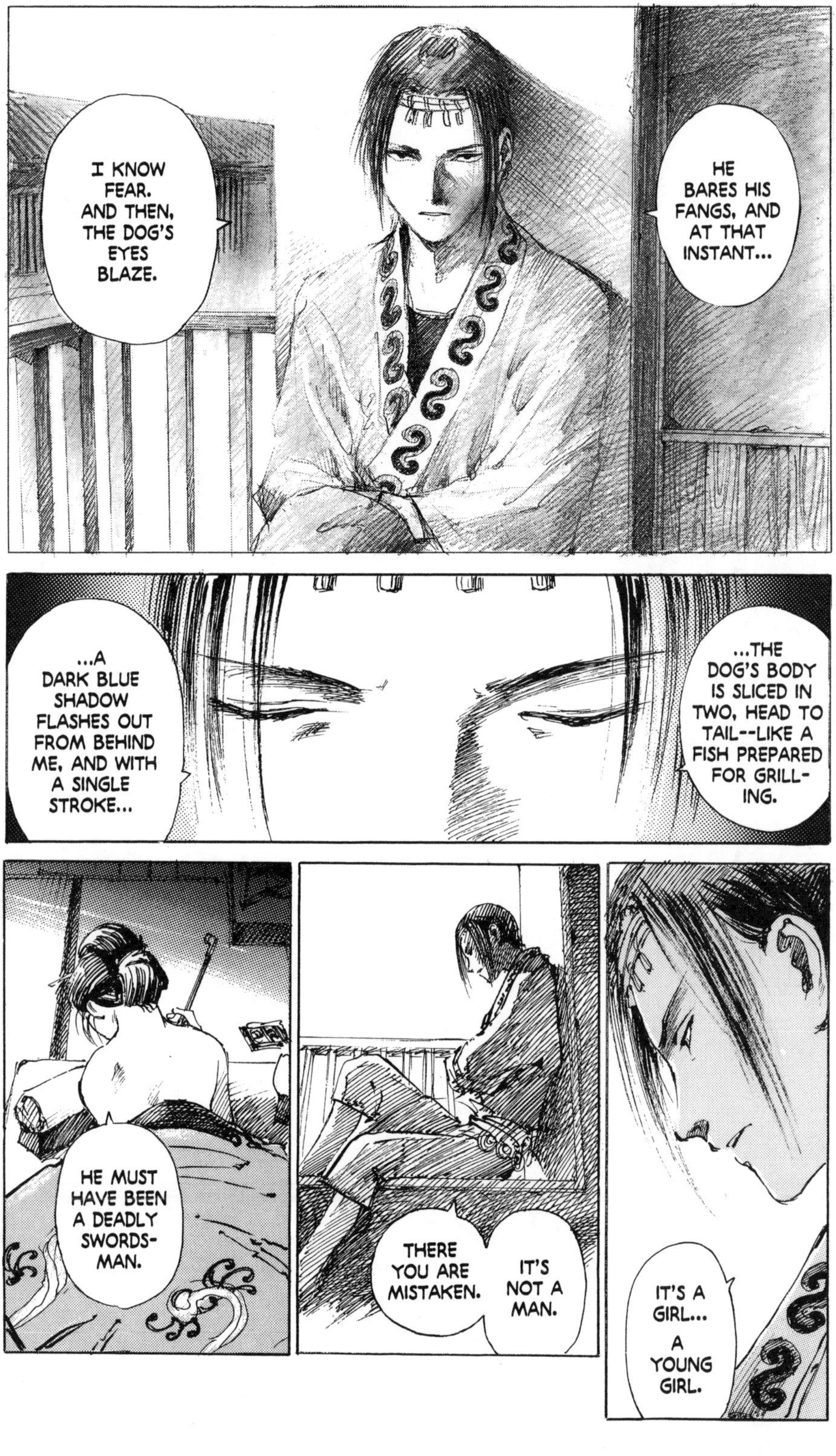
I KNOW FEAR. AND THEN, THE DOG'S EYES BLAZE.
HE BARES HIS FANGS, AND AT THAT INSTANT...
...A DARK BLUE SHADOW FLASHES OUT FROM BEHIND ME, AND WITH A SINGLE STROKE...
...THE DOG'S BODY IS SLICED IN TWO, HEAD TO TAIL--LIKE A FISH PREPARED FOR GRILL-ING.
HE MUST HAVE BEEN A DEADLY SWORDS-MAN.
THERE YOU ARE MISTAKEN.
IT'S NOT A MAN.
IT'S A GIRL...
A YOUNG GIRL.

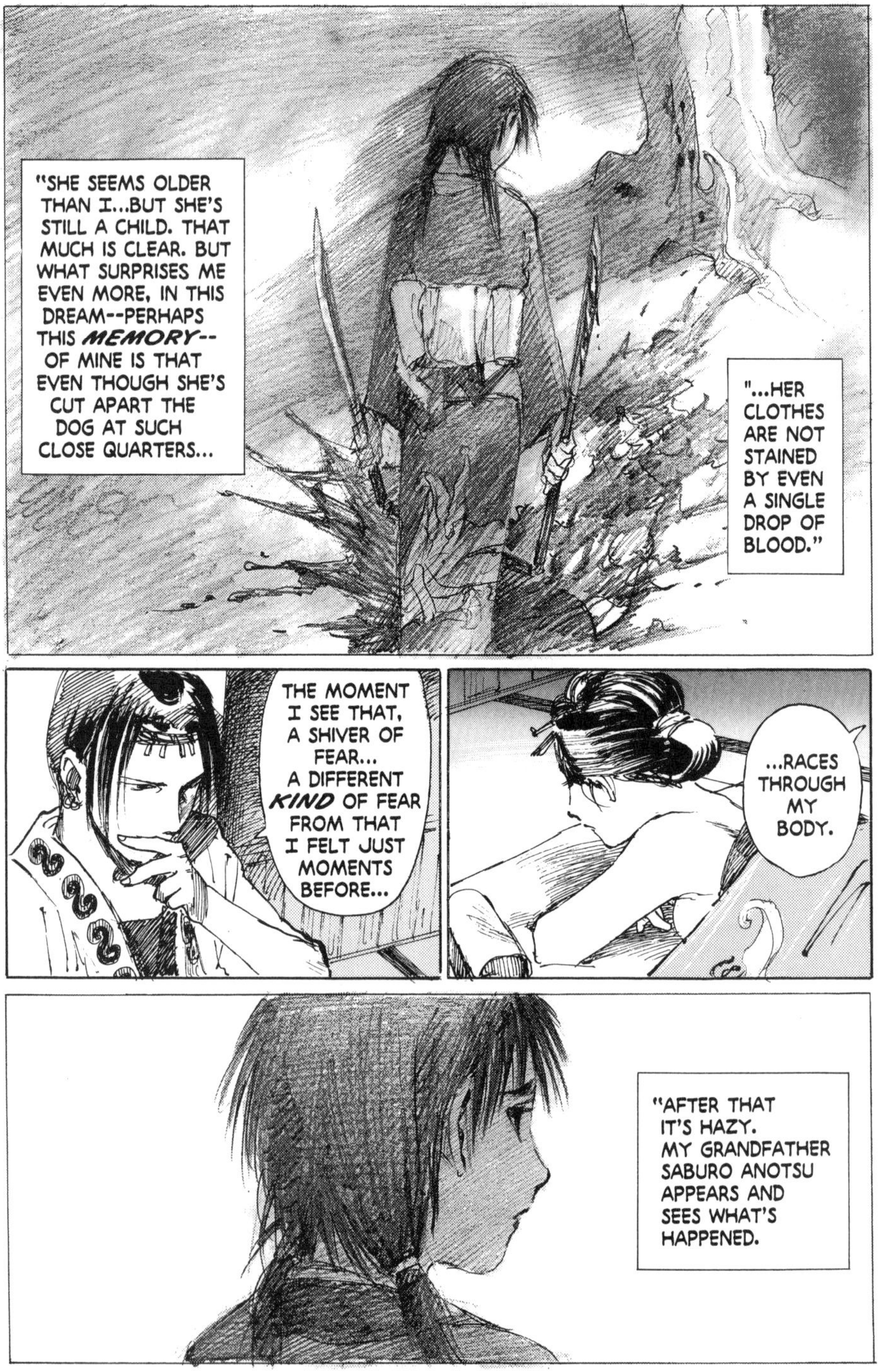
"SHE SEEMS OLDER THAN I...BUT SHE'S STILL A CHILD. THAT MUCH IS CLEAR. BUT WHAT SURPRISES ME EVEN MORE, IN THIS DREAM--PERHAPS THIS MEMORY--OF MINE IS THAT EVEN THOUGH SHE'S CUT APART THE DOG AT SUCH CLOSE QUARTERS...
"...HER CLOTHES ARE NOT STAINED BY EVEN A SINGLE DROP OF BLOOD."
THE MOMENT I SEE THAT, A SHIVER OF FEAR... A DIFFERENT KIND OF FEAR FROM THAT I FELT JUST MOMENTS BEFORE...
...RACES THROUGH MY BODY.
"AFTER THAT IT'S HAZY. MY GRANDFATHER SABURO ANOTSU APPEARS AND SEES WHAT'S HAPPENED.

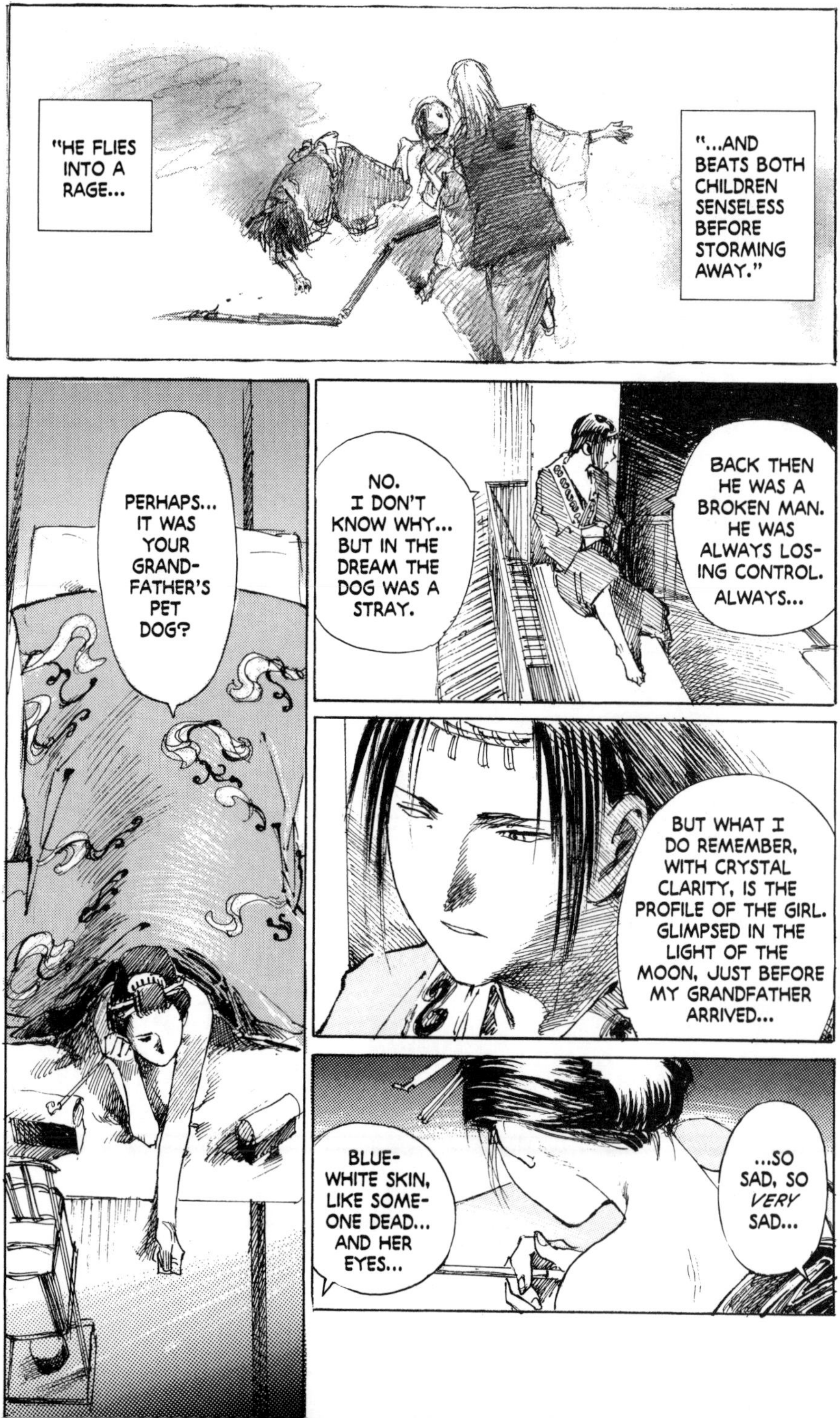
"HE FLIES INTO A RAGE...
"...AND BEATS BOTH CHILDREN SENSELESS BEFORE STORMING AWAY."
PERHAPS... IT WAS YOUR GRANDFATHER'S PET DOG?
NO. I DON'T KNOW WHY... BUT IN THE DREAM THE DOG WAS A STRAY.
BACK THEN HE WAS A BROKEN MAN. HE WAS ALWAYS LOSING CONTROL. ALWAYS...
BUT WHAT I DO REMEMBER, WITH CRYSTAL CLARITY, IS THE PROFILE OF THE GIRL. GLIMPSED IN THE LIGHT OF THE MOON, JUST BEFORE MY GRANDFATHER ARRIVED...
BLUE-WHITE SKIN, LIKE SOMEONE DEAD... AND HER EYES...
...SO SAD, SO *VERY* SAD...

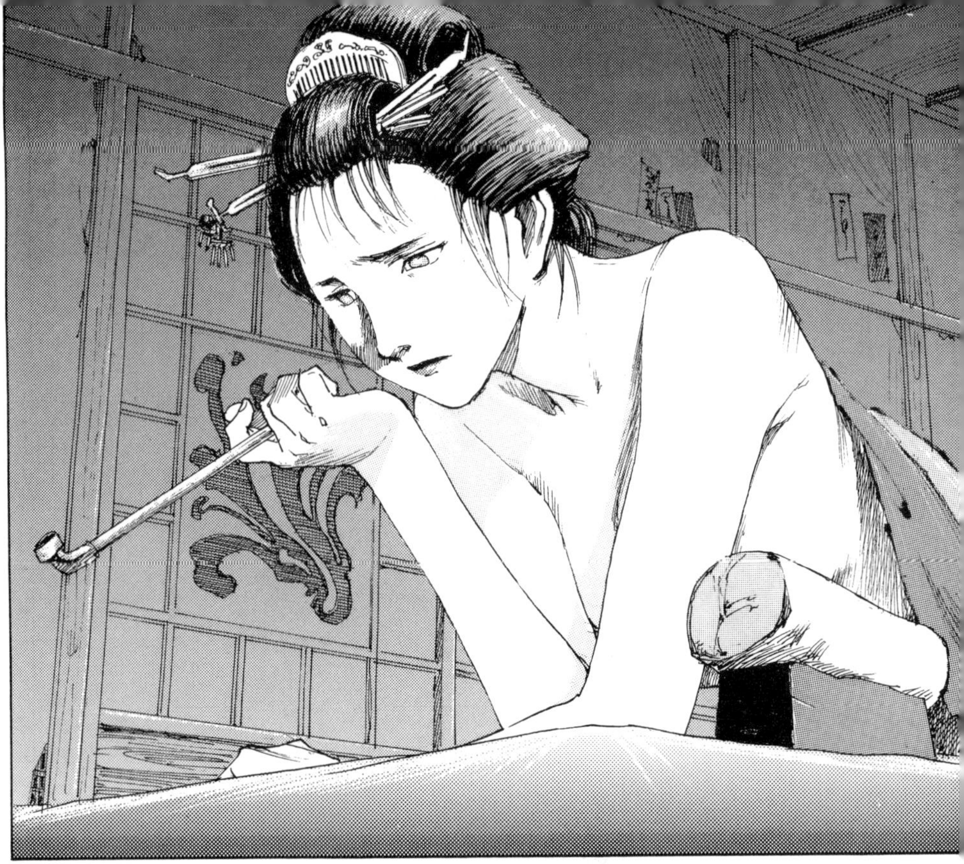

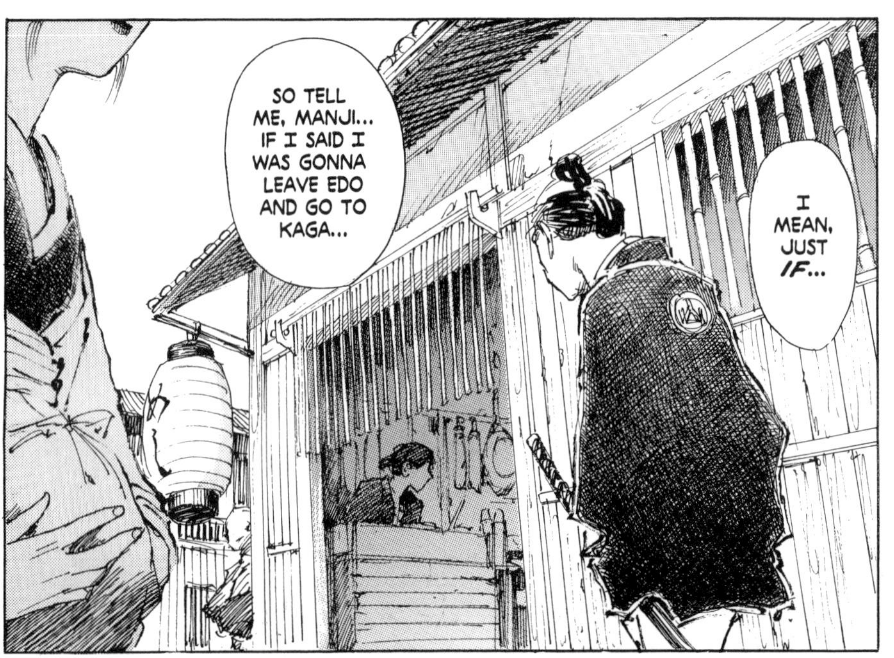
SO TELL ME, MANJI... IF I SAID I WAS GONNA LEAVE EDO AND GO TO KAGA...
I MEAN, JUST *IF*...

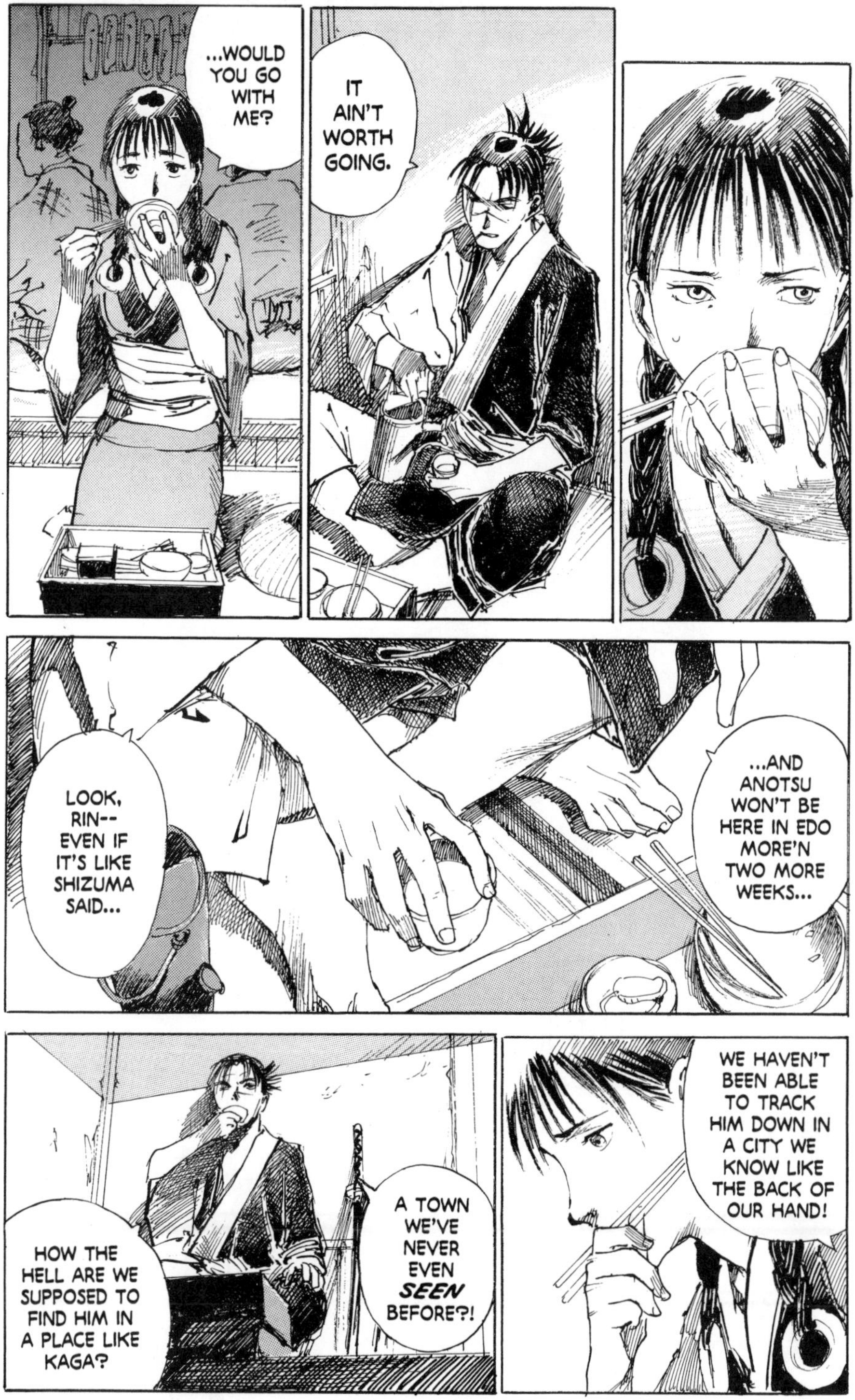
...WOULD YOU GO WITH ME?
IT AIN'T WORTH GOING.
LOOK, RIN-- EVEN IF IT'S LIKE SHIZUMA SAID...
...AND ANOTSU WON'T BE HERE IN EDO MORE'N TWO MORE WEEKS...
HOW THE HELL ARE WE SUPPOSED TO FIND HIM IN A PLACE LIKE KAGA?
A TOWN WE'VE NEVER EVEN *SEEN* BEFORE?!
WE HAVEN'T BEEN ABLE TO TRACK HIM DOWN IN A CITY WE KNOW LIKE THE BACK OF OUR HAND!

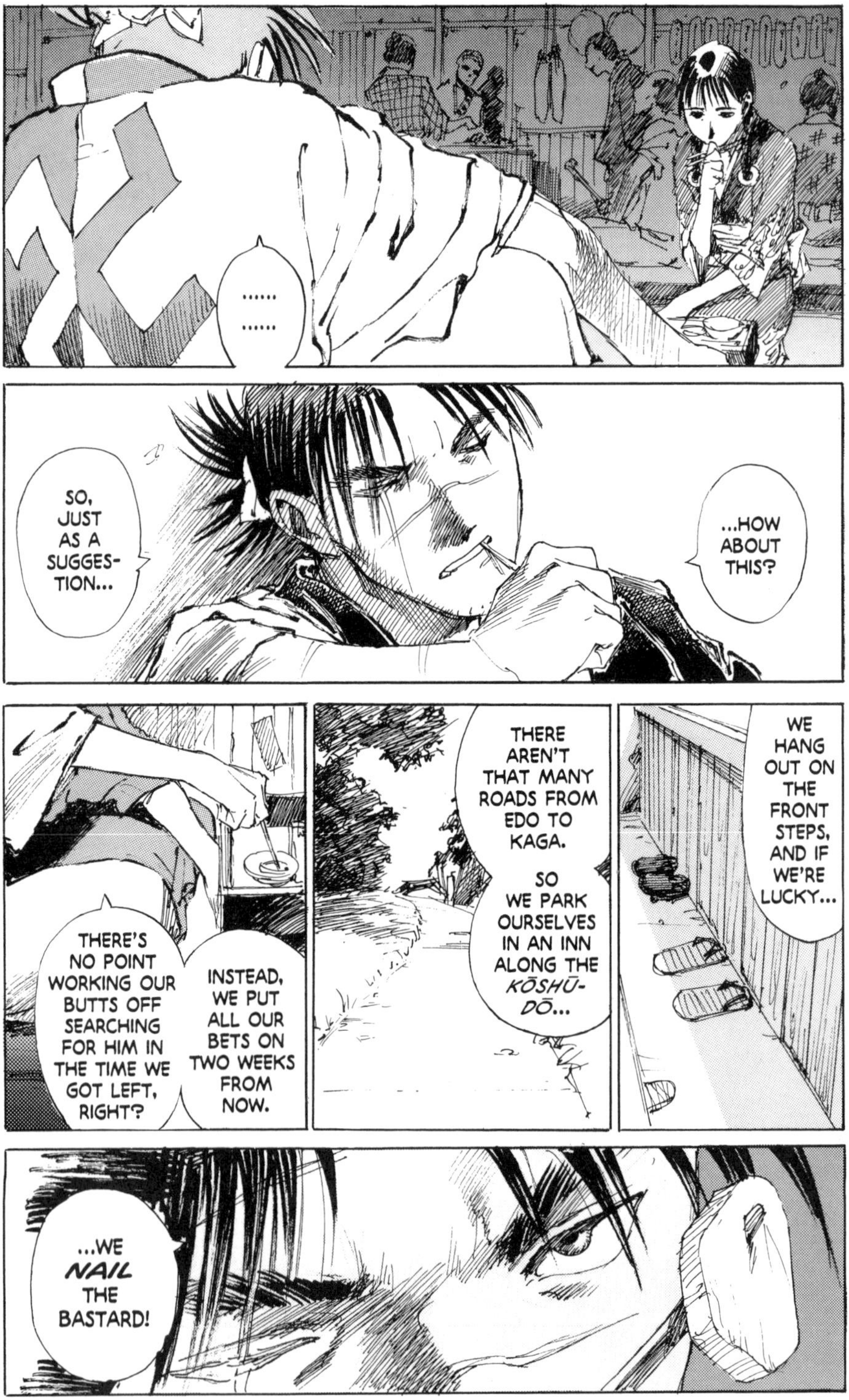
......
......
SO, JUST AS A SUGGES-TION...
...HOW ABOUT THIS?
THERE'S NO POINT WORKING OUR BUTTS OFF SEARCHING FOR HIM IN THE TIME WE GOT LEFT, RIGHT?
INSTEAD, WE PUT ALL OUR BETS ON TWO WEEKS FROM NOW.
THERE AREN'T THAT MANY ROADS FROM EDO TO KAGA.
SO WE PARK OURSELVES IN AN INN ALONG THE *KŌSHŪ-DŌ*...
WE HANG OUT ON THE FRONT STEPS, AND IF WE'RE LUCKY...
...WE ***NAIL*** THE BASTARD!

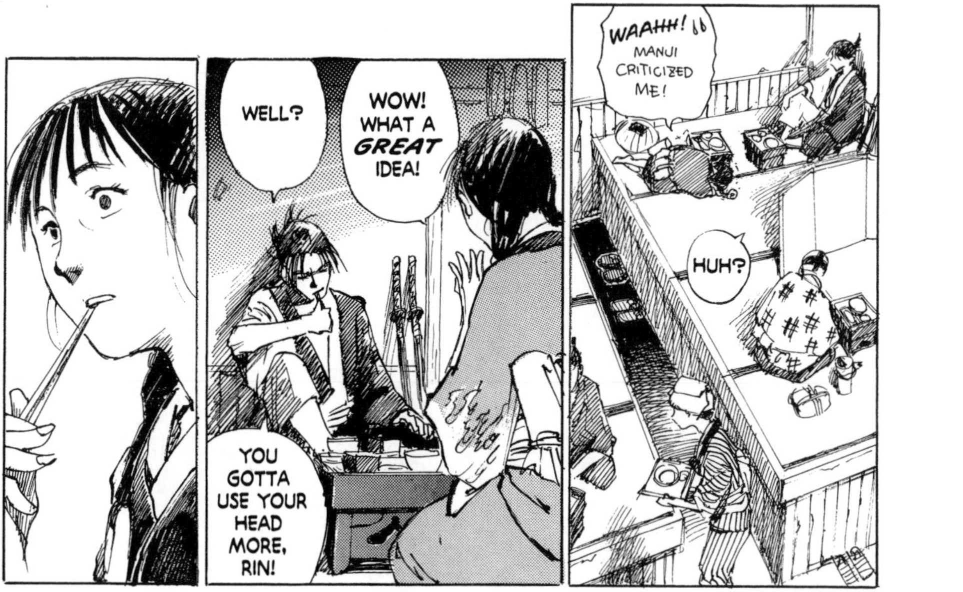
WELL?
WOW! WHAT A GREAT IDEA!
YOU GOTTA USE YOUR HEAD MORE, RIN!
WAAHH! MANJI CRITICIZED ME!
HUH?

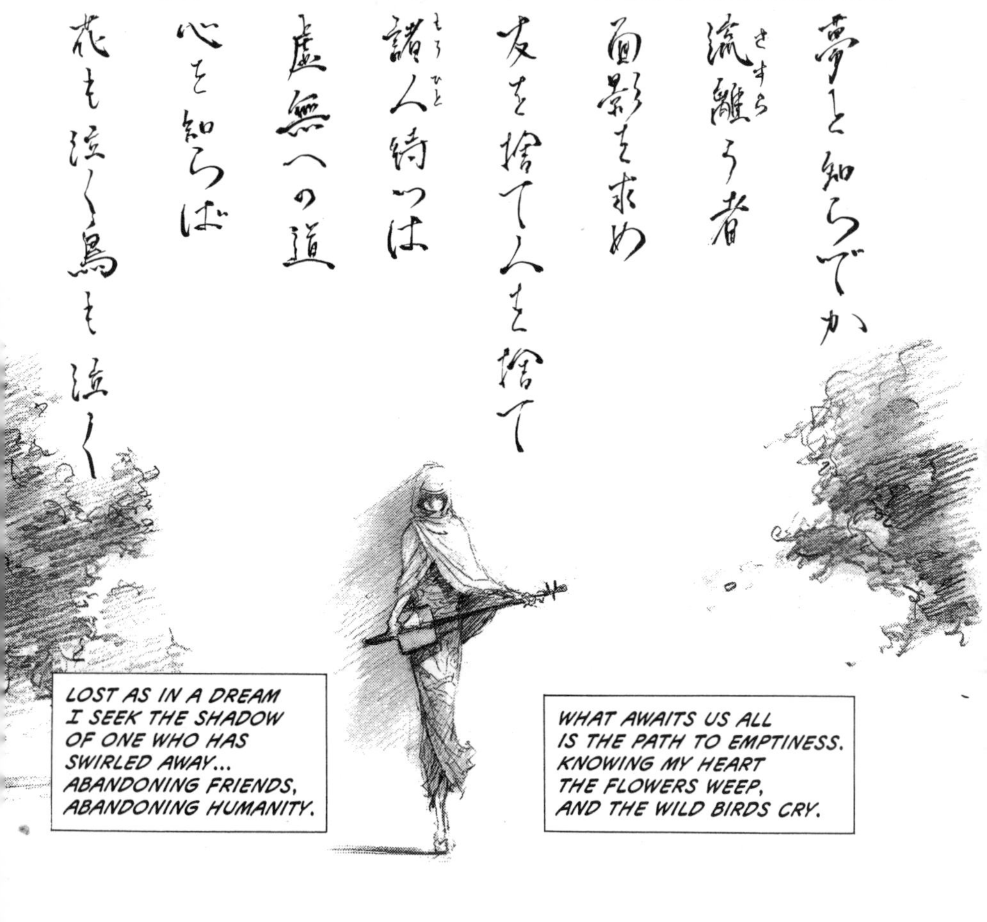
夢と知らでか
流離う者
面影を求め
友を捨て人を捨て
諸人待つは
虚無への道
心を知らば
花も泣く鳥も泣く
LOST AS IN A DREAM
I SEEK THE SHADOW
OF ONE WHO HAS
SWIRLED AWAY...
ABANDONING FRIENDS,
ABANDONING HUMANITY.
WHAT AWAITS US ALL
IS THE PATH TO EMPTINESS.
KNOWING MY HEART
THE FLOWERS WEEP,
AND THE WILD BIRDS CRY.

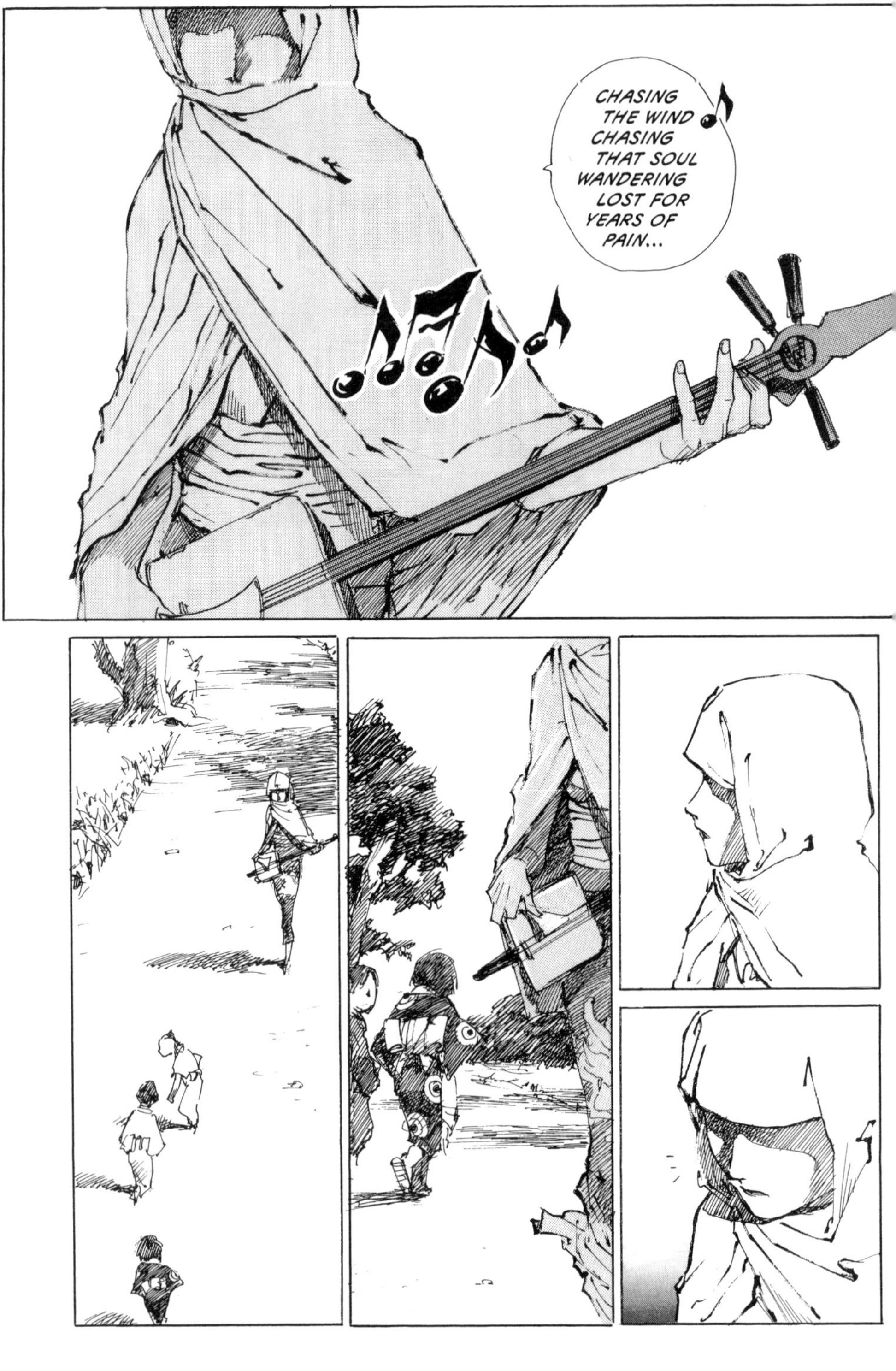
CHASING THE WIND CHASING THAT SOUL WANDERING LOST FOR YEARS OF PAIN...

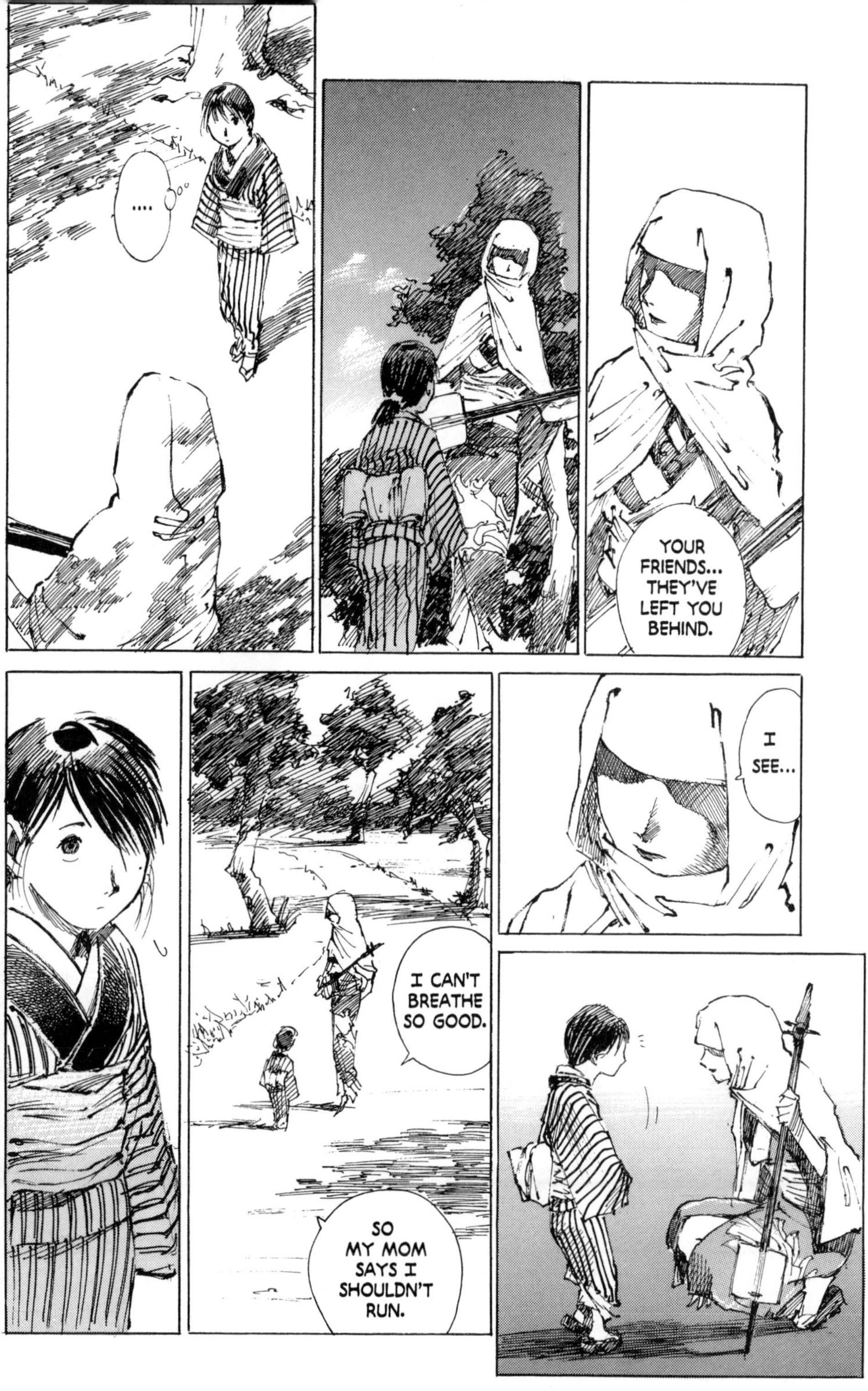
....
YOUR FRIENDS... THEY'VE LEFT YOU BEHIND.
I CAN'T BREATHE SO GOOD.
SO MY MOM SAYS I SHOULDN'T RUN.
I SEE...

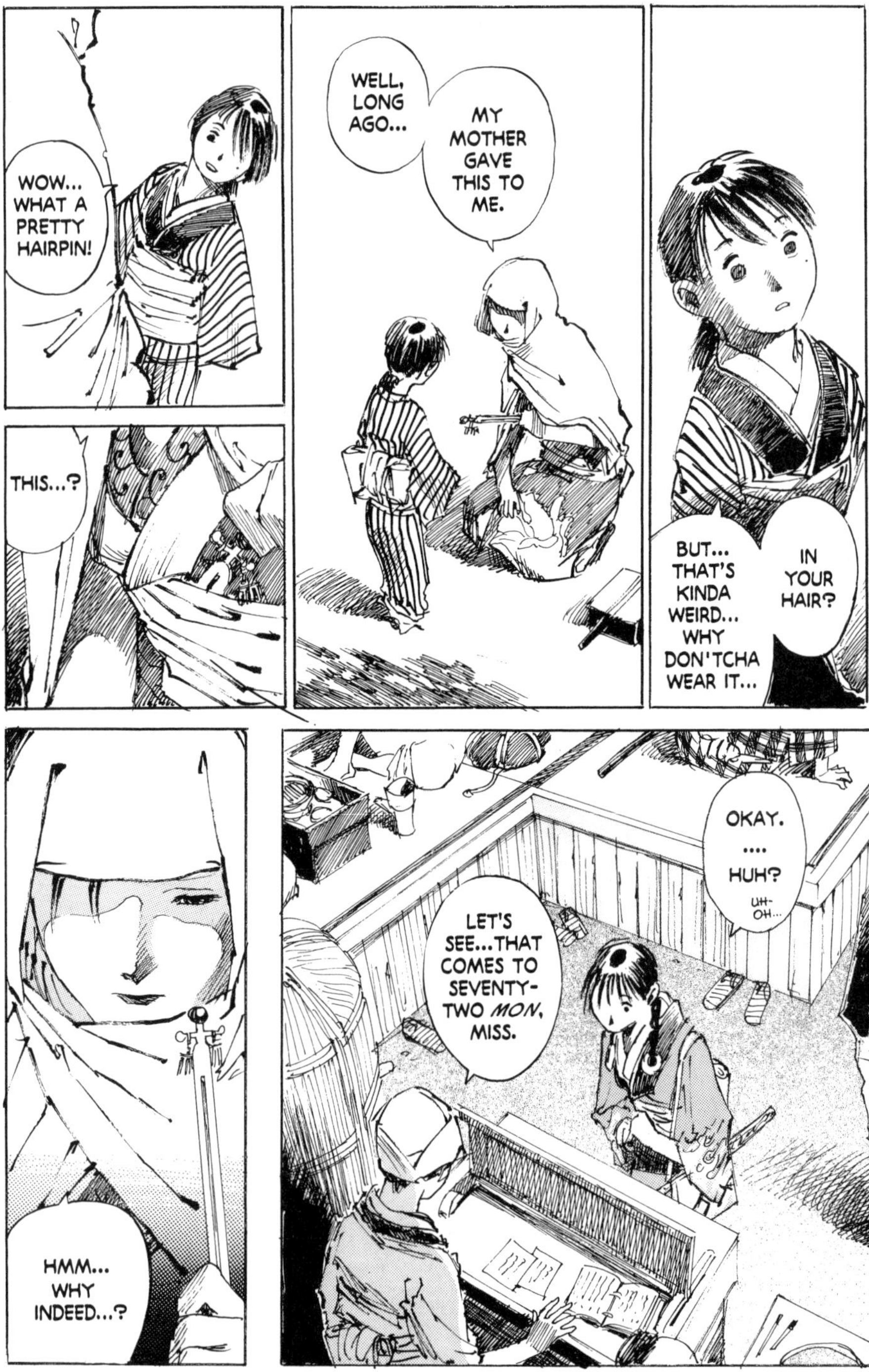
WOW... WHAT A PRETTY HAIRPIN!
THIS...?
WELL, LONG AGO...
MY MOTHER GAVE THIS TO ME.
BUT... THAT'S KINDA WEIRD... WHY DON'TCHA WEAR IT...
IN YOUR HAIR?
HMM... WHY INDEED...?
LET'S SEE...THAT COMES TO SEVENTY-TWO *MON*, MISS.
OKAY.
....
HUH?
UH-OH...

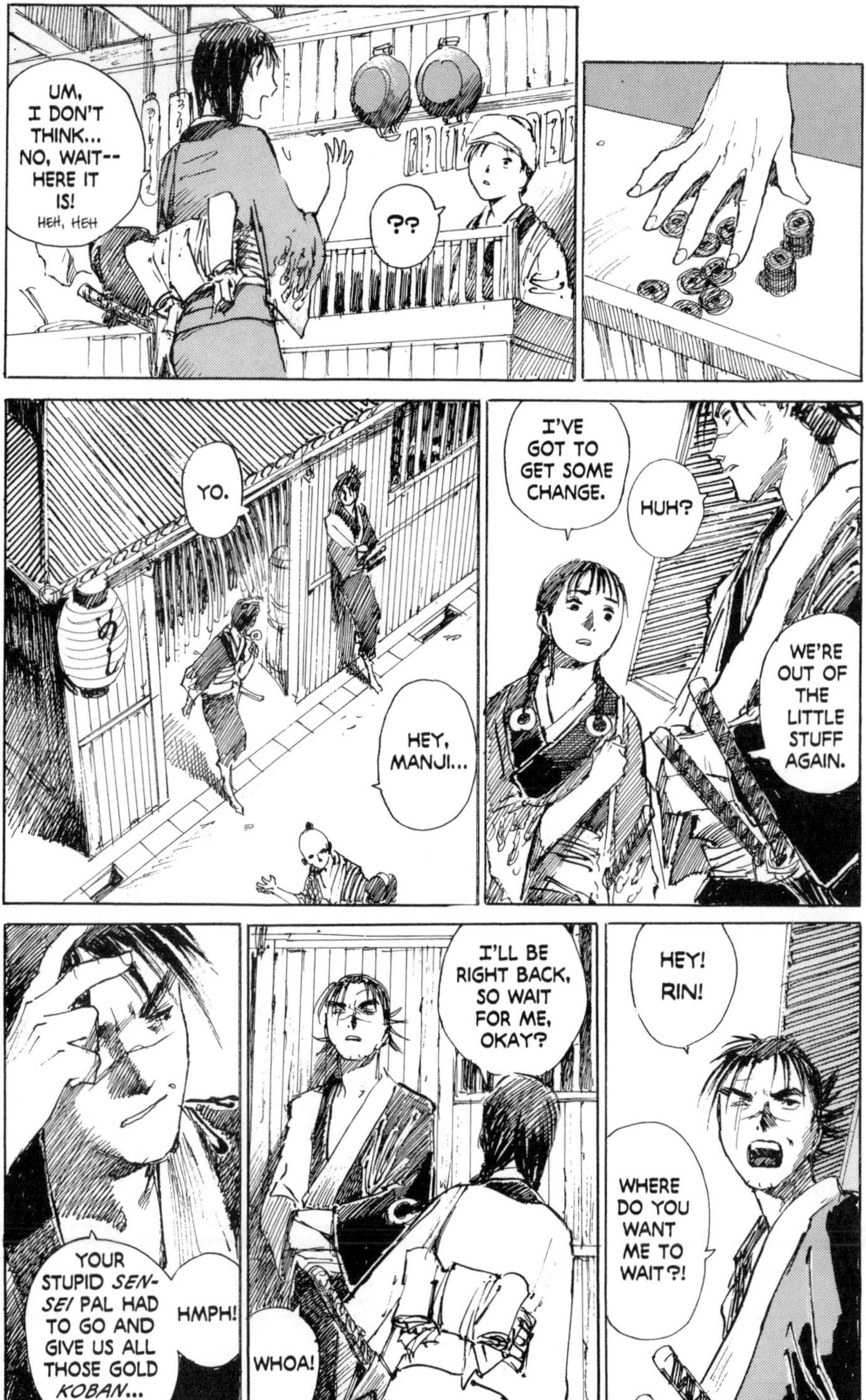
UM, I DON'T THINK... NO, WAIT-- HERE IT IS!
HEH, HEH
??
YO.
HEY, MANJI...
I'VE GOT TO GET SOME CHANGE.
HUH?
WE'RE OUT OF THE LITTLE STUFF AGAIN.
YOUR STUPID *SENSEI* PAL HAD TO GO AND GIVE US ALL THOSE GOLD *KOBAN*...
HMPH!
I'LL BE RIGHT BACK, SO WAIT FOR ME, OKAY?
WHOA!
HEY! RIN!
WHERE DO YOU WANT ME TO WAIT?!

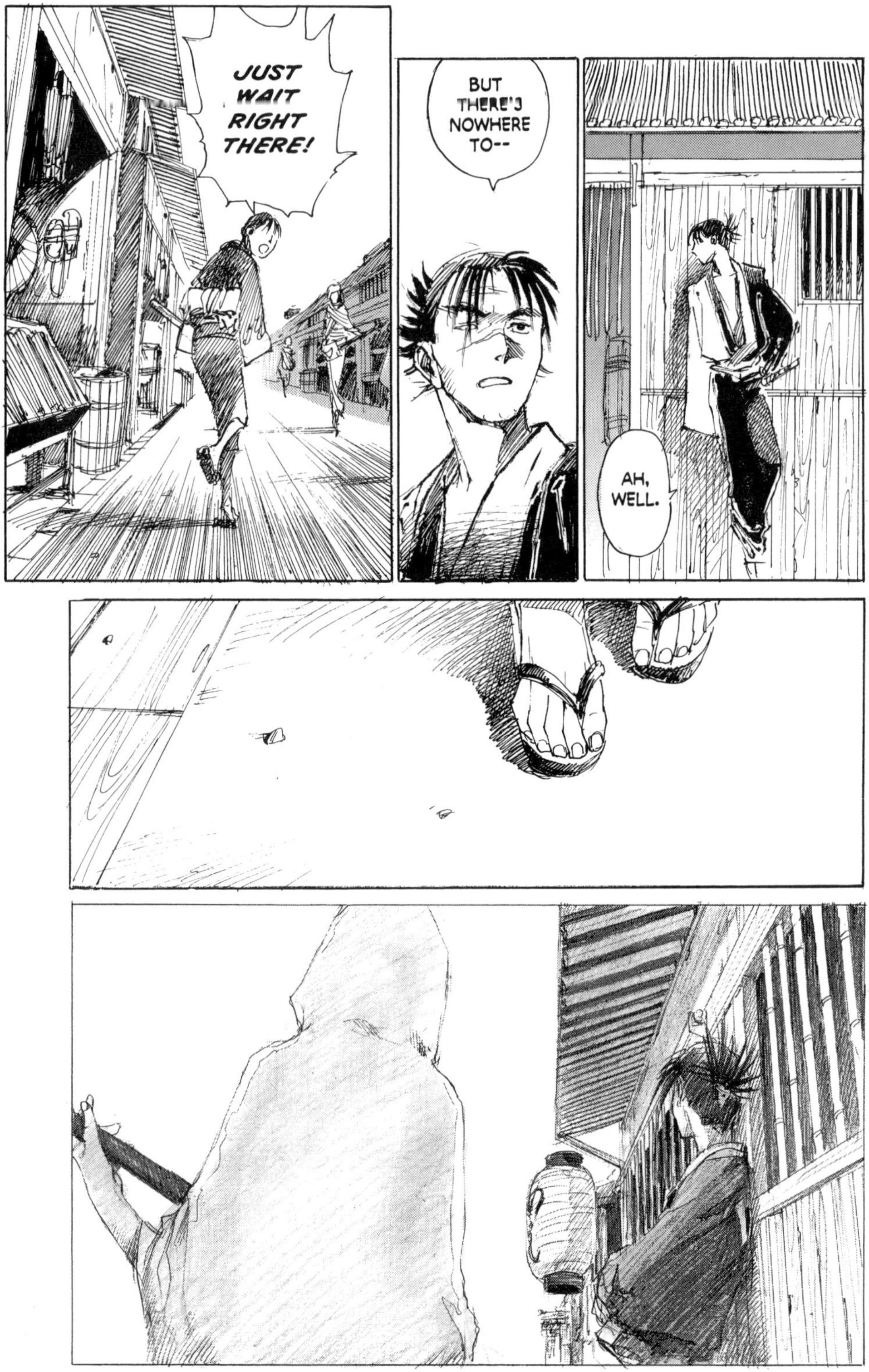
JUST WAIT RIGHT THERE!
BUT THERE'S NOWHERE TO--
AH, WELL.

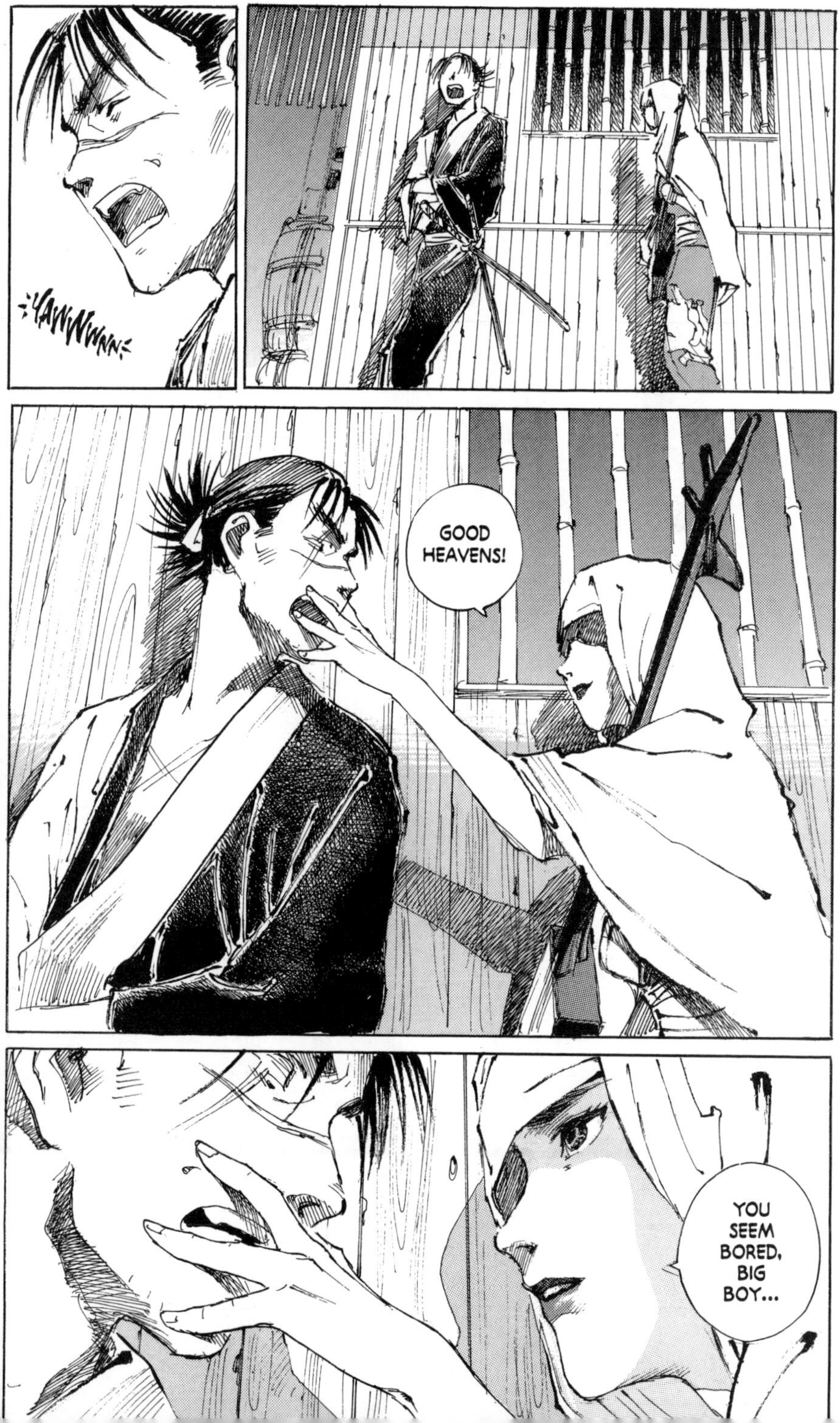
YAWWNWNN
GOOD HEAVENS!
YOU SEEM BORED, BIG BOY...

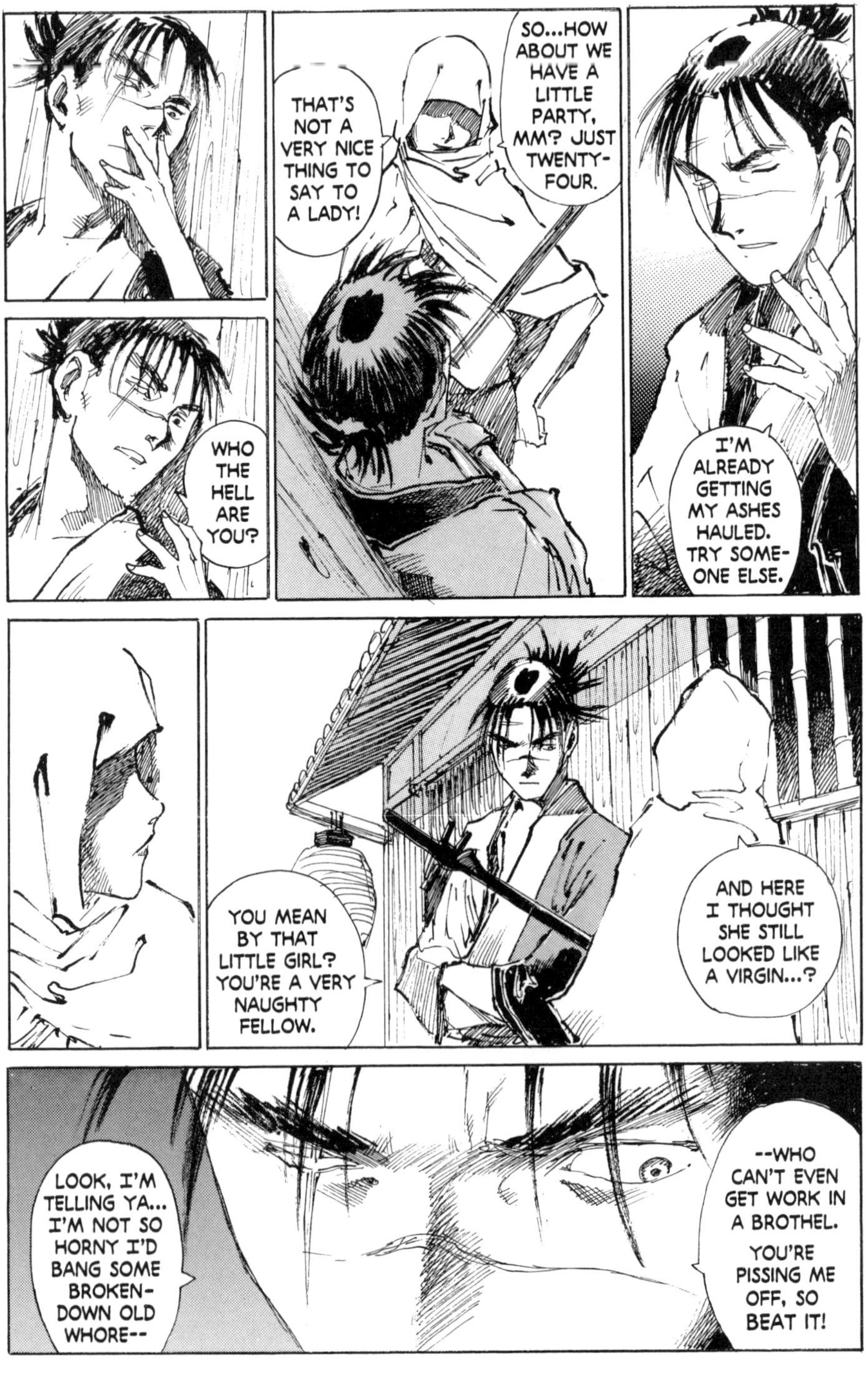
WHO THE HELL ARE YOU?
THAT'S NOT A VERY NICE THING TO SAY TO A LADY!
SO...HOW ABOUT WE HAVE A LITTLE PARTY, MM? JUST TWENTY-FOUR.
I'M ALREADY GETTING MY ASHES HAULED. TRY SOME-ONE ELSE.
YOU MEAN BY THAT LITTLE GIRL? YOU'RE A VERY NAUGHTY FELLOW.
AND HERE I THOUGHT SHE STILL LOOKED LIKE A VIRGIN...?
LOOK, I'M TELLING YA... I'M NOT SO HORNY I'D BANG SOME BROKEN-DOWN OLD WHORE--
--WHO CAN'T EVEN GET WORK IN A BROTHEL.
YOU'RE PISSING ME OFF, SO BEAT IT!

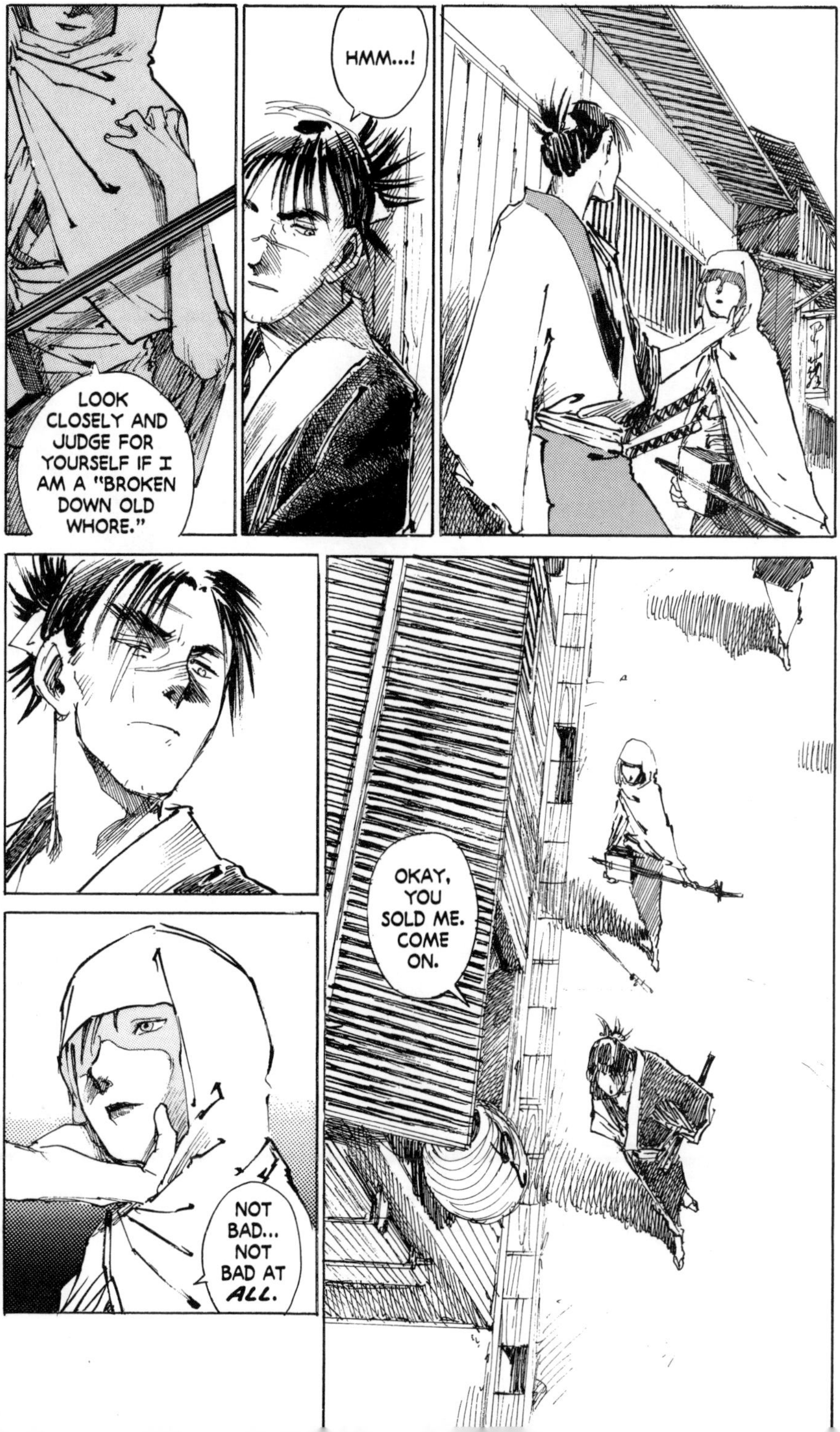
LOOK CLOSELY AND JUDGE FOR YOURSELF IF I AM A "BROKEN DOWN OLD WHORE."
HMM...!
OKAY, YOU SOLD ME. COME ON.
NOT BAD... NOT BAD AT ALL.

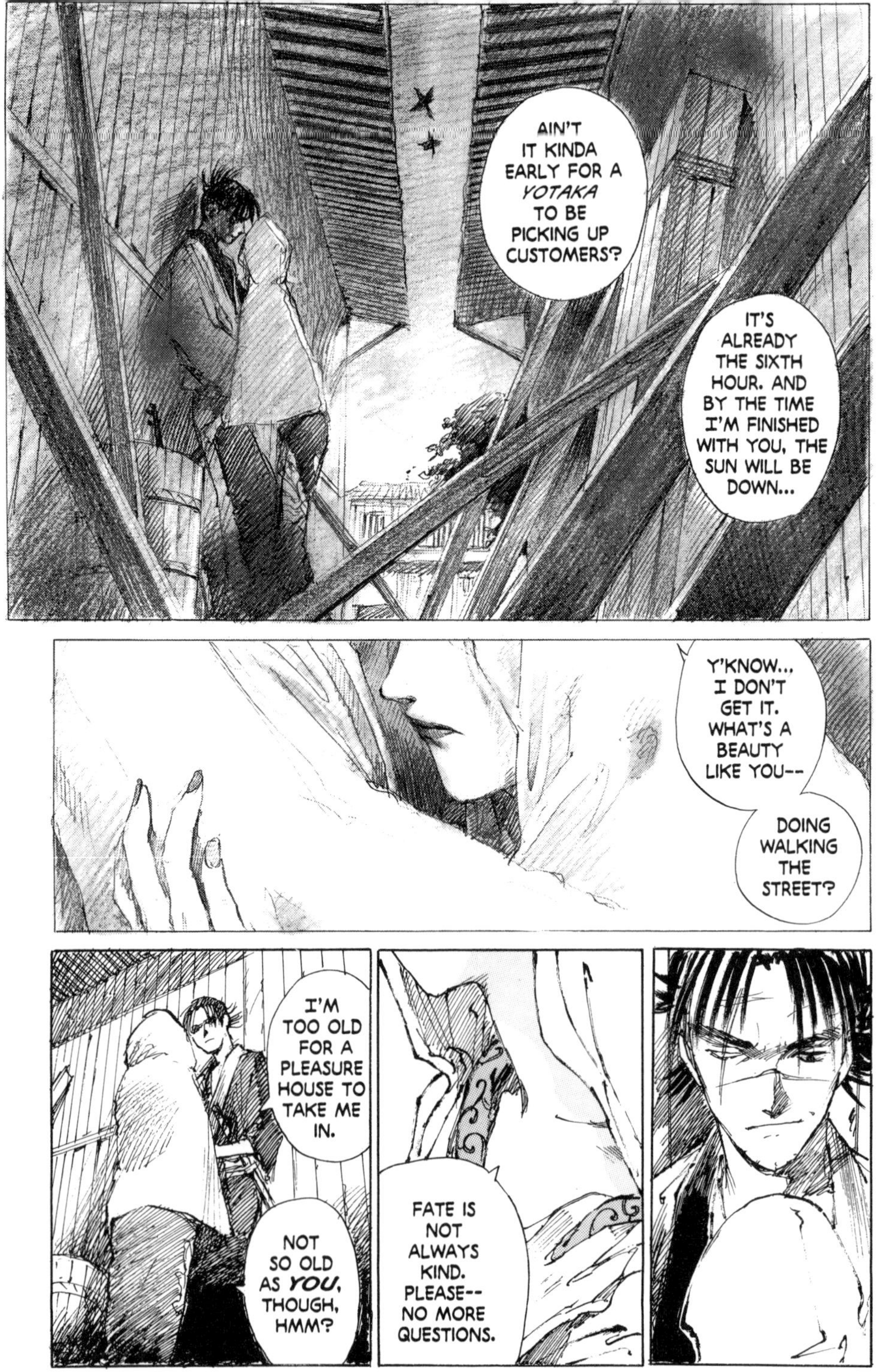
AIN'T IT KINDA EARLY FOR A *YOTAKA* TO BE PICKING UP CUSTOMERS?
IT'S ALREADY THE SIXTH HOUR. AND BY THE TIME I'M FINISHED WITH YOU, THE SUN WILL BE DOWN...
Y'KNOW... I DON'T GET IT. WHAT'S A BEAUTY LIKE YOU--
DOING WALKING THE STREET?
I'M TOO OLD FOR A PLEASURE HOUSE TO TAKE ME IN.
NOT SO OLD AS ***YOU***, THOUGH, HMM?
FATE IS NOT ALWAYS KIND. PLEASE-- NO MORE QUESTIONS.

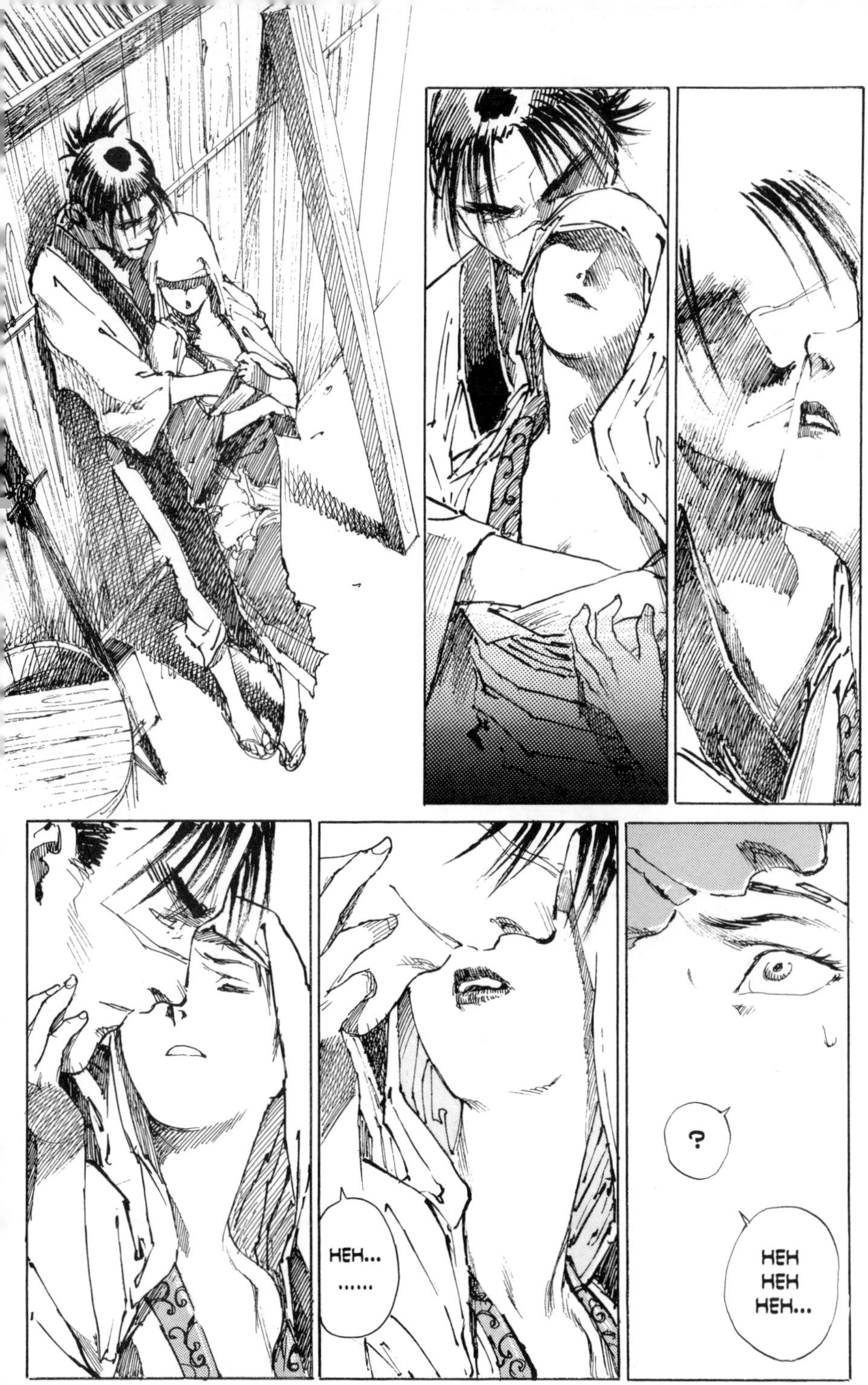
HEH... ......
?
HEH HEH HEH...

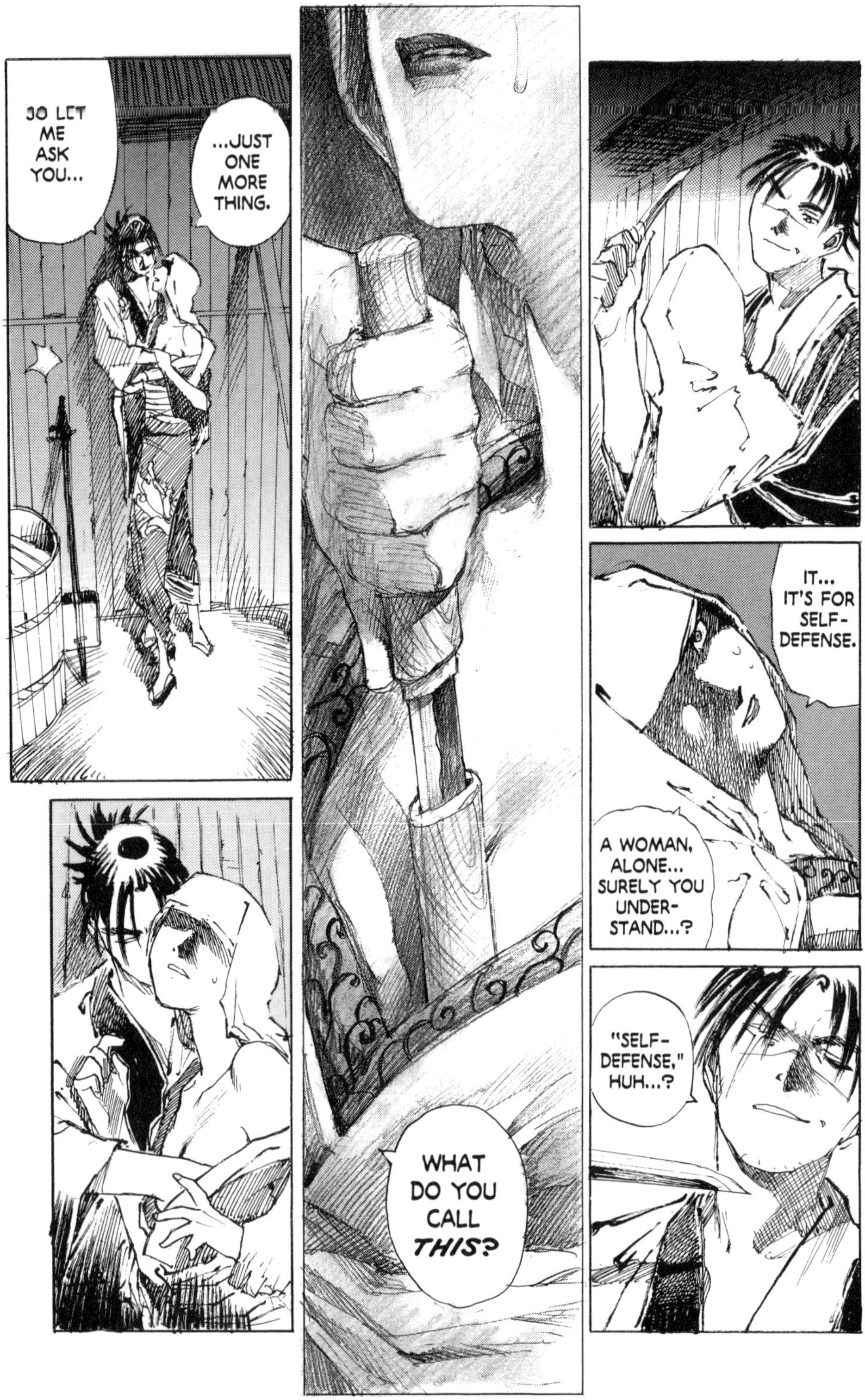
SO LET ME ASK YOU...
...JUST ONE MORE THING.
IT... IT'S FOR SELF-DEFENSE.
A WOMAN, ALONE... SURELY YOU UNDER-STAND...?
WHAT DO YOU CALL *THIS?*
"SELF-DEFENSE," HUH...?

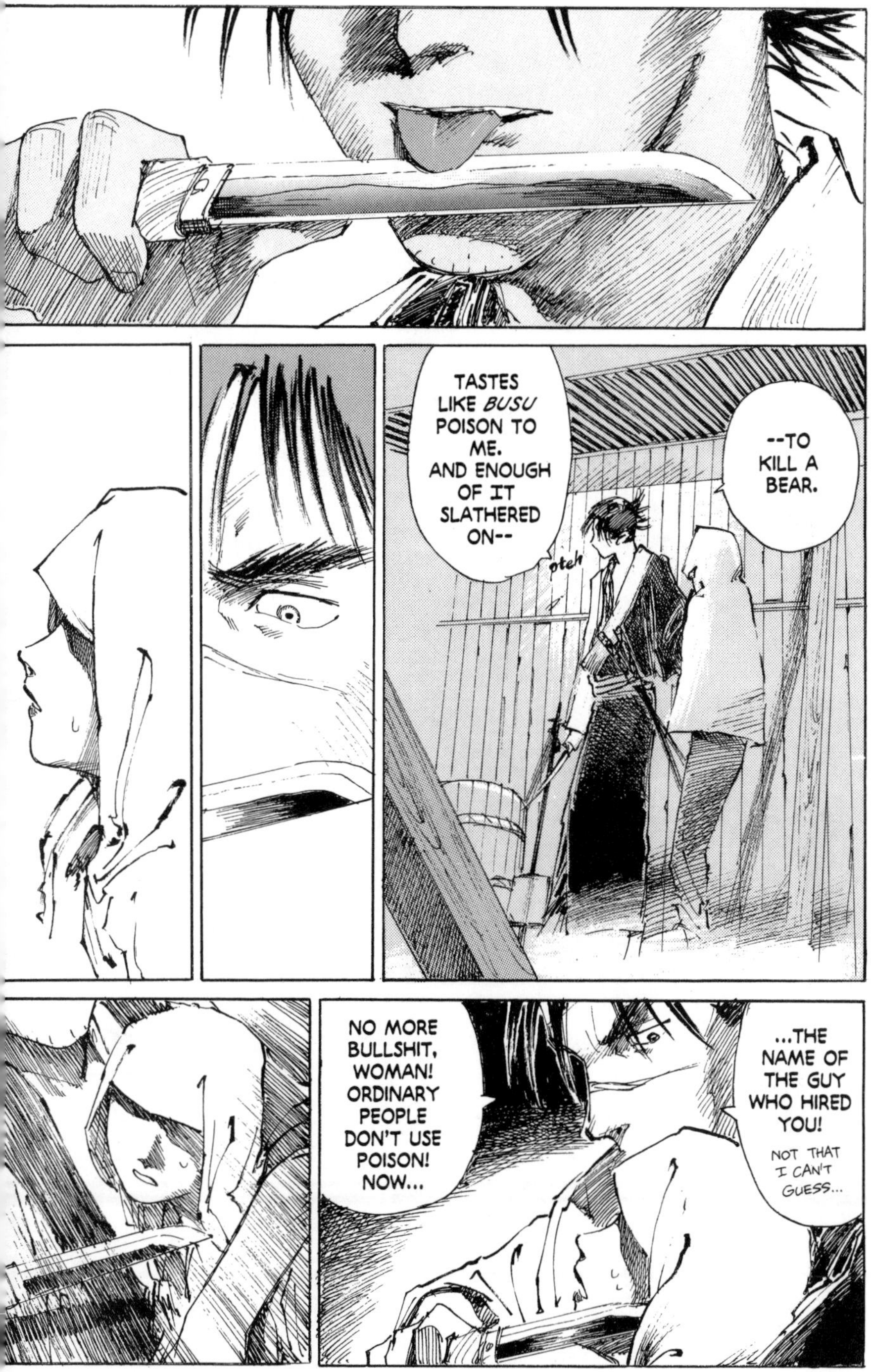
TASTES LIKE *BUSU* POISON TO ME. AND ENOUGH OF IT SLATHERED ON--
pteh
--TO KILL A BEAR.
NO MORE BULLSHIT, WOMAN! ORDINARY PEOPLE DON'T USE POISON! NOW...
...THE NAME OF THE GUY WHO HIRED YOU!
NOT THAT I CAN'T GUESS...

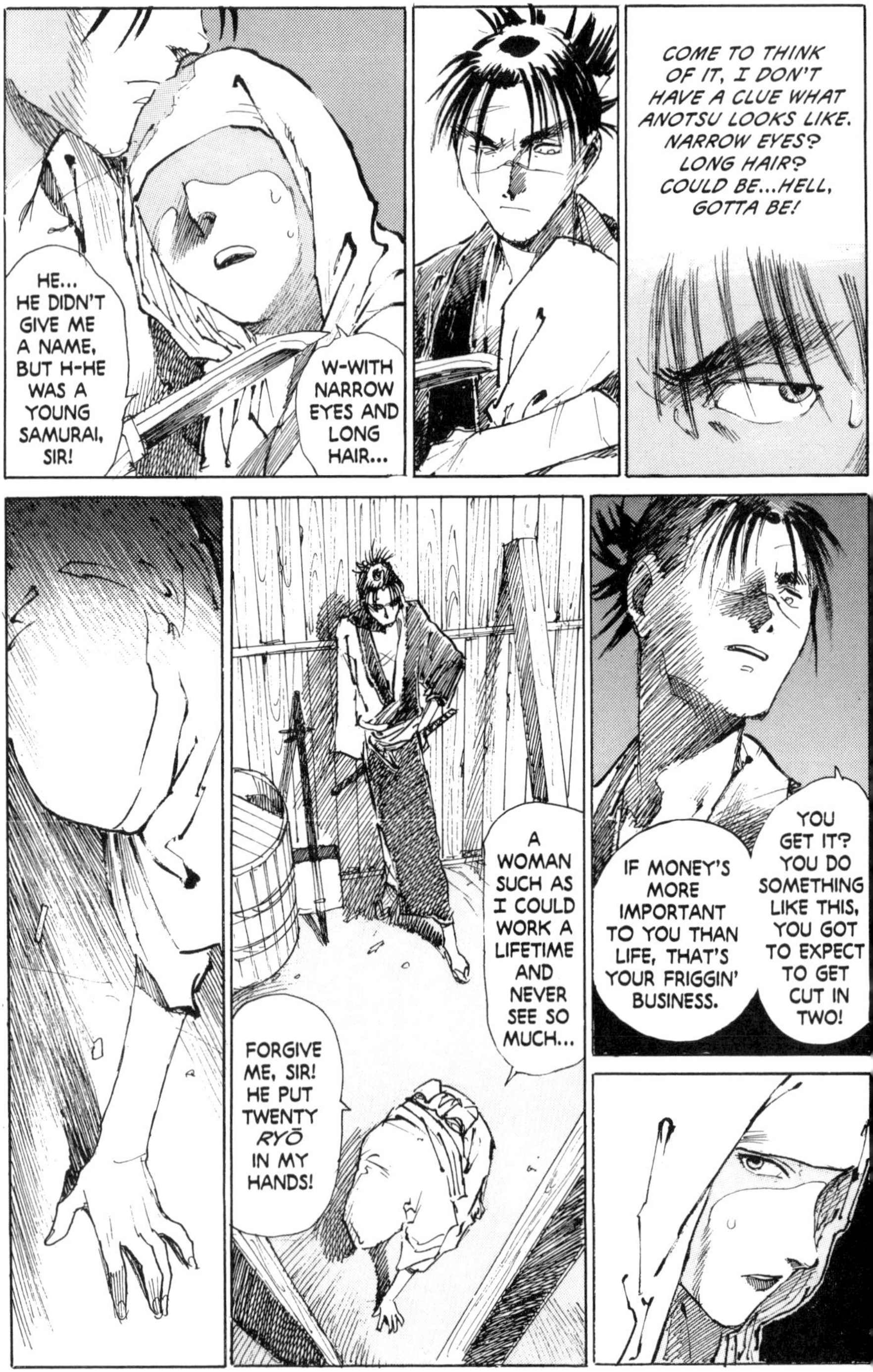
HE... HE DIDN'T GIVE ME A NAME, BUT H-HE WAS A YOUNG SAMURAI, SIR!
W-WITH NARROW EYES AND LONG HAIR...
COME TO THINK OF IT, I DON'T HAVE A CLUE WHAT ANOTSU LOOKS LIKE. NARROW EYES? LONG HAIR? COULD BE...HELL, GOTTA BE!
A WOMAN SUCH AS I COULD WORK A LIFETIME AND NEVER SEE SO MUCH...
FORGIVE ME, SIR! HE PUT TWENTY *RYŌ* IN MY HANDS!
IF MONEY'S MORE IMPORTANT TO YOU THAN LIFE, THAT'S YOUR FRIGGIN' BUSINESS.
YOU GET IT? YOU DO SOMETHING LIKE THIS, YOU GOT TO EXPECT TO GET CUT IN TWO!

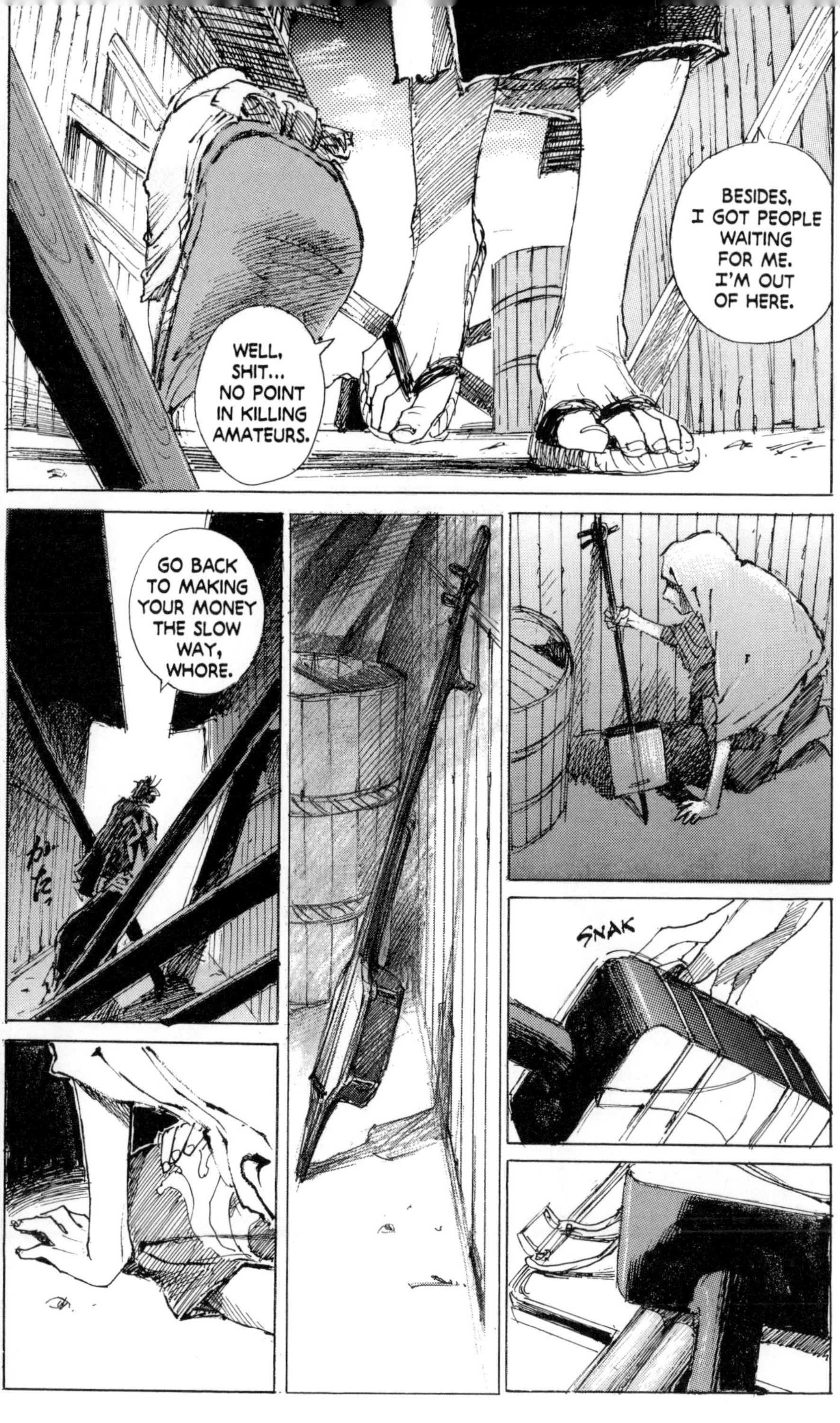
WELL, SHIT... NO POINT IN KILLING AMATEURS.
BESIDES, I GOT PEOPLE WAITING FOR ME. I'M OUT OF HERE.
GO BACK TO MAKING YOUR MONEY THE SLOW WAY, WHORE.
SNAK

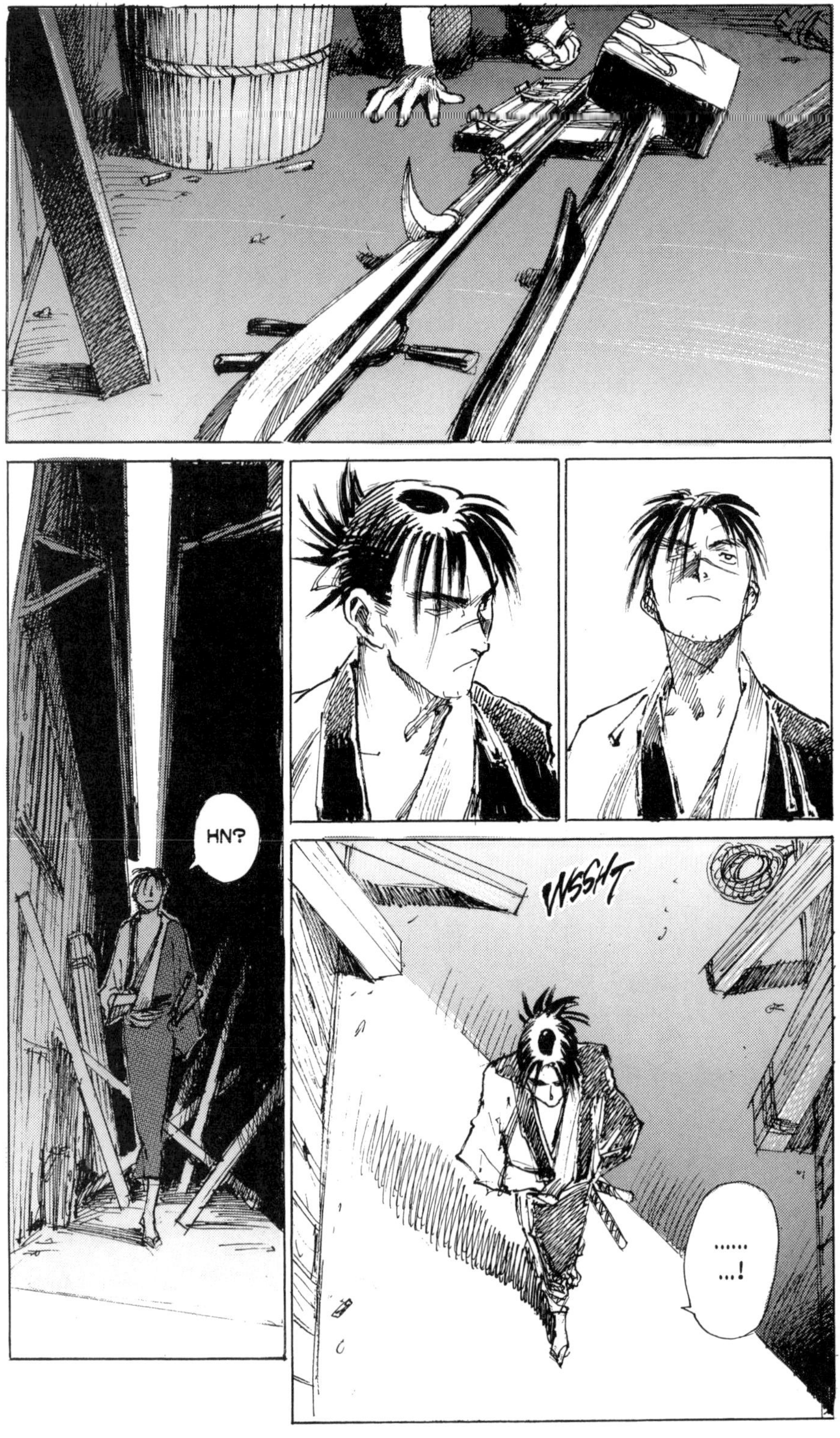
HN?
WSSHT
......
...!

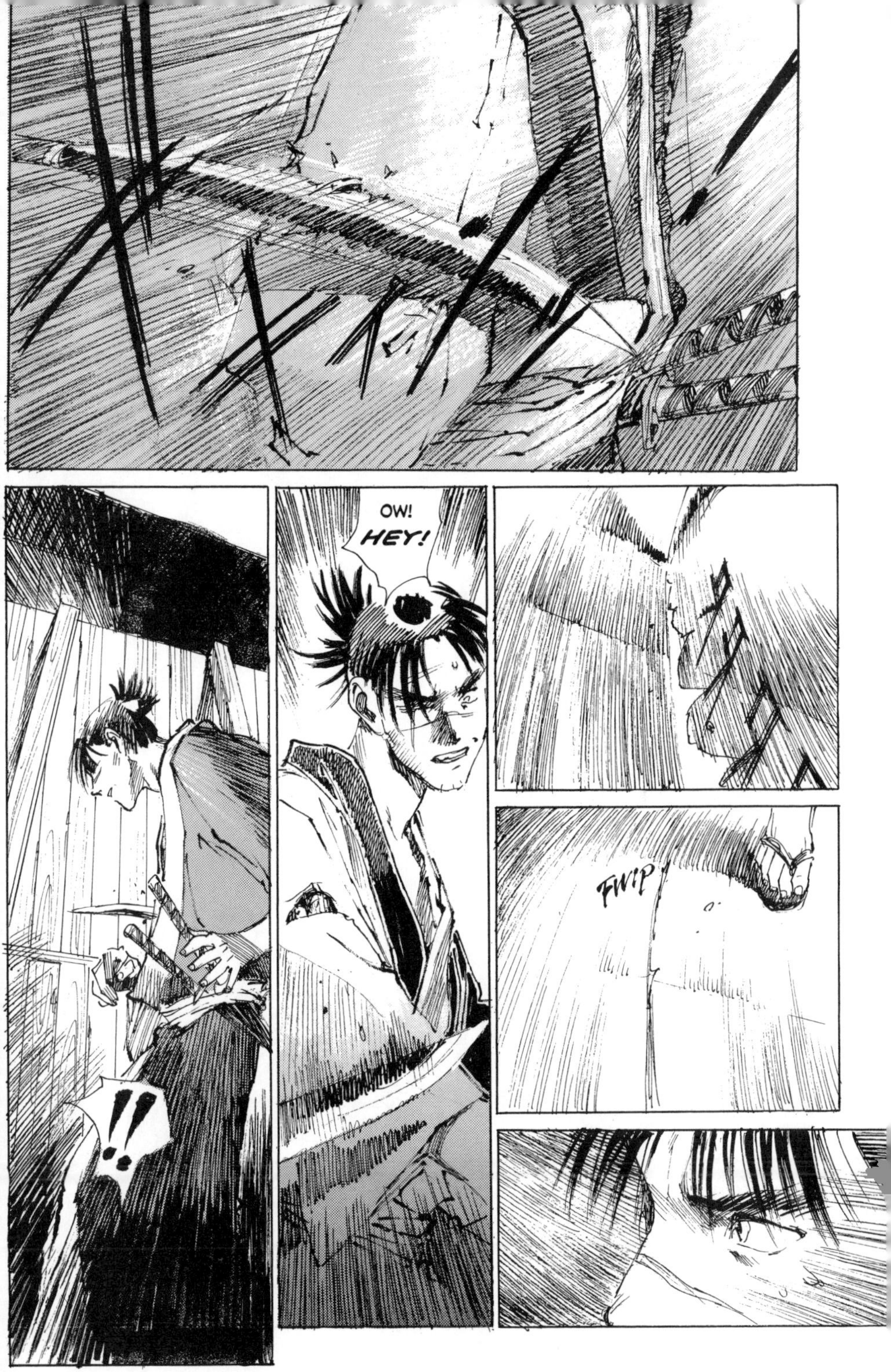

!!
OW!
HEY!
FWIP

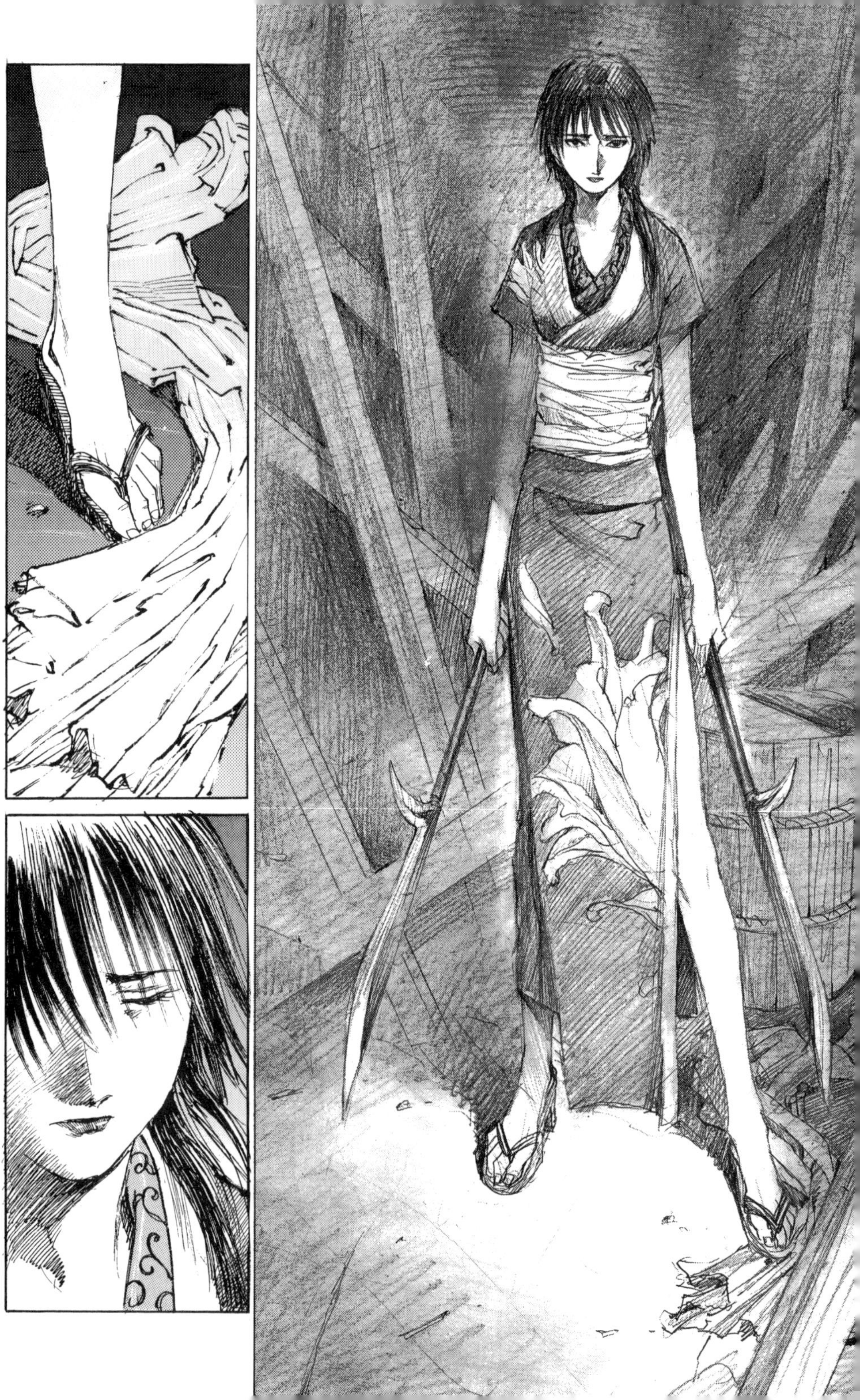

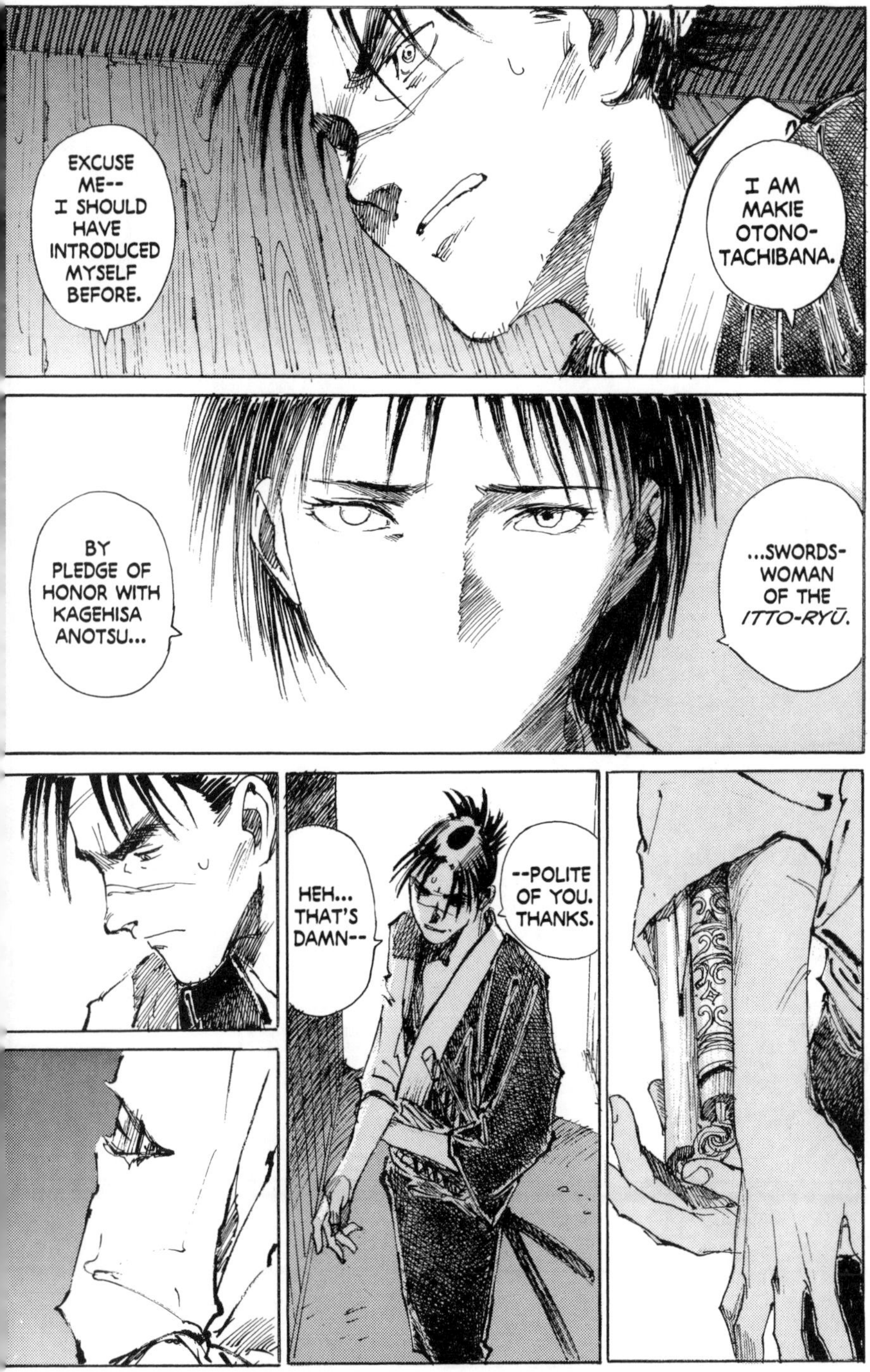
EXCUSE ME-- I SHOULD HAVE INTRODUCED MYSELF BEFORE.
I AM MAKIE OTONO-TACHIBANA.
BY PLEDGE OF HONOR WITH KAGEHISA ANOTSU...
...SWORDS-WOMAN OF THE *ITTO-RYŪ*.
HEH... THAT'S DAMN--
--POLITE OF YOU. THANKS.

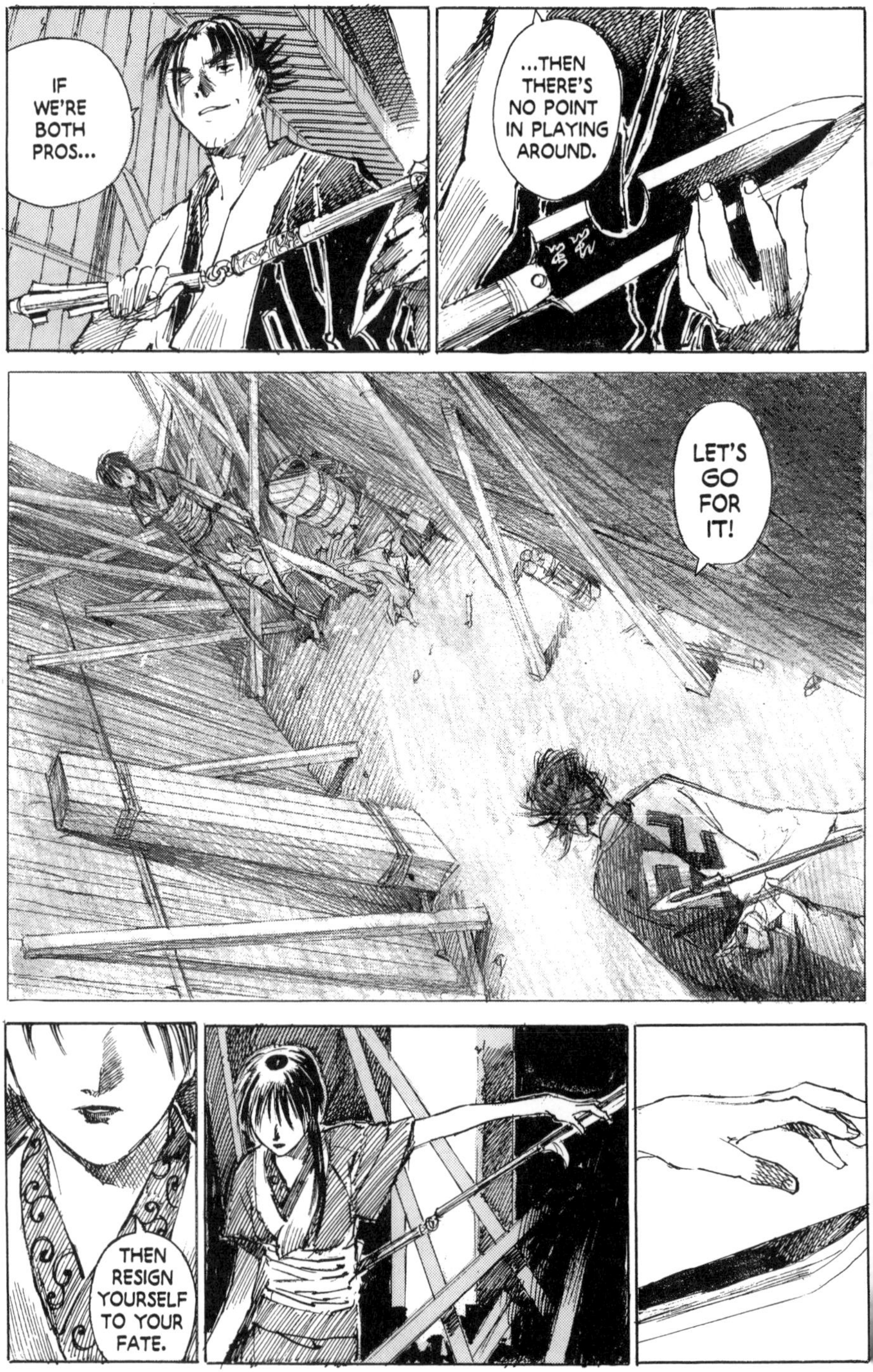
IF WE'RE BOTH PROS...
...THEN THERE'S NO POINT IN PLAYING AROUND.
LET'S GO FOR IT!
THEN RESIGN YOURSELF TO YOUR FATE.

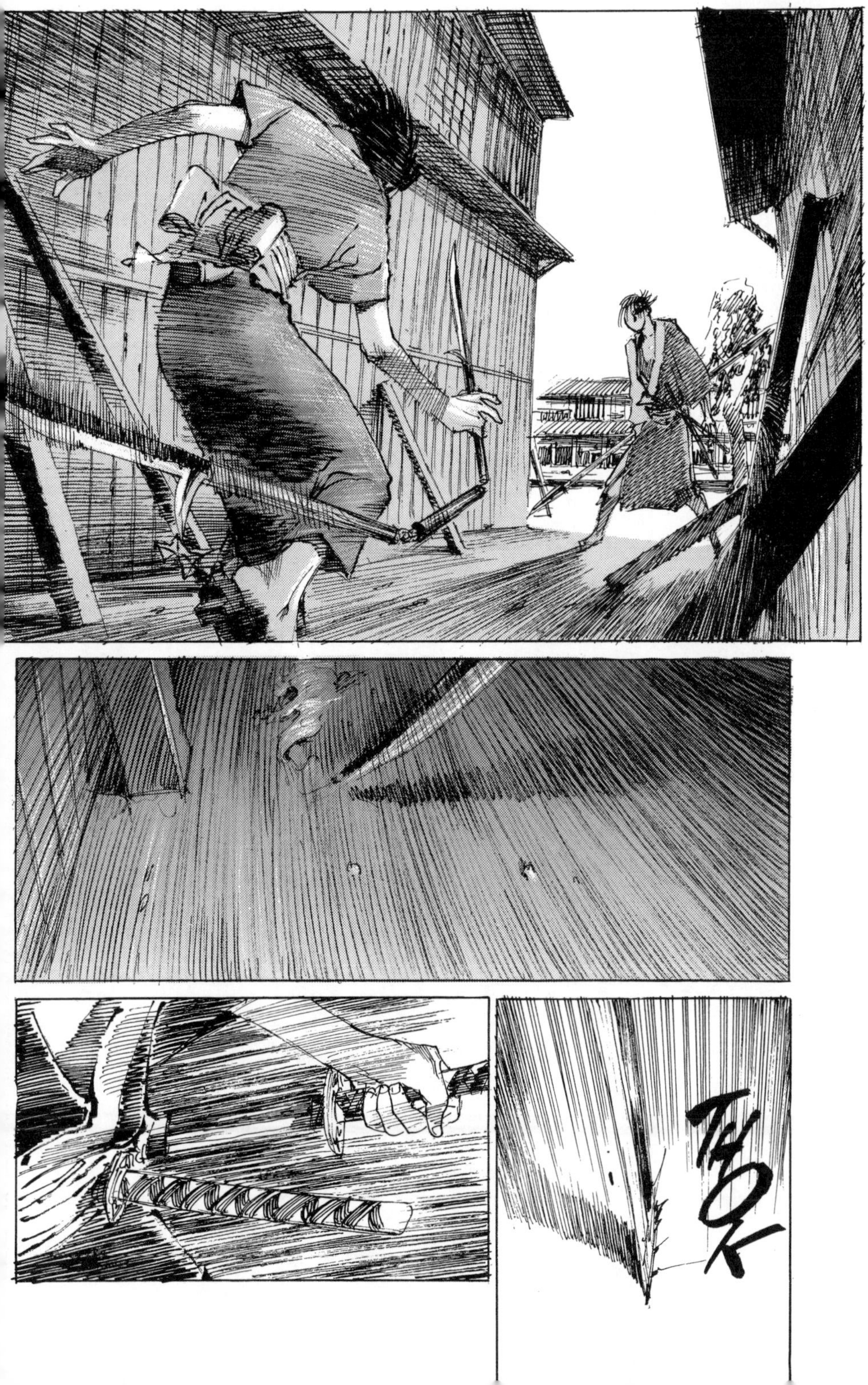
THOK

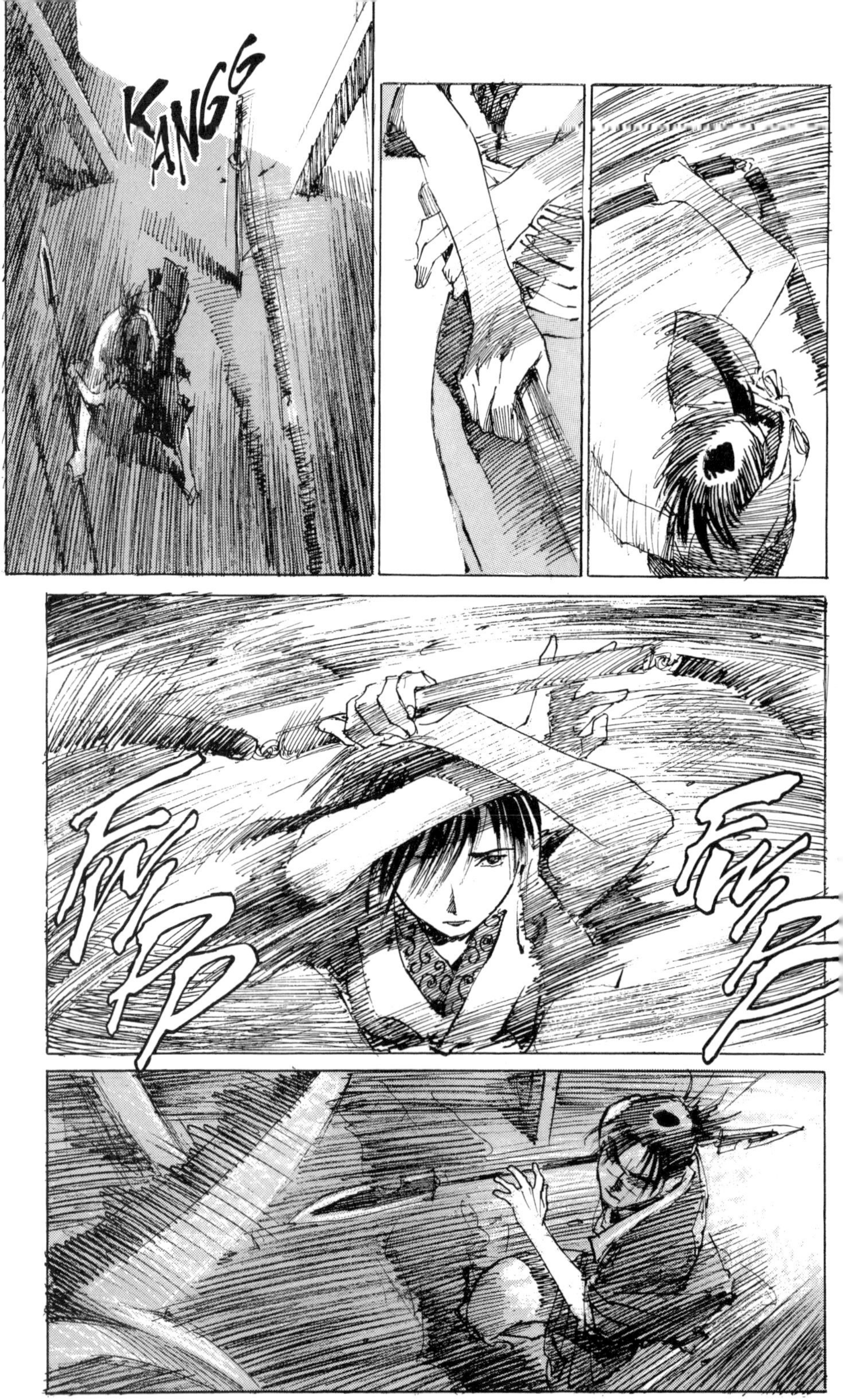
KANGG
FWPP
FWPP

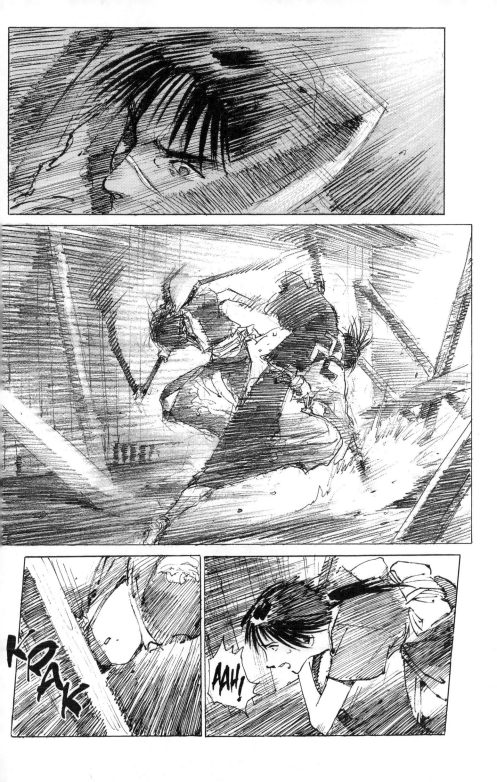

KRAK

AAH!

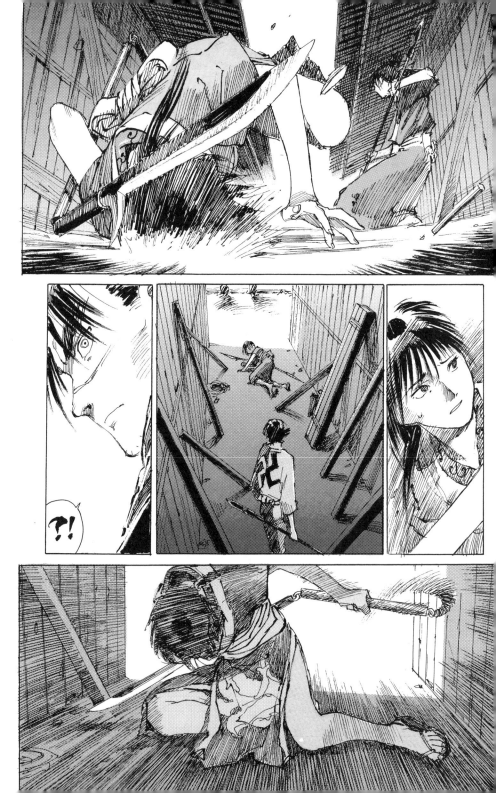

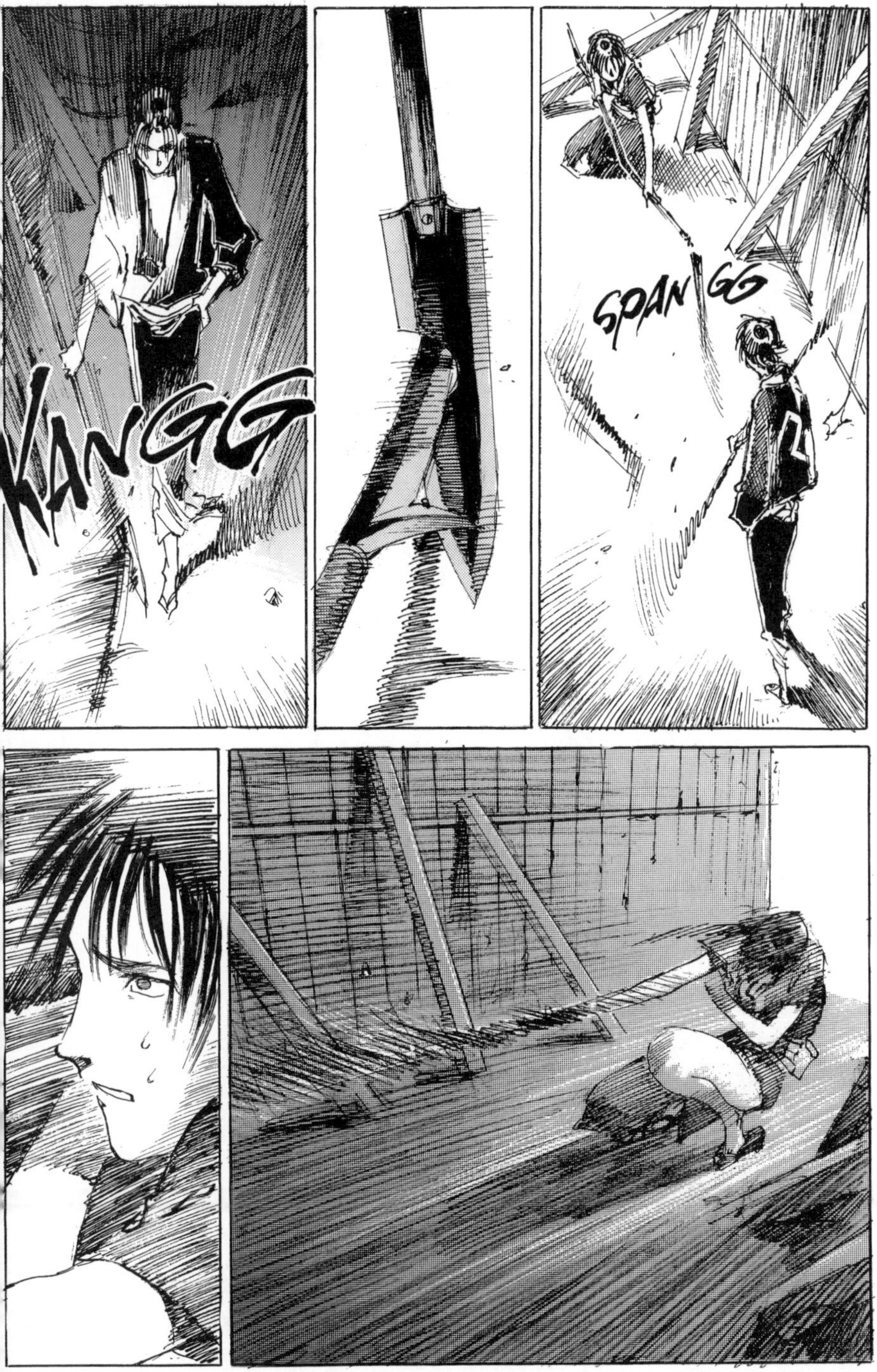
KANGG
SPANGG

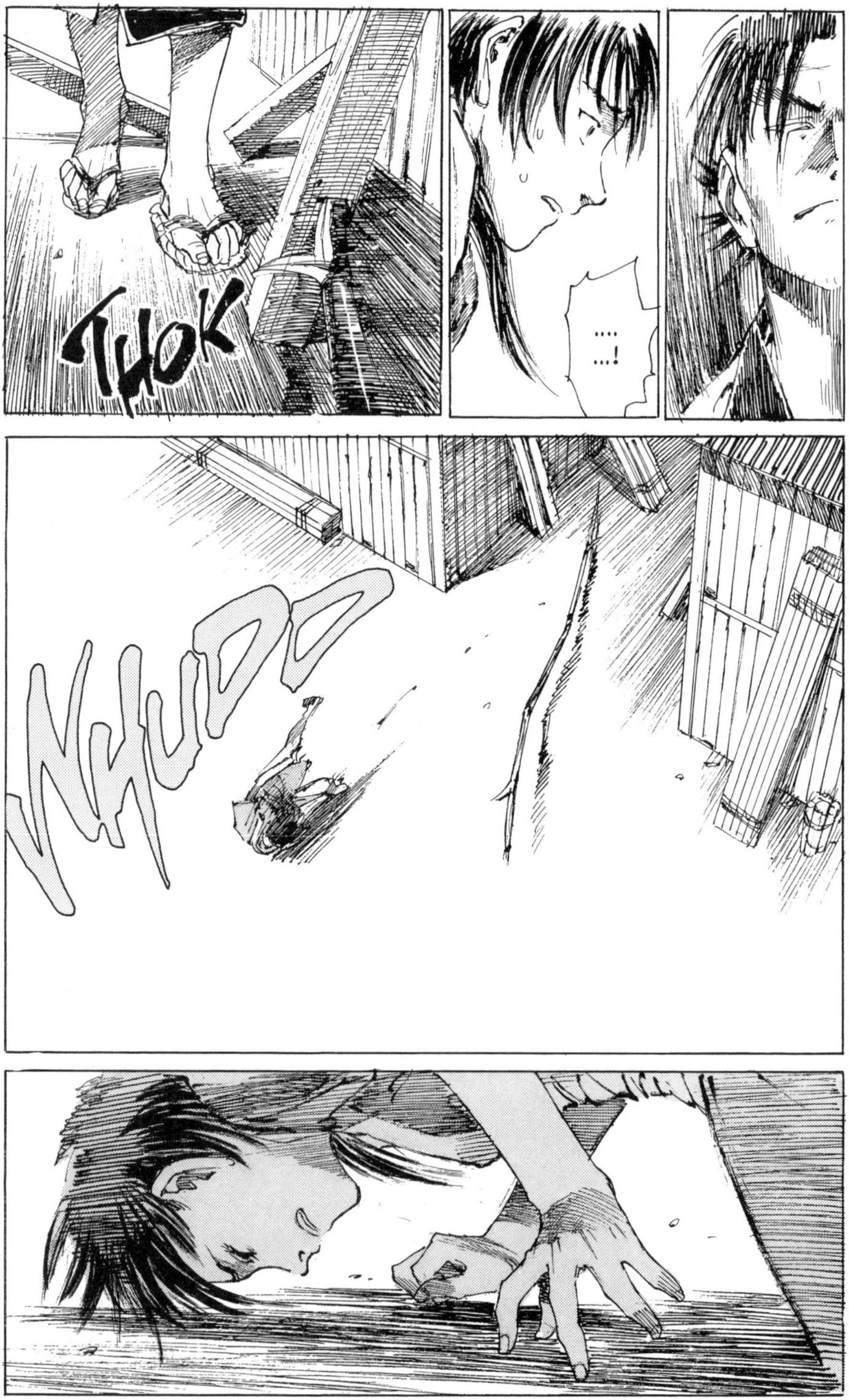
THOK
……
…!
WHUDD

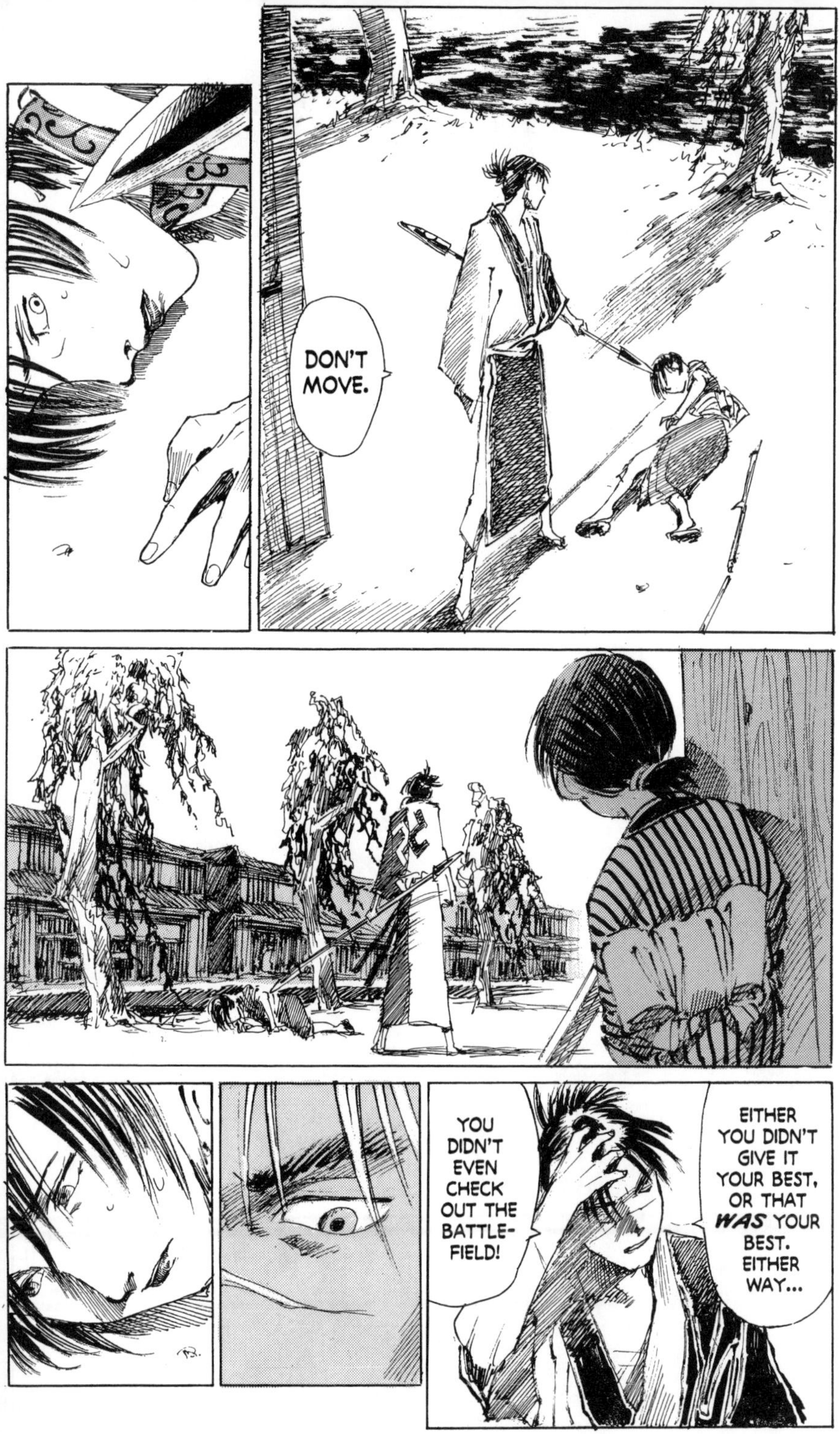
DON'T MOVE.
YOU DIDN'T EVEN CHECK OUT THE BATTLE-FIELD!
EITHER YOU DIDN'T GIVE IT YOUR BEST, OR THAT *WAS* YOUR BEST. EITHER WAY...

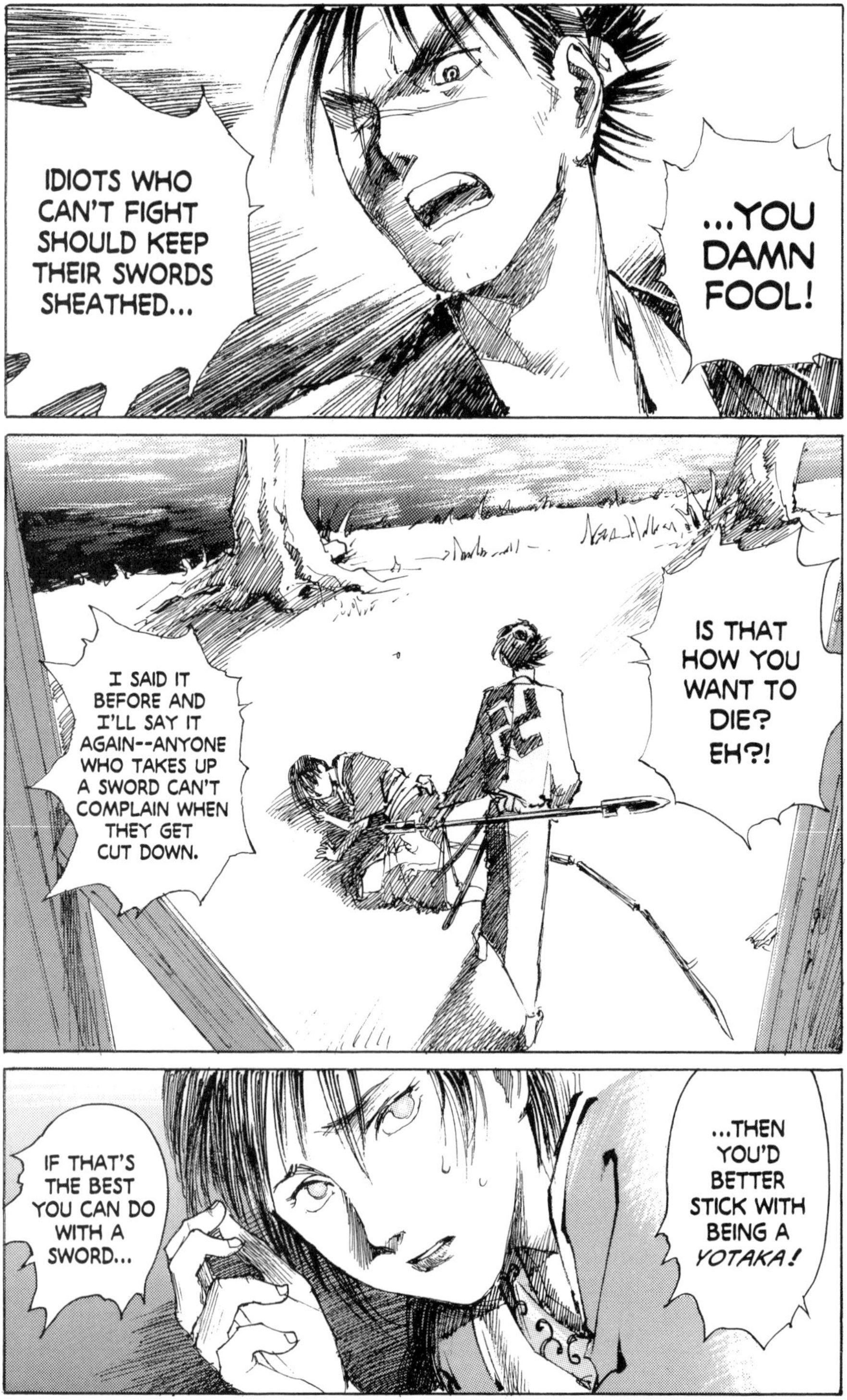
IDIOTS WHO CAN'T FIGHT SHOULD KEEP THEIR SWORDS SHEATHED...
...YOU DAMN FOOL!
I SAID IT BEFORE AND I'LL SAY IT AGAIN--ANYONE WHO TAKES UP A SWORD CAN'T COMPLAIN WHEN THEY GET CUT DOWN.
IS THAT HOW YOU WANT TO DIE? EH?!
IF THAT'S THE BEST YOU CAN DO WITH A SWORD...
...THEN YOU'D BETTER STICK WITH BEING A *YOTAKA!*

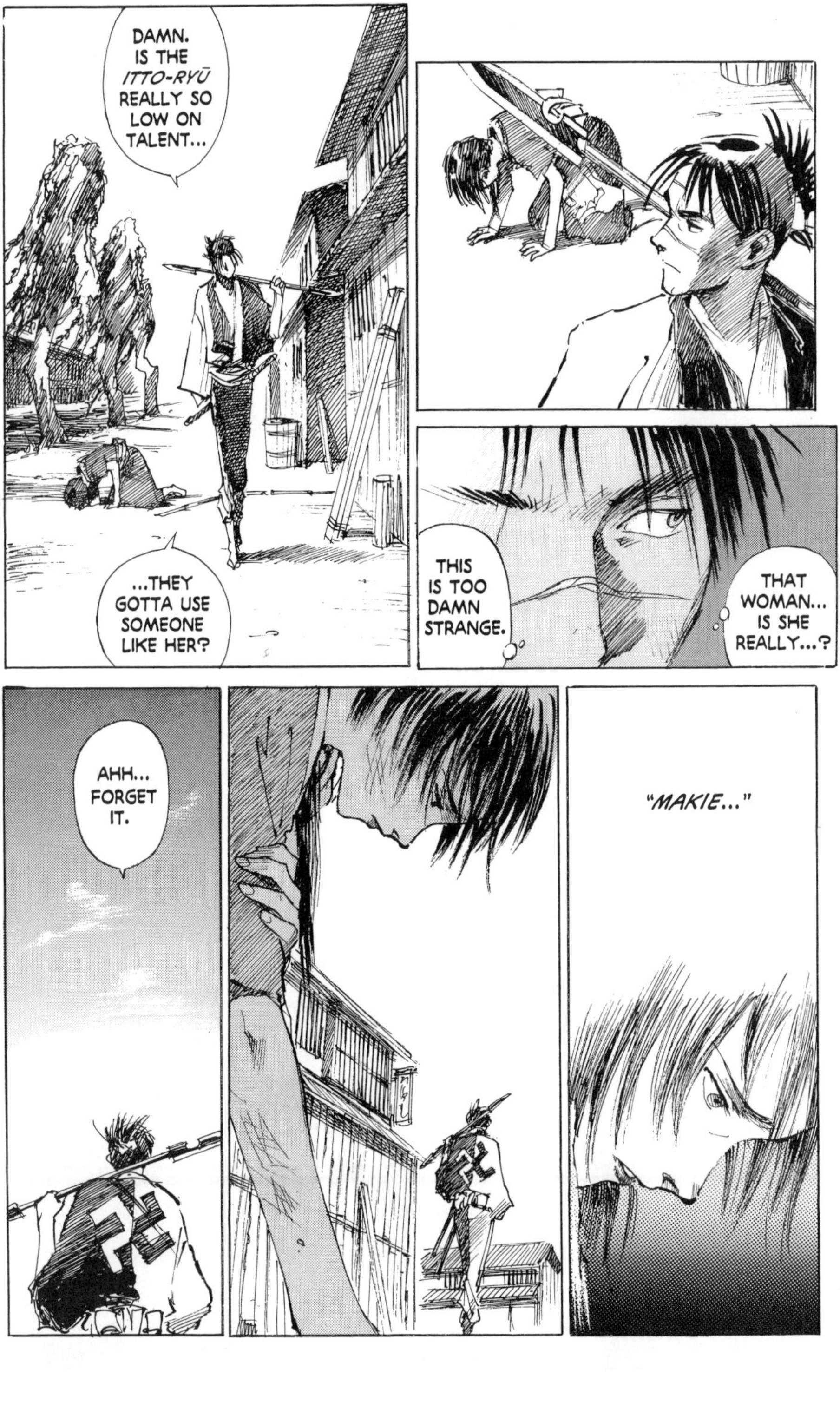
DAMN. IS THE *ITTO-RYŪ* REALLY SO LOW ON TALENT...
...THEY GOTTA USE SOMEONE LIKE HER?
THIS IS TOO DAMN STRANGE.
THAT WOMAN... IS SHE REALLY...?
AHH... FORGET IT.
"MAKIE..."

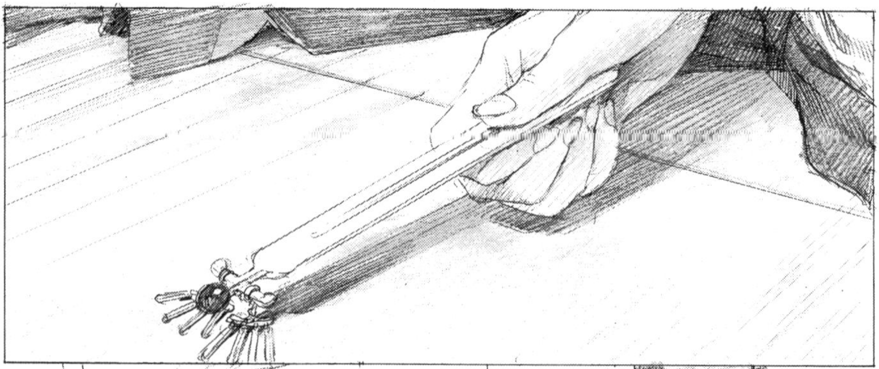
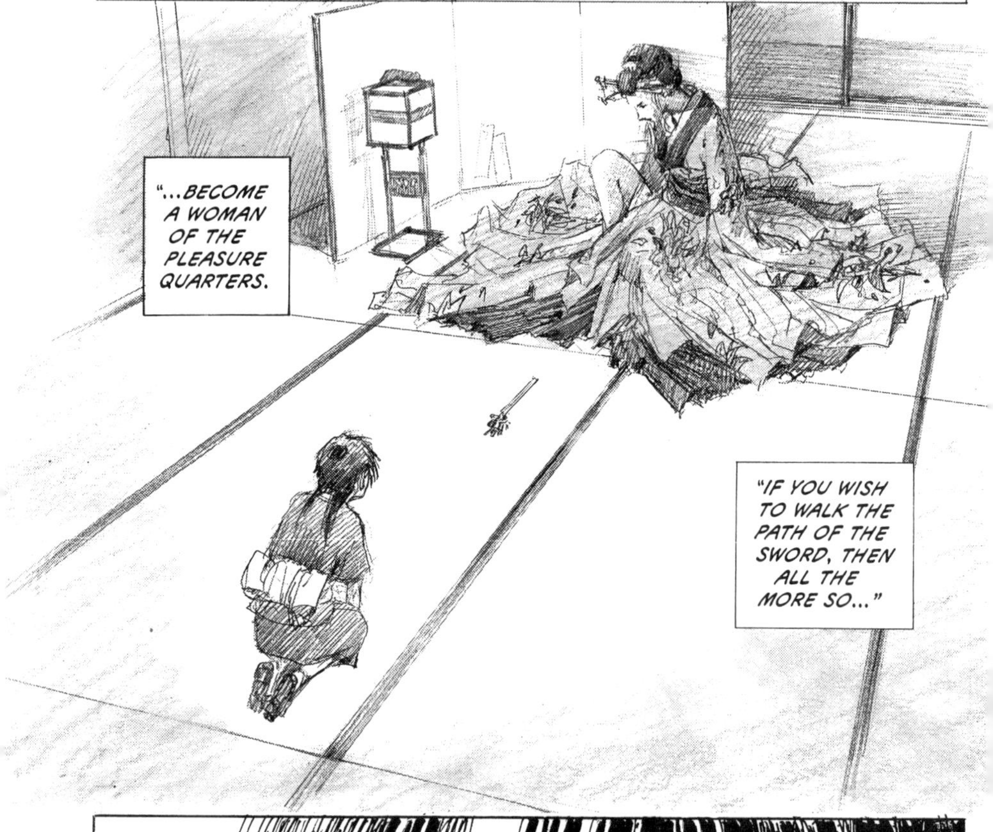
"...BECOME A WOMAN OF THE PLEASURE QUARTERS.
"IF YOU WISH TO WALK THE PATH OF THE SWORD, THEN ALL THE MORE SO..."
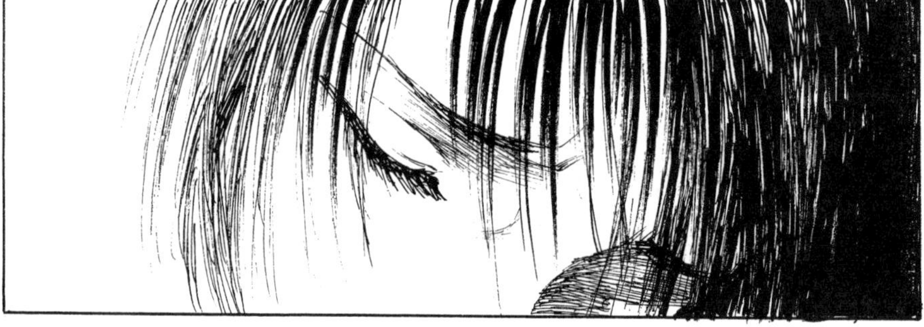

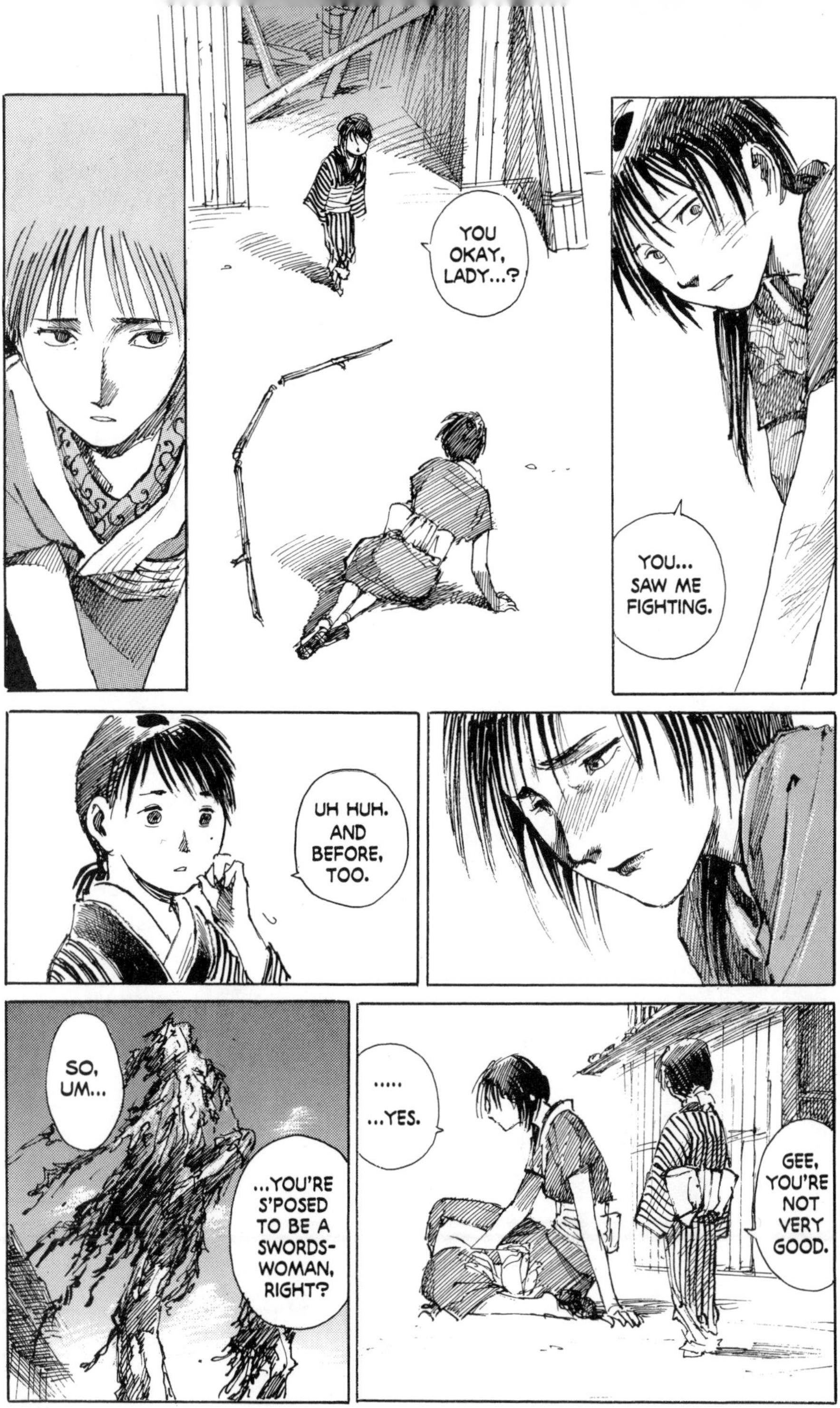
YOU OKAY, LADY...?
YOU... SAW ME FIGHTING.
UH HUH. AND BEFORE, TOO.
SO, UM...
...YOU'RE S'POSED TO BE A SWORDS-WOMAN, RIGHT?
.....
...YES.
GEE, YOU'RE NOT VERY GOOD.

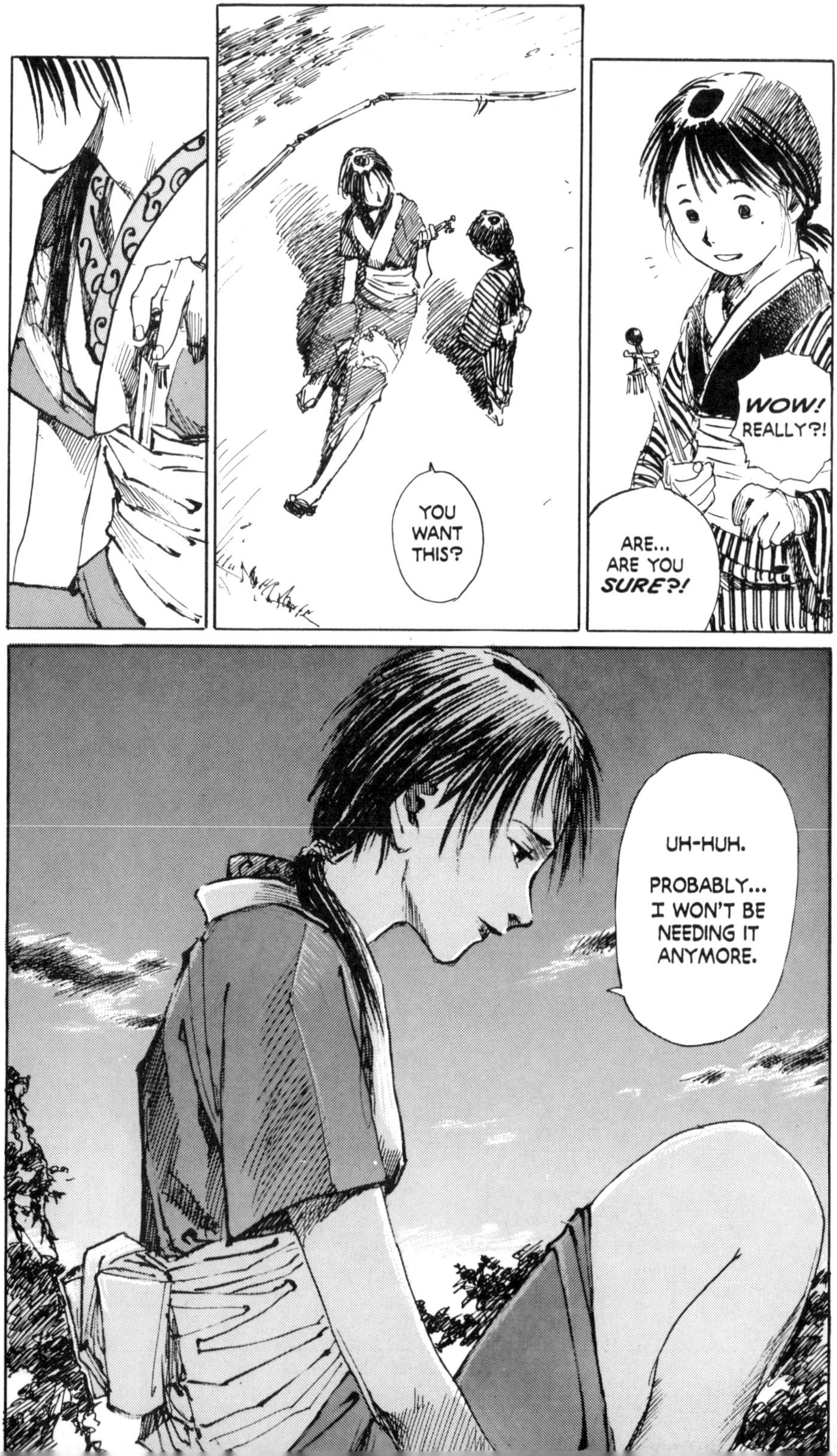
YOU WANT THIS?
WOW! REALLY?!
ARE... ARE YOU SURE?!
UH-HUH.
PROBABLY... I WON'T BE NEEDING IT ANYMORE.

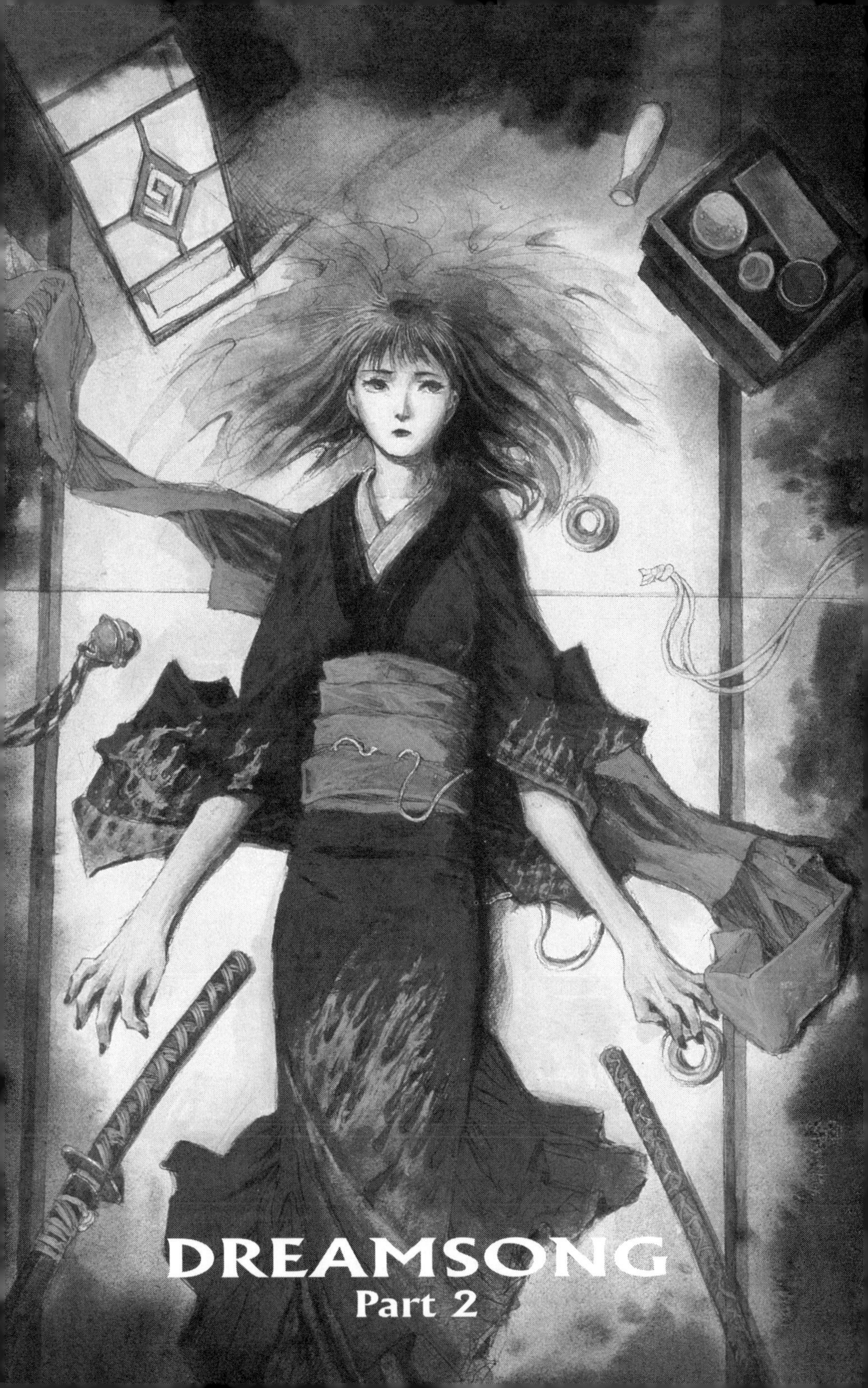

DREAMSONG
Part 2

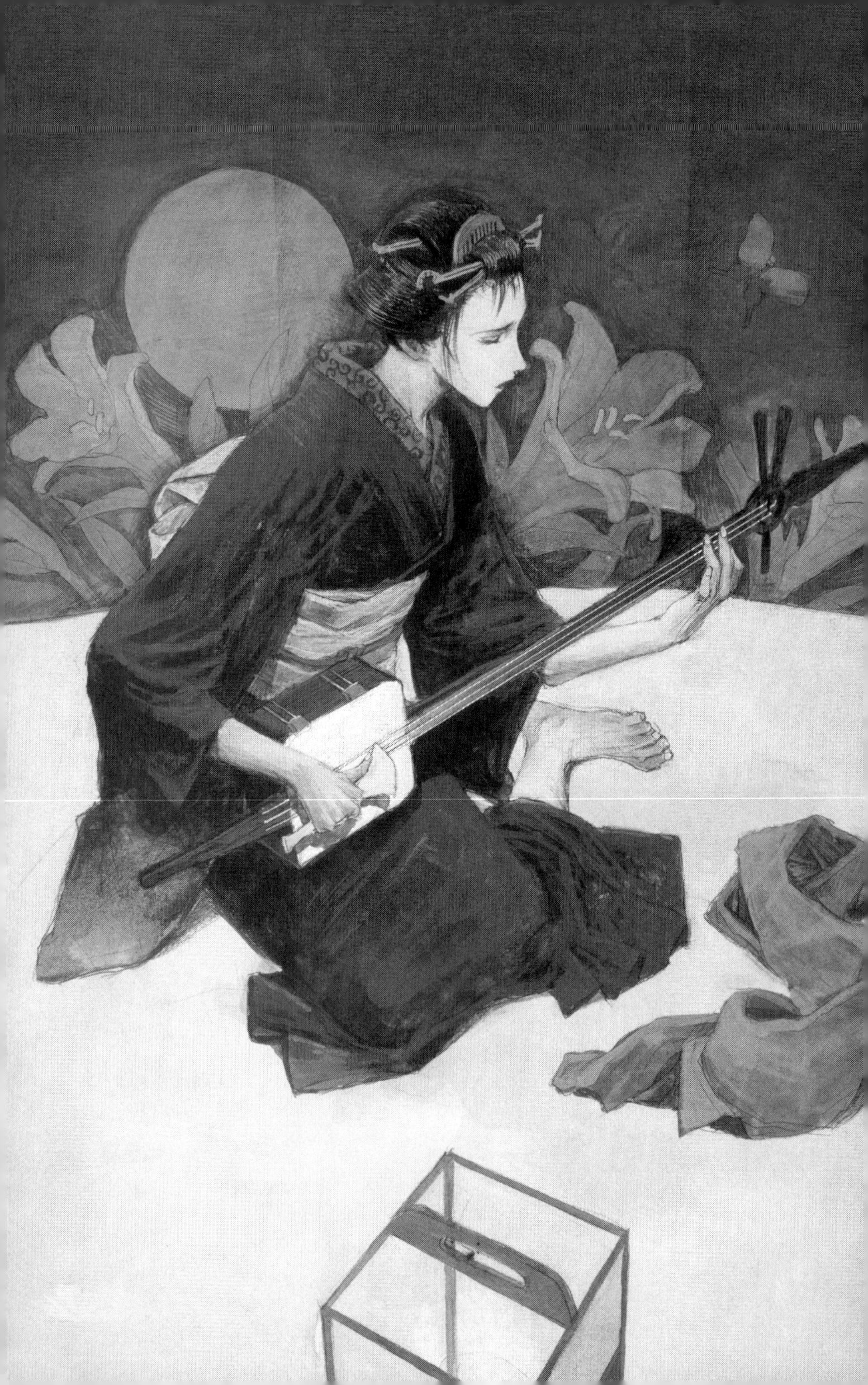

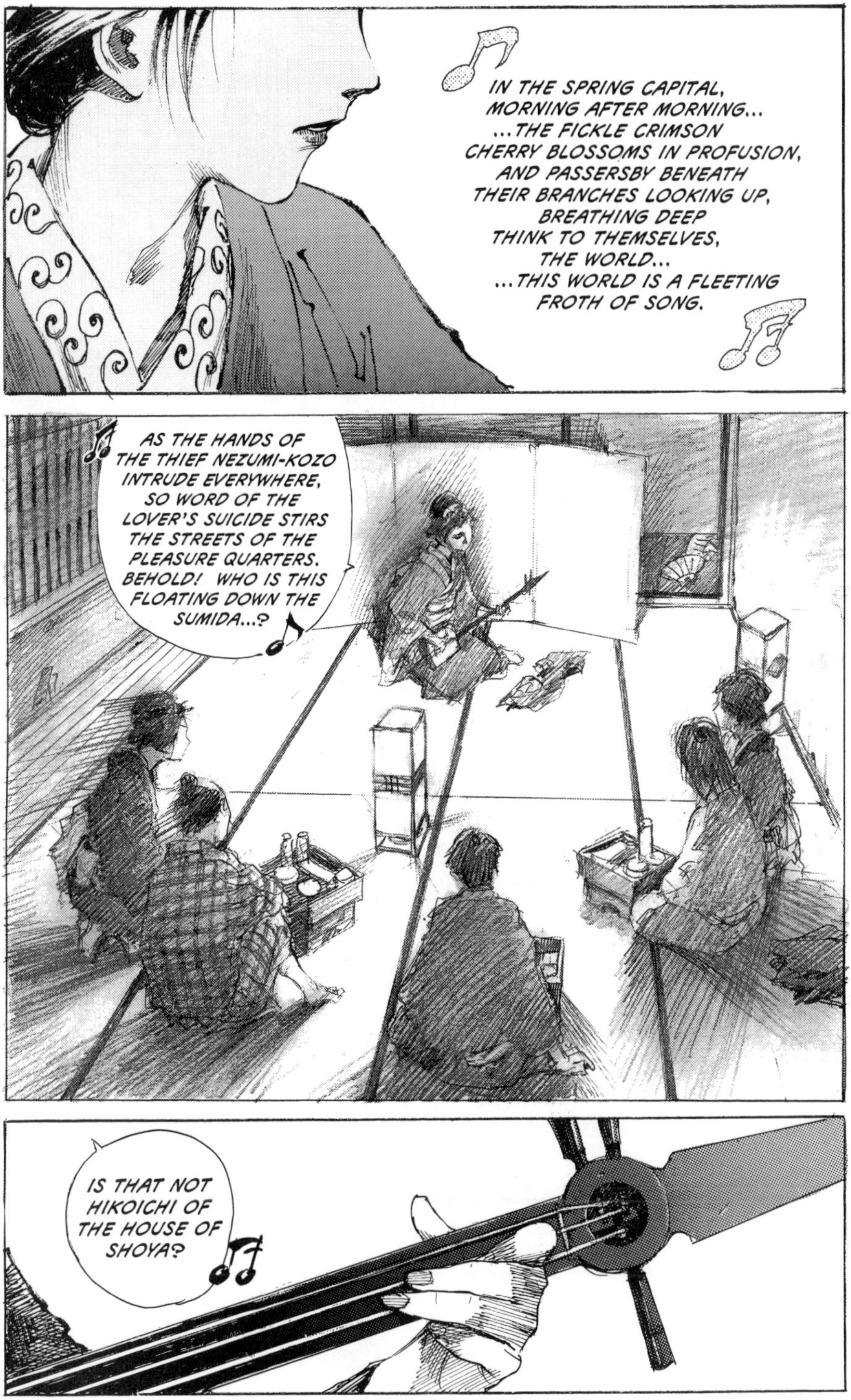
IN THE SPRING CAPITAL, MORNING AFTER MORNING... ...THE FICKLE CRIMSON CHERRY BLOSSOMS IN PROFUSION, AND PASSERSBY BENEATH THEIR BRANCHES LOOKING UP, BREATHING DEEP THINK TO THEMSELVES, THE WORLD... ...THIS WORLD IS A FLEETING FROTH OF SONG.
AS THE HANDS OF THE THIEF NEZUMI-KOZO INTRUDE EVERYWHERE, SO WORD OF THE LOVER'S SUICIDE STIRS THE STREETS OF THE PLEASURE QUARTERS. BEHOLD! WHO IS THIS FLOATING DOWN THE SUMIDA...?
IS THAT NOT HIKOICHI OF THE HOUSE OF SHOYA?

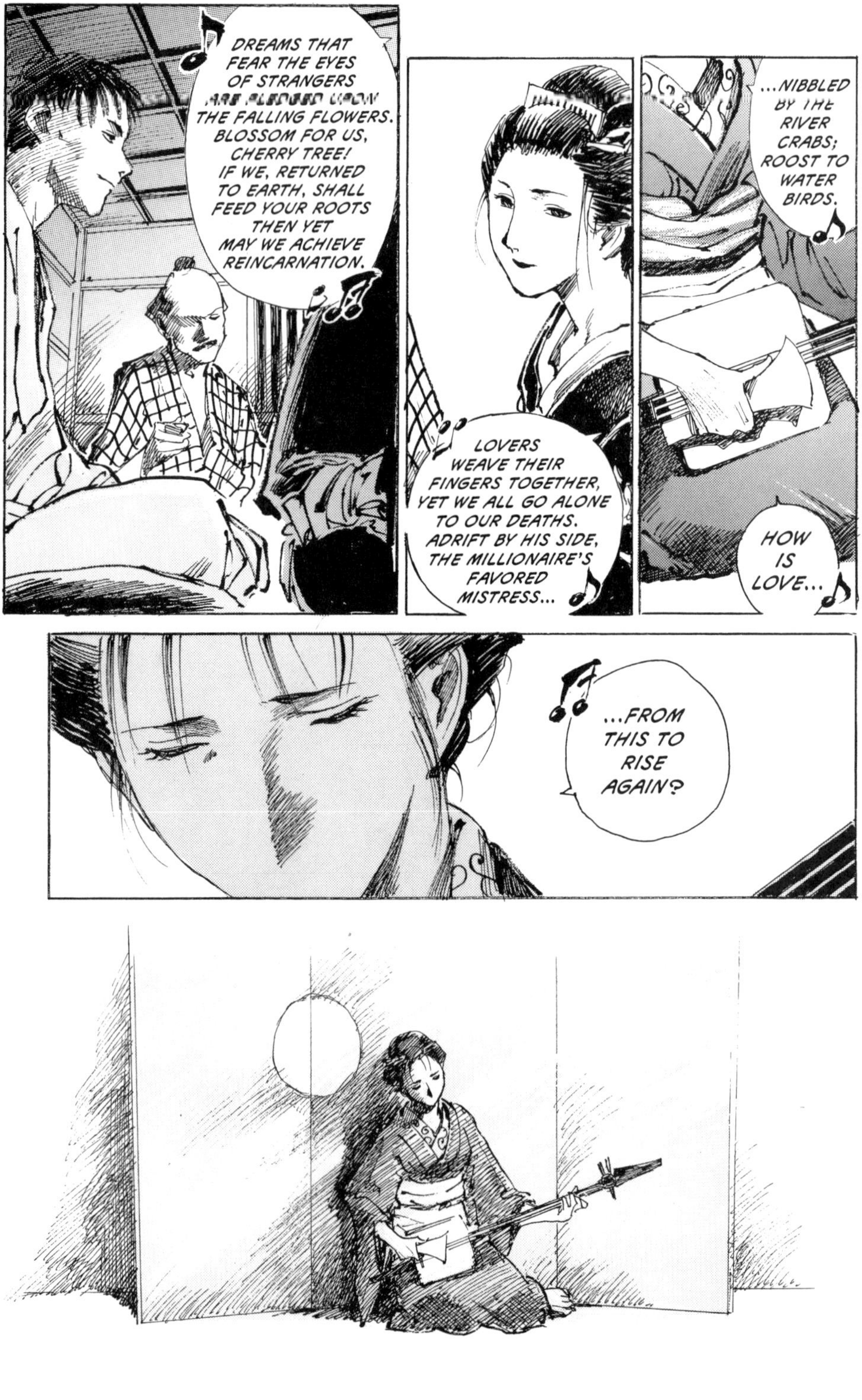
DREAMS THAT FEAR THE EYES OF STRANGERS ARE PLEDGED UPON THE FALLING FLOWERS. BLOSSOM FOR US, CHERRY TREE! IF WE, RETURNED TO EARTH, SHALL FEED YOUR ROOTS THEN YET MAY WE ACHIEVE REINCARNATION.
LOVERS WEAVE THEIR FINGERS TOGETHER, YET WE ALL GO ALONE TO OUR DEATHS. ADRIFT BY HIS SIDE, THE MILLIONAIRE'S FAVORED MISTRESS...
...NIBBLED BY THE RIVER CRABS; ROOST TO WATER BIRDS.
HOW IS LOVE...
...FROM THIS TO RISE AGAIN?

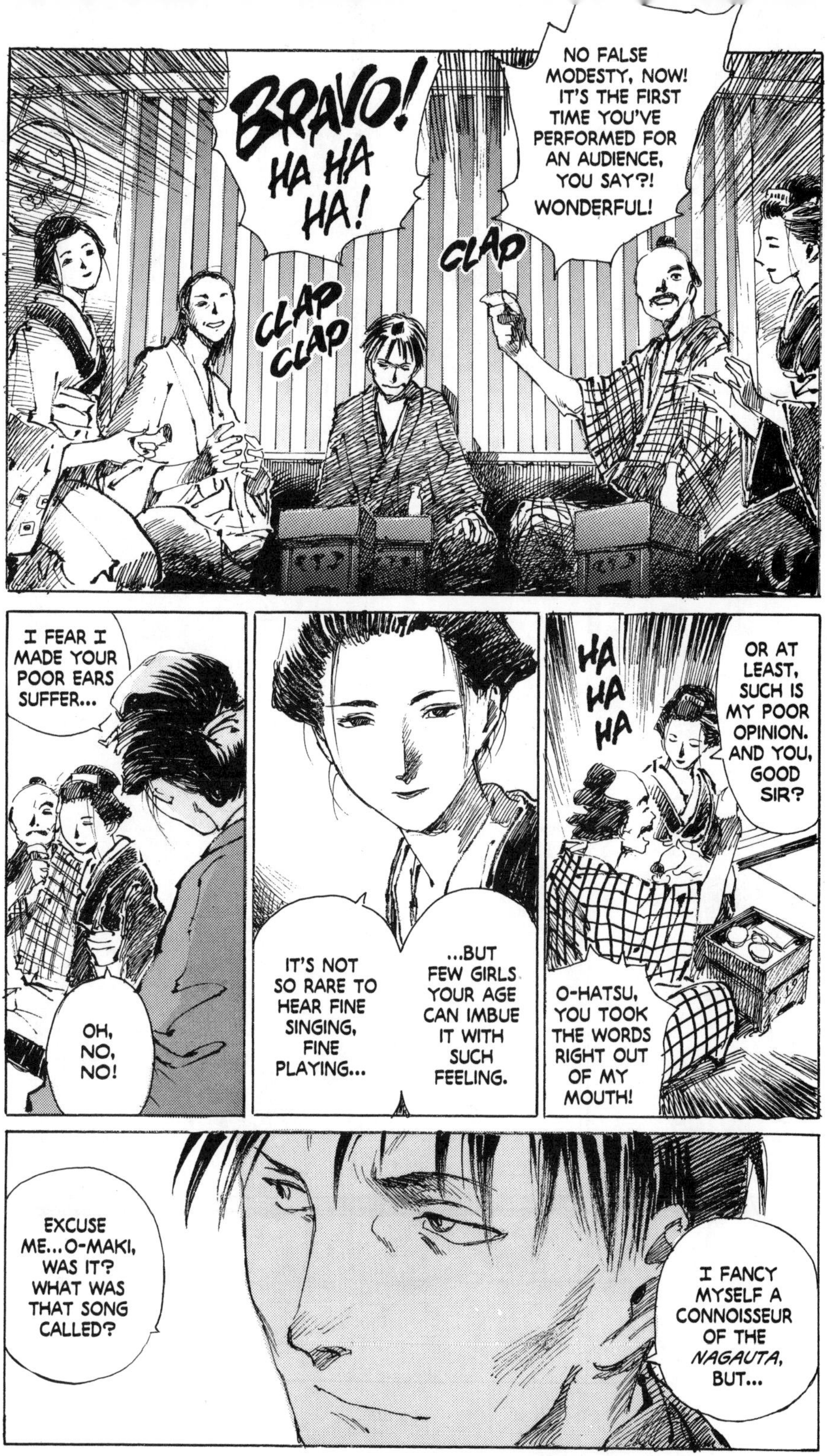
BRAVO! HA HA HA!
NO FALSE MODESTY, NOW! IT'S THE FIRST TIME YOU'VE PERFORMED FOR AN AUDIENCE, YOU SAY?! WONDERFUL!
CLAP
CLAP CLAP
I FEAR I MADE YOUR POOR EARS SUFFER...
OH, NO, NO!
IT'S NOT SO RARE TO HEAR FINE SINGING, FINE PLAYING...
...BUT FEW GIRLS YOUR AGE CAN IMBUE IT WITH SUCH FEELING.
HA HA HA
OR AT LEAST, SUCH IS MY POOR OPINION. AND YOU, GOOD SIR?
O-HATSU, YOU TOOK THE WORDS RIGHT OUT OF MY MOUTH!
EXCUSE ME...O-MAKI, WAS IT? WHAT WAS THAT SONG CALLED?
I FANCY MYSELF A CONNOISSEUR OF THE *NAGAUTA*, BUT...

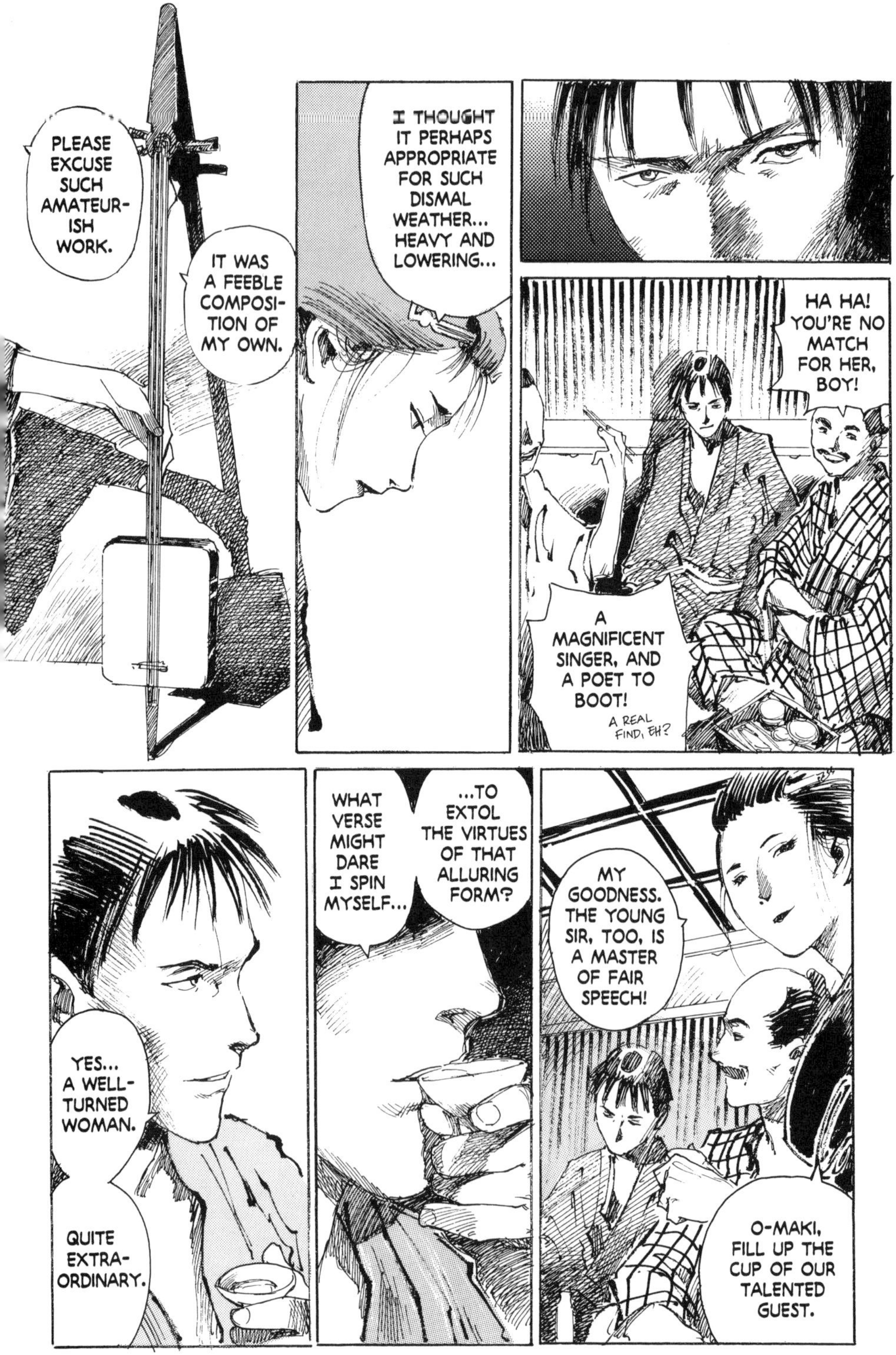
PLEASE EXCUSE SUCH AMATEURISH WORK.
IT WAS A FEEBLE COMPOSITION OF MY OWN.
I THOUGHT IT PERHAPS APPROPRIATE FOR SUCH DISMAL WEATHER... HEAVY AND LOWERING...
HA HA! YOU'RE NO MATCH FOR HER, BOY!
A MAGNIFICENT SINGER, AND A POET TO BOOT!
A REAL FIND, EH?
YES... A WELL-TURNED WOMAN.
QUITE EXTRAORDINARY.
WHAT VERSE MIGHT DARE I SPIN MYSELF...
...TO EXTOL THE VIRTUES OF THAT ALLURING FORM?
MY GOODNESS. THE YOUNG SIR, TOO, IS A MASTER OF FAIR SPEECH!
O-MAKI, FILL UP THE CUP OF OUR TALENTED GUEST.

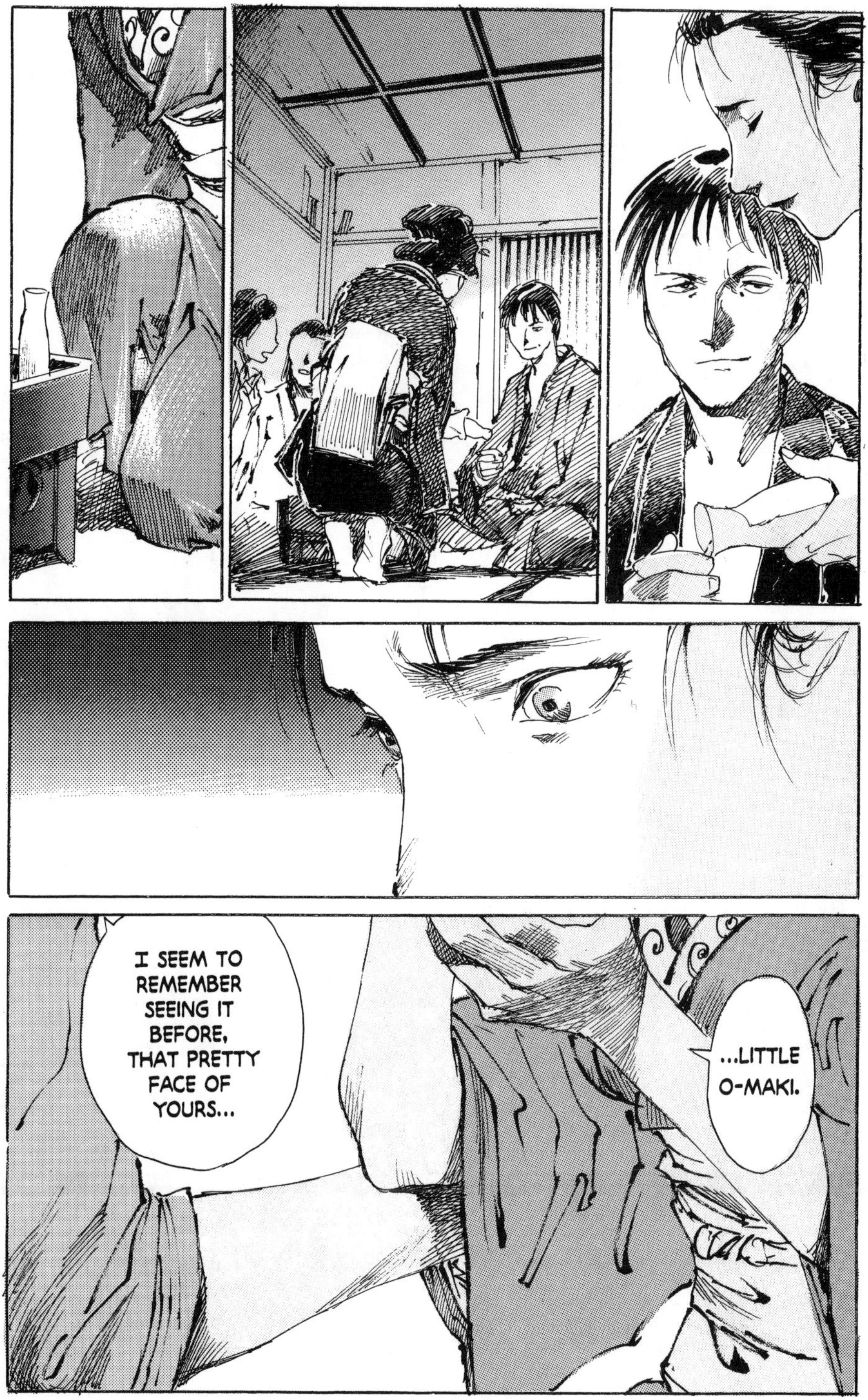
I SEEM TO REMEMBER SEEING IT BEFORE, THAT PRETTY FACE OF YOURS...
...LITTLE O-MAKI.

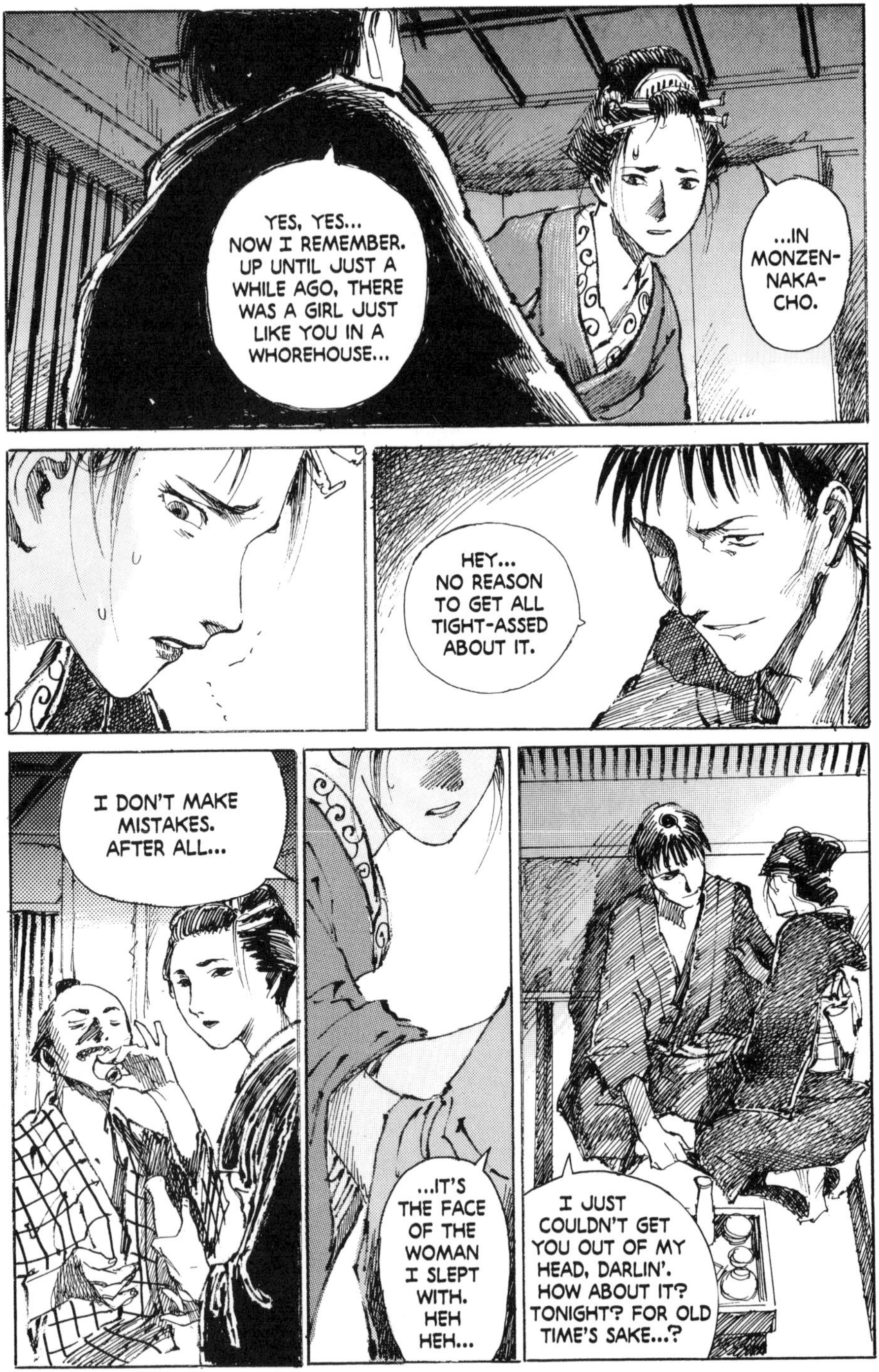
YES, YES... NOW I REMEMBER. UP UNTIL JUST A WHILE AGO, THERE WAS A GIRL JUST LIKE YOU IN A WHOREHOUSE...
...IN MONZEN-NAKA-CHO.
HEY... NO REASON TO GET ALL TIGHT-ASSED ABOUT IT.
I DON'T MAKE MISTAKES. AFTER ALL...
...IT'S THE FACE OF THE WOMAN I SLEPT WITH. HEH HEH...
I JUST COULDN'T GET YOU OUT OF MY HEAD, DARLIN'. HOW ABOUT IT? TONIGHT? FOR OLD TIME'S SAKE...?

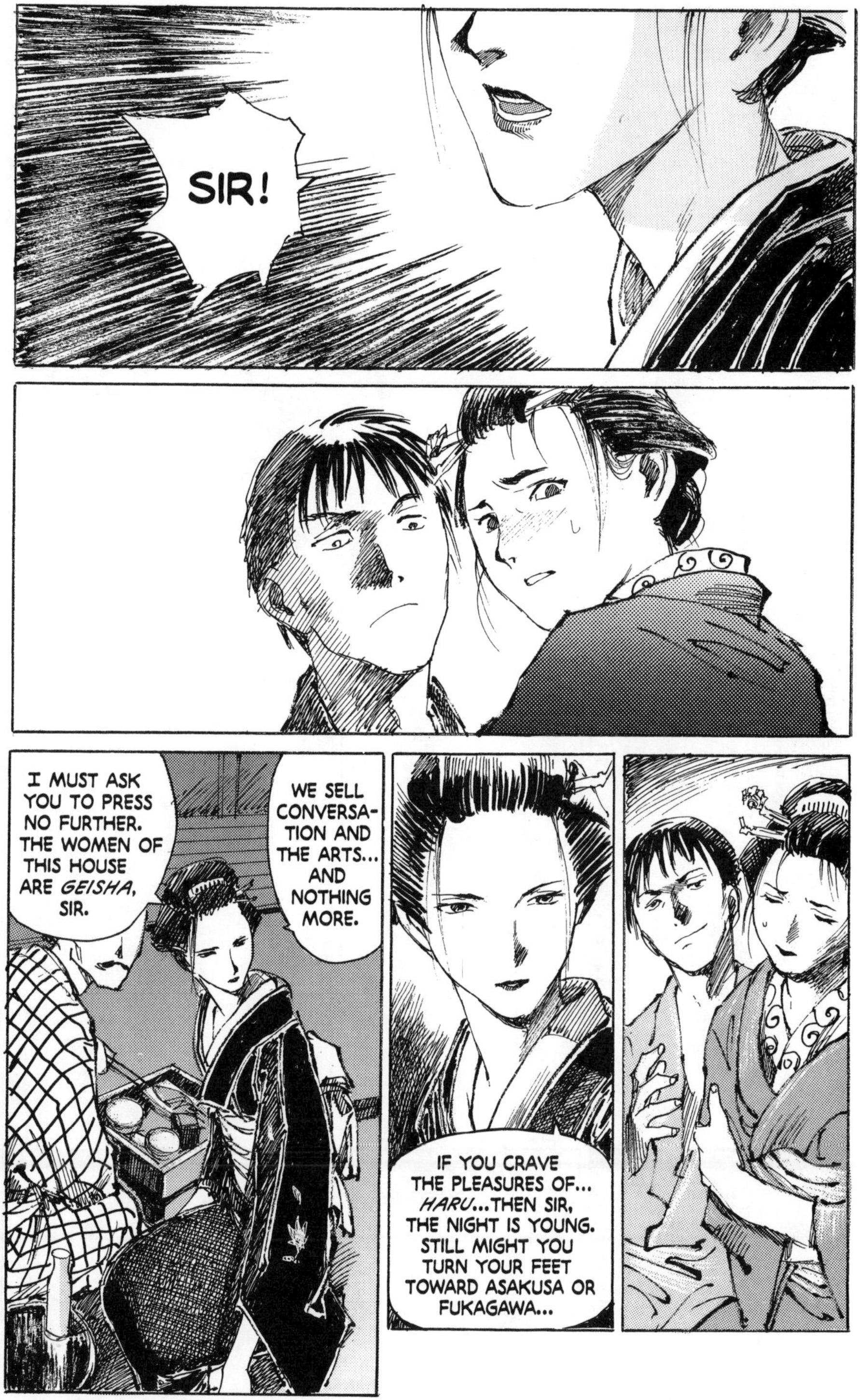
SIR!
I MUST ASK YOU TO PRESS NO FURTHER. THE WOMEN OF THIS HOUSE ARE *GEISHA*, SIR.
WE SELL CONVERSATION AND THE ARTS... AND NOTHING MORE.
IF YOU CRAVE THE PLEASURES OF... *HARU*...THEN SIR, THE NIGHT IS YOUNG. STILL MIGHT YOU TURN YOUR FEET TOWARD ASAKUSA OR FUKAGAWA...

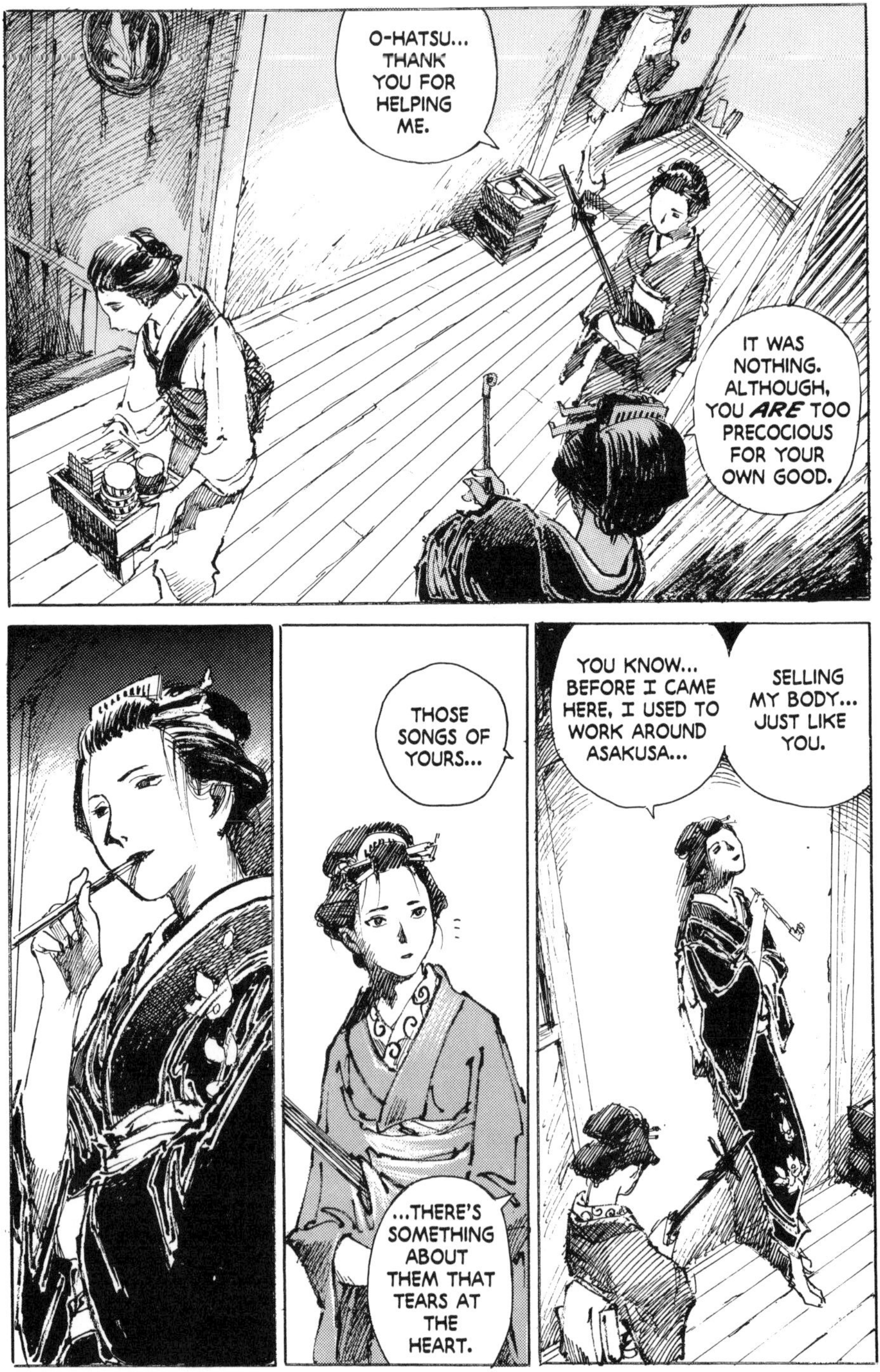
O-HATSU... THANK YOU FOR HELPING ME.
IT WAS NOTHING. ALTHOUGH, YOU *ARE* TOO PRECOCIOUS FOR YOUR OWN GOOD.
THOSE SONGS OF YOURS...
...THERE'S SOMETHING ABOUT THEM THAT TEARS AT THE HEART.
YOU KNOW... BEFORE I CAME HERE, I USED TO WORK AROUND ASAKUSA...
SELLING MY BODY... JUST LIKE YOU.

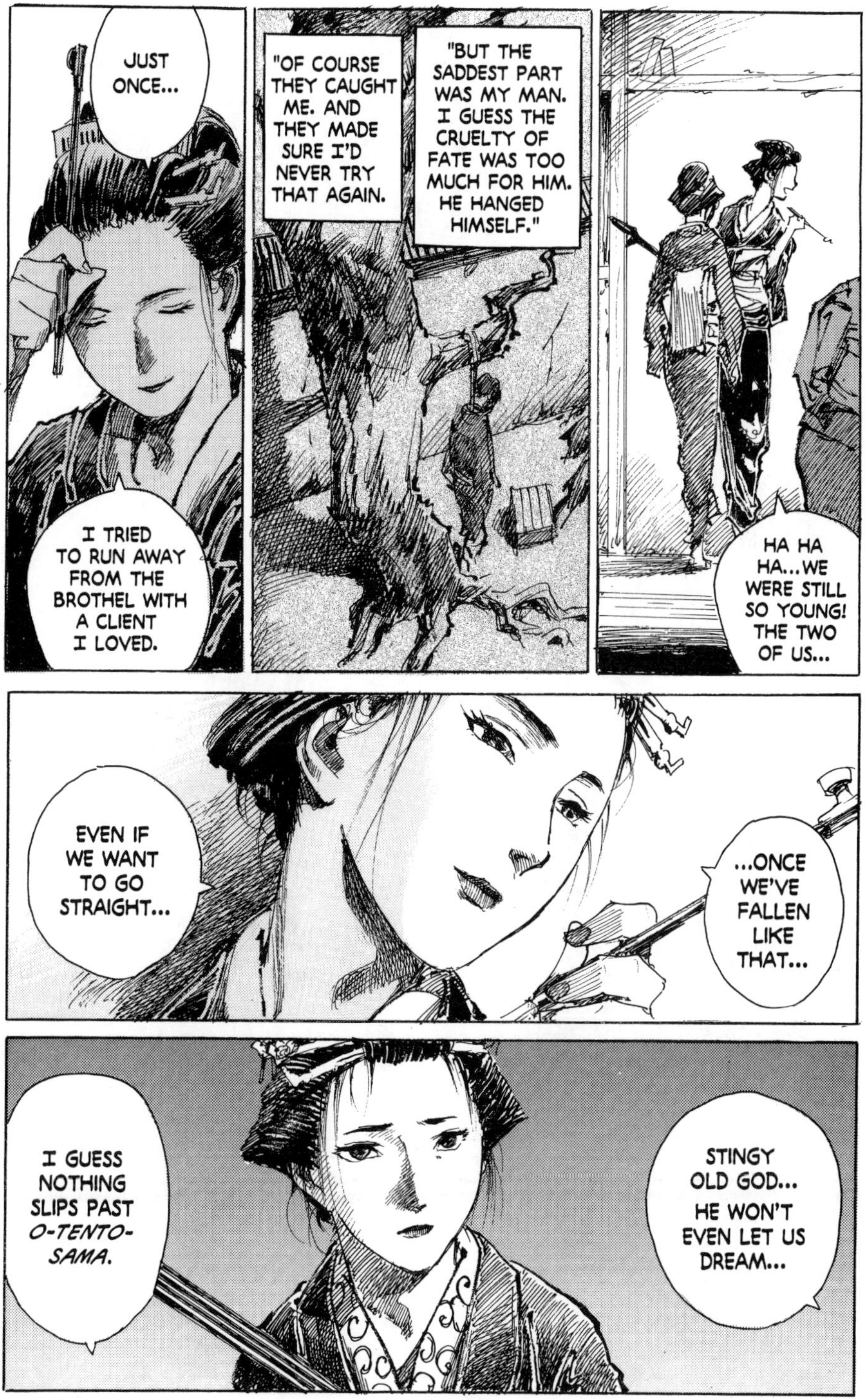
JUST ONCE...
I TRIED TO RUN AWAY FROM THE BROTHEL WITH A CLIENT I LOVED.
"OF COURSE THEY CAUGHT ME. AND THEY MADE SURE I'D NEVER TRY THAT AGAIN.
"BUT THE SADDEST PART WAS MY MAN. I GUESS THE CRUELTY OF FATE WAS TOO MUCH FOR HIM. HE HANGED HIMSELF."
HA HA HA...WE WERE STILL SO YOUNG! THE TWO OF US...
EVEN IF WE WANT TO GO STRAIGHT...
...ONCE WE'VE FALLEN LIKE THAT...
I GUESS NOTHING SLIPS PAST *O-TENTO-SAMA*.
STINGY OLD GOD...
HE WON'T EVEN LET US DREAM...

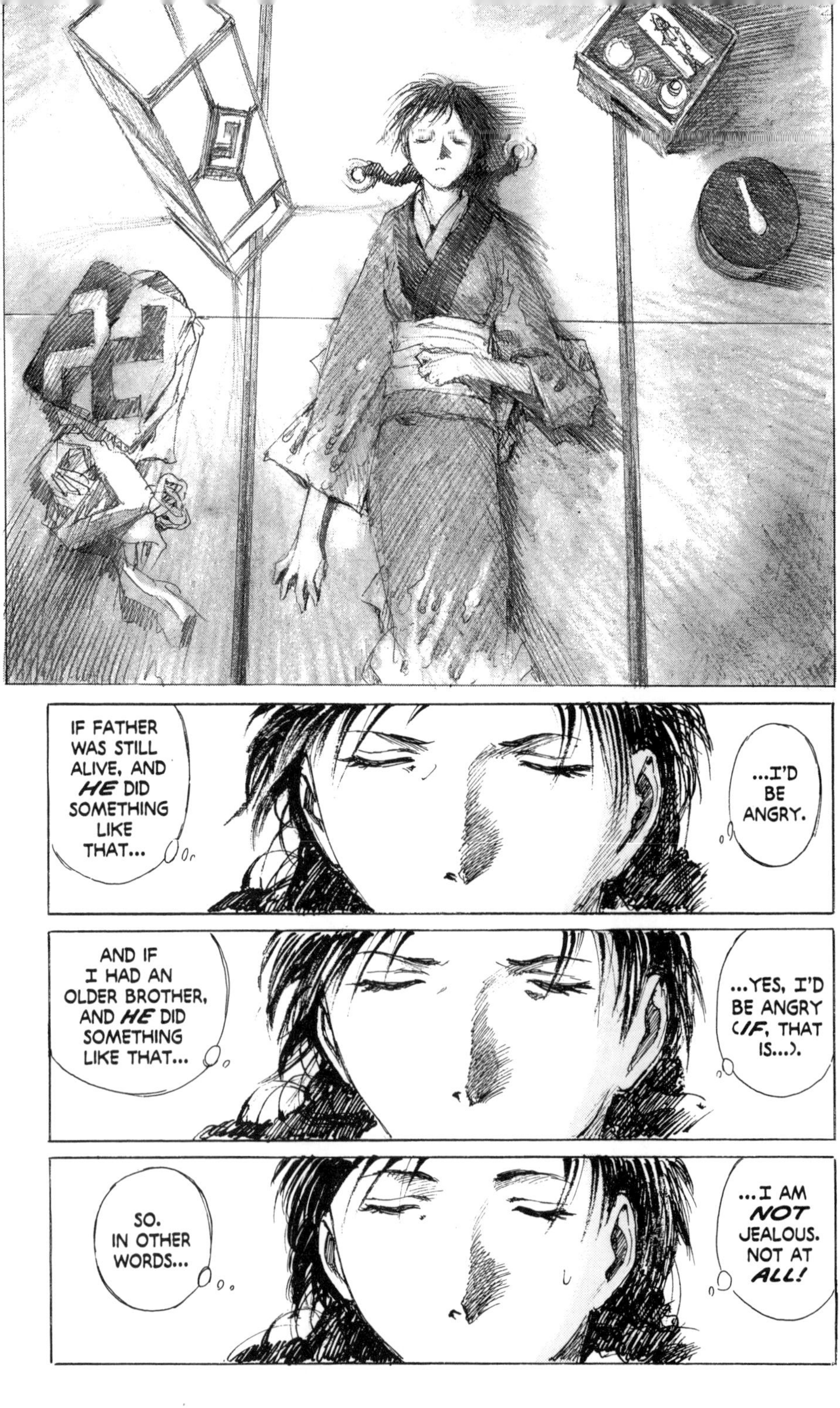
IF FATHER WAS STILL ALIVE, AND HE DID SOMETHING LIKE THAT...
...I'D BE ANGRY.
AND IF I HAD AN OLDER BROTHER, AND HE DID SOMETHING LIKE THAT...
...YES, I'D BE ANGRY (IF, THAT IS...).
SO. IN OTHER WORDS...
...I AM NOT JEALOUS. NOT AT ALL!

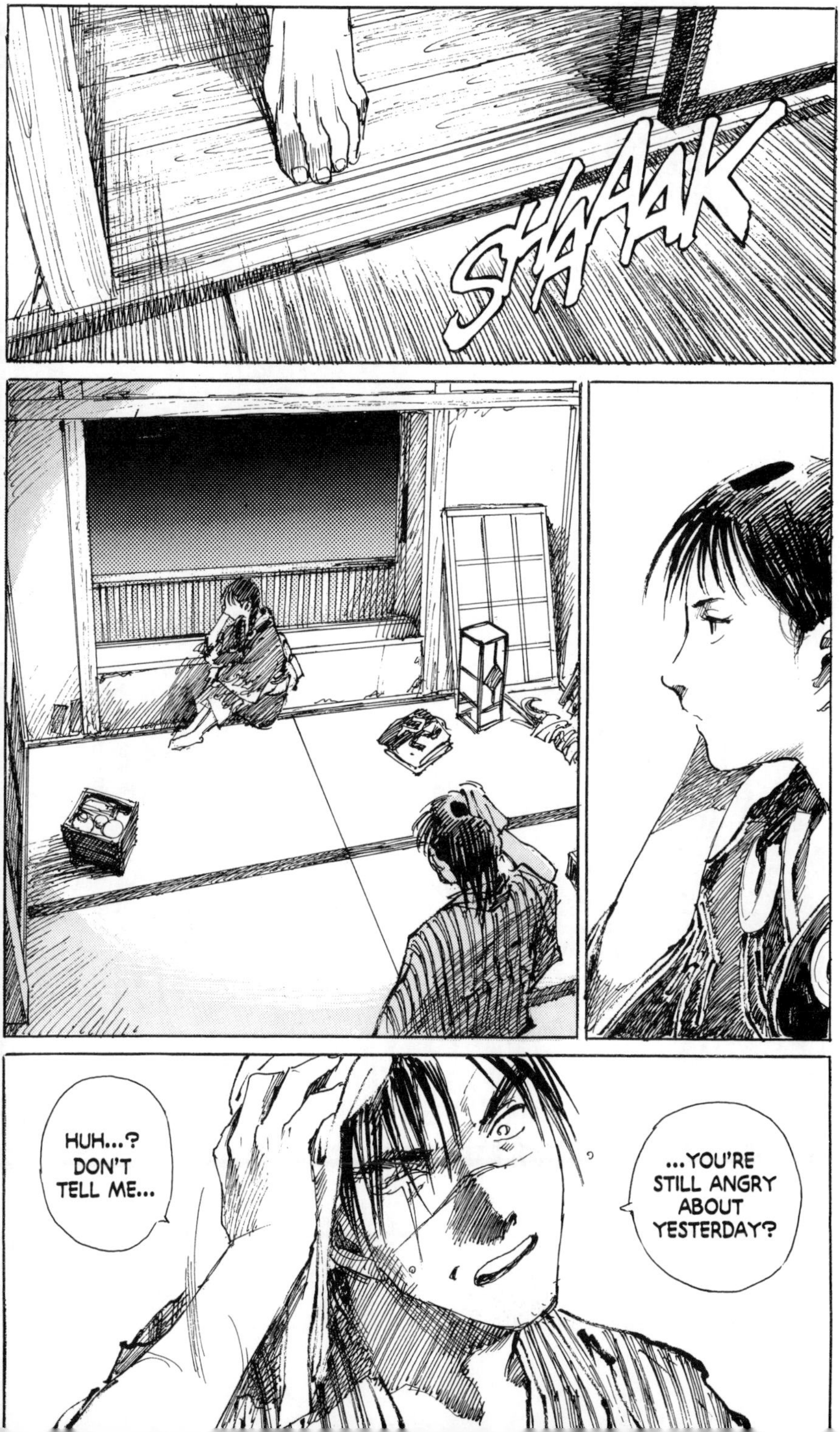
SHAAK
HUH...? DON'T TELL ME...
...YOU'RE STILL ANGRY ABOUT YESTERDAY?

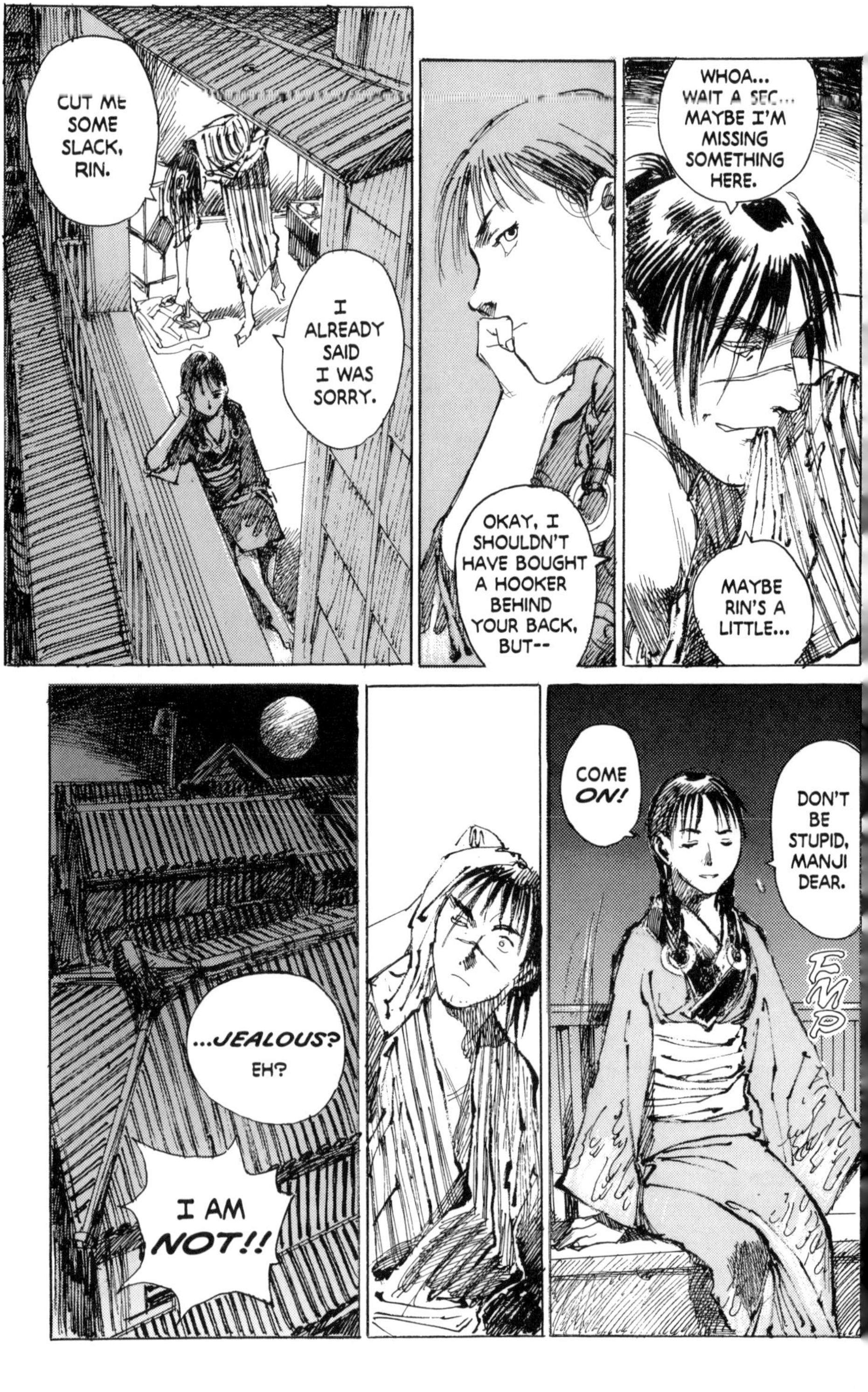
CUT ME SOME SLACK, RIN.
I ALREADY SAID I WAS SORRY.
OKAY, I SHOULDN'T HAVE BOUGHT A HOOKER BEHIND YOUR BACK, BUT--
WHOA... WAIT A SEC... MAYBE I'M MISSING SOMETHING HERE.
MAYBE RIN'S A LITTLE...
...JEALOUS? EH?
I AM NOT!!
COME ON!
DON'T BE STUPID, MANJI DEAR.
FMP

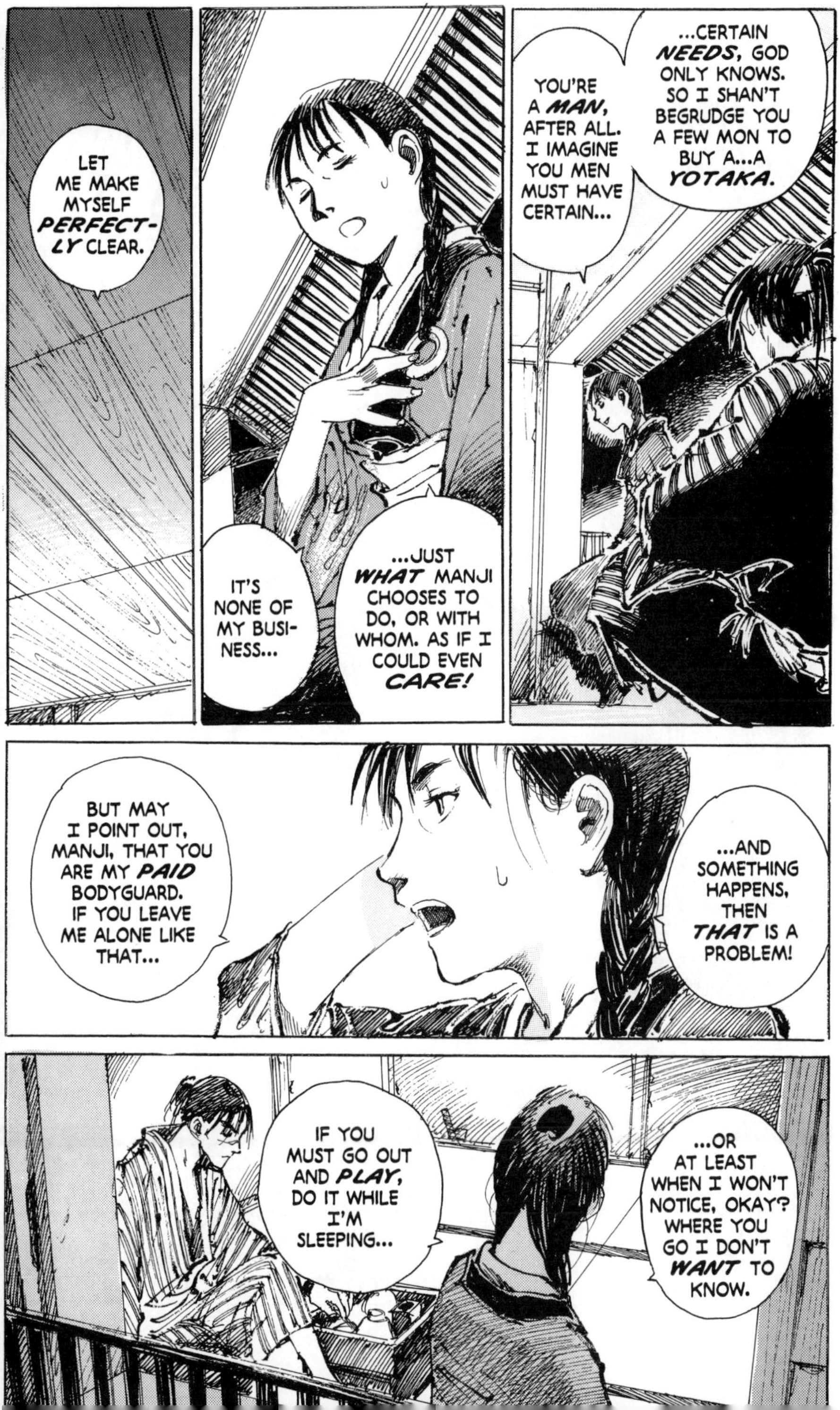
LET ME MAKE MYSELF PERFECTLY CLEAR.
IT'S NONE OF MY BUSINESS...
...JUST WHAT MANJI CHOOSES TO DO, OR WITH WHOM. AS IF I COULD EVEN CARE!
YOU'RE A MAN, AFTER ALL. I IMAGINE YOU MEN MUST HAVE CERTAIN...
...CERTAIN NEEDS, GOD ONLY KNOWS. SO I SHAN'T BEGRUDGE YOU A FEW MON TO BUY A...A YOTAKA.
BUT MAY I POINT OUT, MANJI, THAT YOU ARE MY PAID BODYGUARD. IF YOU LEAVE ME ALONE LIKE THAT...
...AND SOMETHING HAPPENS, THEN THAT IS A PROBLEM!
IF YOU MUST GO OUT AND PLAY, DO IT WHILE I'M SLEEPING...
...OR AT LEAST WHEN I WON'T NOTICE, OKAY? WHERE YOU GO I DON'T WANT TO KNOW.

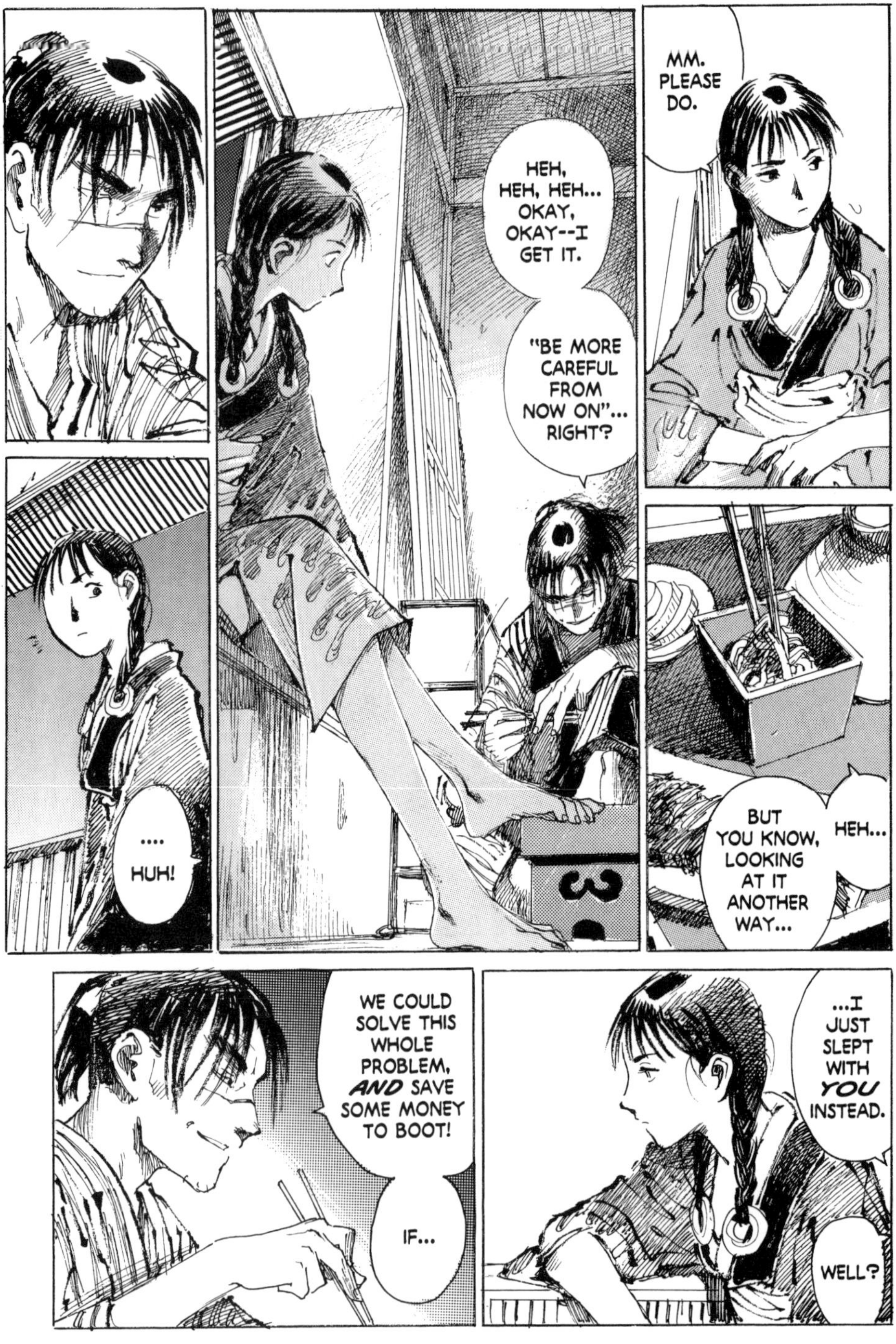
HEH, HEH, HEH... OKAY, OKAY--I GET IT.
"BE MORE CAREFUL FROM NOW ON"... RIGHT?
MM. PLEASE DO.
.... HUH!
HEH...
BUT YOU KNOW, LOOKING AT IT ANOTHER WAY...
WE COULD SOLVE THIS WHOLE PROBLEM, AND SAVE SOME MONEY TO BOOT!
IF...
...I JUST SLEPT WITH YOU INSTEAD.
WELL?

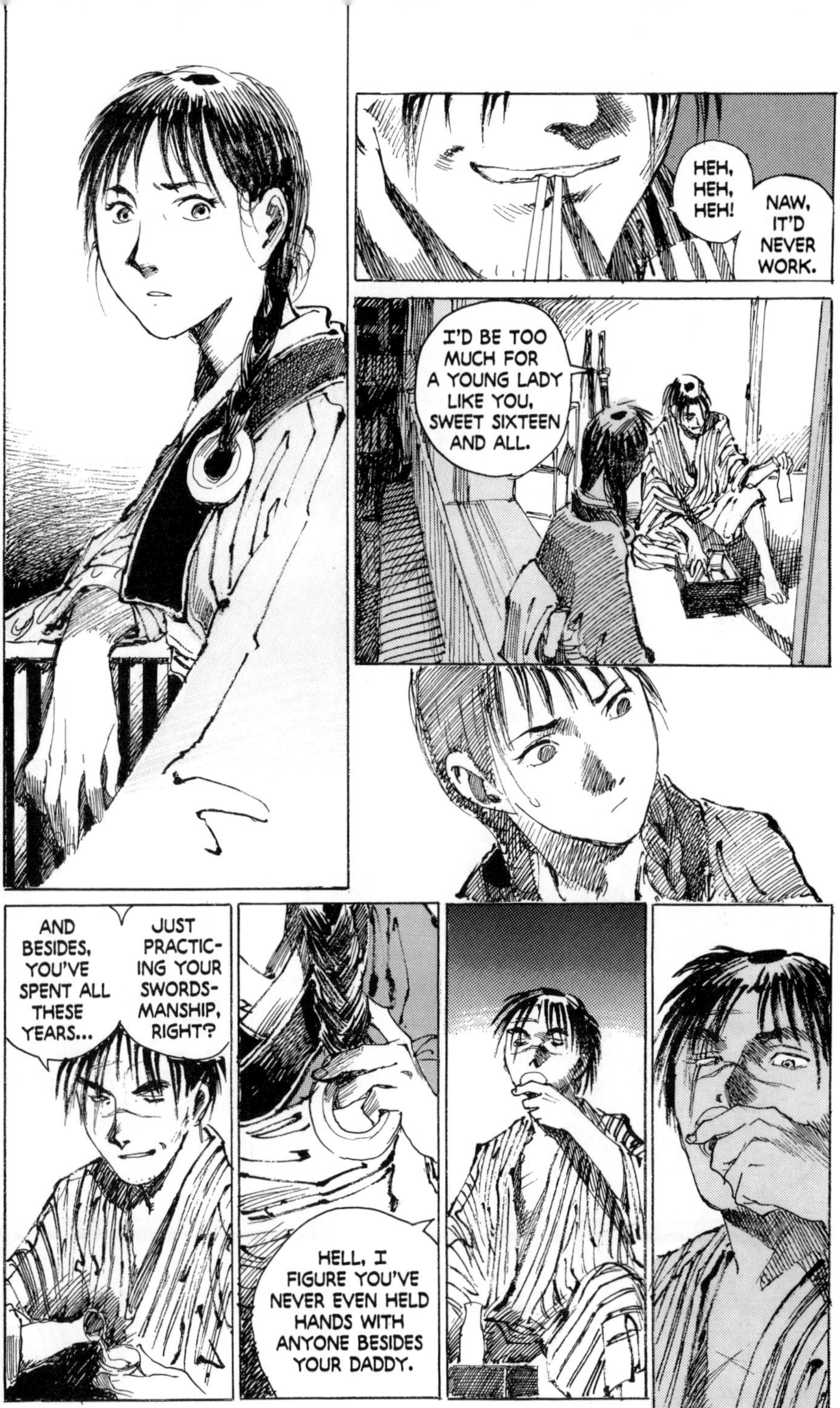
HEH, HEH, HEH!
NAW, IT'D NEVER WORK.
I'D BE TOO MUCH FOR A YOUNG LADY LIKE YOU, SWEET SIXTEEN AND ALL.
AND BESIDES, YOU'VE SPENT ALL THESE YEARS...
JUST PRACTICING YOUR SWORDSMANSHIP, RIGHT?
HELL, I FIGURE YOU'VE NEVER EVEN HELD HANDS WITH ANYONE BESIDES YOUR DADDY.

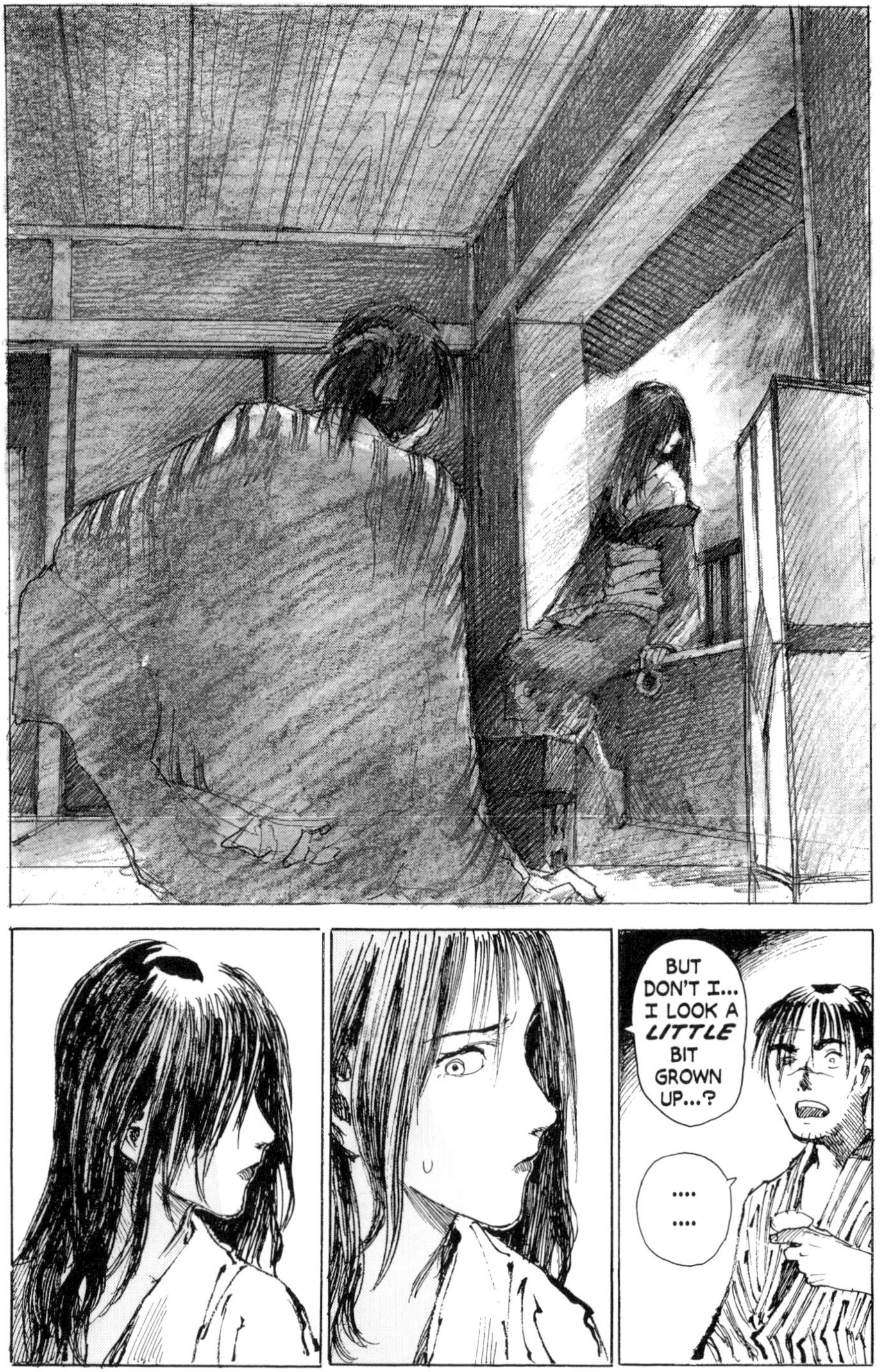
BUT DON'T I... I LOOK A *LITTLE* BIT GROWN UP...?
....
....

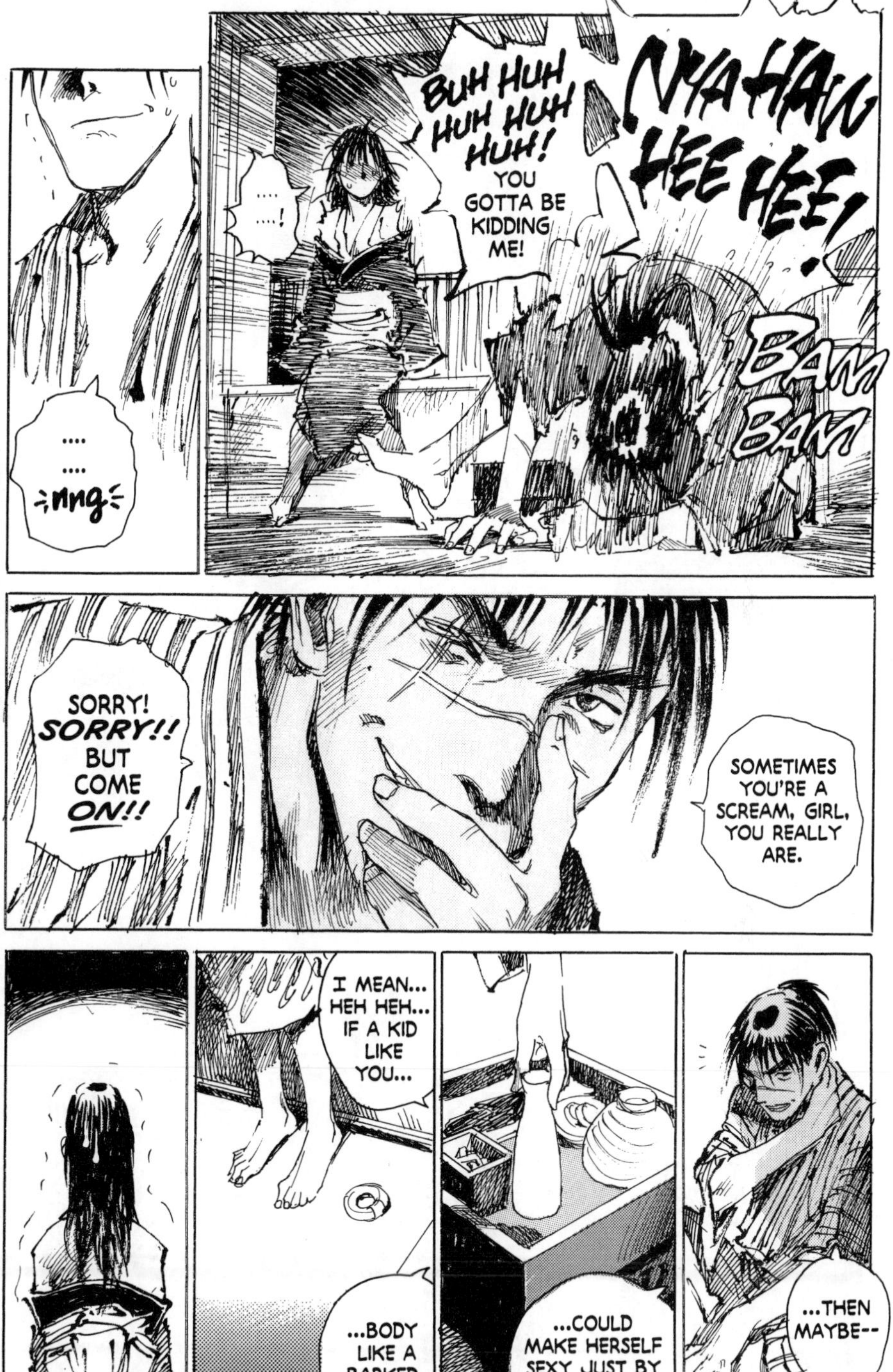
....
....
nng
....
....!
BUH HUH HUH HUH HUH! YOU GOTTA BE KIDDING ME!
NYA HAW HEE HEE!
BAM BAM
SORRY! SORRY!! BUT COME ON!!
SOMETIMES YOU'RE A SCREAM, GIRL, YOU REALLY ARE.
I MEAN... HEH HEH... IF A KID LIKE YOU...
...BODY LIKE A BARKED TWIG...
...COULD MAKE HERSELF SEXY JUST BY LETTING DOWN HER HAIR...
...THEN MAYBE--

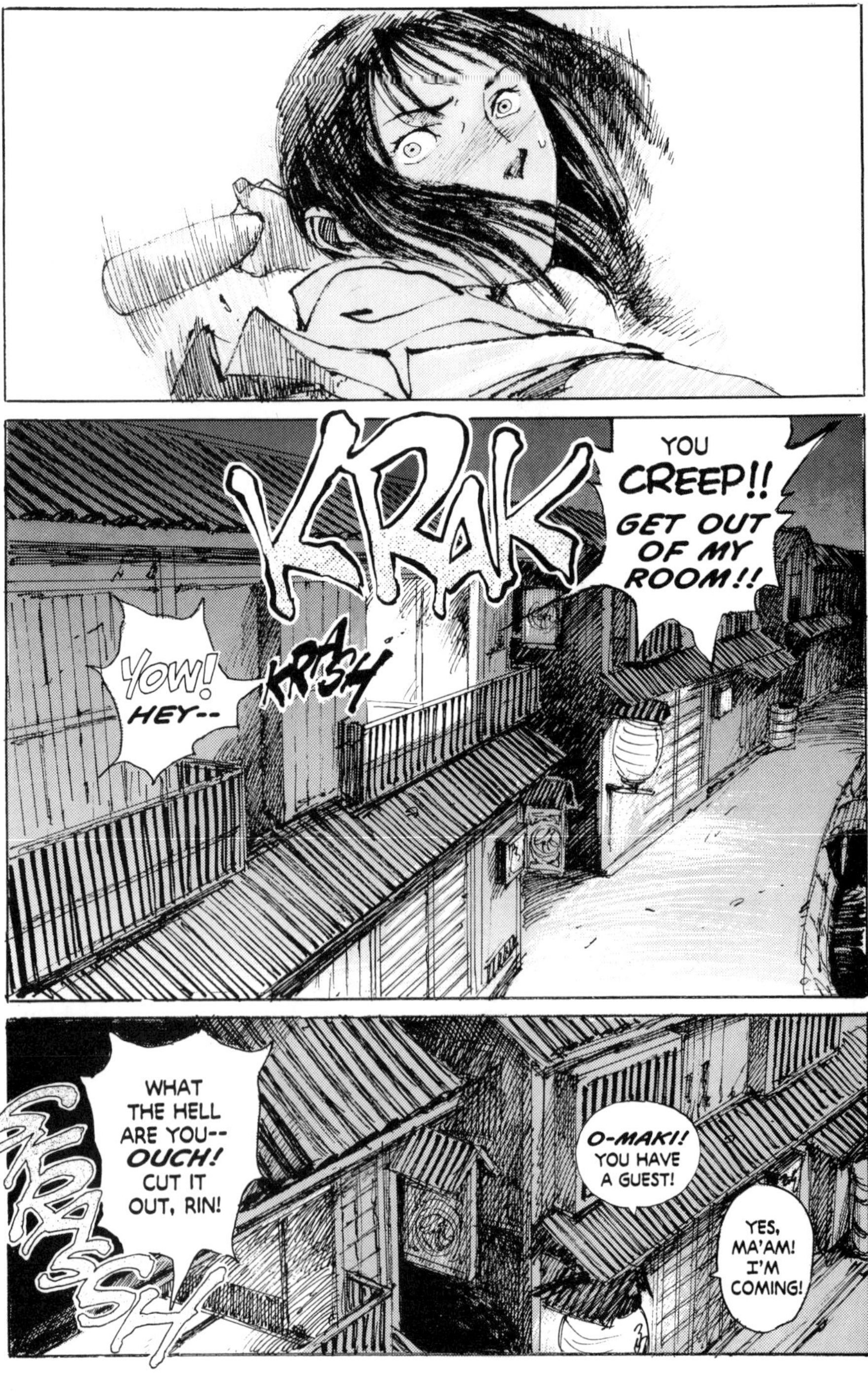
KRAK
YOU CREEP!! GET OUT OF MY ROOM!!
YOW! HEY--
KRASH
SKRASH
WHAT THE HELL ARE YOU-- OUCH! CUT IT OUT, RIN!
O-MAKI! YOU HAVE A GUEST!
YES, MA'AM! I'M COMING!

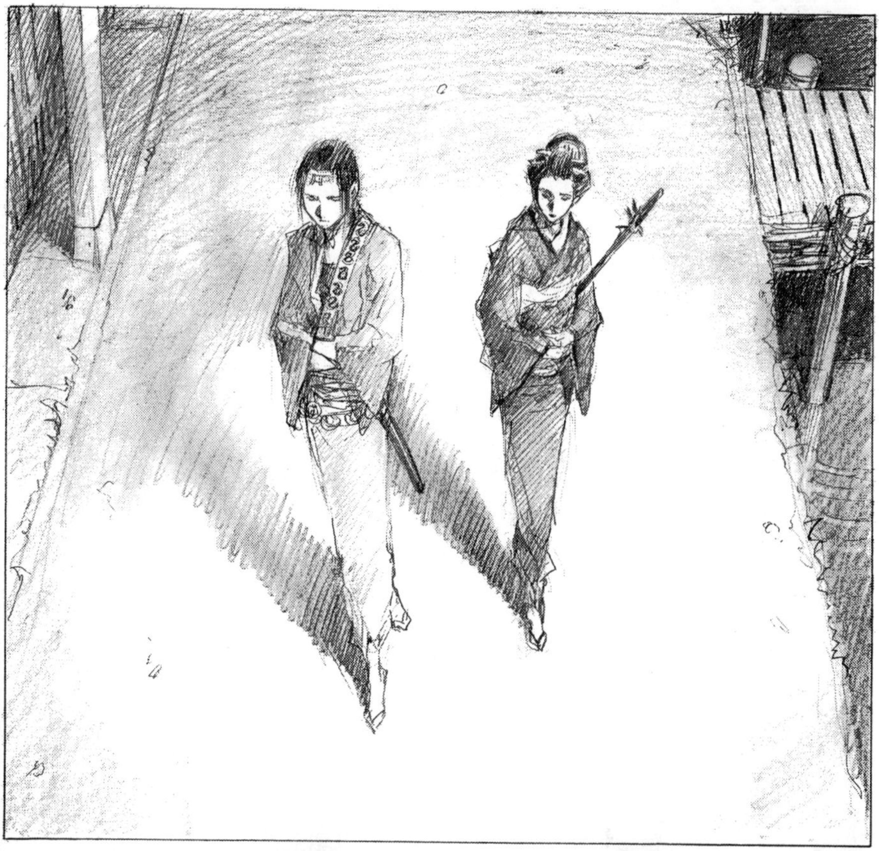

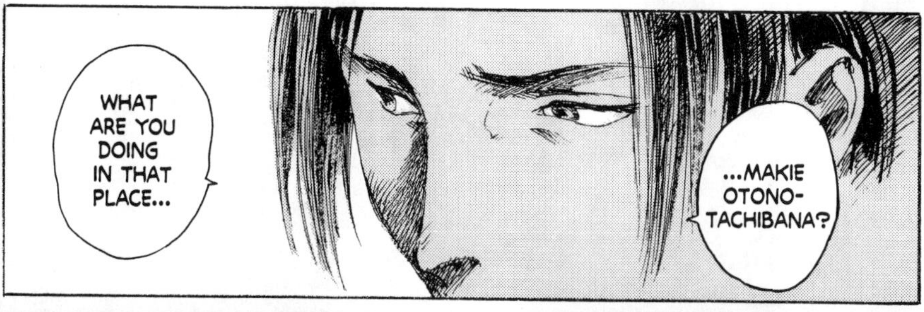
WHAT ARE YOU DOING IN THAT PLACE...
...MAKIE OTONO-TACHIBANA?

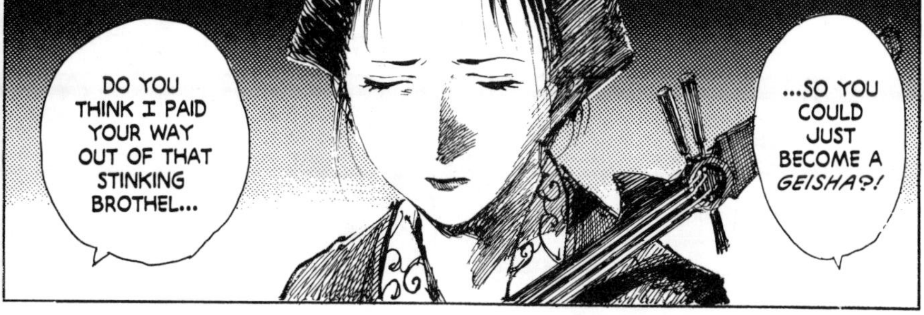
DO YOU THINK I PAID YOUR WAY OUT OF THAT STINKING BROTHEL...
...SO YOU COULD JUST BECOME A *GEISHA*?!

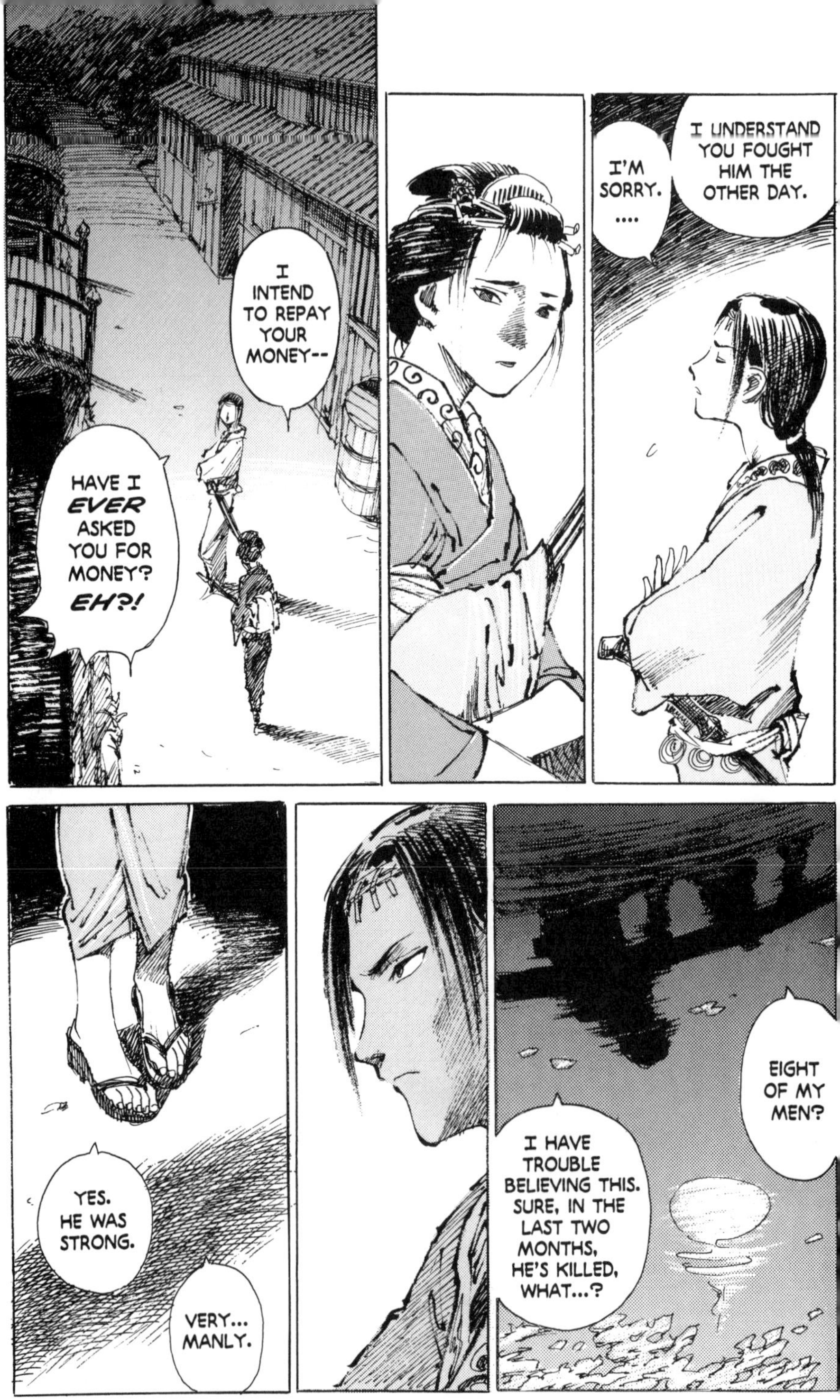
I INTEND TO REPAY YOUR MONEY--
HAVE I *EVER* ASKED YOU FOR MONEY? *EH?!*
I UNDERSTAND YOU FOUGHT HIM THE OTHER DAY.
I'M SORRY. ....
YES. HE WAS STRONG.
VERY... MANLY.
I HAVE TROUBLE BELIEVING THIS. SURE, IN THE LAST TWO MONTHS, HE'S KILLED, WHAT...?
EIGHT OF MY MEN?

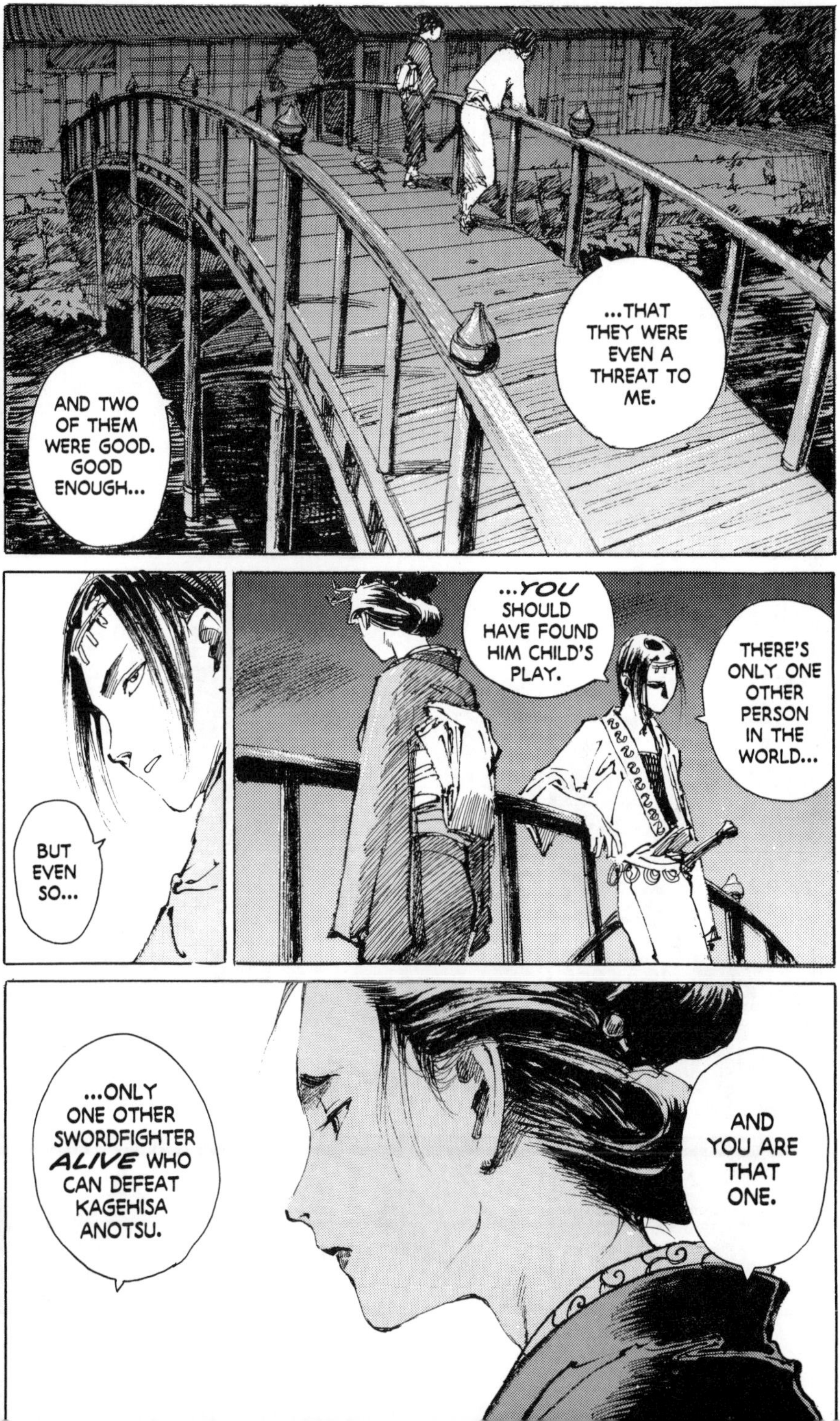
AND TWO OF THEM WERE GOOD. GOOD ENOUGH...
...THAT THEY WERE EVEN A THREAT TO ME.
BUT EVEN SO...
...YOU SHOULD HAVE FOUND HIM CHILD'S PLAY.
THERE'S ONLY ONE OTHER PERSON IN THE WORLD...
...ONLY ONE OTHER SWORDFIGHTER ALIVE WHO CAN DEFEAT KAGEHISA ANOTSU.
AND YOU ARE THAT ONE.

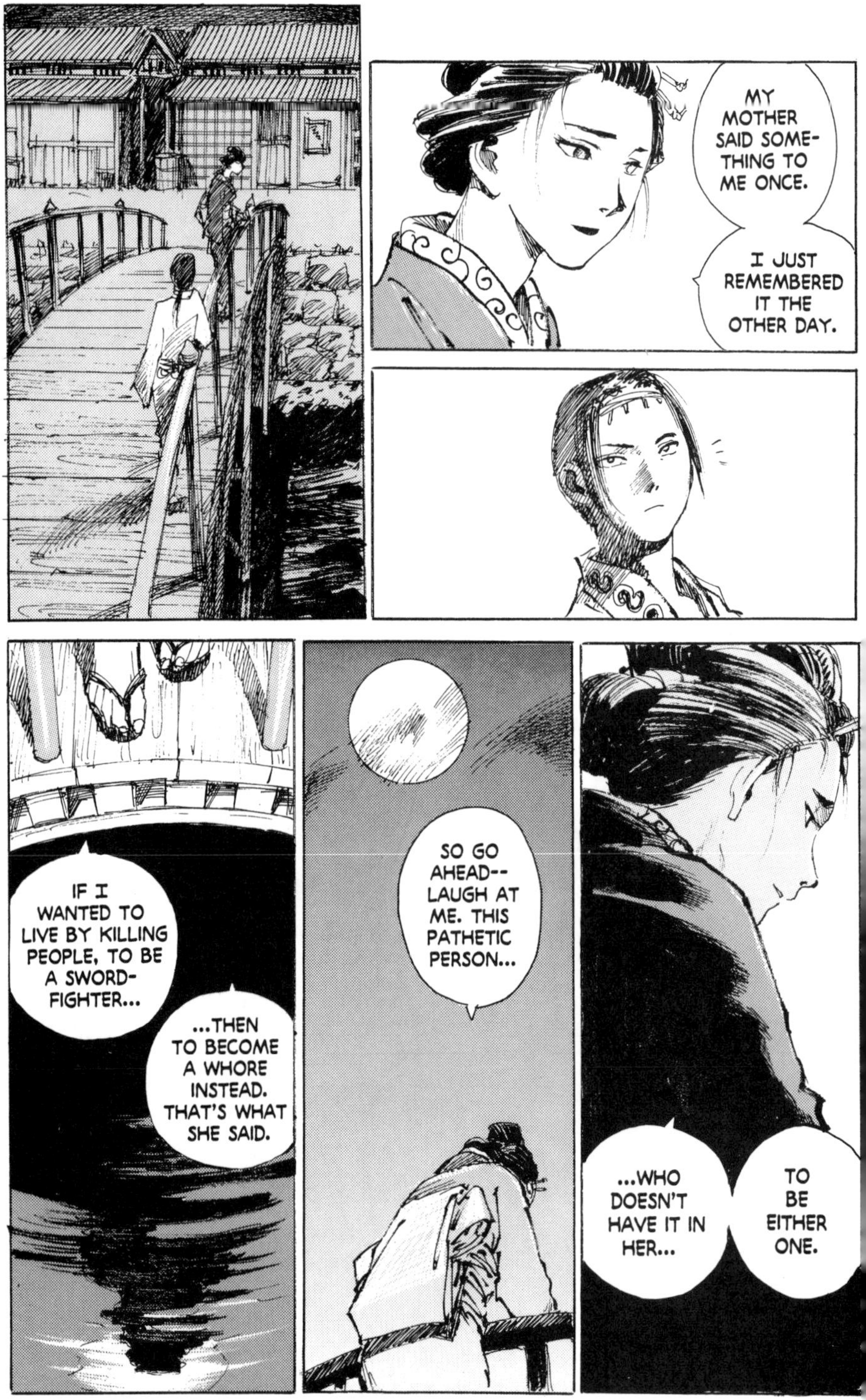
MY MOTHER SAID SOMETHING TO ME ONCE.
I JUST REMEMBERED IT THE OTHER DAY.
IF I WANTED TO LIVE BY KILLING PEOPLE, TO BE A SWORD-FIGHTER...
...THEN TO BECOME A WHORE INSTEAD. THAT'S WHAT SHE SAID.
SO GO AHEAD--LAUGH AT ME. THIS PATHETIC PERSON...
...WHO DOESN'T HAVE IT IN HER...
TO BE EITHER ONE.

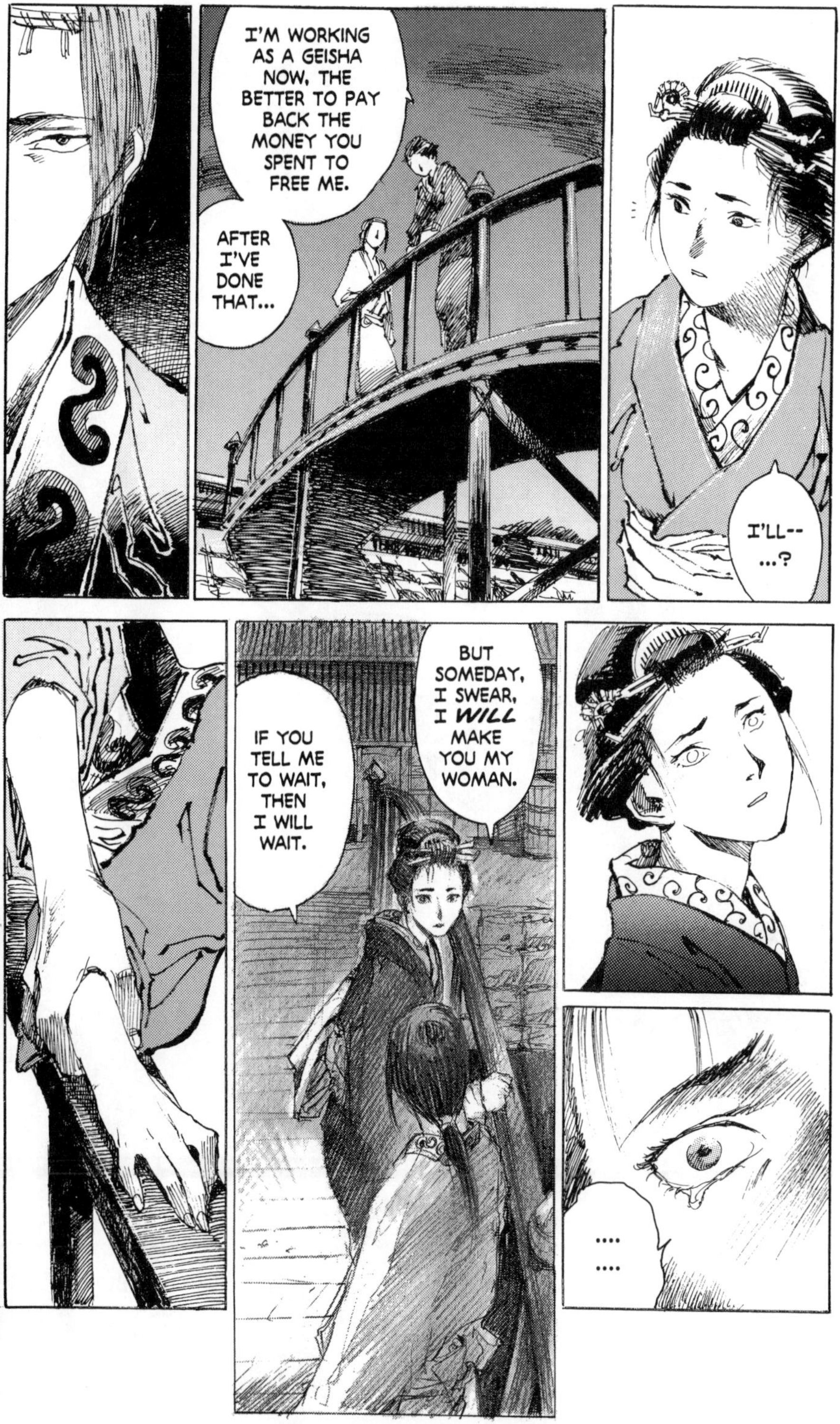
I'M WORKING AS A GEISHA NOW, THE BETTER TO PAY BACK THE MONEY YOU SPENT TO FREE ME.
AFTER I'VE DONE THAT...
I'LL-- ...?
IF YOU TELL ME TO WAIT, THEN I WILL WAIT.
BUT SOMEDAY, I SWEAR, I WILL MAKE YOU MY WOMAN.
....

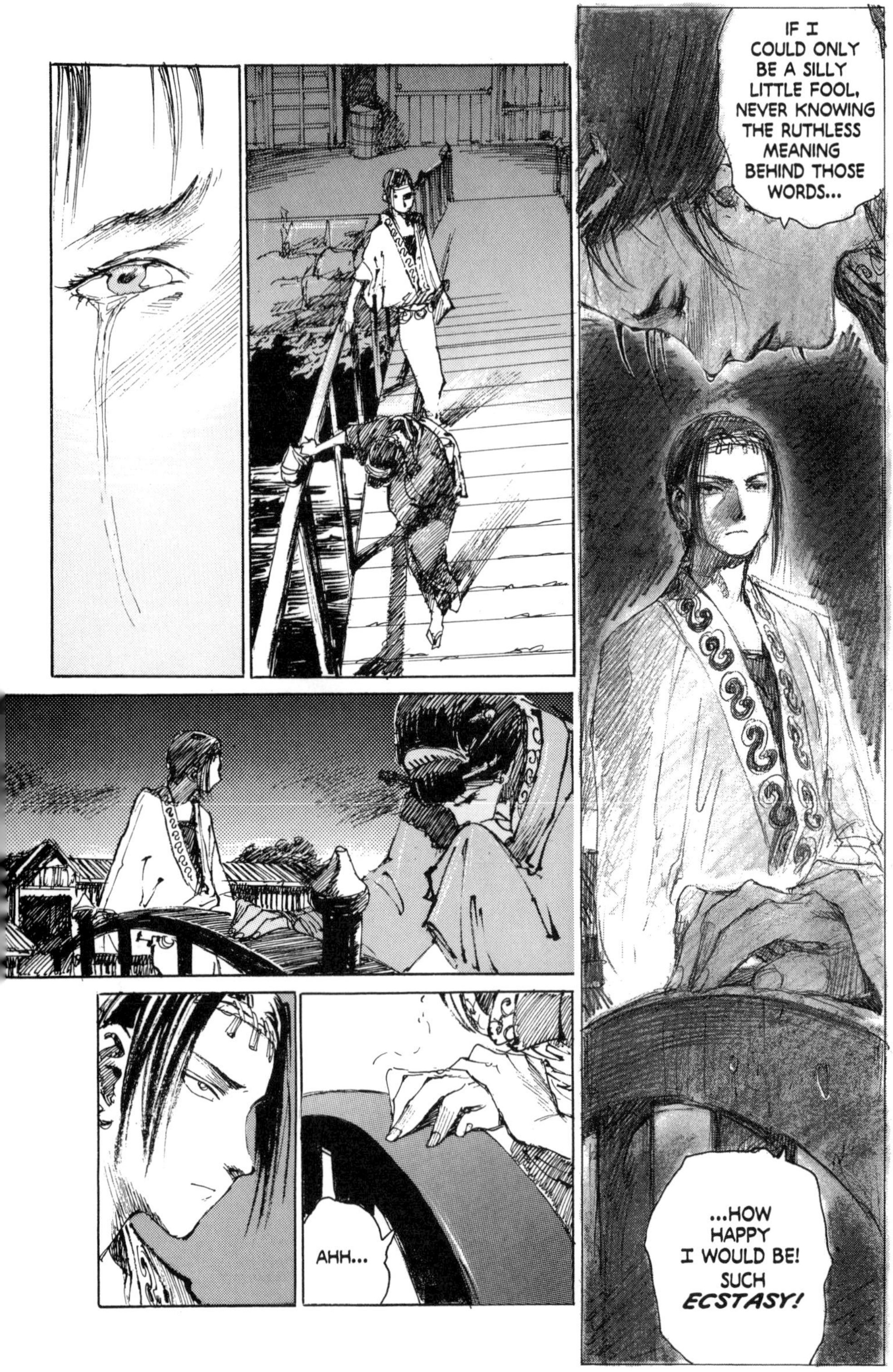
IF I COULD ONLY BE A SILLY LITTLE FOOL, NEVER KNOWING THE RUTHLESS MEANING BEHIND THOSE WORDS...
AHH...
...HOW HAPPY I WOULD BE! SUCH ***ECSTASY!***

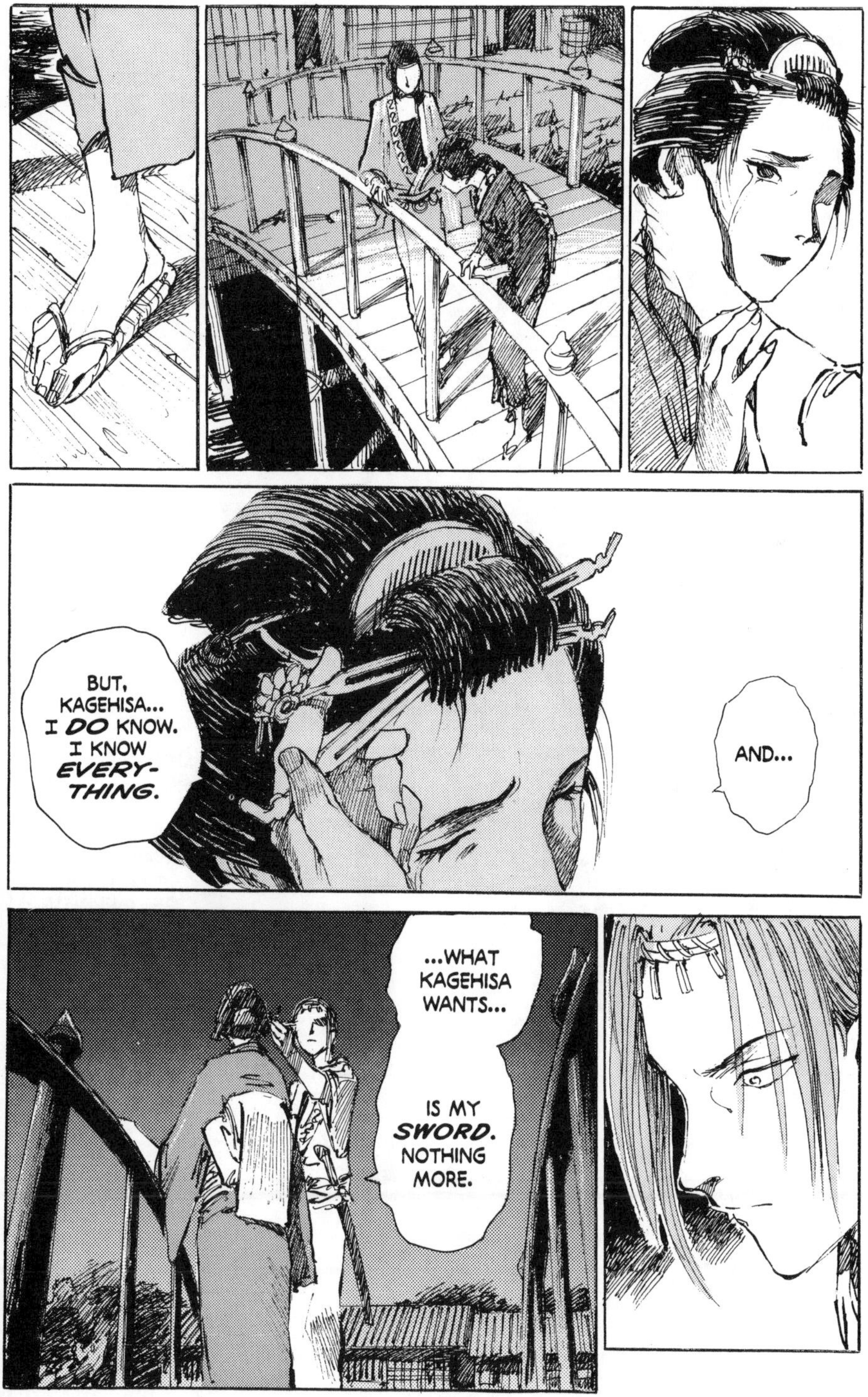
BUT, KAGEHISA... I DO KNOW. I KNOW EVERYTHING.
AND...
...WHAT KAGEHISA WANTS...
IS MY SWORD. NOTHING MORE.

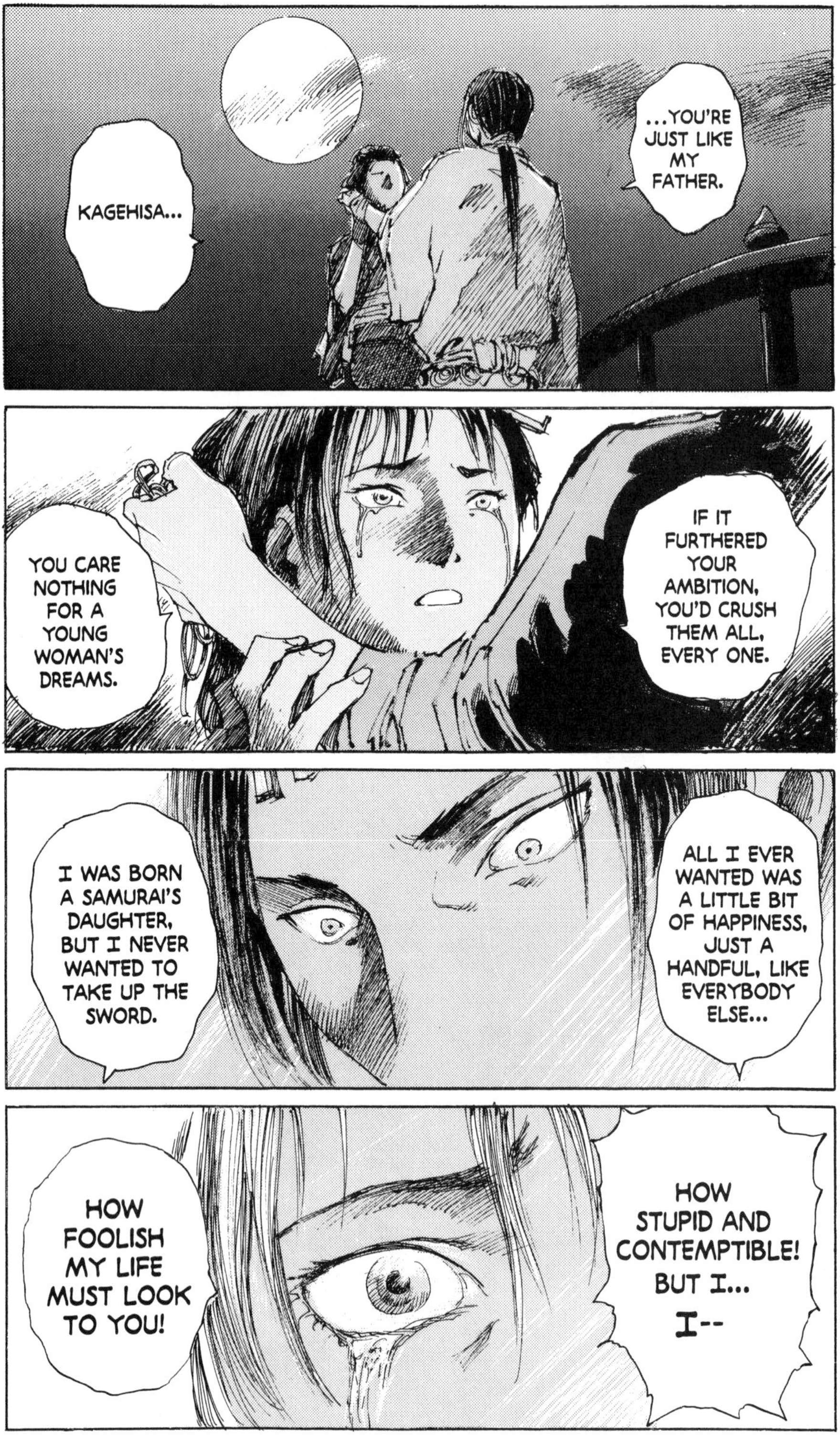
KAGEHISA...
...YOU'RE JUST LIKE MY FATHER.
YOU CARE NOTHING FOR A YOUNG WOMAN'S DREAMS.
IF IT FURTHERED YOUR AMBITION, YOU'D CRUSH THEM ALL, EVERY ONE.
I WAS BORN A SAMURAI'S DAUGHTER, BUT I NEVER WANTED TO TAKE UP THE SWORD.
ALL I EVER WANTED WAS A LITTLE BIT OF HAPPINESS, JUST A HANDFUL, LIKE EVERYBODY ELSE...
HOW FOOLISH MY LIFE MUST LOOK TO YOU!
HOW STUPID AND CONTEMPTIBLE! BUT I...
I--

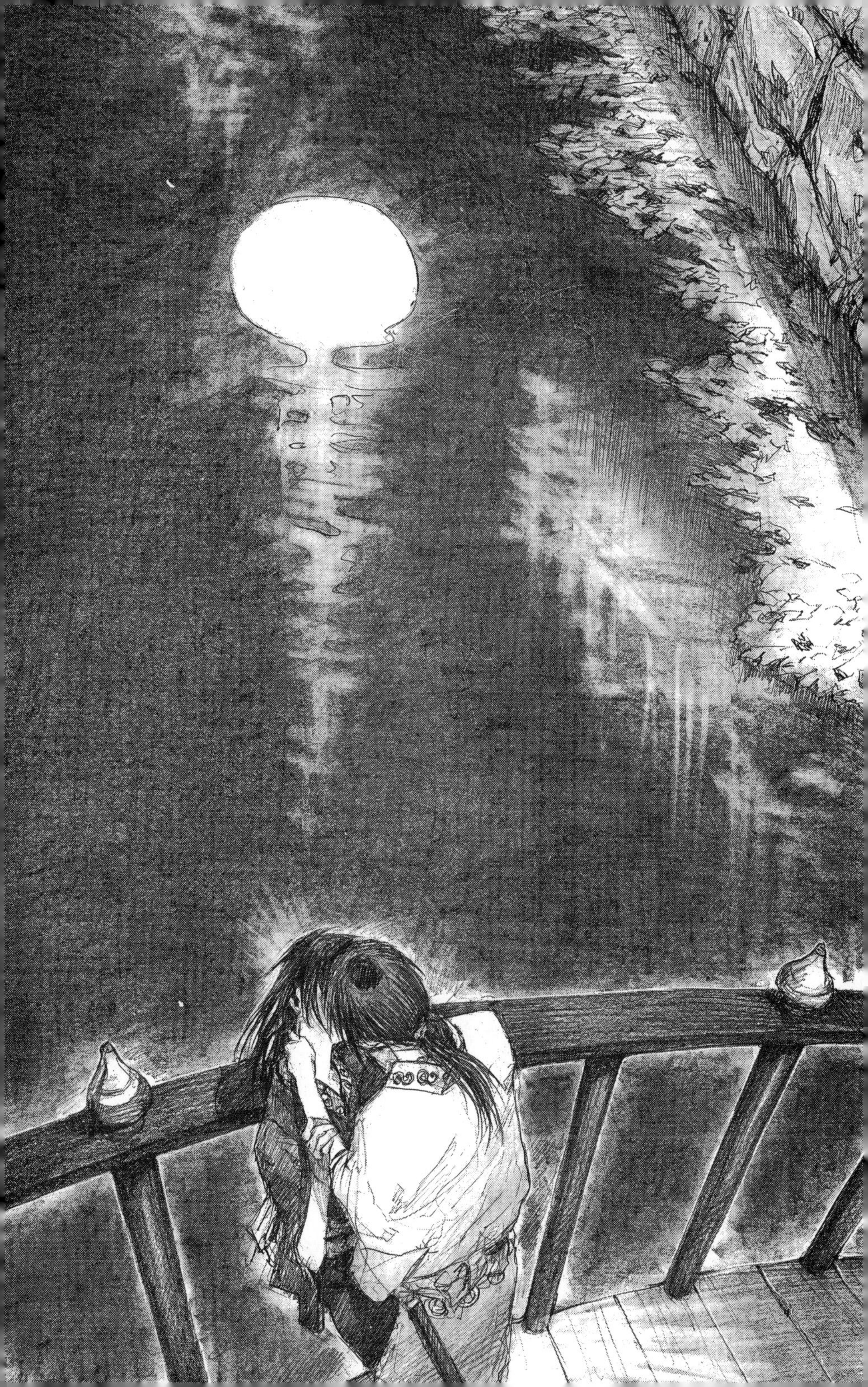

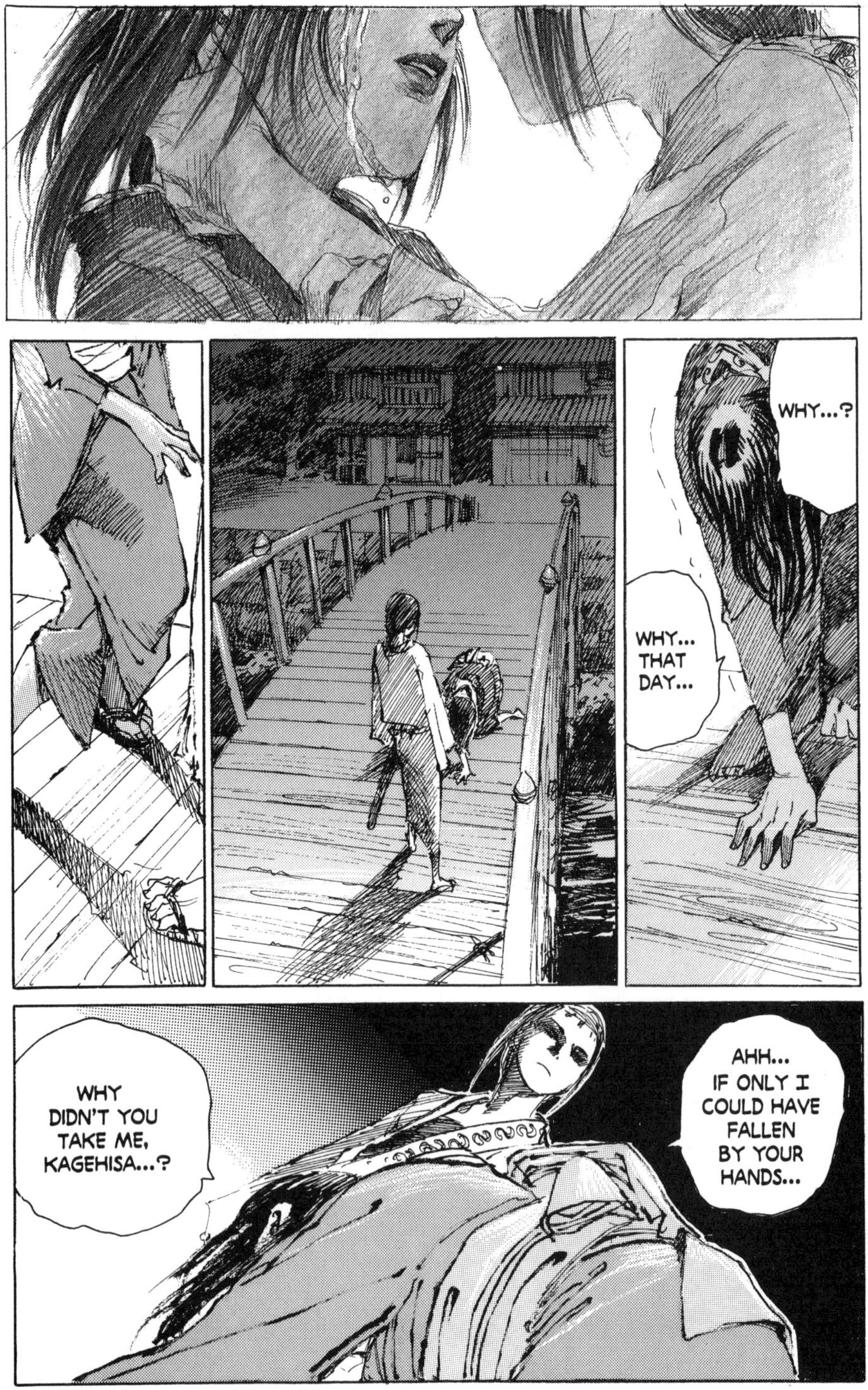
WHY...?
WHY... THAT DAY...
WHY DIDN'T YOU TAKE ME, KAGEHISA...?
AHH... IF ONLY I COULD HAVE FALLEN BY YOUR HANDS...

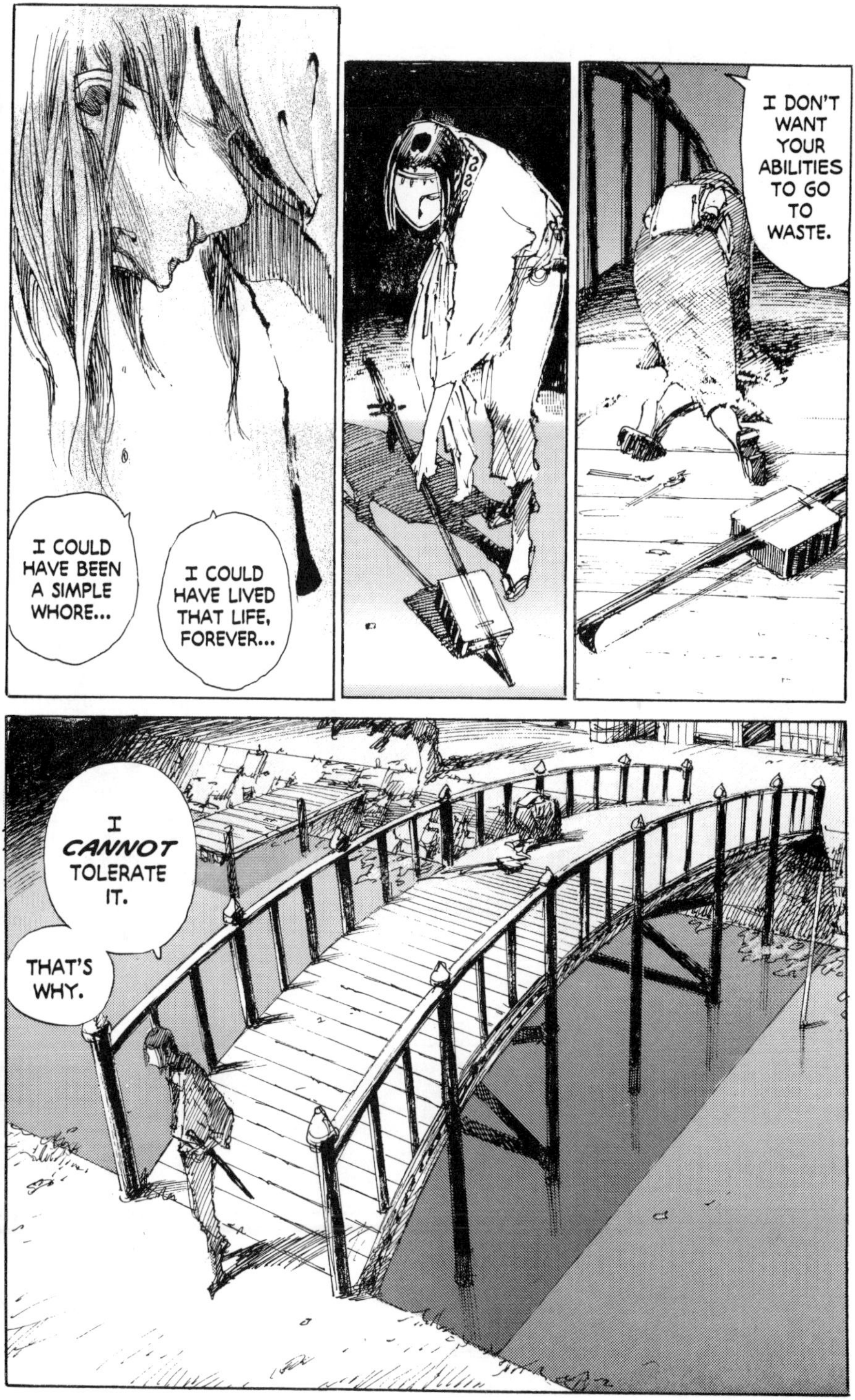
I COULD HAVE BEEN A SIMPLE WHORE...
I COULD HAVE LIVED THAT LIFE, FOREVER...
I DON'T WANT YOUR ABILITIES TO GO TO WASTE.
I *CANNOT* TOLERATE IT.
THAT'S WHY.

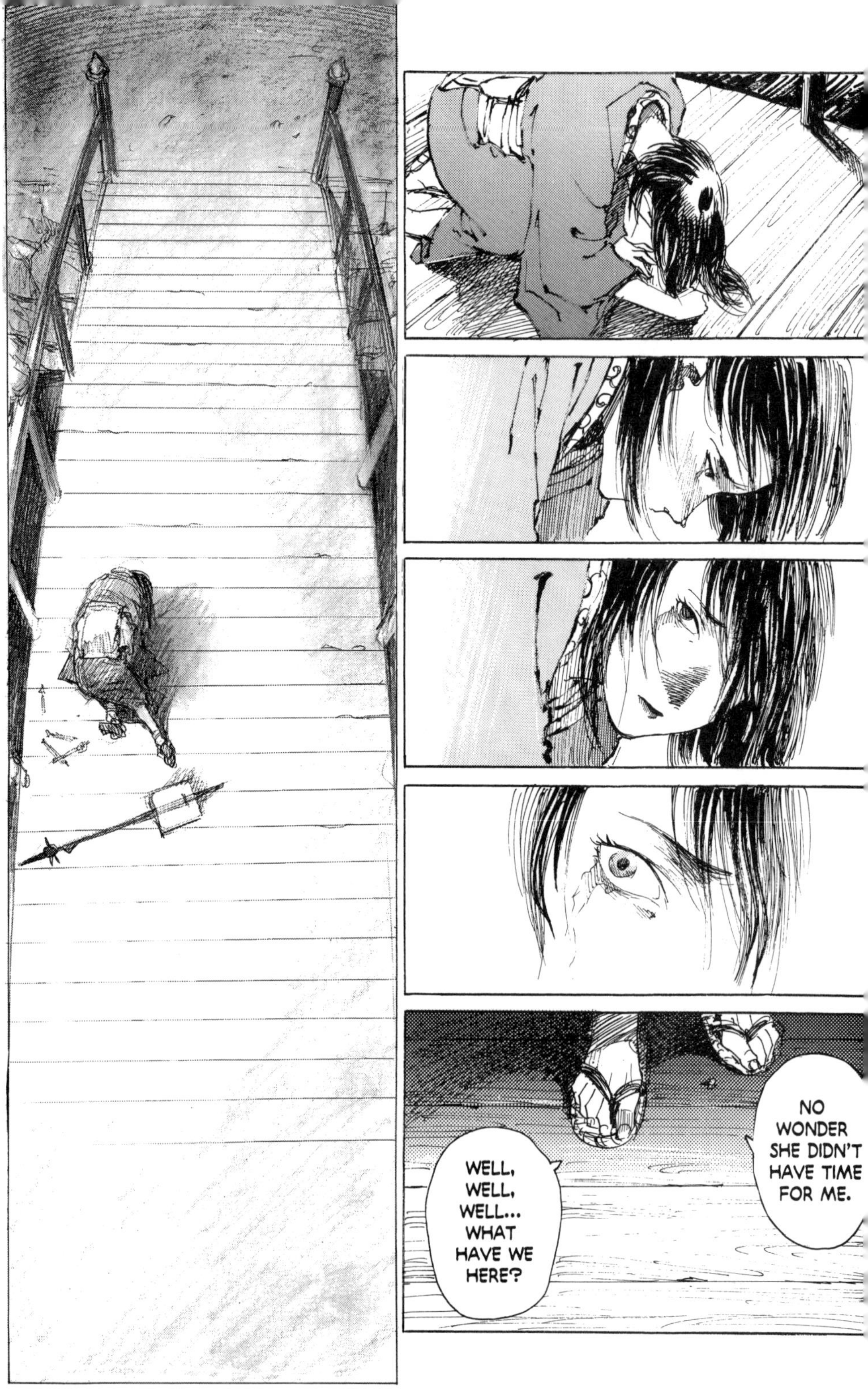
WELL, WELL, WELL... WHAT HAVE WE HERE?
NO WONDER SHE DIDN'T HAVE TIME FOR ME.

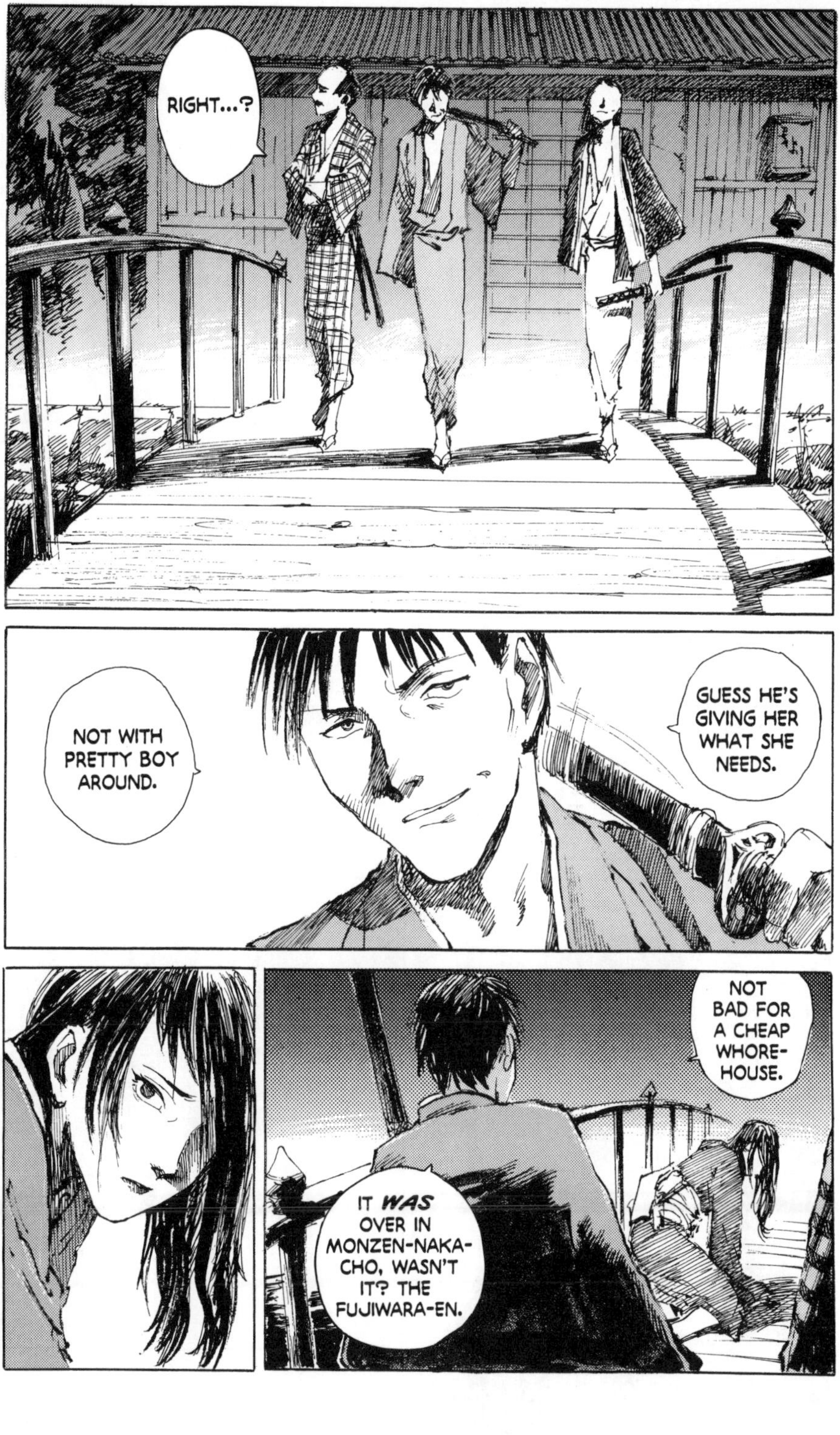
RIGHT...?
NOT WITH PRETTY BOY AROUND.
GUESS HE'S GIVING HER WHAT SHE NEEDS.
NOT BAD FOR A CHEAP WHORE-HOUSE.
IT *WAS* OVER IN MONZEN-NAKA-CHO, WASN'T IT? THE FUJIWARA-EN.

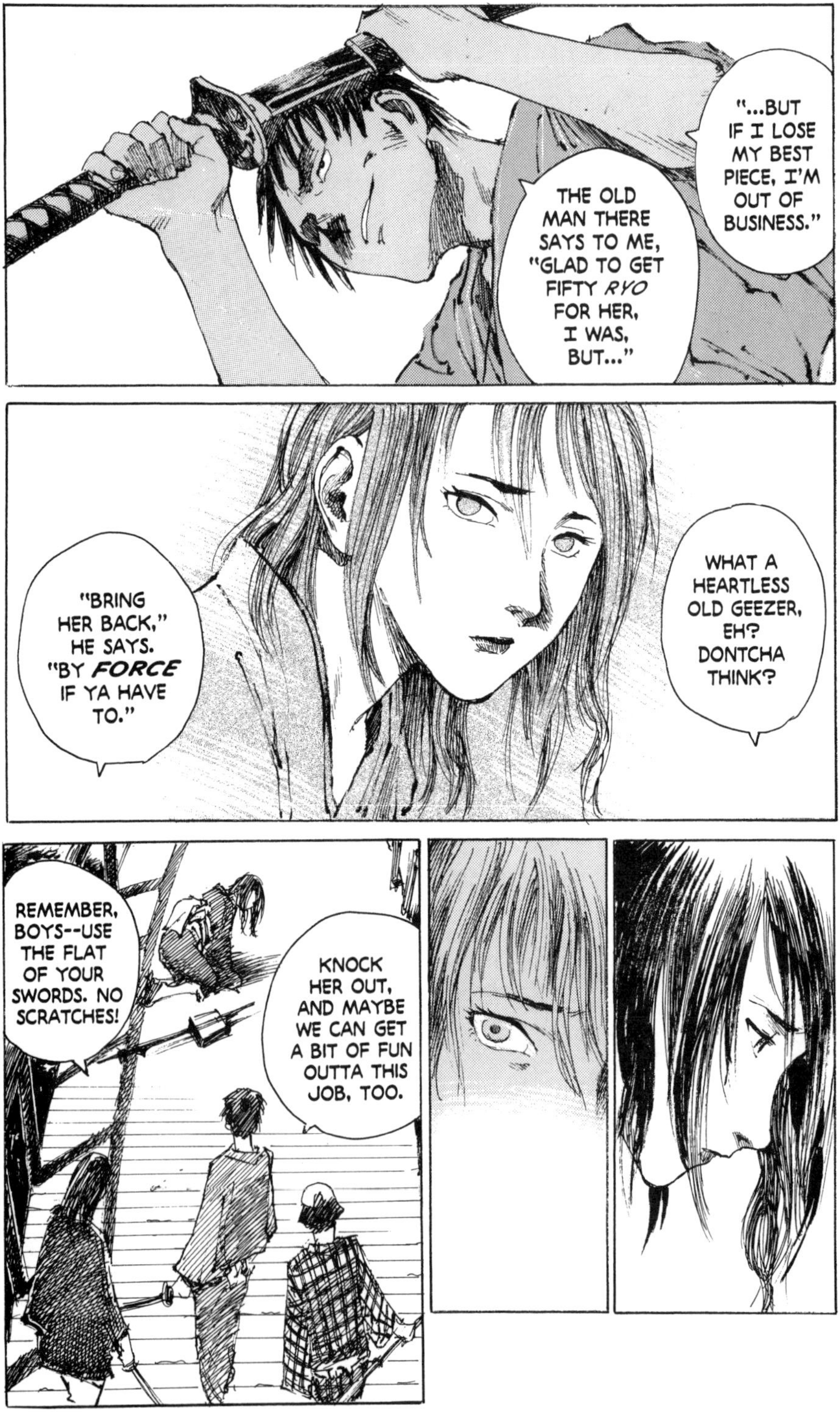
THE OLD MAN THERE SAYS TO ME, "GLAD TO GET FIFTY *RYO* FOR HER, I WAS, BUT..."
"...BUT IF I LOSE MY BEST PIECE, I'M OUT OF BUSINESS."
"BRING HER BACK," HE SAYS. "BY ***FORCE*** IF YA HAVE TO."
WHAT A HEARTLESS OLD GEEZER, EH? DONTCHA THINK?
REMEMBER, BOYS--USE THE FLAT OF YOUR SWORDS. NO SCRATCHES!
KNOCK HER OUT, AND MAYBE WE CAN GET A BIT OF FUN OUTTA THIS JOB, TOO.

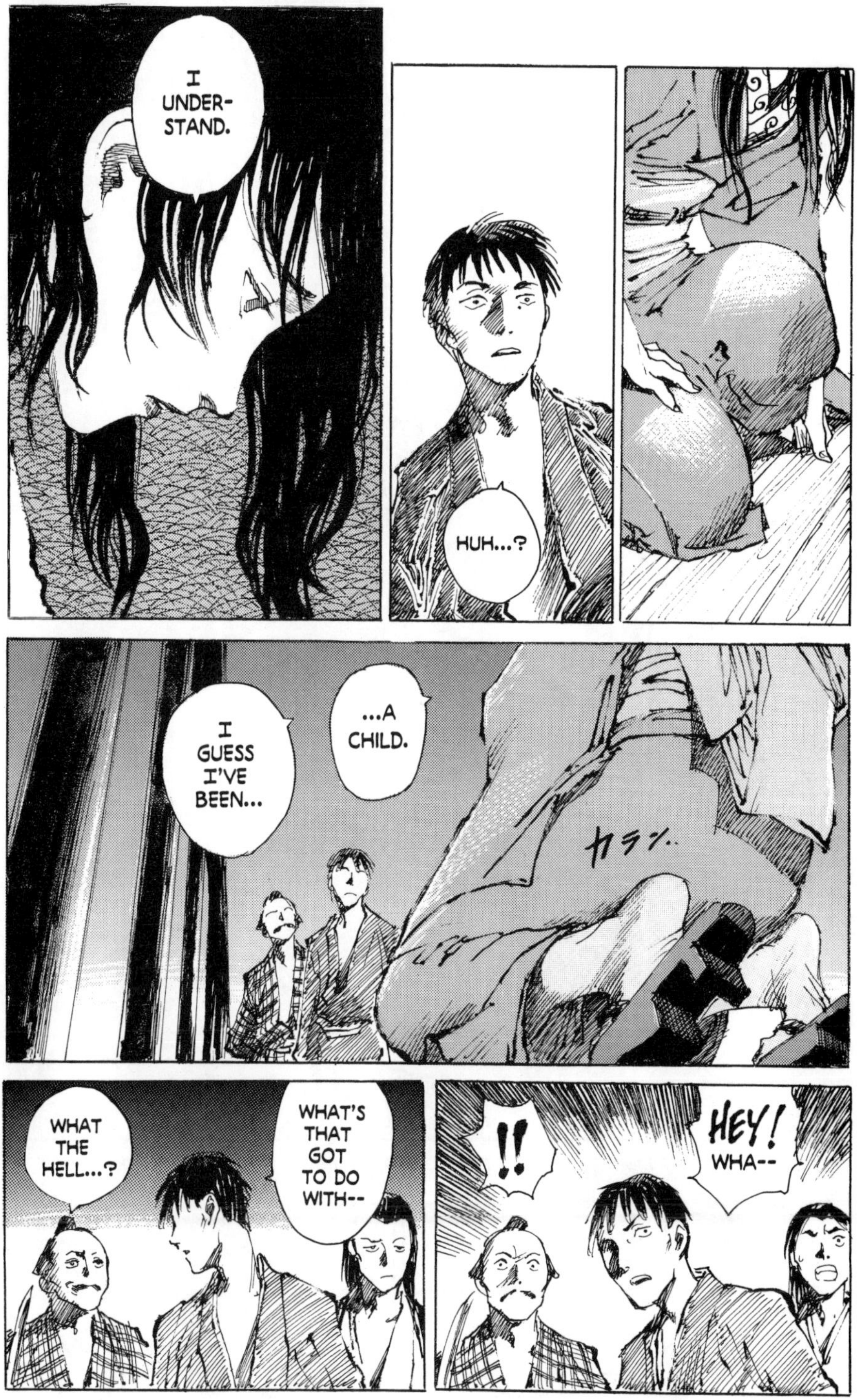
I UNDER-STAND.
HUH...?
I GUESS I'VE BEEN...
...A CHILD.
カラン..
WHAT THE HELL...?
WHAT'S THAT GOT TO DO WITH--
!!
HEY! WHA--

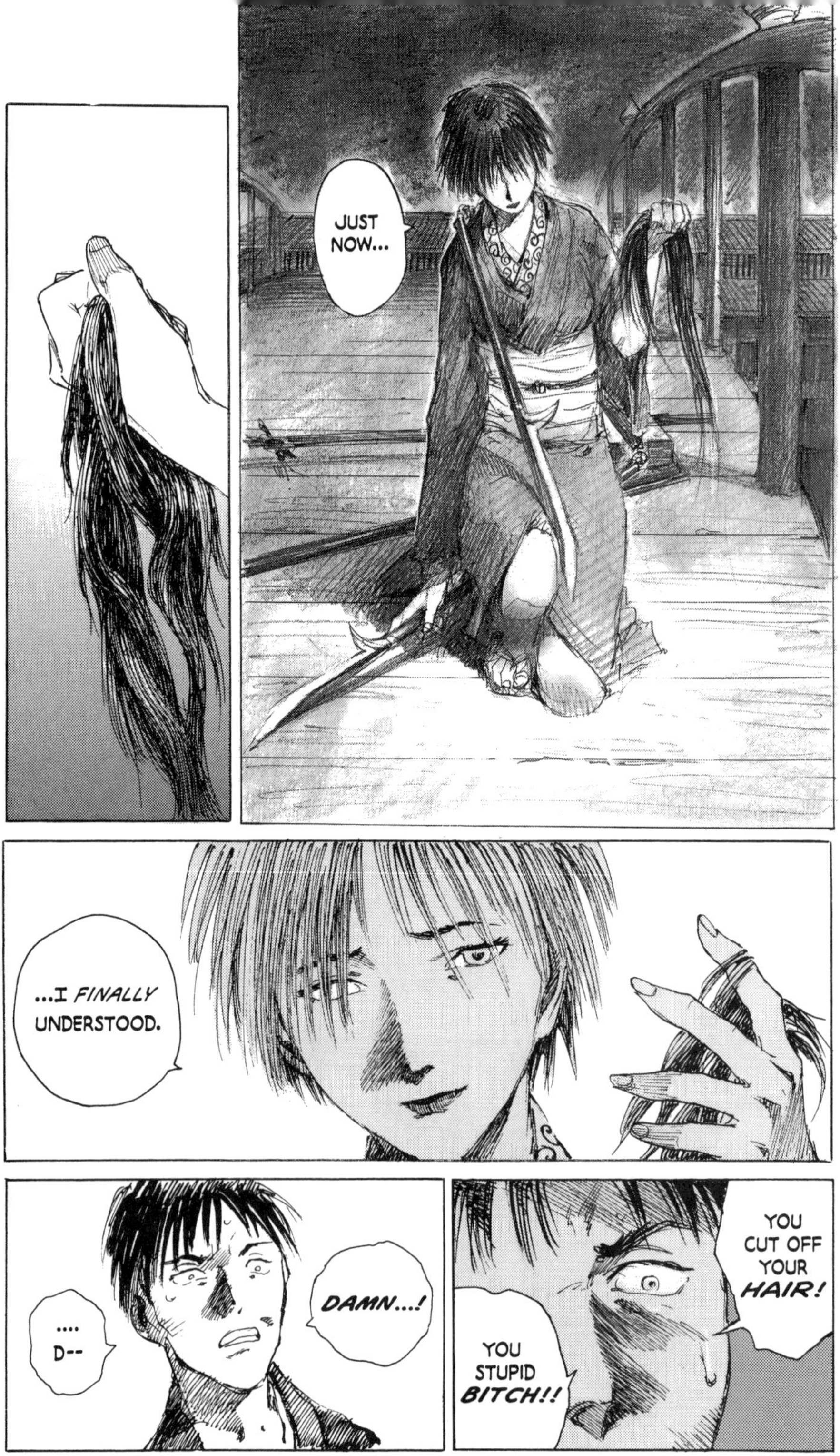
JUST NOW...
...I *FINALLY* UNDERSTOOD.
....D--
DAMN...!
YOU CUT OFF YOUR *HAIR!*
YOU STUPID *BITCH!!*

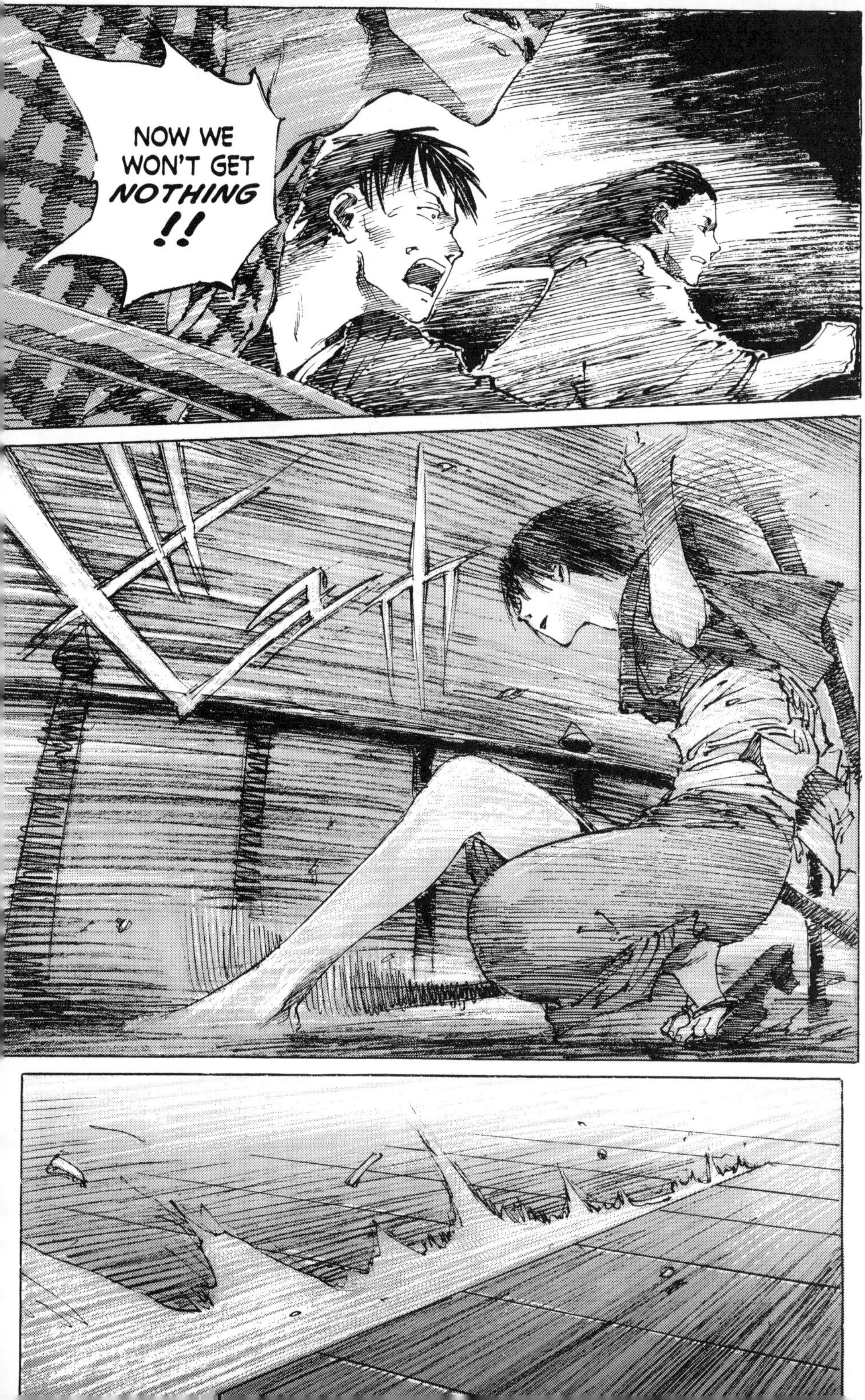
NOW WE WON'T GET NOTHING !!

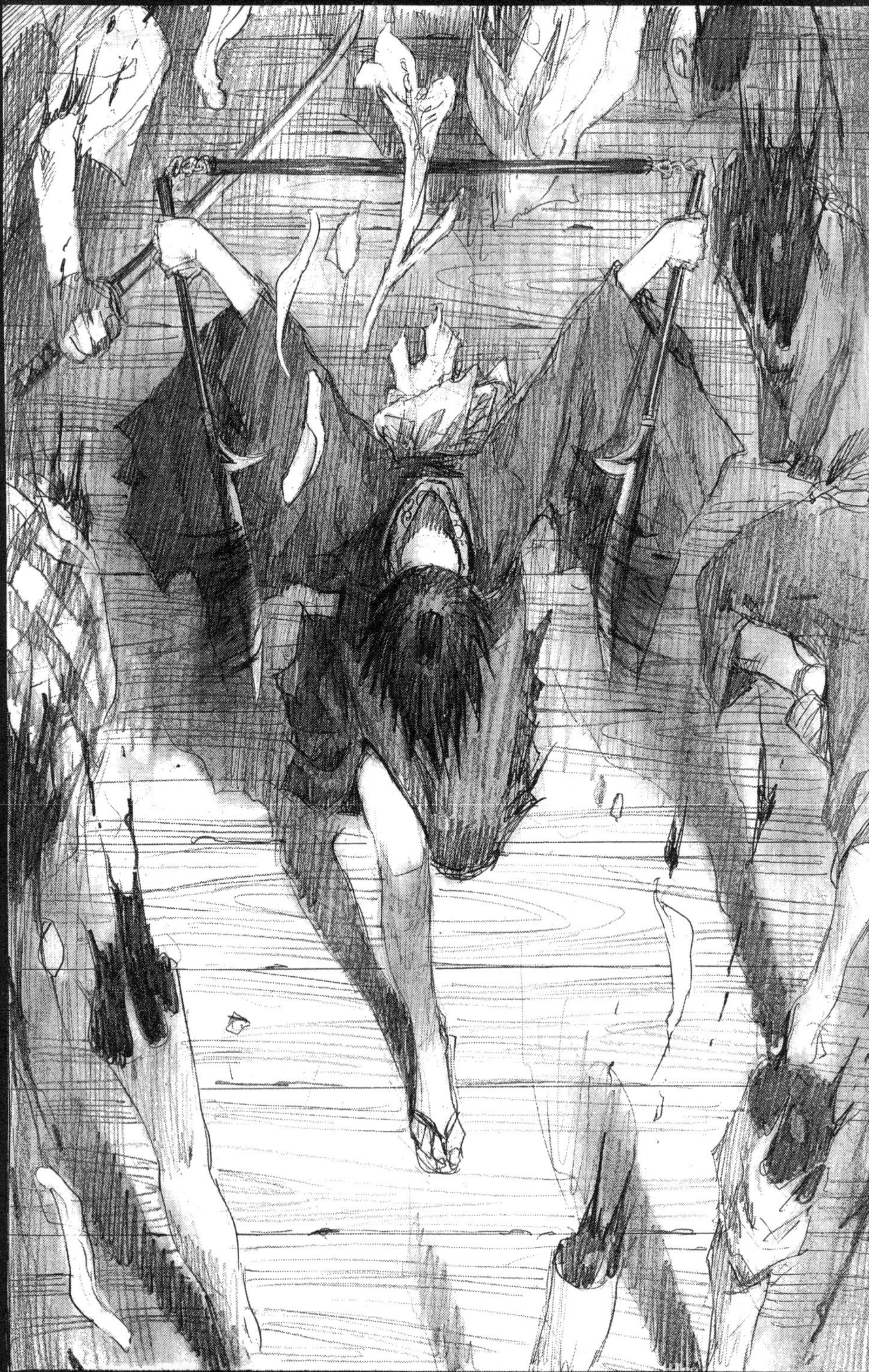

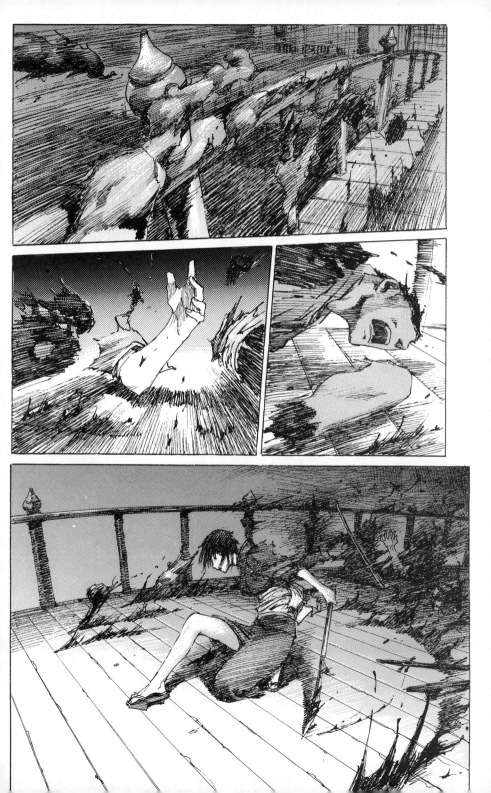

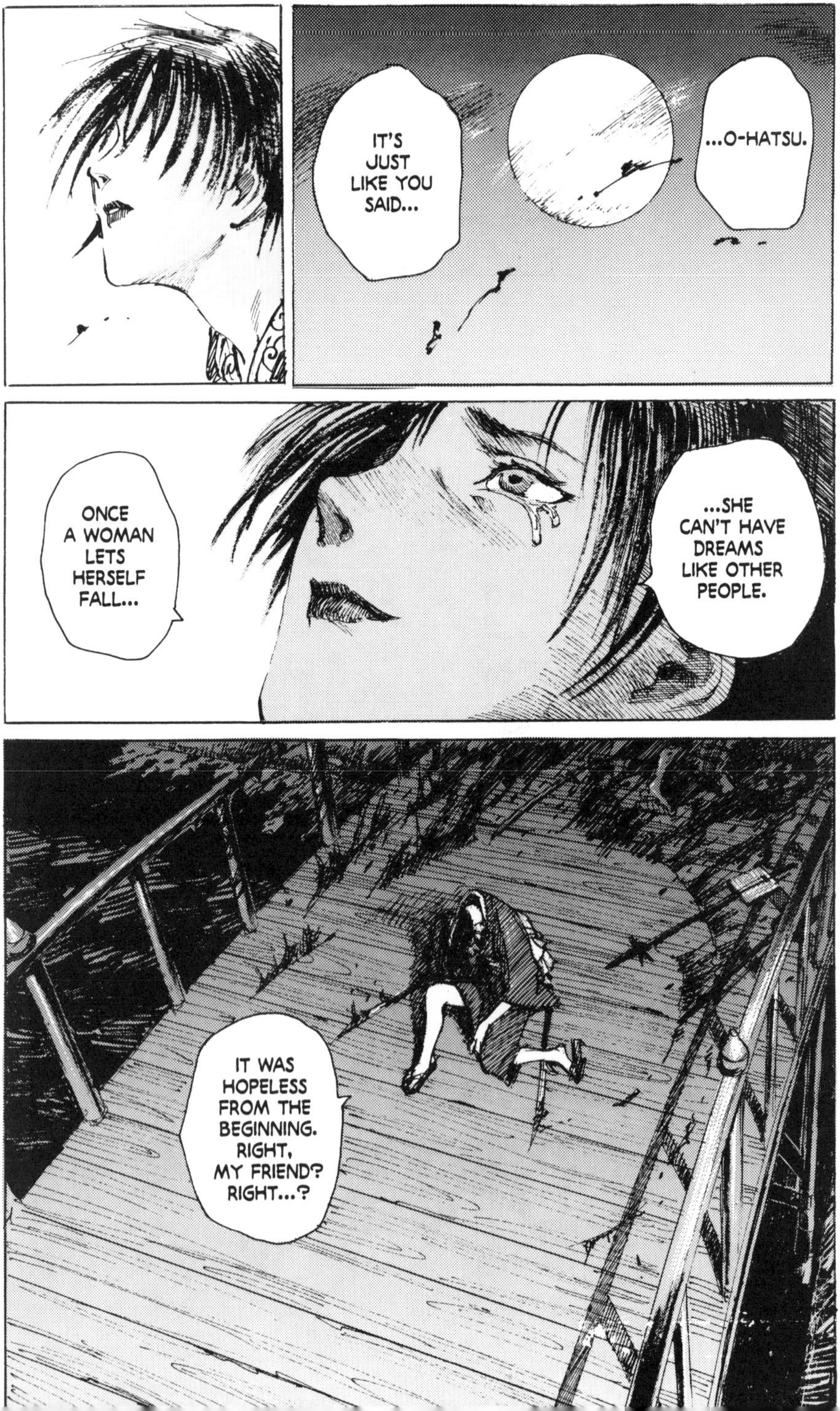
IT'S JUST LIKE YOU SAID...
...O-HATSU.
ONCE A WOMAN LETS HERSELF FALL...
...SHE CAN'T HAVE DREAMS LIKE OTHER PEOPLE.
IT WAS HOPELESS FROM THE BEGINNING. RIGHT, MY FRIEND? RIGHT...?

DREAMSONG
Part 3

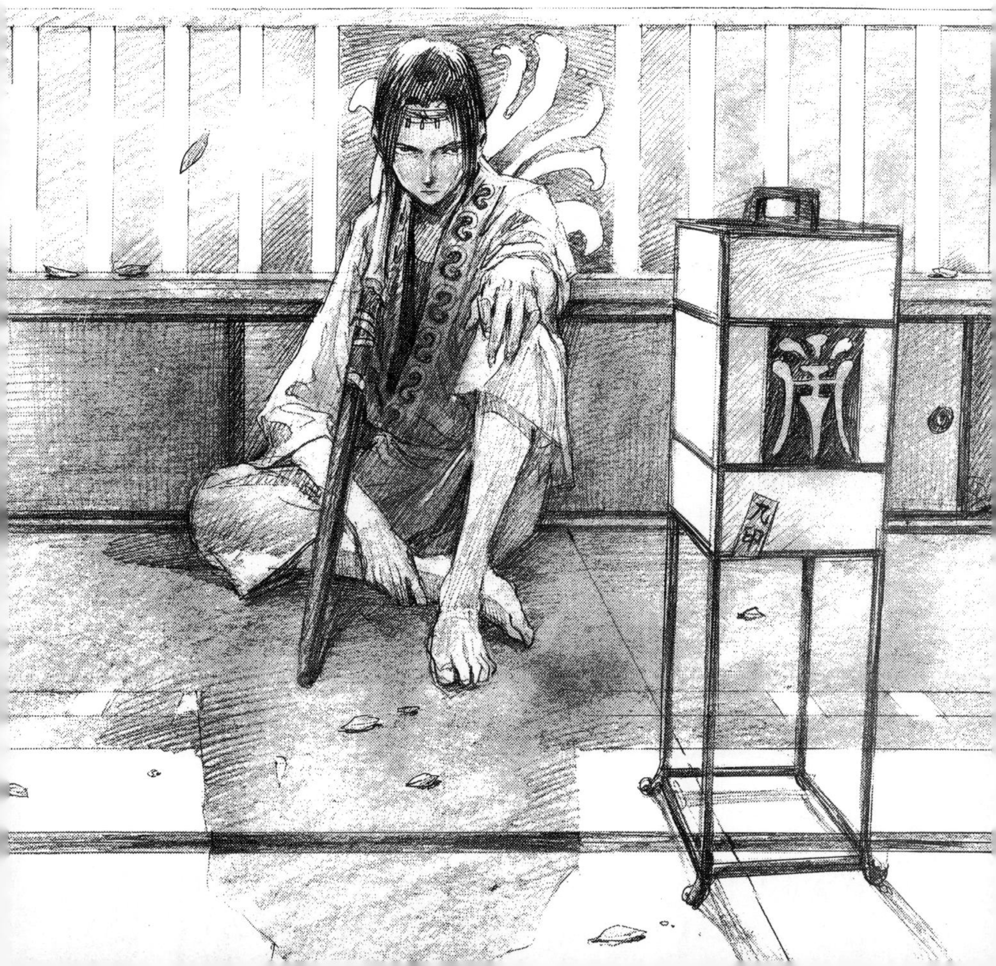

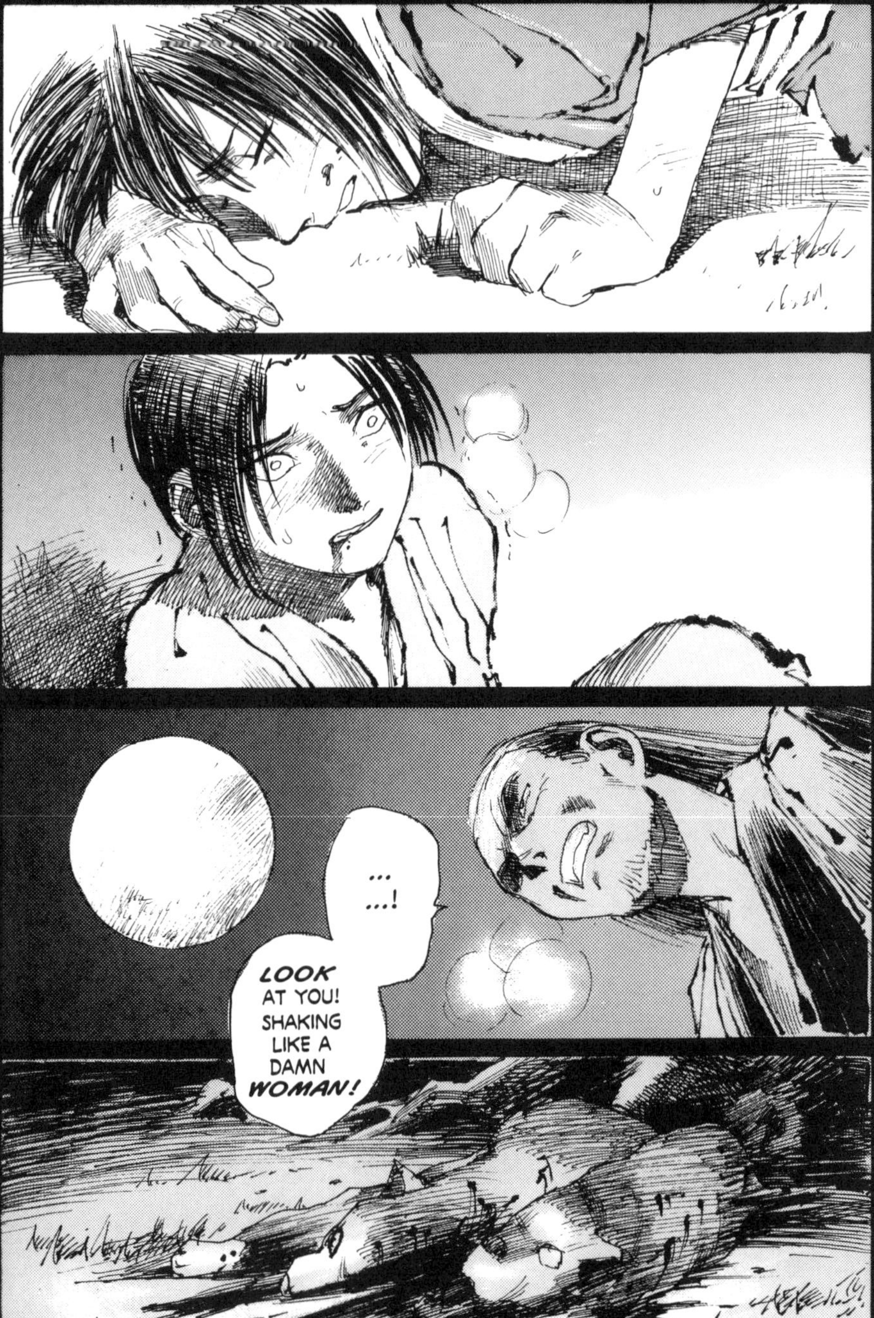
...
...!
LOOK AT YOU! SHAKING LIKE A DAMN WOMAN!

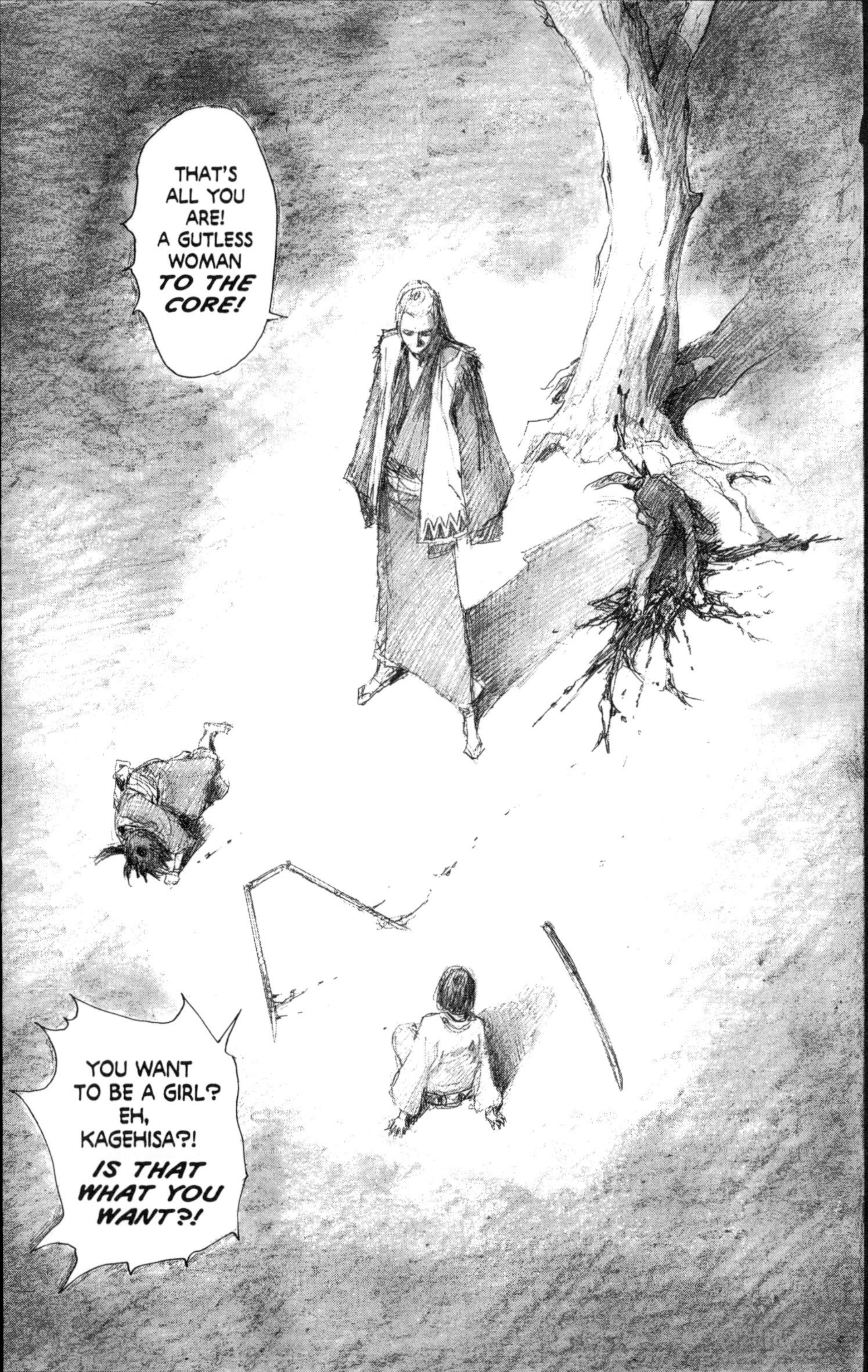
THAT'S ALL YOU ARE! A GUTLESS WOMAN ***TO THE CORE!***
YOU WANT TO BE A GIRL? EH, KAGEHISA?! ***IS THAT WHAT YOU WANT?!***

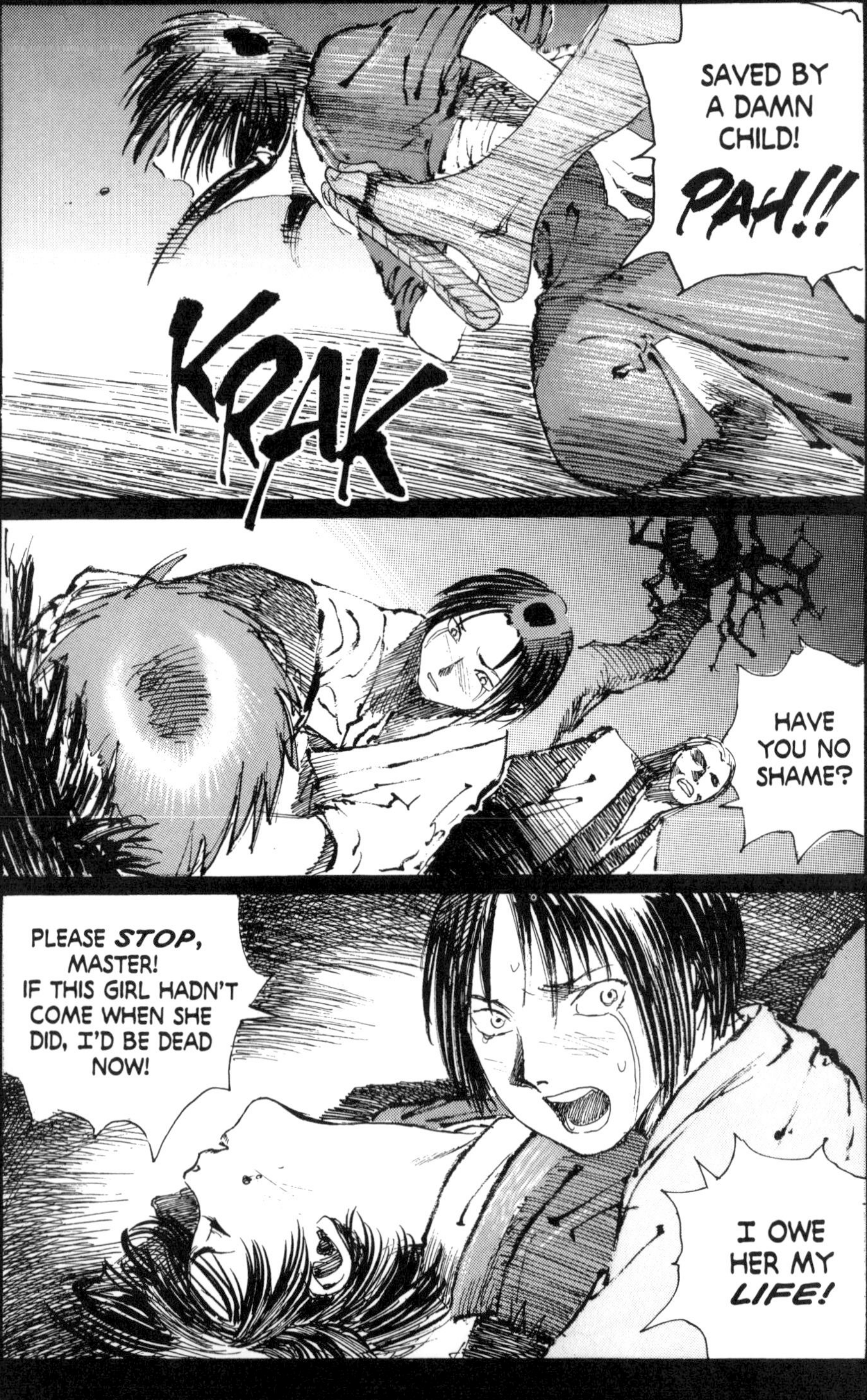
SAVED BY A DAMN CHILD!
PAH!!
KRAK
HAVE YOU NO SHAME?
PLEASE *STOP*, MASTER! IF THIS GIRL HADN'T COME WHEN SHE DID, I'D BE DEAD NOW!
I OWE HER MY *LIFE!*

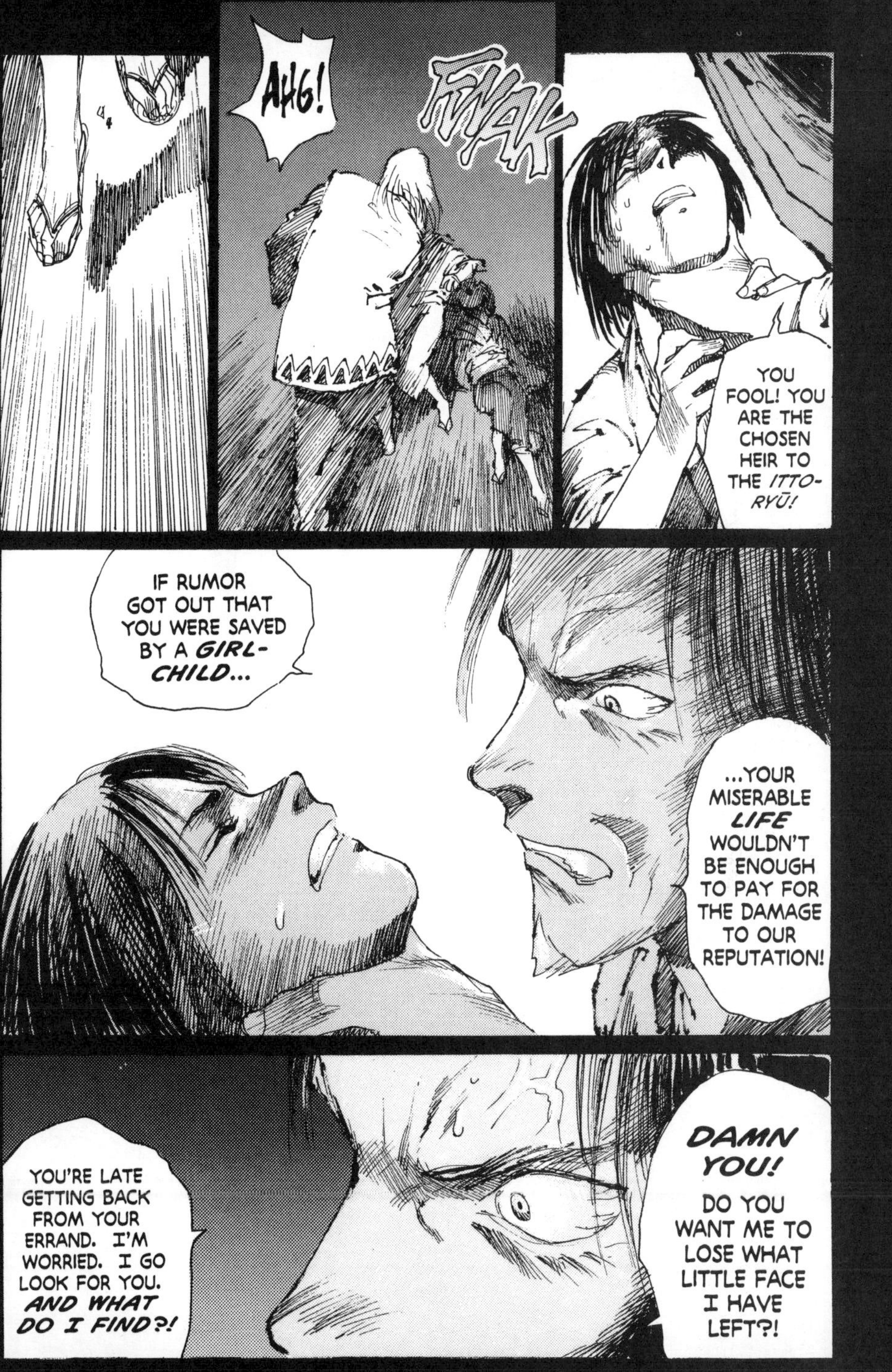
AHG!
FWAK
YOU FOOL! YOU ARE THE CHOSEN HEIR TO THE *ITTO-RYŪ!*
IF RUMOR GOT OUT THAT YOU WERE SAVED BY A ***GIRL-CHILD...***
...YOUR MISERABLE ***LIFE*** WOULDN'T BE ENOUGH TO PAY FOR THE DAMAGE TO OUR REPUTATION!
YOU'RE LATE GETTING BACK FROM YOUR ERRAND. I'M WORRIED. I GO LOOK FOR YOU. ***AND WHAT DO I FIND?!***
DAMN YOU!
DO YOU WANT ME TO LOSE WHAT LITTLE FACE I HAVE LEFT?!

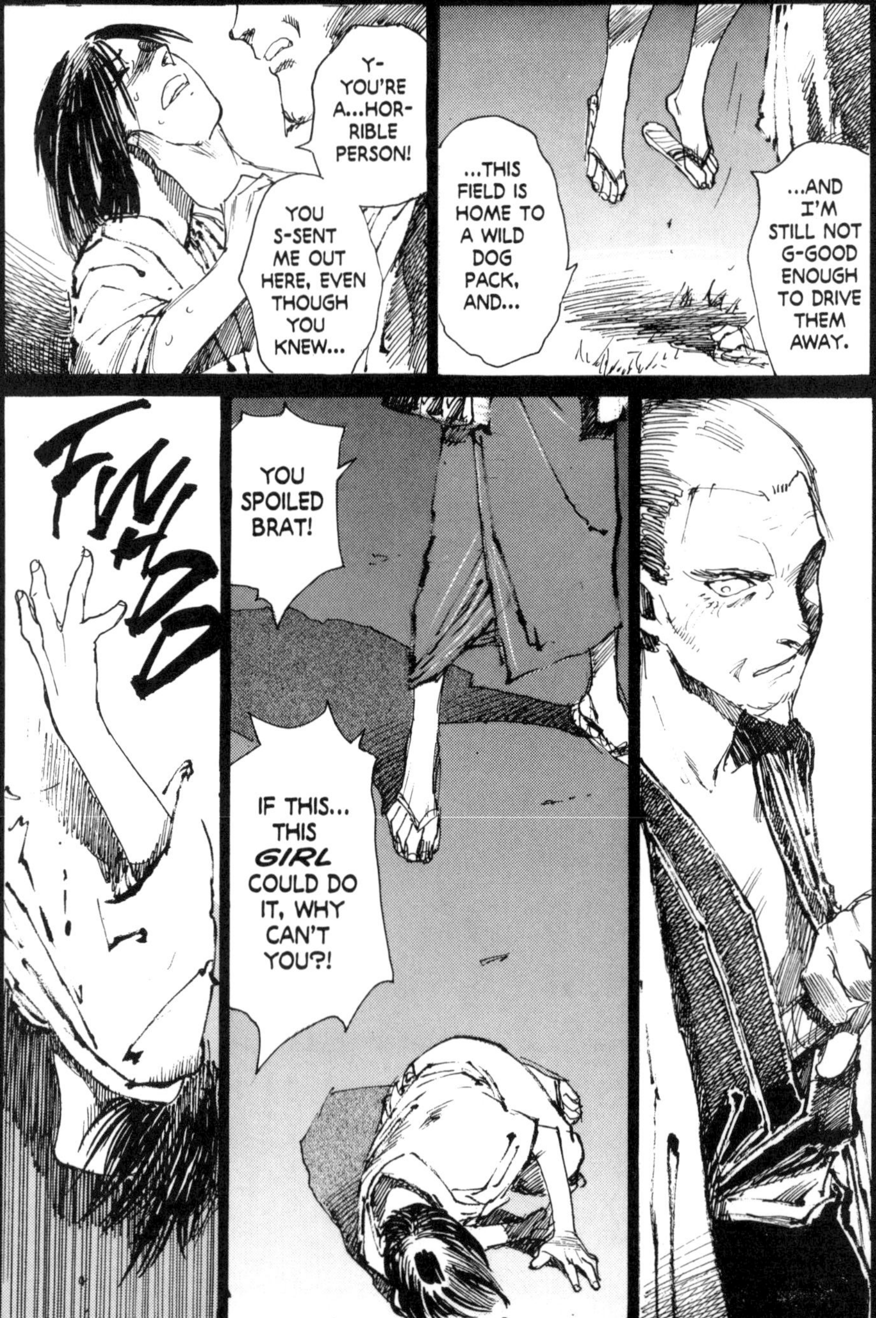
Y-YOU'RE A...HORRIBLE PERSON!
YOU S-SENT ME OUT HERE, EVEN THOUGH YOU KNEW...
...THIS FIELD IS HOME TO A WILD DOG PACK, AND...
...AND I'M STILL NOT G-GOOD ENOUGH TO DRIVE THEM AWAY.
FWHOO
YOU SPOILED BRAT!
IF THIS... THIS GIRL COULD DO IT, WHY CAN'T YOU?!

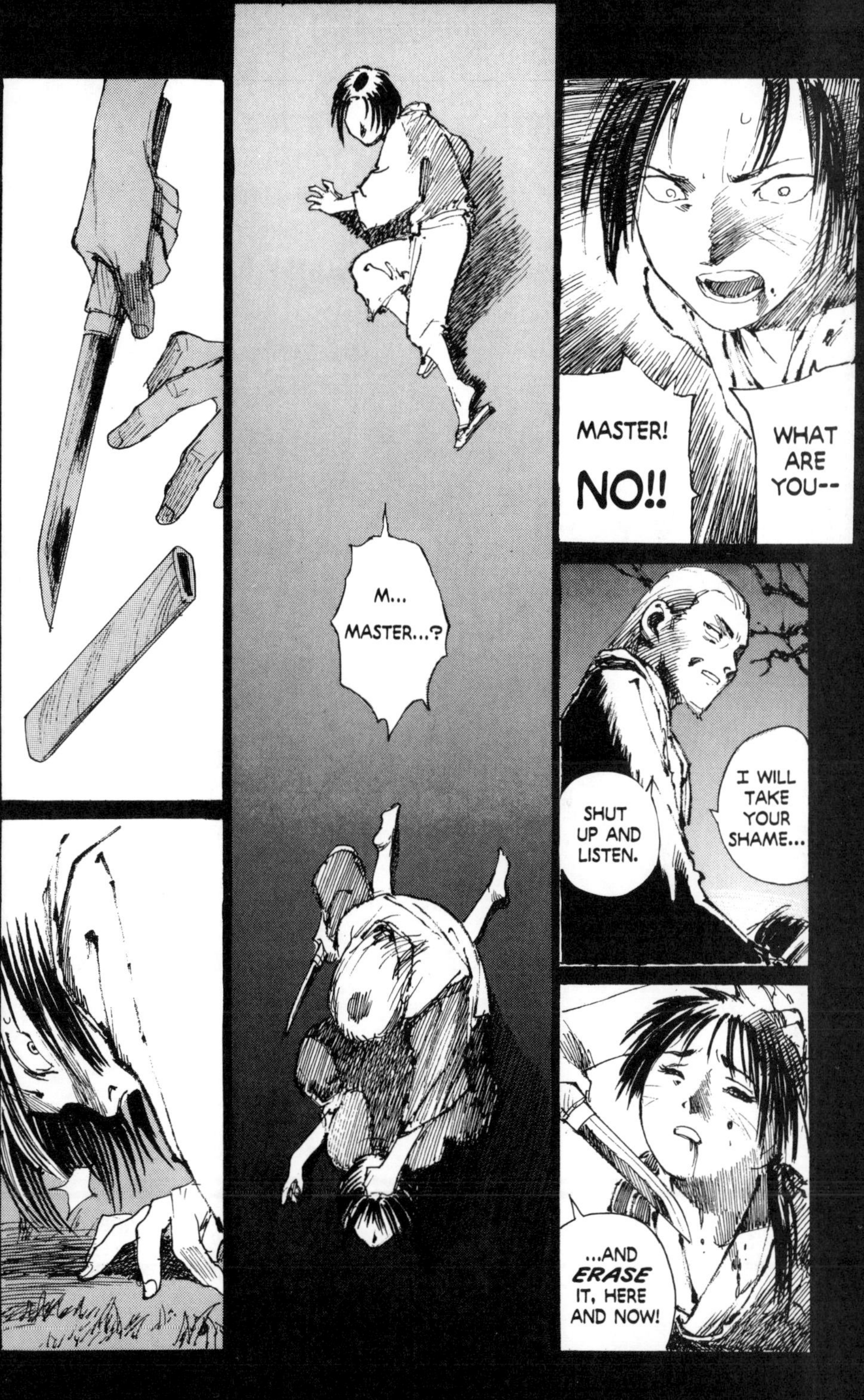
M... MASTER...?
MASTER! NO!!
WHAT ARE YOU--
SHUT UP AND LISTEN.
I WILL TAKE YOUR SHAME...
...AND *ERASE* IT, HERE AND NOW!

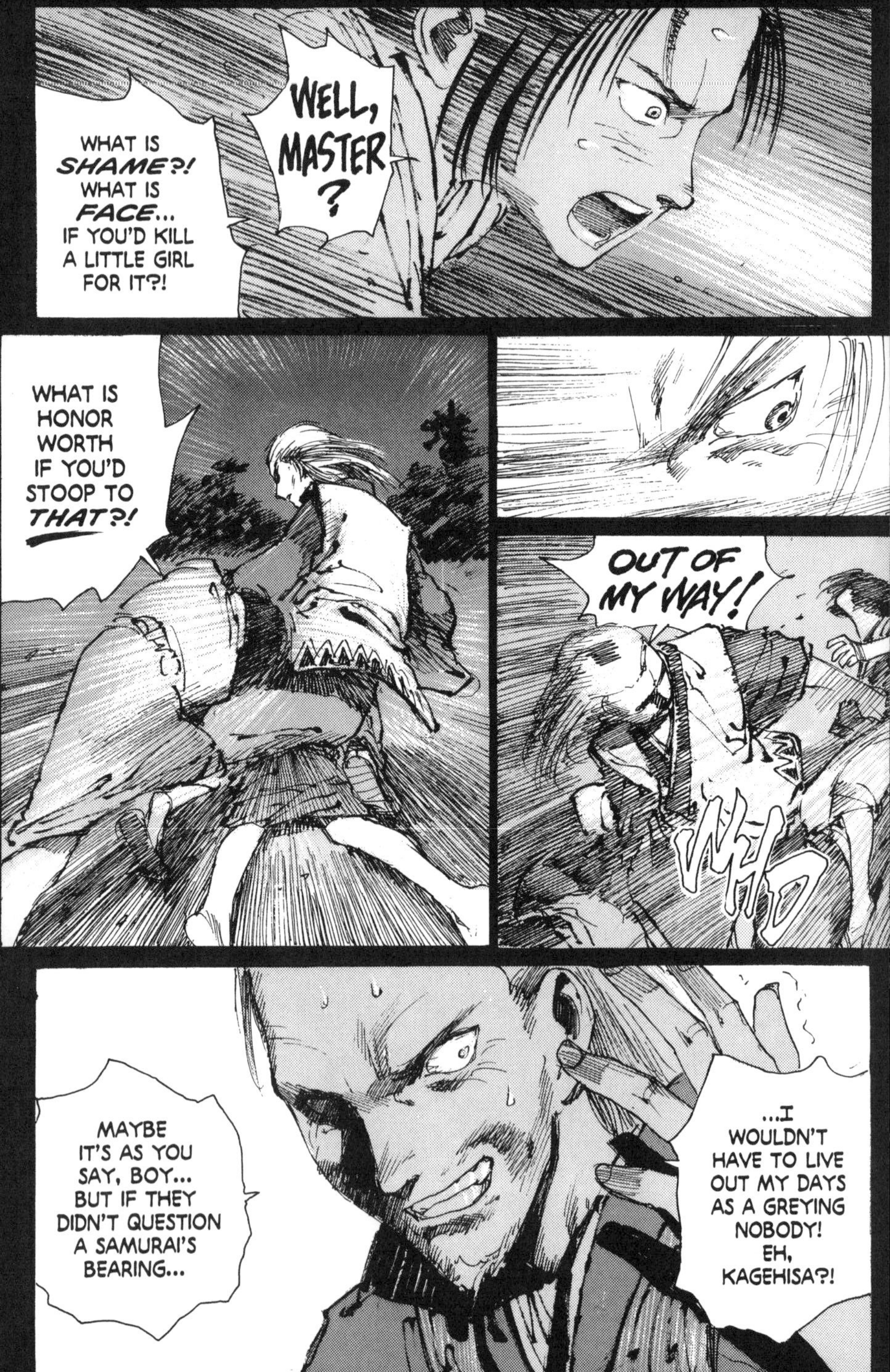
WHAT IS *SHAME?!* WHAT IS *FACE*... IF YOU'D KILL A LITTLE GIRL FOR IT?!
WELL, MASTER?
WHAT IS HONOR WORTH IF YOU'D STOOP TO *THAT?!*
OUT OF MY WAY!
WHD
MAYBE IT'S AS YOU SAY, BOY... BUT IF THEY DIDN'T QUESTION A SAMURAI'S BEARING...
...I WOULDN'T HAVE TO LIVE OUT MY DAYS AS A GREYING NOBODY! EH, KAGEHISA?!

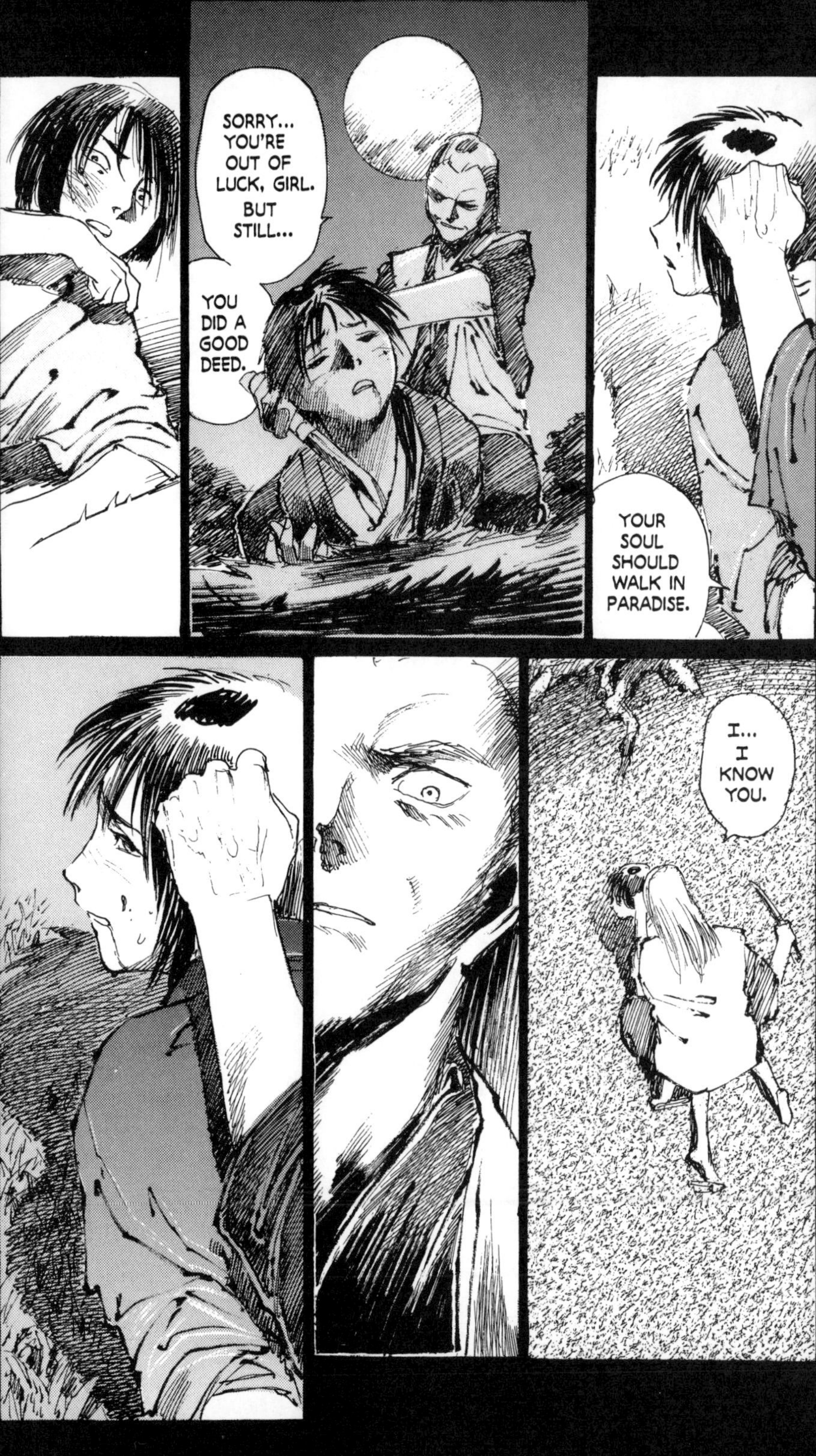
SORRY... YOU'RE OUT OF LUCK, GIRL.
BUT STILL...
YOU DID A GOOD DEED.
YOUR SOUL SHOULD WALK IN PARADISE.
I... I KNOW YOU.

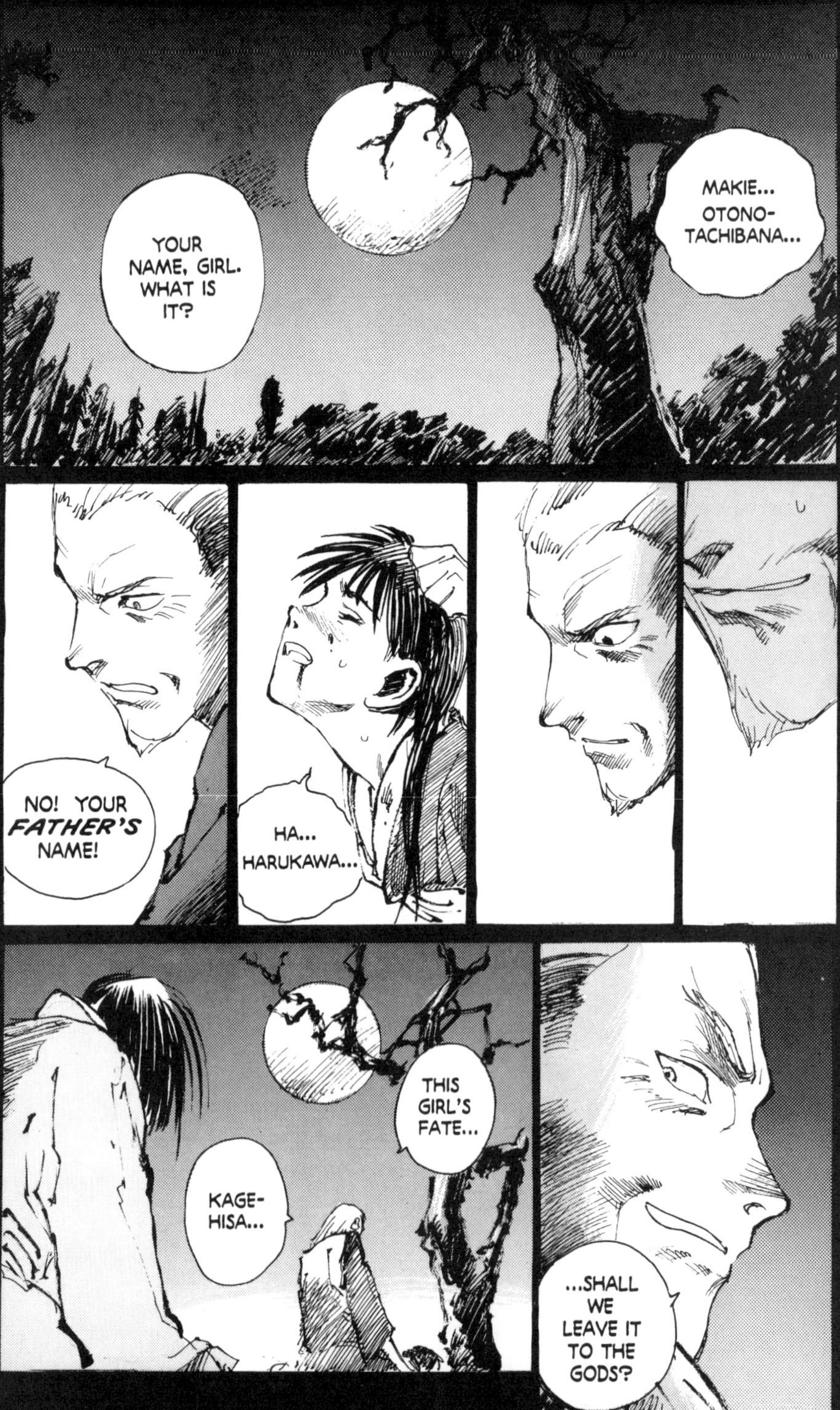
YOUR NAME, GIRL. WHAT IS IT?
MAKIE... OTONO-TACHIBANA...
NO! YOUR *FATHER'S* NAME!
HA... HARUKAWA...
THIS GIRL'S FATE...
KAGE-HISA...
...SHALL WE LEAVE IT TO THE GODS?

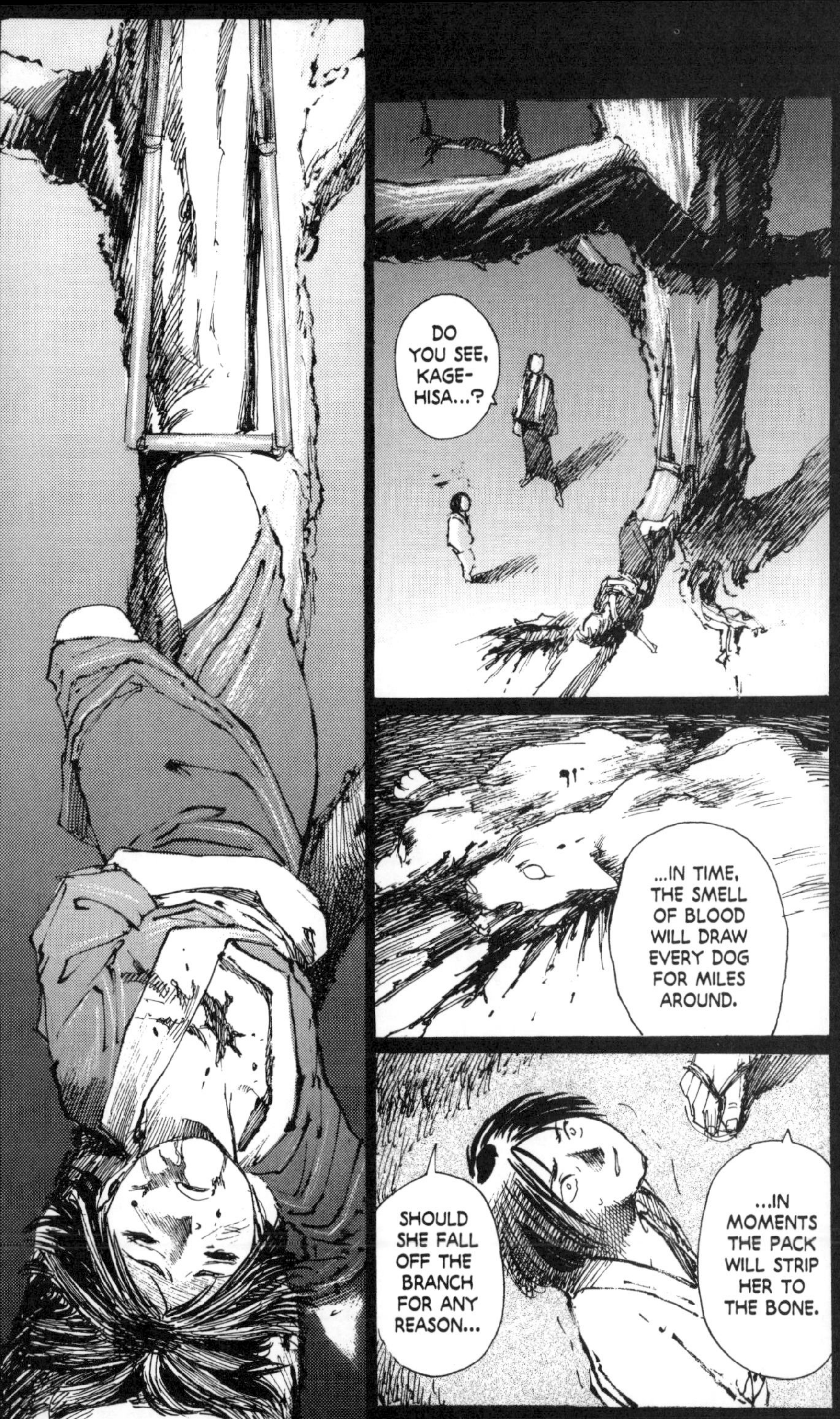
DO YOU SEE, KAGE-HISA...?
...IN TIME, THE SMELL OF BLOOD WILL DRAW EVERY DOG FOR MILES AROUND.
SHOULD SHE FALL OFF THE BRANCH FOR ANY REASON...
...IN MOMENTS THE PACK WILL STRIP HER TO THE BONE.

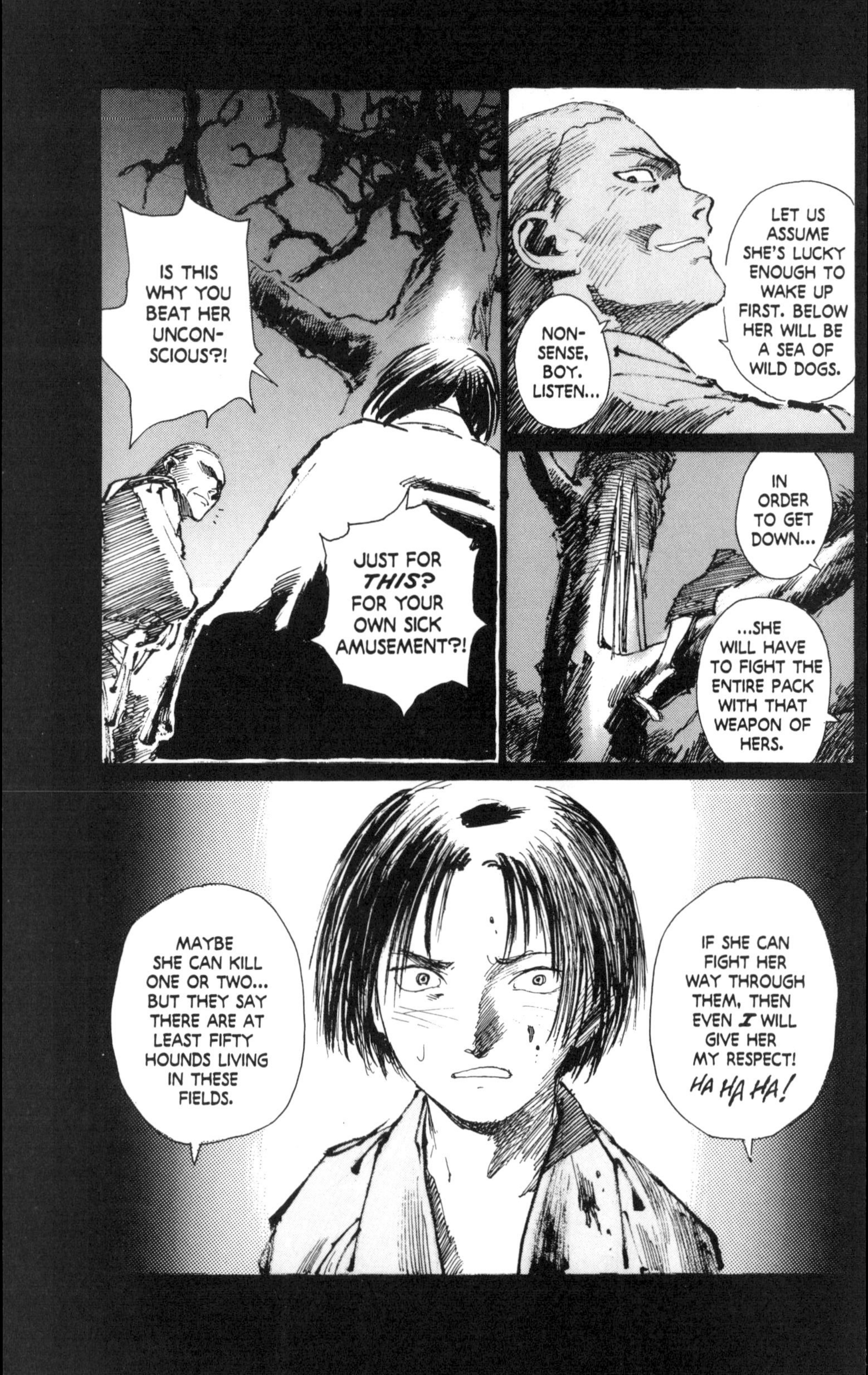
IS THIS WHY YOU BEAT HER UNCON-SCIOUS?!
JUST FOR *THIS?* FOR YOUR OWN SICK AMUSEMENT?!
NON-SENSE, BOY. LISTEN...
LET US ASSUME SHE'S LUCKY ENOUGH TO WAKE UP FIRST. BELOW HER WILL BE A SEA OF WILD DOGS.
IN ORDER TO GET DOWN...
...SHE WILL HAVE TO FIGHT THE ENTIRE PACK WITH THAT WEAPON OF HERS.
MAYBE SHE CAN KILL ONE OR TWO... BUT THEY SAY THERE ARE AT LEAST FIFTY HOUNDS LIVING IN THESE FIELDS.
IF SHE CAN FIGHT HER WAY THROUGH THEM, THEN EVEN *I* WILL GIVE HER MY RESPECT!
HA HA HA!

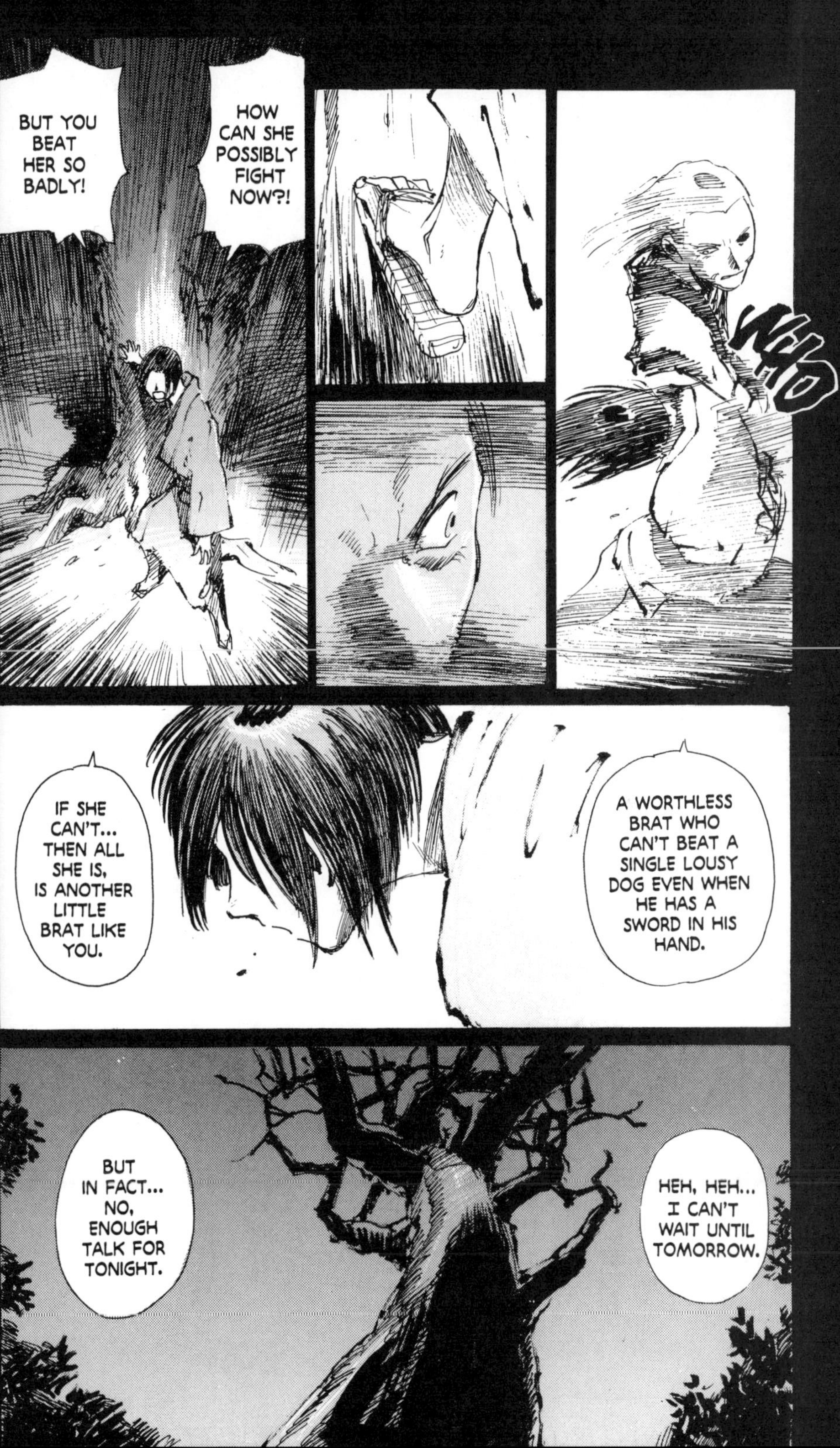

BUT YOU BEAT HER SO BADLY!
HOW CAN SHE POSSIBLY FIGHT NOW?!
WHO
IF SHE CAN'T... THEN ALL SHE IS, IS ANOTHER LITTLE BRAT LIKE YOU.
A WORTHLESS BRAT WHO CAN'T BEAT A SINGLE LOUSY DOG EVEN WHEN HE HAS A SWORD IN HIS HAND.
BUT IN FACT... NO, ENOUGH TALK FOR TONIGHT.
HEH, HEH... I CAN'T WAIT UNTIL TOMORROW.

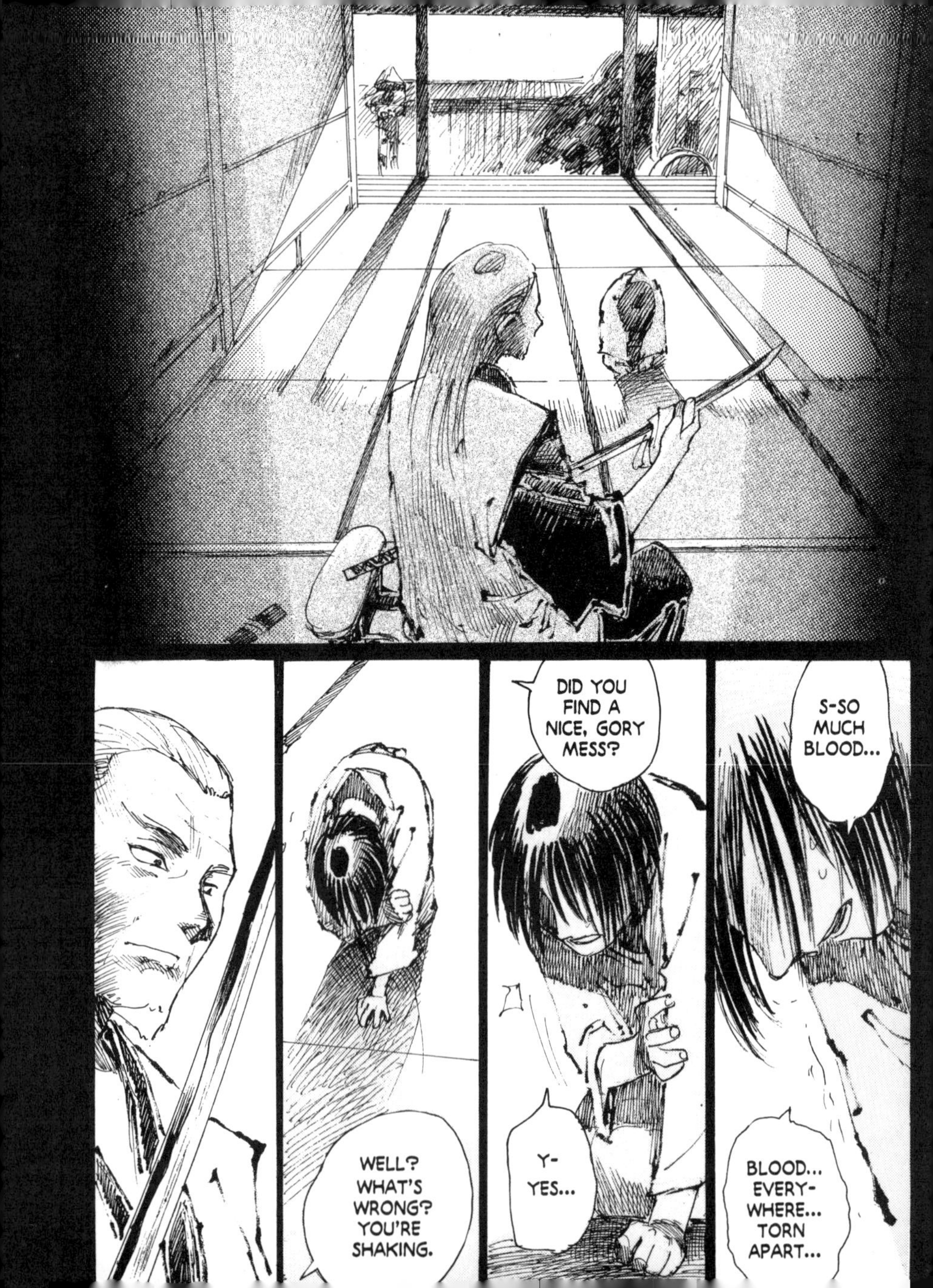
WELL? WHAT'S WRONG? YOU'RE SHAKING.
DID YOU FIND A NICE, GORY MESS?
Y- YES...
S-SO MUCH BLOOD...
BLOOD... EVERY-WHERE... TORN APART...

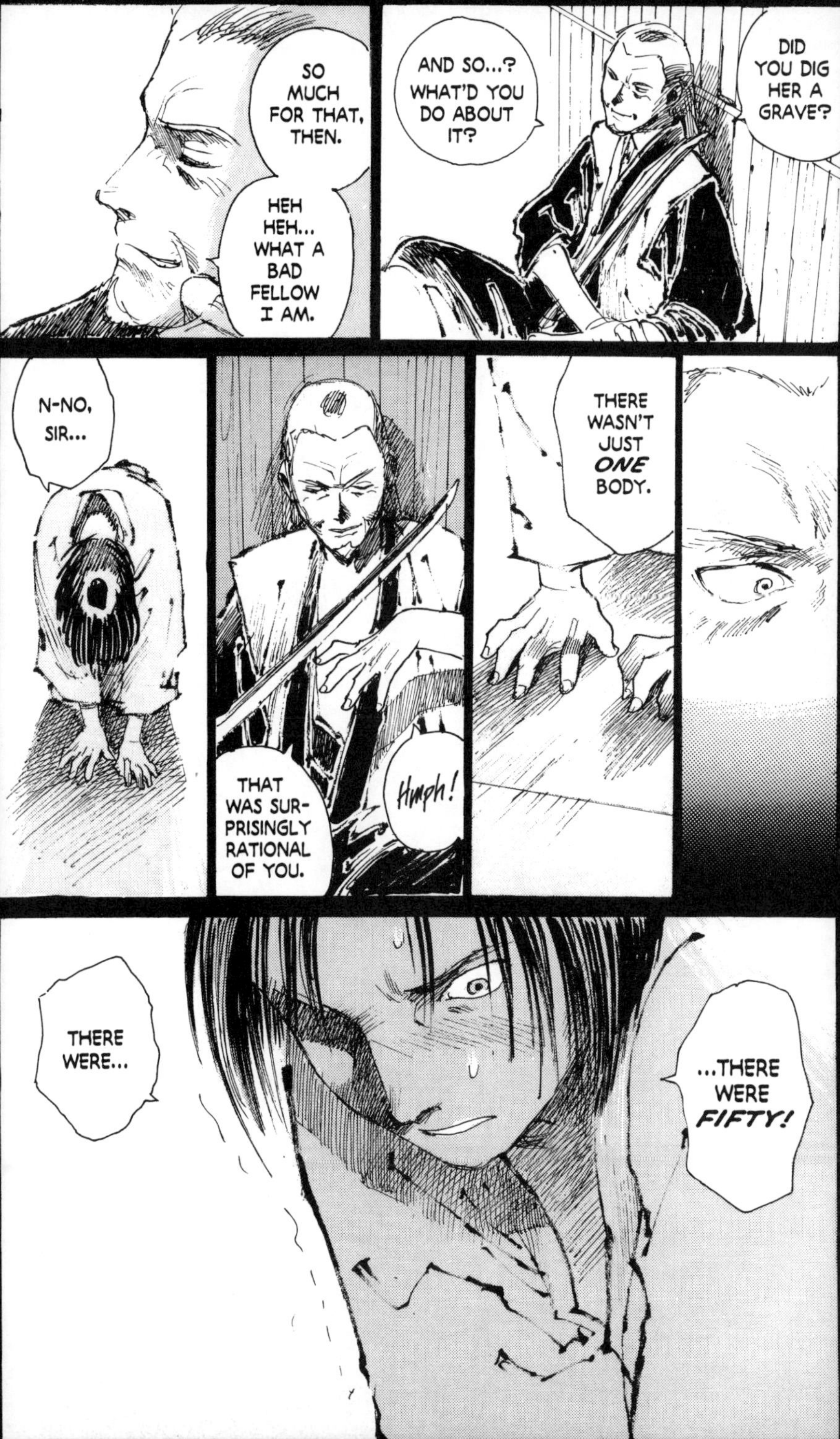
SO MUCH FOR THAT, THEN.
HEH HEH... WHAT A BAD FELLOW I AM.
AND SO...? WHAT'D YOU DO ABOUT IT?
DID YOU DIG HER A GRAVE?
N-NO, SIR...
THAT WAS SUR-PRISINGLY RATIONAL OF YOU.
Hmph!
THERE WASN'T JUST *ONE* BODY.
THERE WERE...
...THERE WERE *FIFTY!*

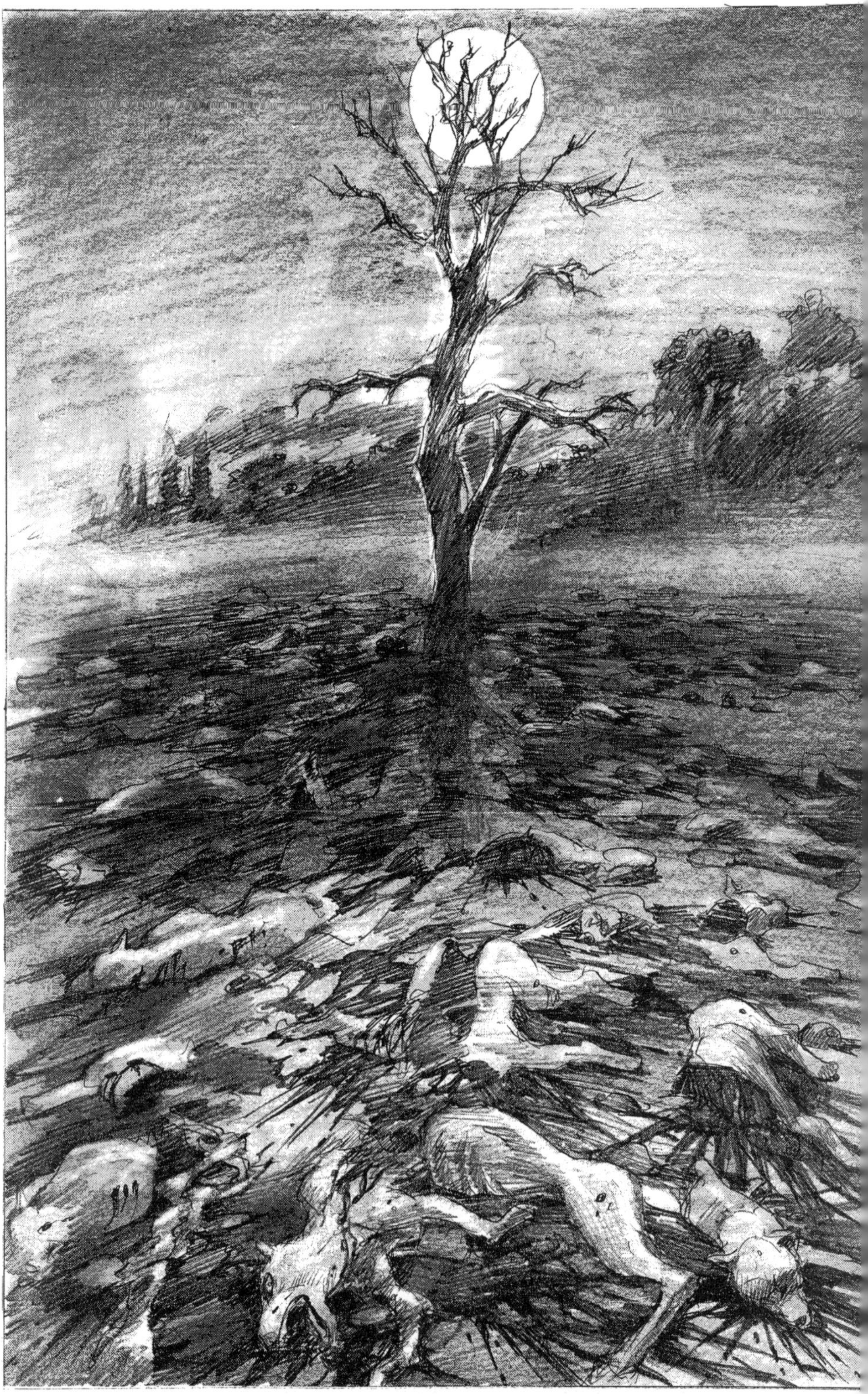

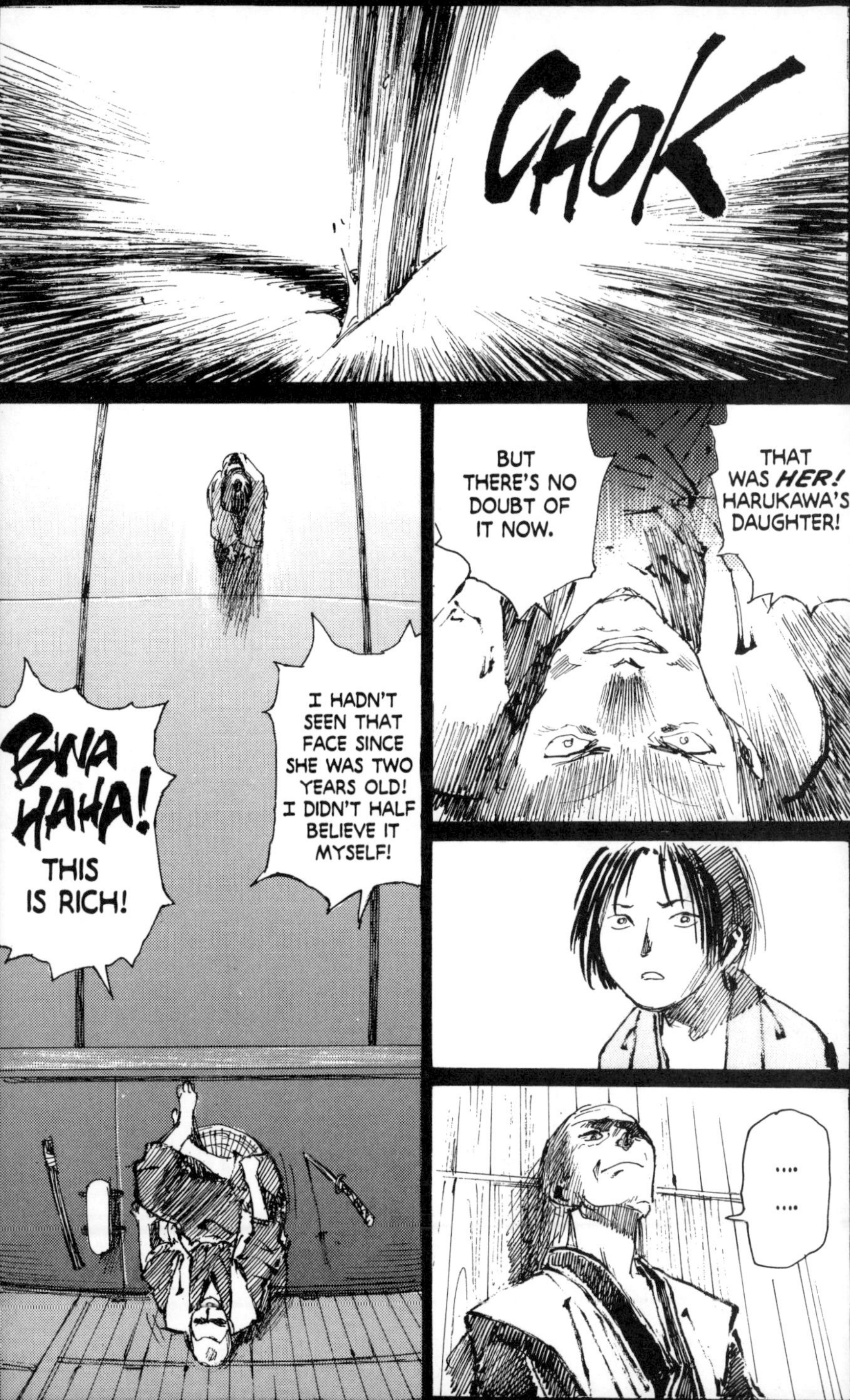
CHOK
BWA HAHA! THIS IS RICH!
I HADN'T SEEN THAT FACE SINCE SHE WAS TWO YEARS OLD! I DIDN'T HALF BELIEVE IT MYSELF!
BUT THERE'S NO DOUBT OF IT NOW.
THAT WAS *HER!* HARUKAWA'S DAUGHTER!
....
....

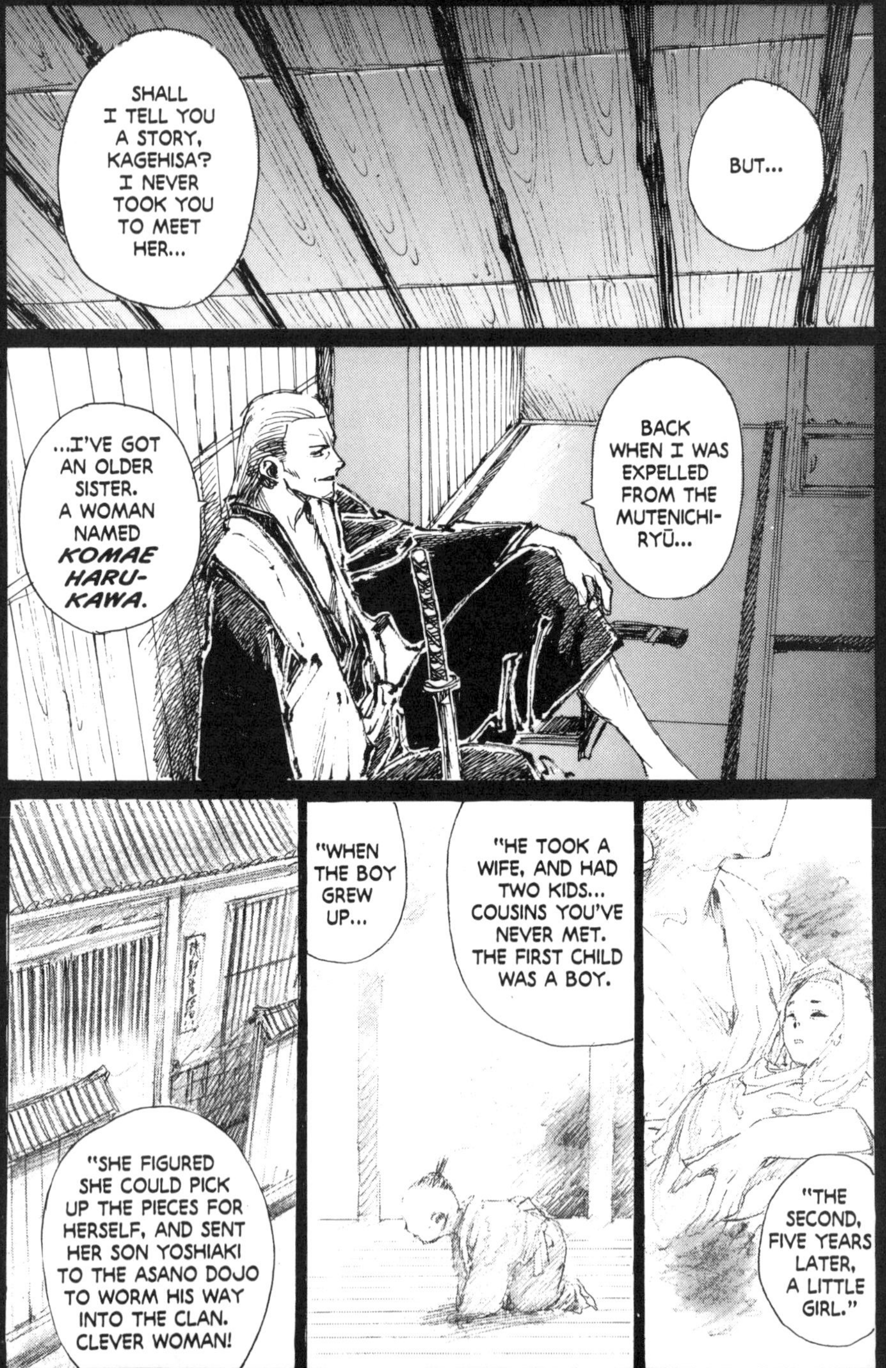
SHALL I TELL YOU A STORY, KAGEHISA? I NEVER TOOK YOU TO MEET HER...
BUT...
...I'VE GOT AN OLDER SISTER. A WOMAN NAMED *KOMAE HARUKAWA*.
BACK WHEN I WAS EXPELLED FROM THE MUTENICHI-RYŪ...
"SHE FIGURED SHE COULD PICK UP THE PIECES FOR HERSELF, AND SENT HER SON YOSHIAKI TO THE ASANO DOJO TO WORM HIS WAY INTO THE CLAN. CLEVER WOMAN!
"WHEN THE BOY GREW UP...
"HE TOOK A WIFE, AND HAD TWO KIDS... COUSINS YOU'VE NEVER MET. THE FIRST CHILD WAS A BOY.
"THE SECOND, FIVE YEARS LATER, A LITTLE GIRL."

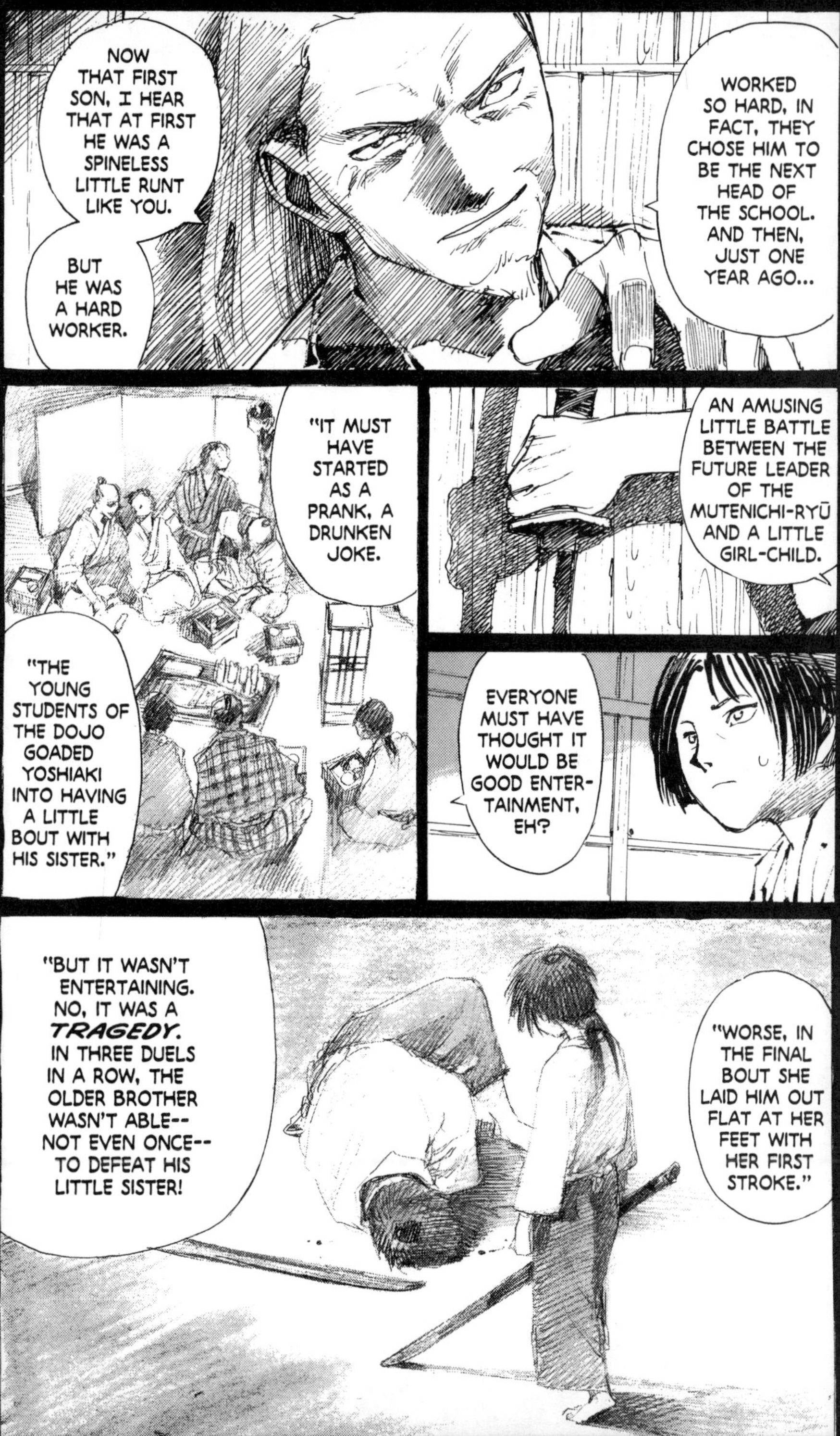
NOW THAT FIRST SON, I HEAR THAT AT FIRST HE WAS A SPINELESS LITTLE RUNT LIKE YOU.
BUT HE WAS A HARD WORKER.
WORKED SO HARD, IN FACT, THEY CHOSE HIM TO BE THE NEXT HEAD OF THE SCHOOL. AND THEN, JUST ONE YEAR AGO...
"IT MUST HAVE STARTED AS A PRANK, A DRUNKEN JOKE.
"THE YOUNG STUDENTS OF THE DOJO GOADED YOSHIAKI INTO HAVING A LITTLE BOUT WITH HIS SISTER."
AN AMUSING LITTLE BATTLE BETWEEN THE FUTURE LEADER OF THE MUTENICHI-RYŪ AND A LITTLE GIRL-CHILD.
EVERYONE MUST HAVE THOUGHT IT WOULD BE GOOD ENTERTAINMENT, EH?
"BUT IT WASN'T ENTERTAINING. NO, IT WAS A ***TRAGEDY***. IN THREE DUELS IN A ROW, THE OLDER BROTHER WASN'T ABLE--NOT EVEN ONCE--TO DEFEAT HIS LITTLE SISTER!
"WORSE, IN THE FINAL BOUT SHE LAID HIM OUT FLAT AT HER FEET WITH HER FIRST STROKE."

AT THAT MOMENT, EVERYONE AT THE PARTY KNEW, BEYOND A DOUBT--THE SAMURAI BLOODLINE OF THE HARUKAWA CLAN, UNBROKEN FOR GENERATIONS...

IF YOU REALIZED YOU COULDN'T BEAT A WOMAN...

...A *GIRL*...

...IF IT WAS YOU, WHAT WOULD YOU DO...?

I WOULD ERASE THIS TERRIBLE INSULT...

...BY FINDING *SOME WAY* TO DEFEAT HER.

...HAD BEEN RECEIVED NOT BY THE ELDEST SON, BUT BY THE *DAUGHTER!* A GIRL WHO COULD NEVER BE A WARRIOR!

OH, REALLY? BUT YOSHIAKI'S BOY DIDN'T SEE IT THAT WAY.

NO...

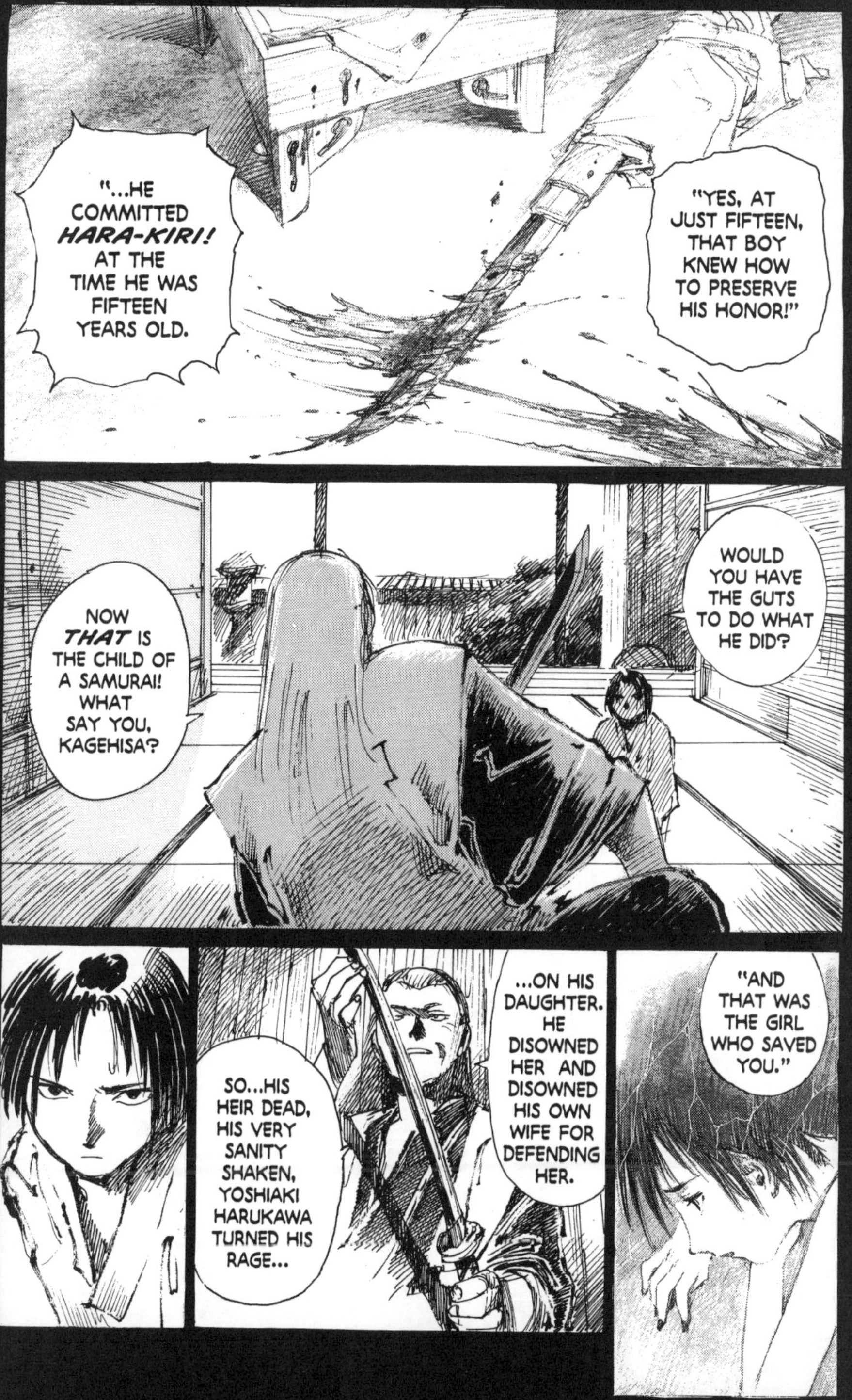
"...HE COMMITTED HARA-KIRI! AT THE TIME HE WAS FIFTEEN YEARS OLD.
"YES, AT JUST FIFTEEN, THAT BOY KNEW HOW TO PRESERVE HIS HONOR!"
NOW THAT IS THE CHILD OF A SAMURAI! WHAT SAY YOU, KAGEHISA?
WOULD YOU HAVE THE GUTS TO DO WHAT HE DID?
SO...HIS HEIR DEAD, HIS VERY SANITY SHAKEN, YOSHIAKI HARUKAWA TURNED HIS RAGE...
...ON HIS DAUGHTER. HE DISOWNED HER AND DISOWNED HIS OWN WIFE FOR DEFENDING HER.
"AND THAT WAS THE GIRL WHO SAVED YOU."

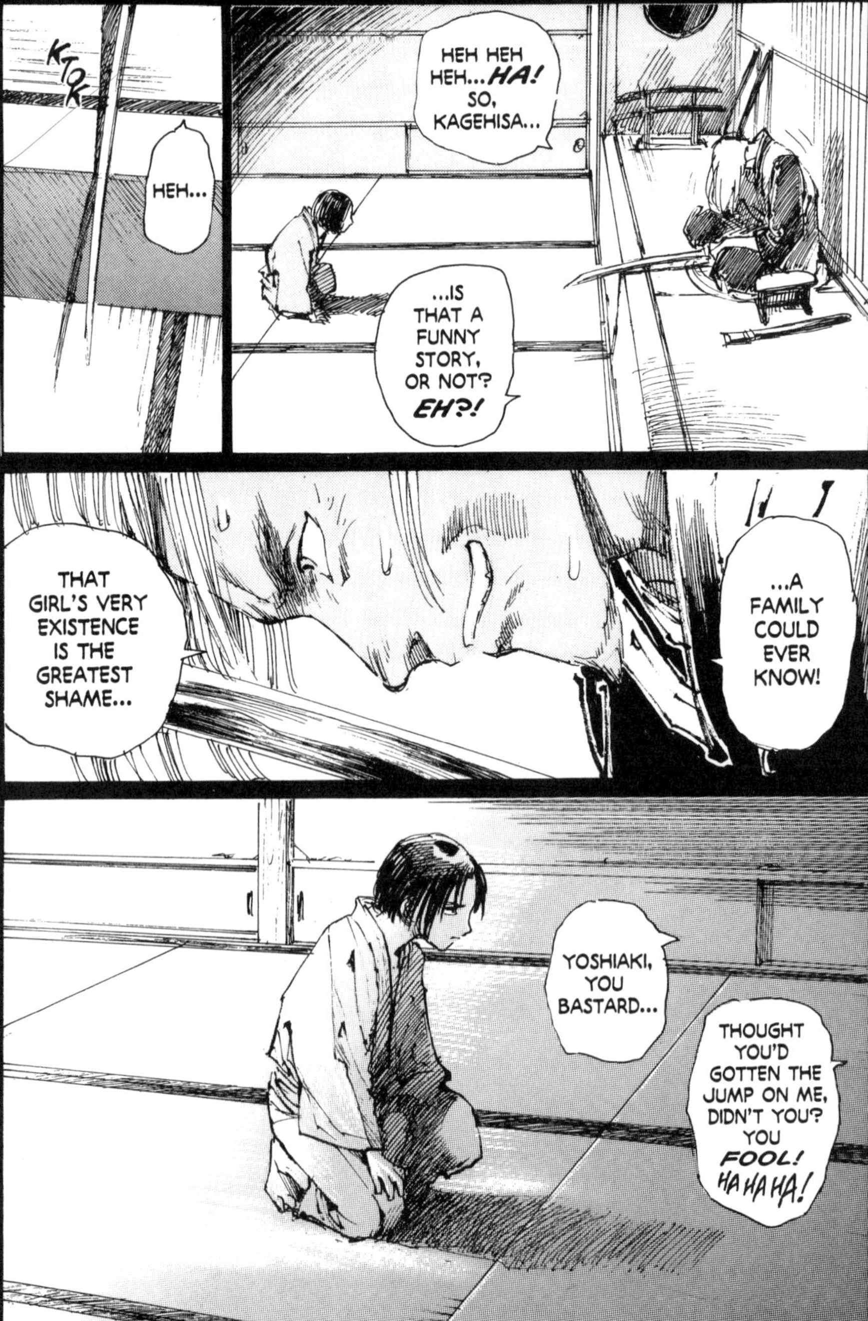
KTOK
HEH...
HEH HEH HEH...HA! SO, KAGEHISA...
...IS THAT A FUNNY STORY, OR NOT? EH?!
THAT GIRL'S VERY EXISTENCE IS THE GREATEST SHAME...
...A FAMILY COULD EVER KNOW!
YOSHIAKI, YOU BASTARD...
THOUGHT YOU'D GOTTEN THE JUMP ON ME, DIDN'T YOU? YOU FOOL! HA HA HA!

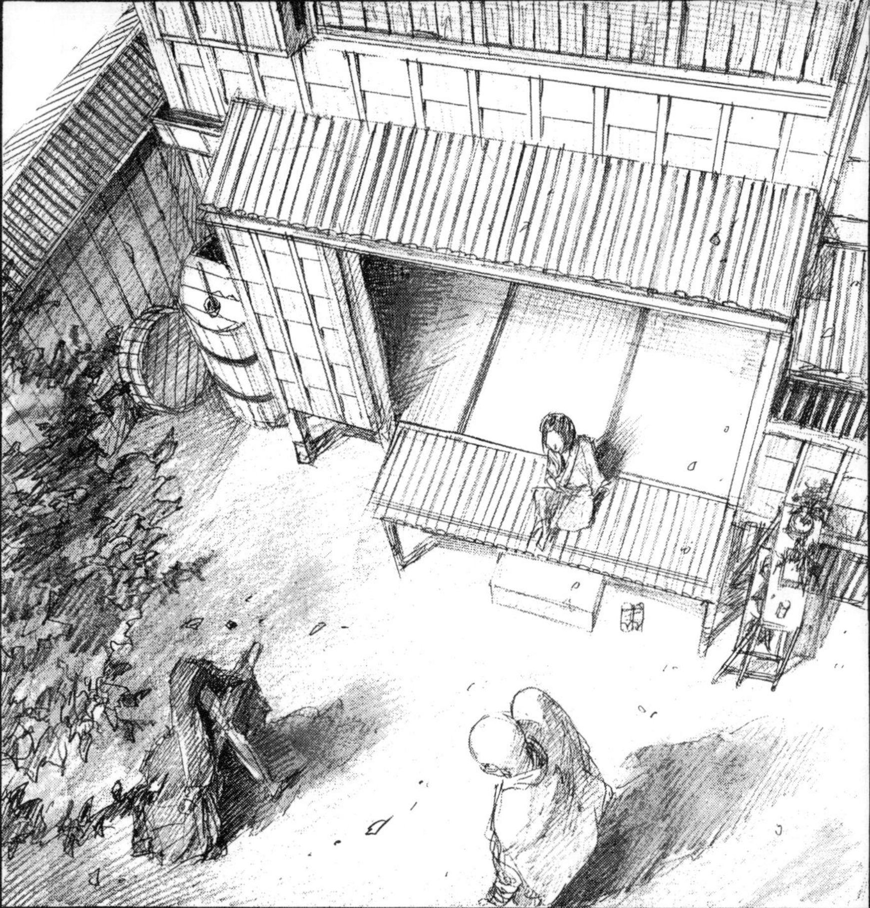

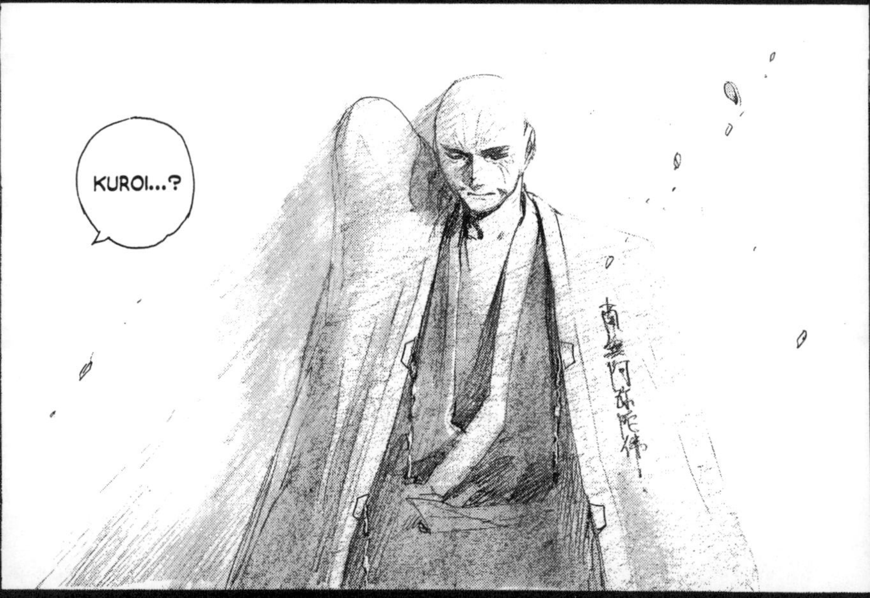
KUROI...?
南無阿弥陀佛…

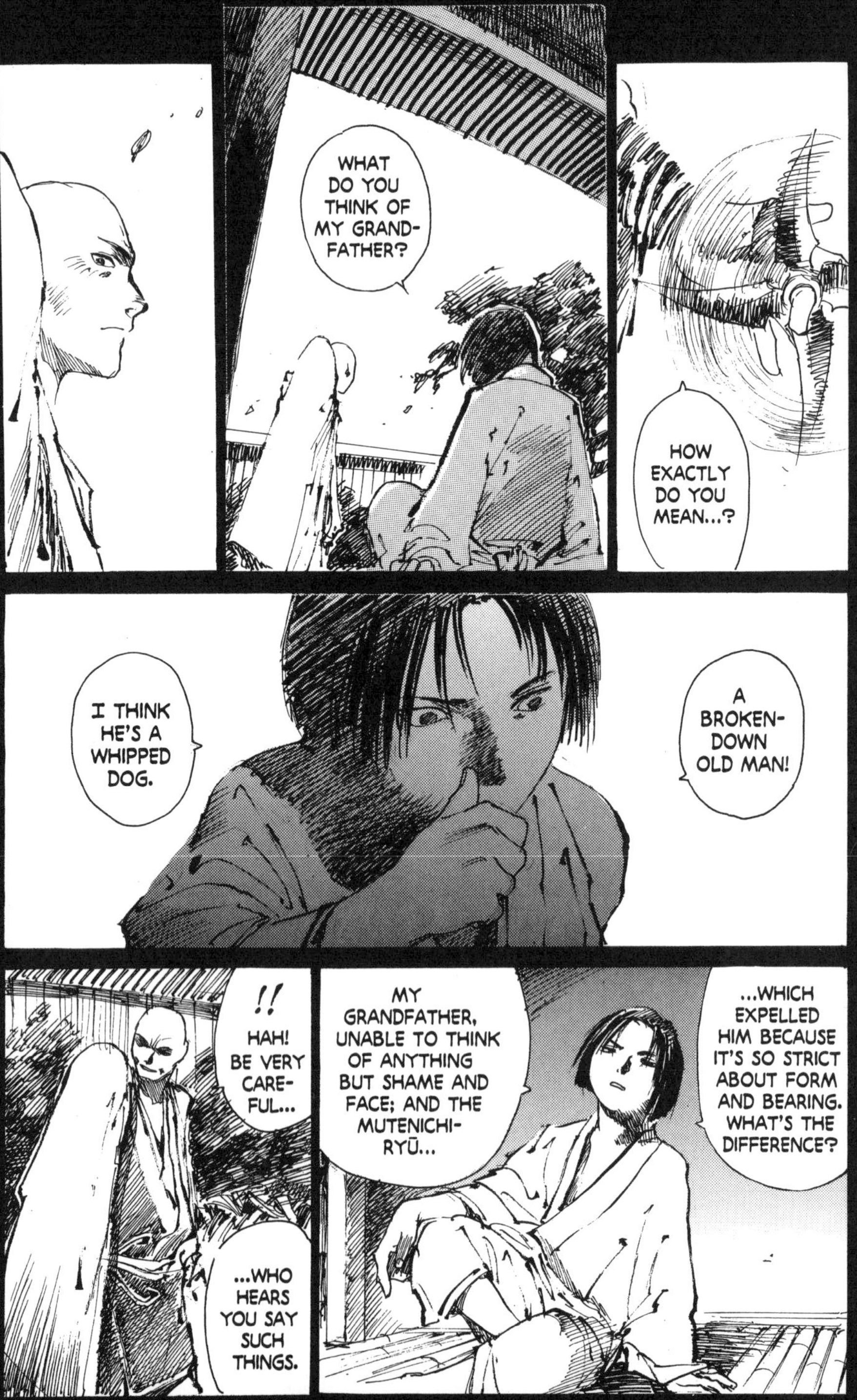
WHAT DO YOU THINK OF MY GRAND-FATHER?
HOW EXACTLY DO YOU MEAN...?
I THINK HE'S A WHIPPED DOG.
A BROKEN-DOWN OLD MAN!
!!
HAH! BE VERY CARE-FUL...
...WHO HEARS YOU SAY SUCH THINGS.
MY GRANDFATHER, UNABLE TO THINK OF ANYTHING BUT SHAME AND FACE; AND THE MUTENICHI-RYŪ...
...WHICH EXPELLED HIM BECAUSE IT'S SO STRICT ABOUT FORM AND BEARING. WHAT'S THE DIFFERENCE?

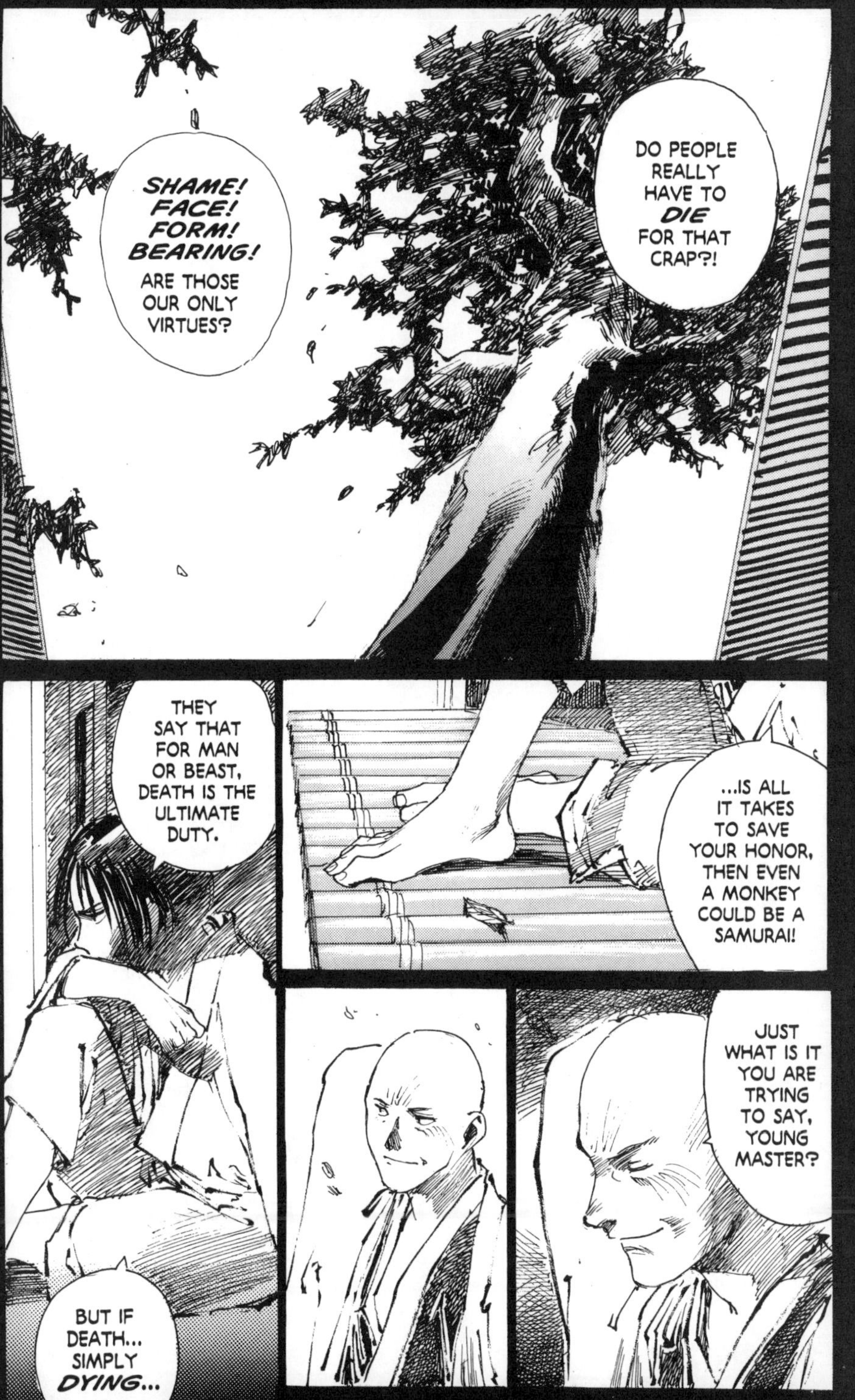
SHAME! FACE! FORM! BEARING! ARE THOSE OUR ONLY VIRTUES?
DO PEOPLE REALLY HAVE TO DIE FOR THAT CRAP?!
THEY SAY THAT FOR MAN OR BEAST, DEATH IS THE ULTIMATE DUTY.
BUT IF DEATH... SIMPLY DYING...
...IS ALL IT TAKES TO SAVE YOUR HONOR, THEN EVEN A MONKEY COULD BE A SAMURAI!
JUST WHAT IS IT YOU ARE TRYING TO SAY, YOUNG MASTER?

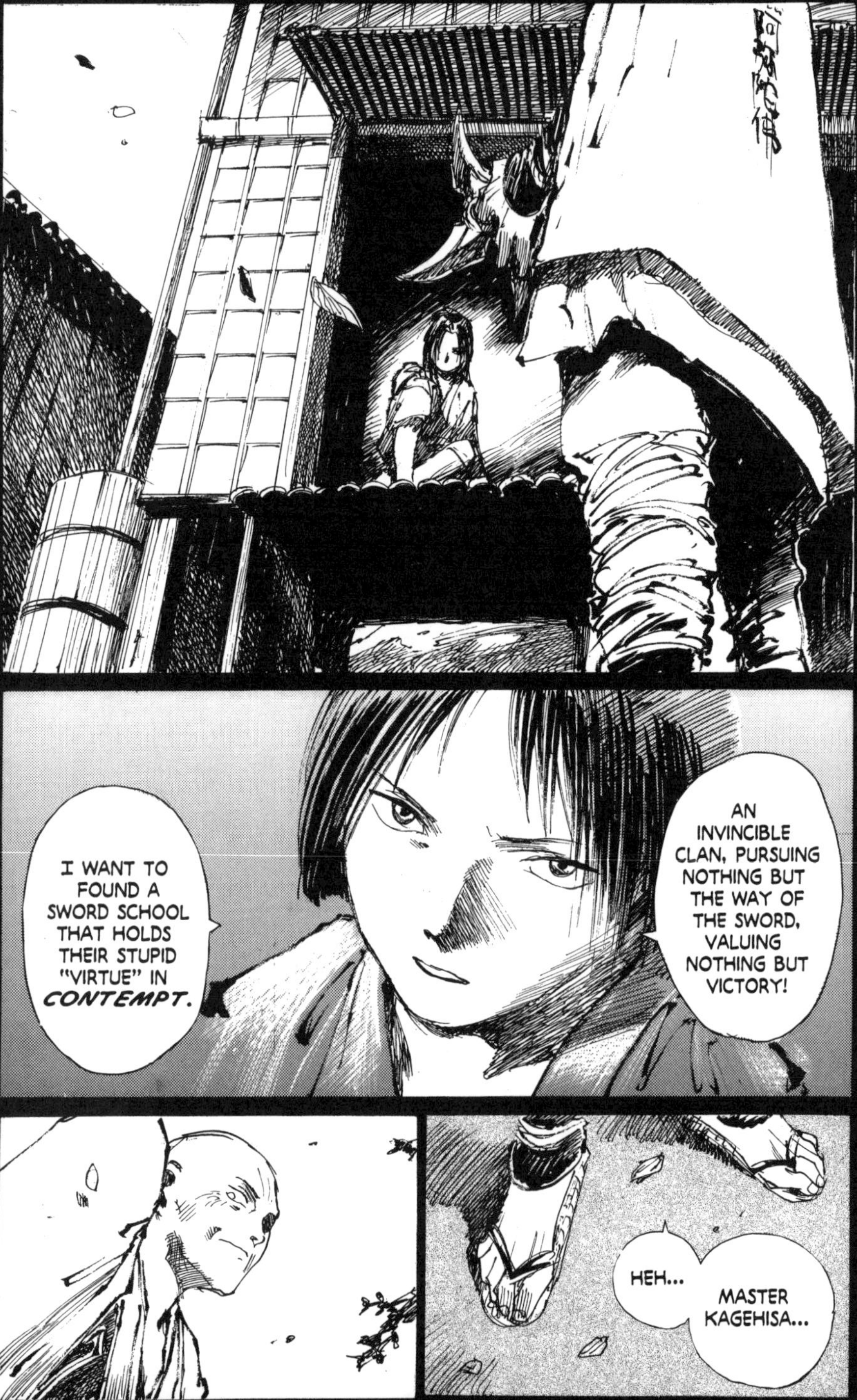
I WANT TO FOUND A SWORD SCHOOL THAT HOLDS THEIR STUPID "VIRTUE" IN *CONTEMPT*.
AN INVINCIBLE CLAN, PURSUING NOTHING BUT THE WAY OF THE SWORD, VALUING NOTHING BUT VICTORY!
HEH...
MASTER KAGEHISA...

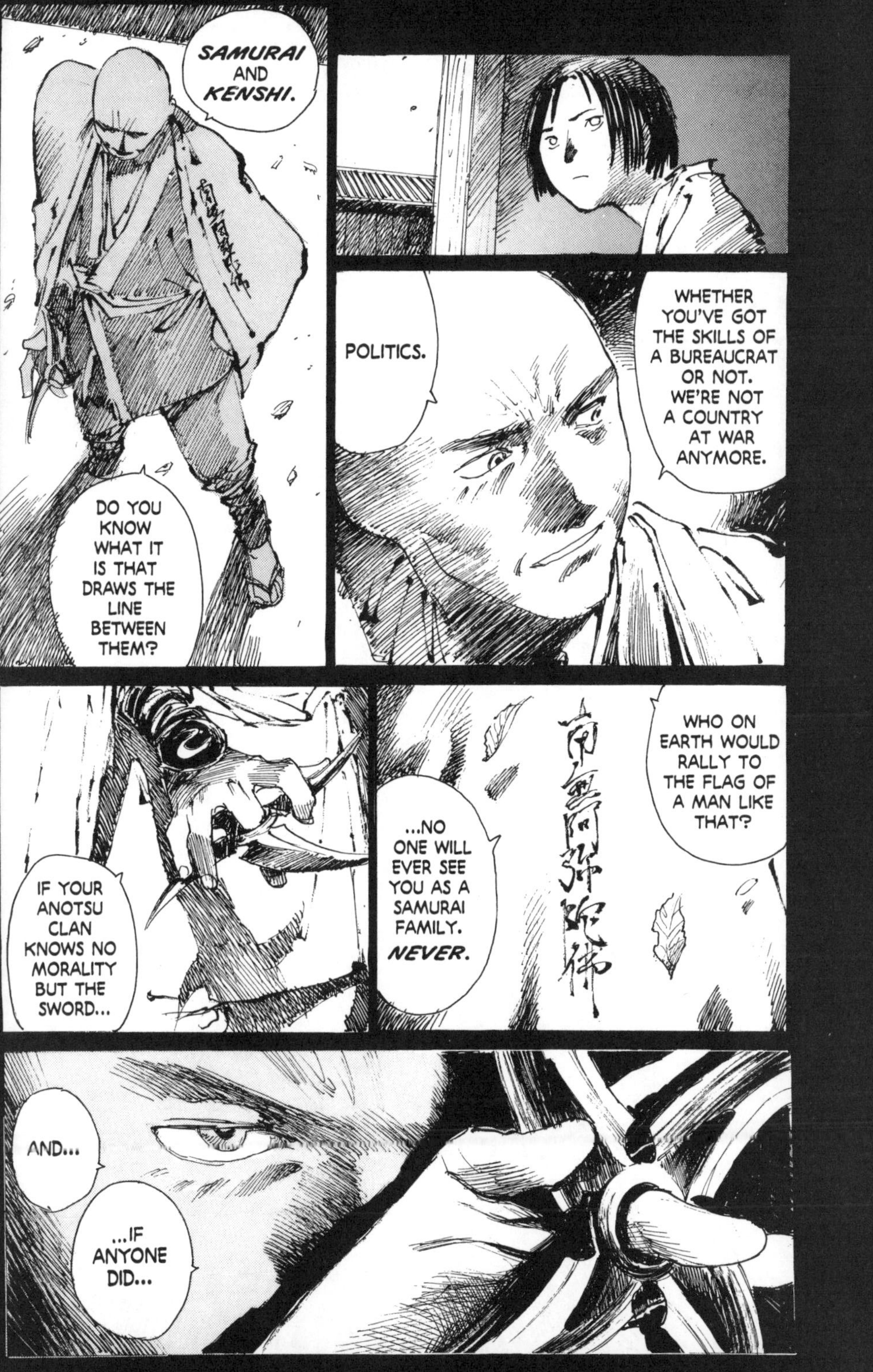
SAMURAI AND KENSHI.
DO YOU KNOW WHAT IT IS THAT DRAWS THE LINE BETWEEN THEM?
POLITICS.
WHETHER YOU'VE GOT THE SKILLS OF A BUREAUCRAT OR NOT. WE'RE NOT A COUNTRY AT WAR ANYMORE.
IF YOUR ANOTSU CLAN KNOWS NO MORALITY BUT THE SWORD...
...NO ONE WILL EVER SEE YOU AS A SAMURAI FAMILY. NEVER.
WHO ON EARTH WOULD RALLY TO THE FLAG OF A MAN LIKE THAT?
AND...
...IF ANYONE DID...

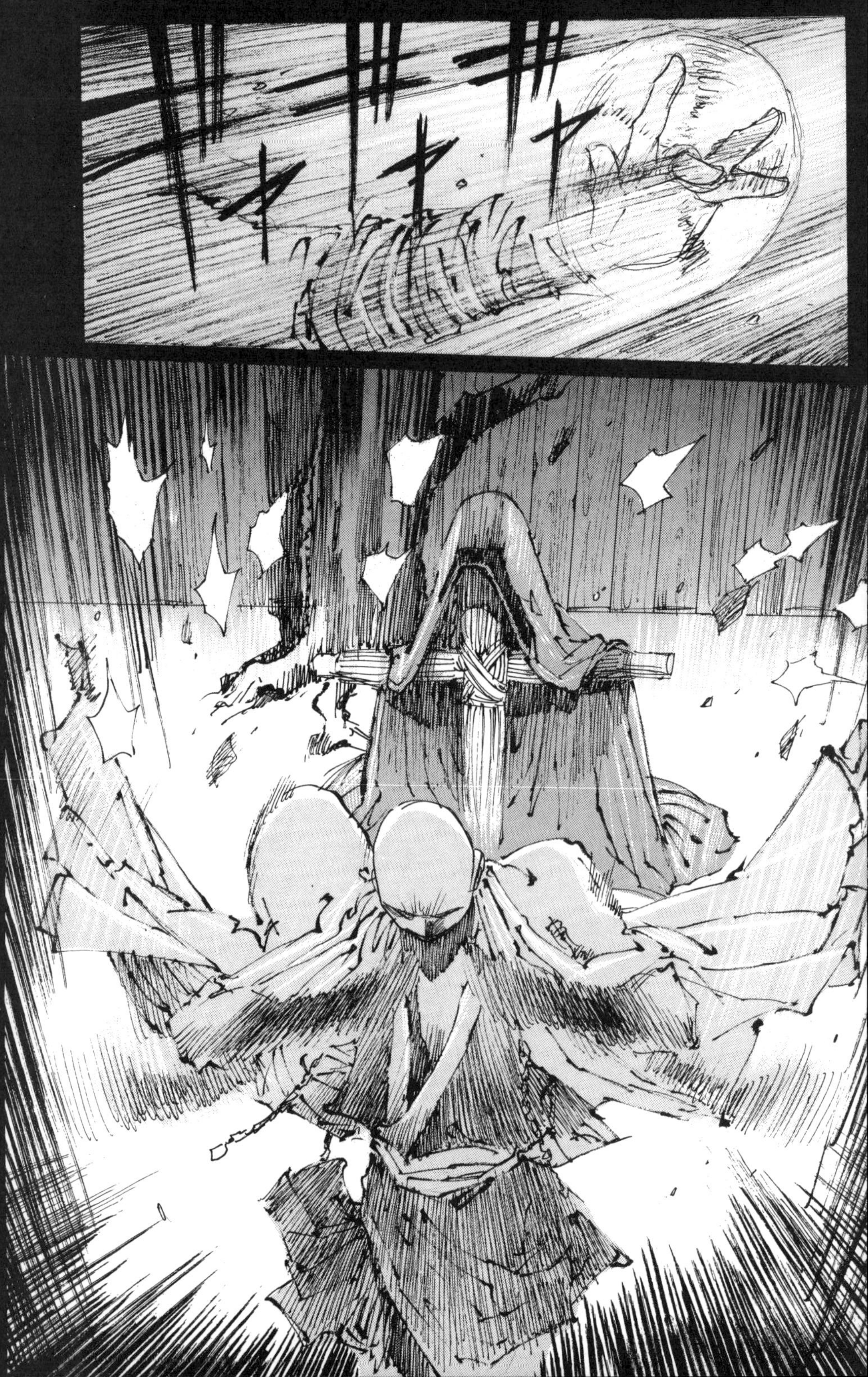

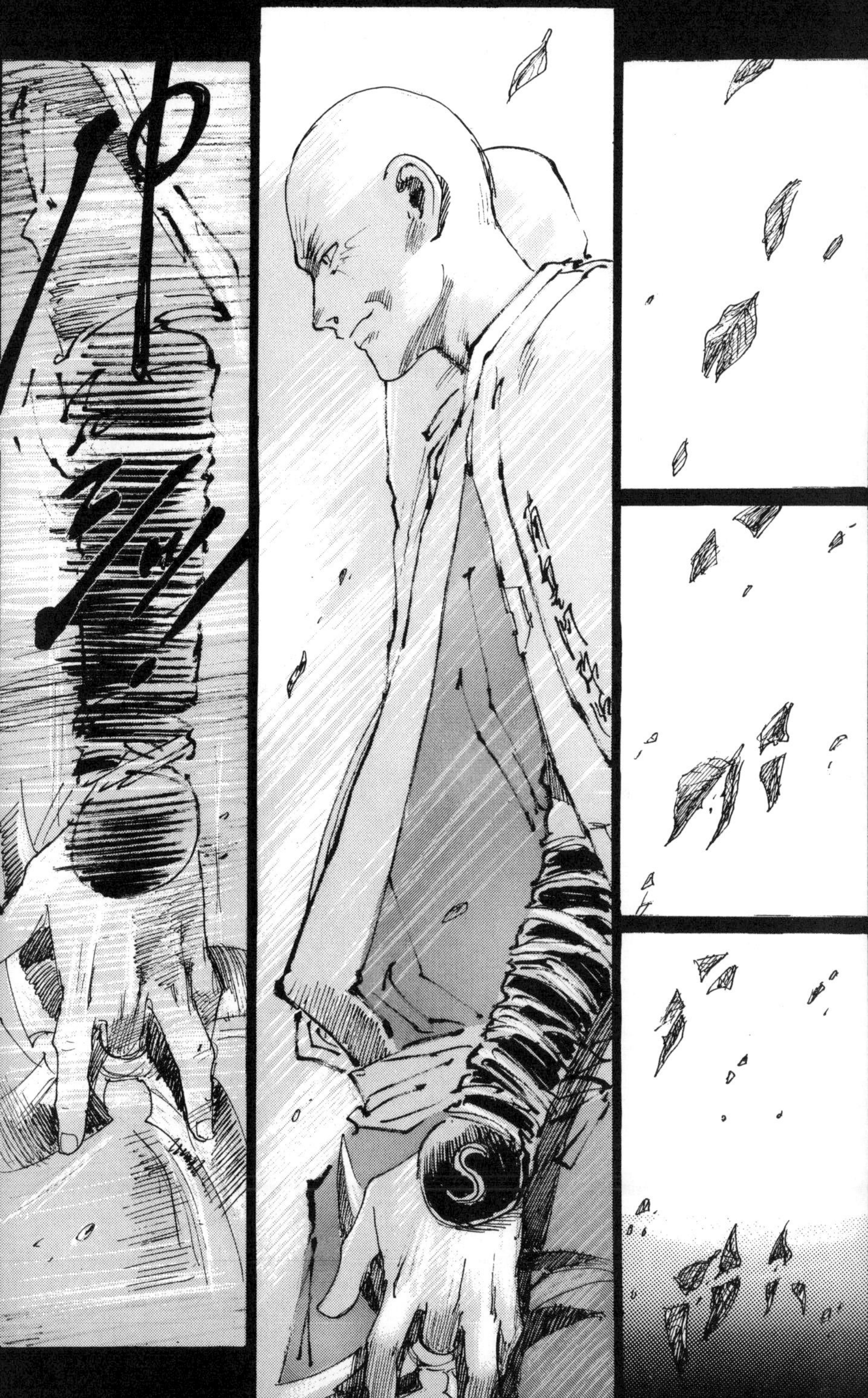

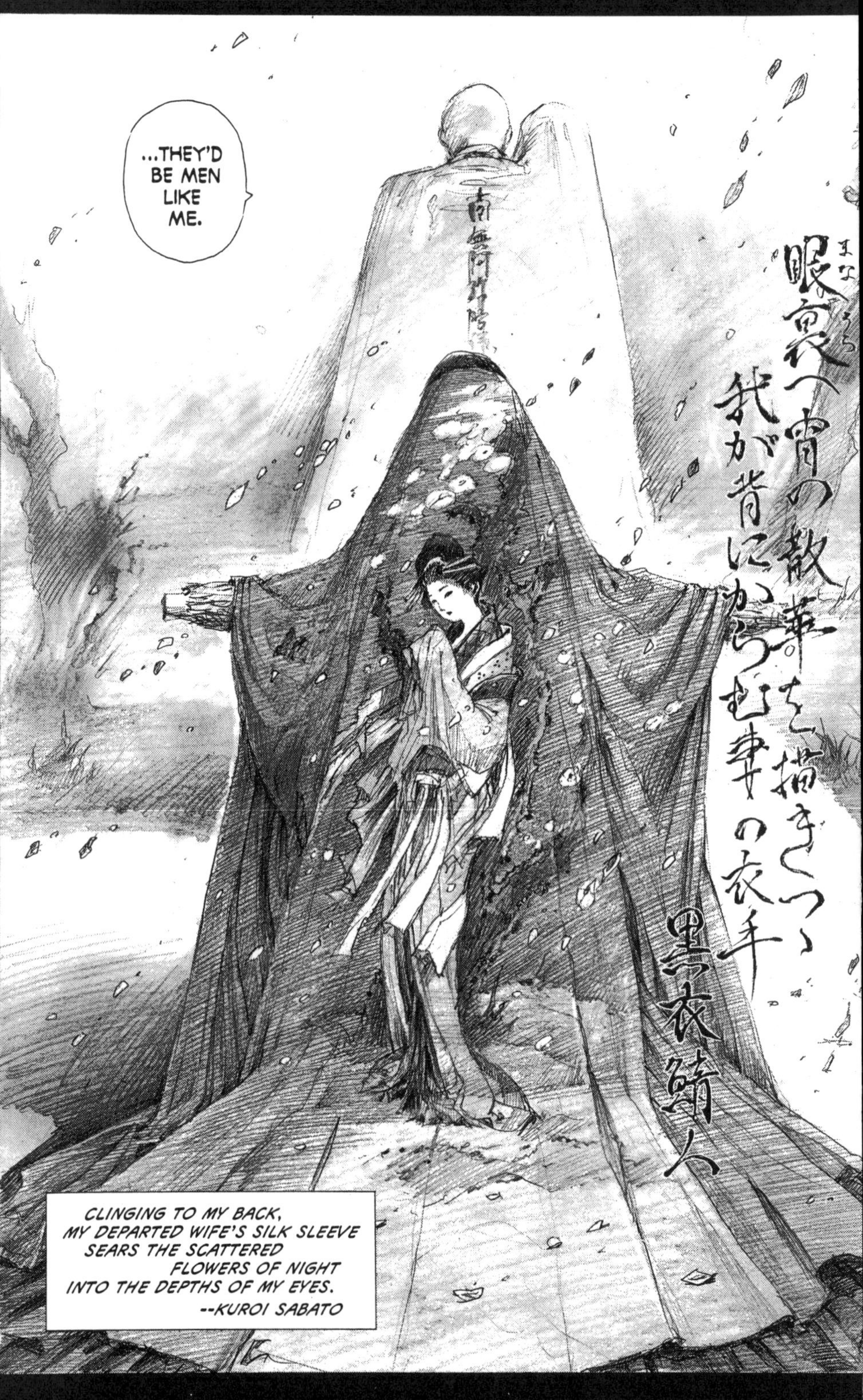
...THEY'D BE MEN LIKE ME.
眼裏へ宵の散華を描きつつ
我が背にからむ妻の衣手
黒衣鯖人
CLINGING TO MY BACK,
MY DEPARTED WIFE'S SILK SLEEVE
SEARS THE SCATTERED
FLOWERS OF NIGHT
INTO THE DEPTHS OF MY EYES.
--KUROI SABATO

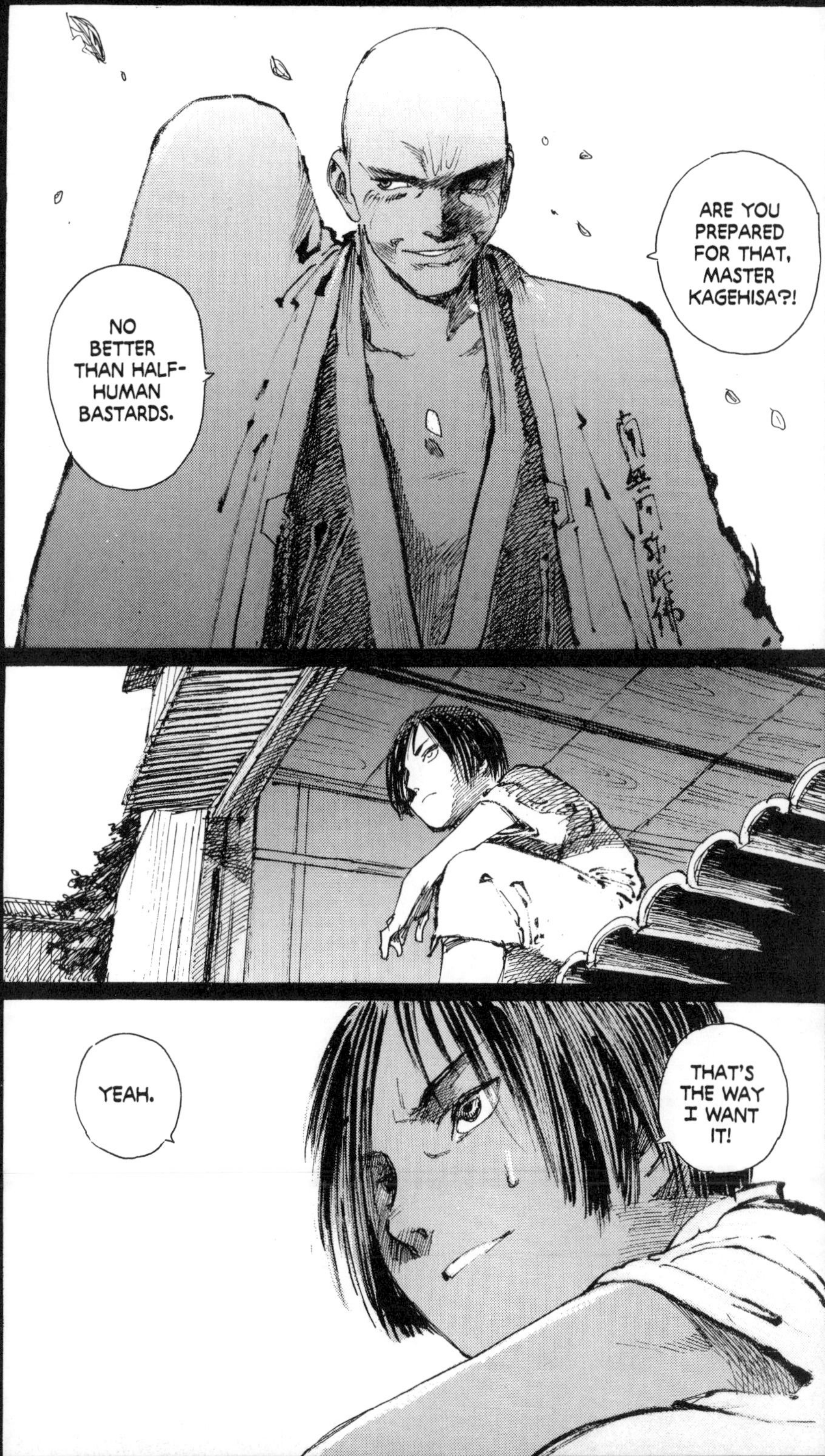
NO BETTER THAN HALF-HUMAN BASTARDS.
ARE YOU PREPARED FOR THAT, MASTER KAGEHISA?!
YEAH.
THAT'S THE WAY I WANT IT!

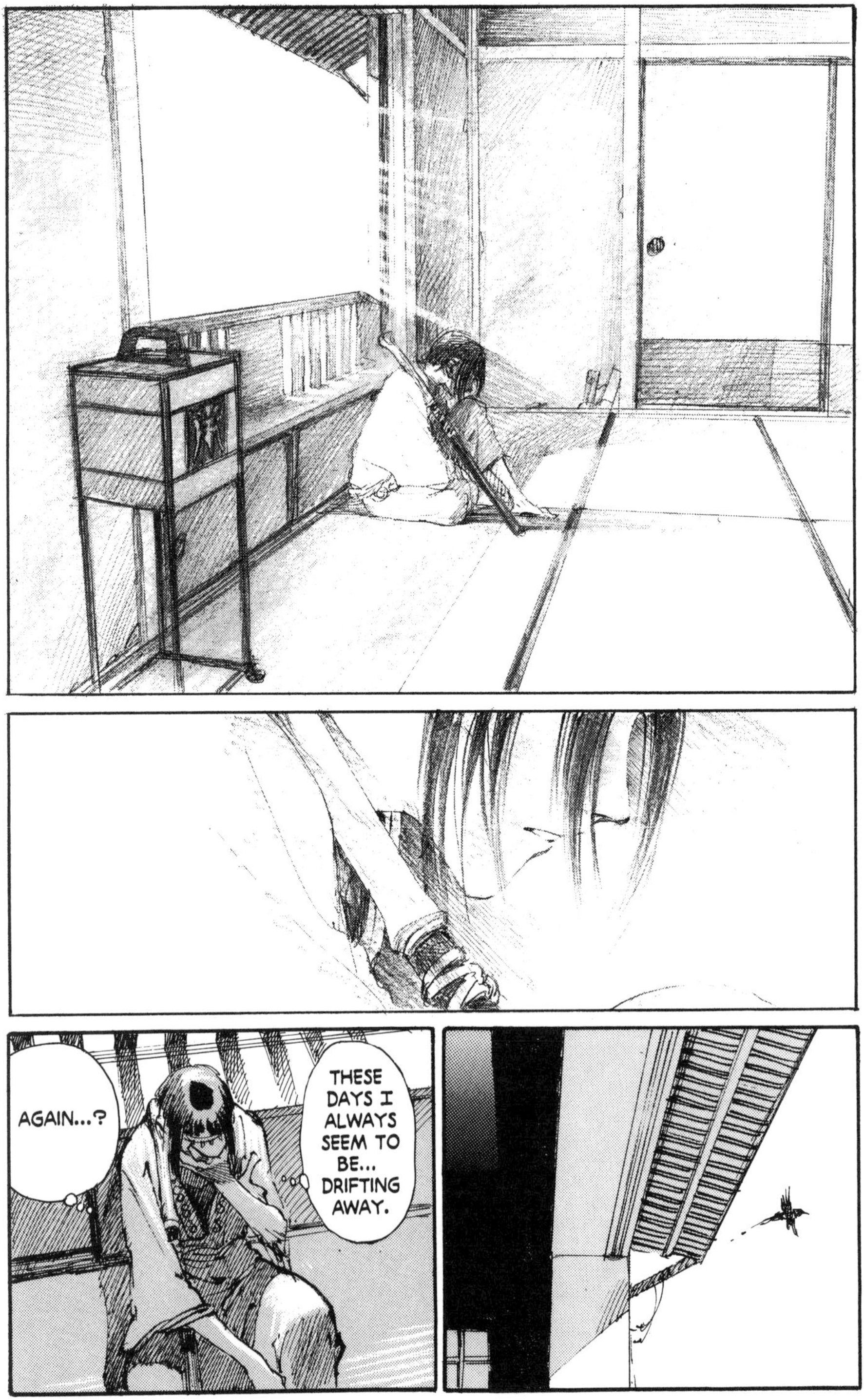
AGAIN...?
THESE DAYS I ALWAYS SEEM TO BE... DRIFTING AWAY.

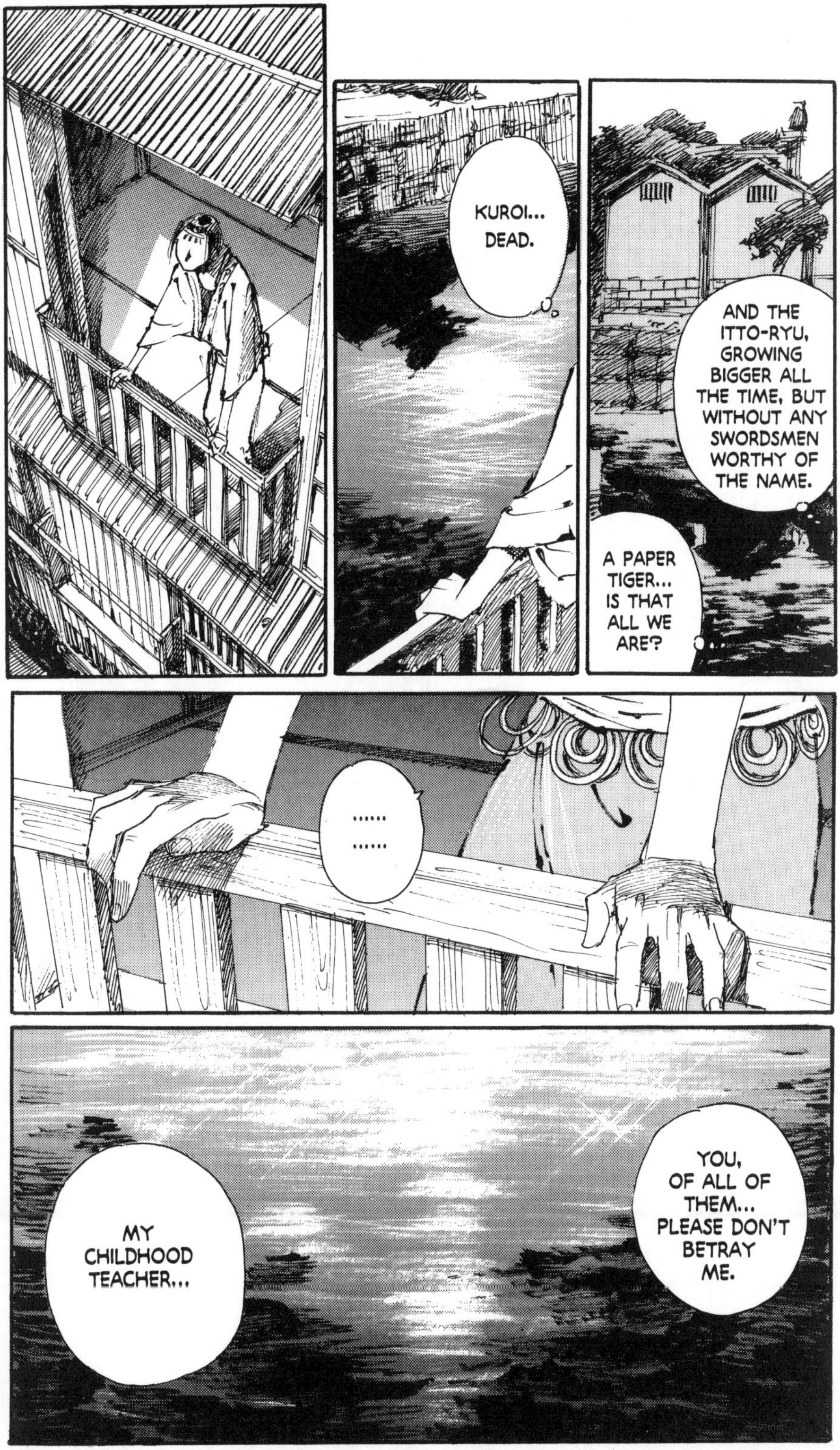

KUROI... DEAD.
AND THE ITTO-RYU, GROWING BIGGER ALL THE TIME, BUT WITHOUT ANY SWORDSMEN WORTHY OF THE NAME.
A PAPER TIGER... IS THAT ALL WE ARE?
....
MY CHILDHOOD TEACHER...
YOU, OF ALL OF THEM... PLEASE DON'T BETRAY ME.

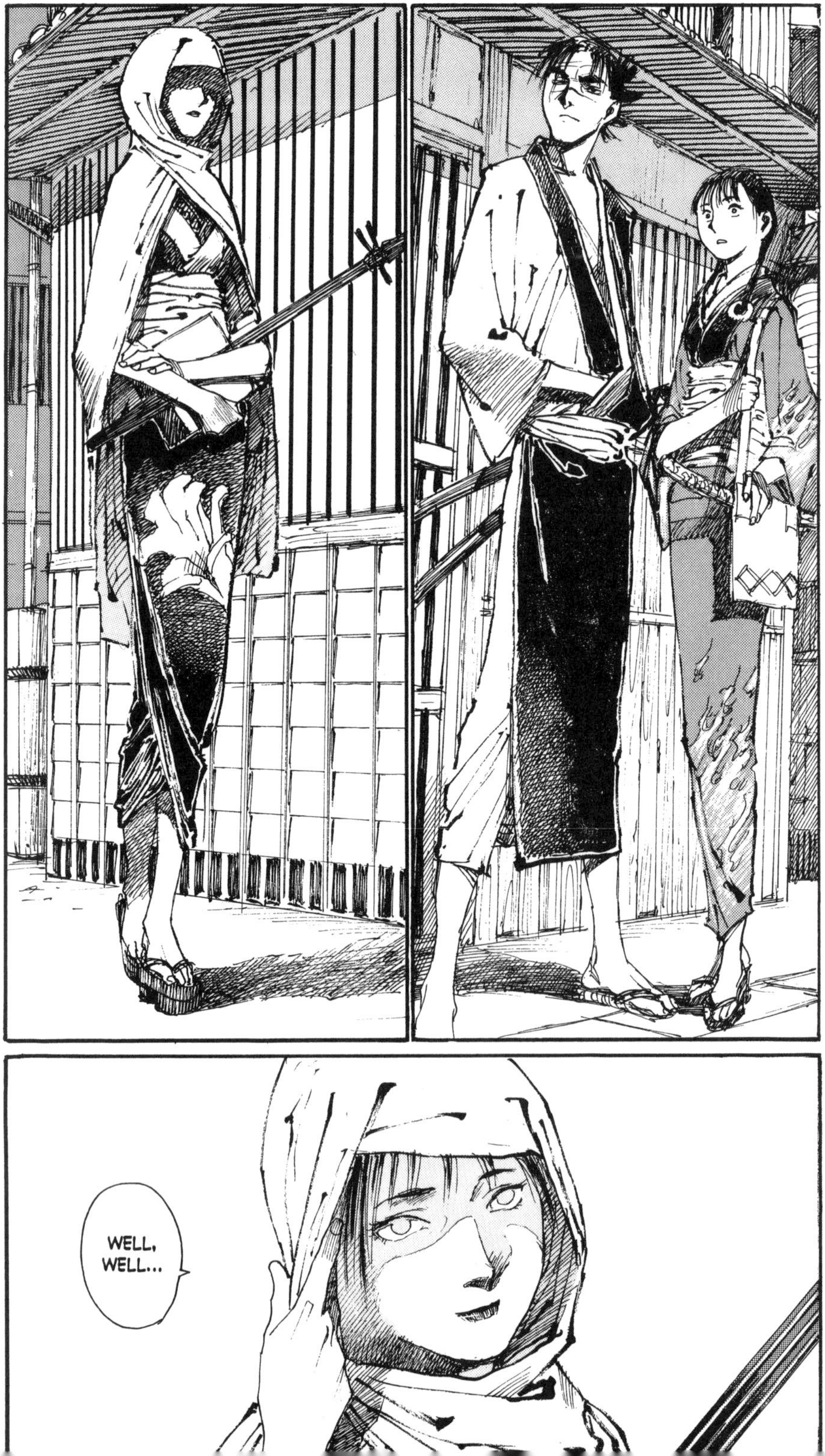
WELL, WELL...

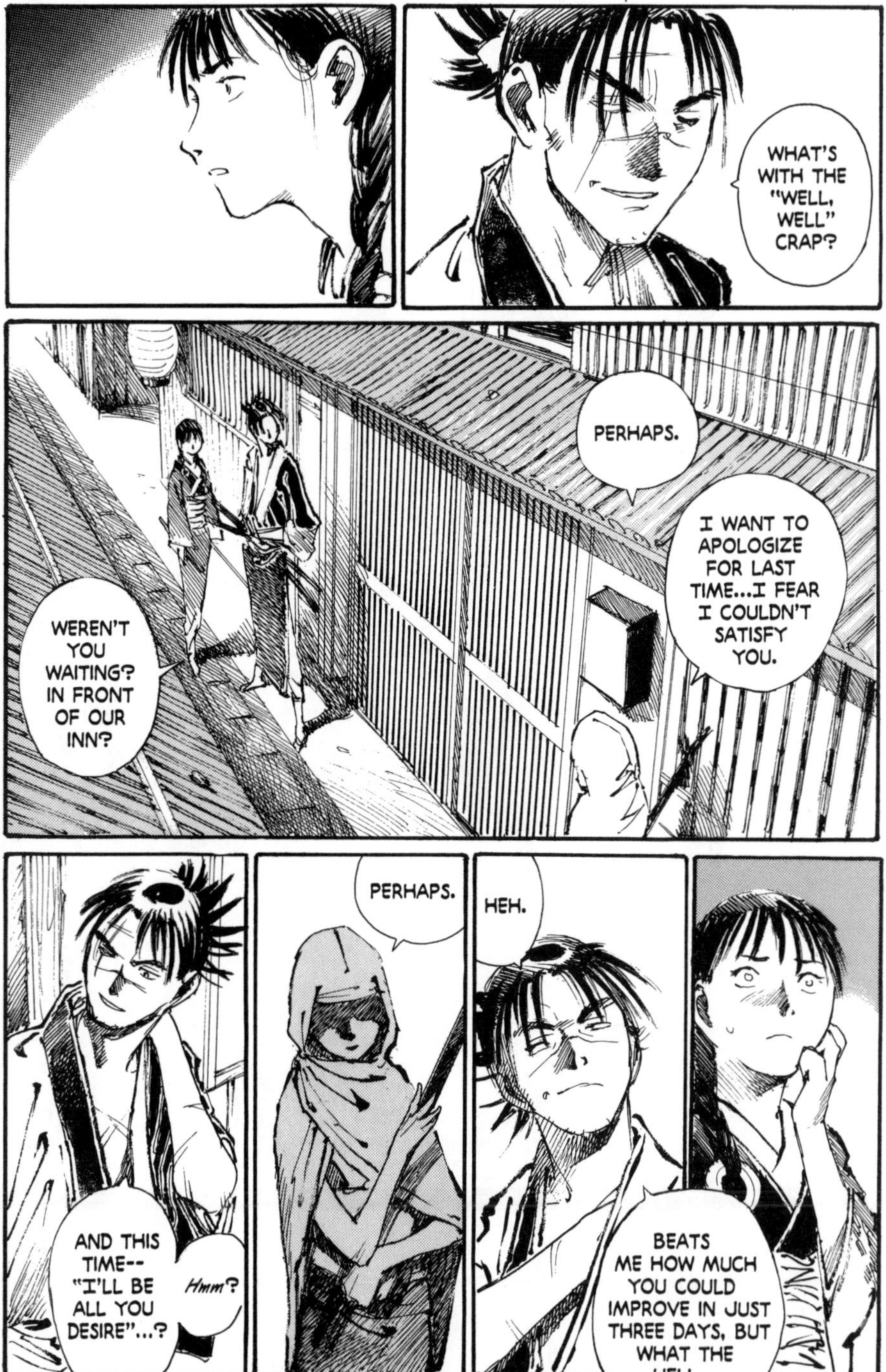
WHAT'S WITH THE "WELL, WELL" CRAP?
WEREN'T YOU WAITING? IN FRONT OF OUR INN?
PERHAPS.
I WANT TO APOLOGIZE FOR LAST TIME...I FEAR I COULDN'T SATISFY YOU.
AND THIS TIME-- "I'LL BE ALL YOU DESIRE"...?
Hmm?
PERHAPS.
HEH.
BEATS ME HOW MUCH YOU COULD IMPROVE IN JUST THREE DAYS, BUT WHAT THE HELL...

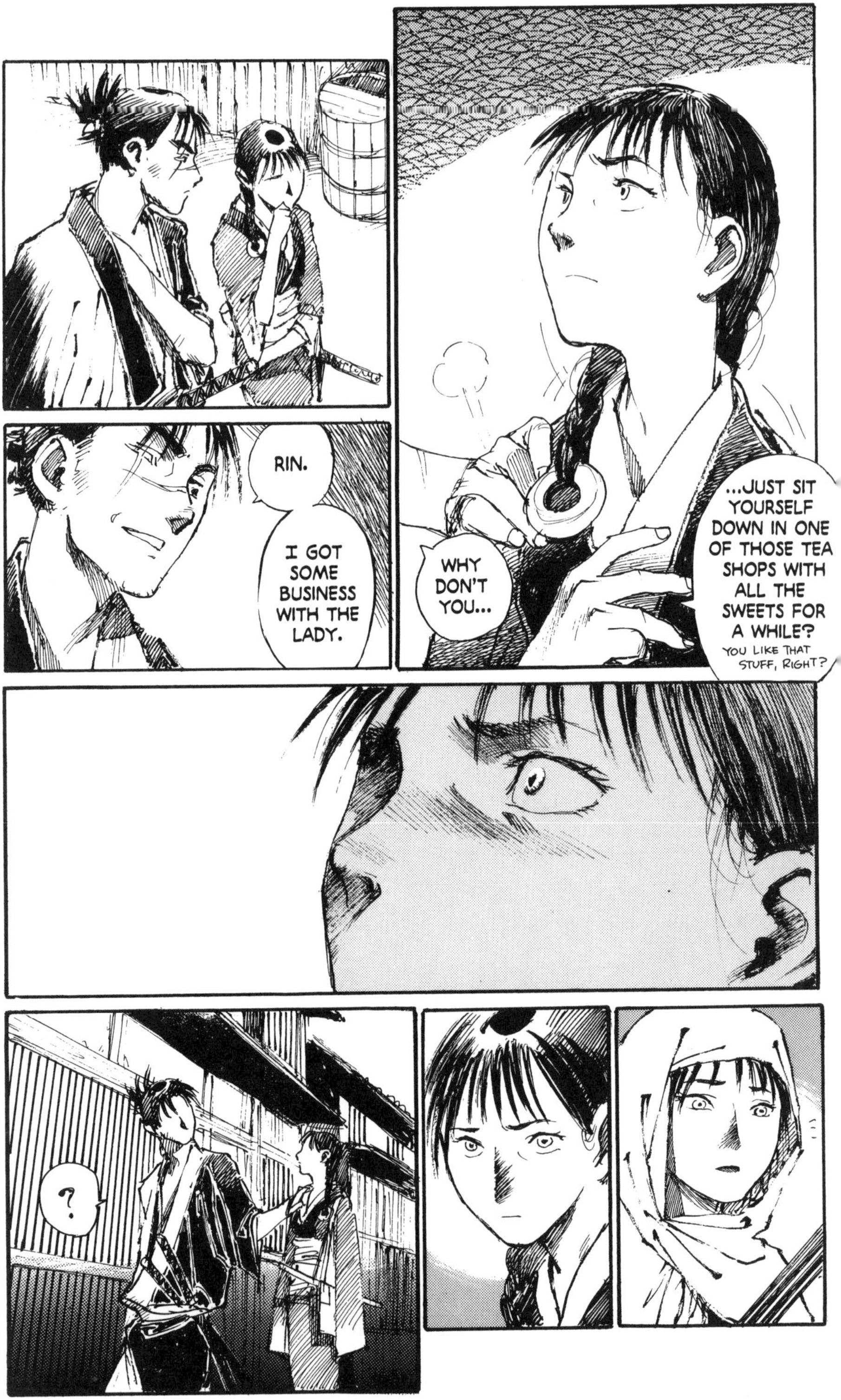
RIN.
I GOT SOME BUSINESS WITH THE LADY.
WHY DON'T YOU...
...JUST SIT YOURSELF DOWN IN ONE OF THOSE TEA SHOPS WITH ALL THE SWEETS FOR A WHILE?
YOU LIKE THAT STUFF, RIGHT?
?

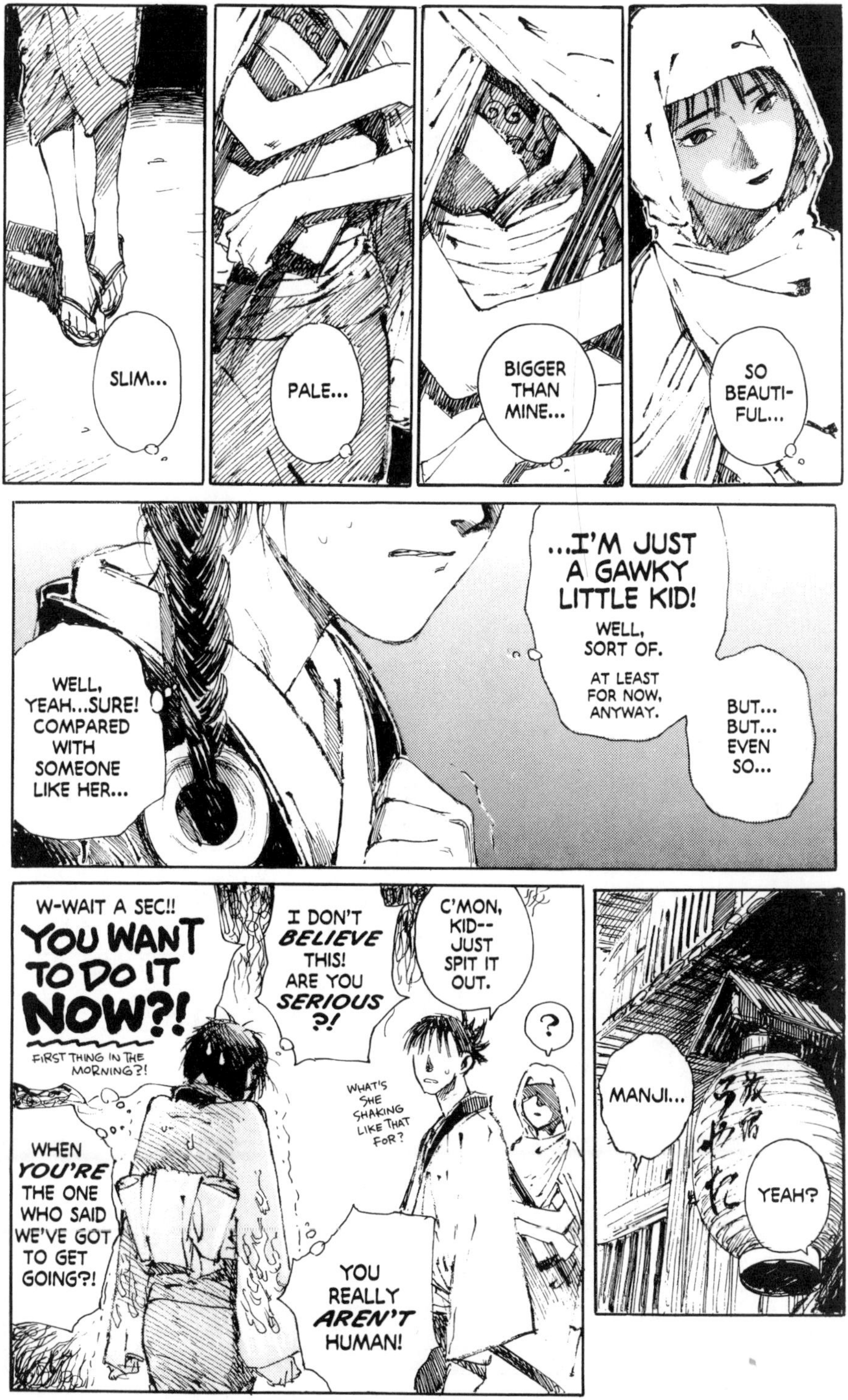
SLIM...
PALE...
BIGGER THAN MINE...
SO BEAUTI-FUL...
WELL, YEAH...SURE! COMPARED WITH SOMEONE LIKE HER...
...I'M JUST A GAWKY LITTLE KID!
WELL, SORT OF.
AT LEAST FOR NOW, ANYWAY.
BUT... BUT... EVEN SO...
W-WAIT A SEC!! YOU WANT TO DO IT NOW?!
FIRST THING IN THE MORNING?!
WHEN YOU'RE THE ONE WHO SAID WE'VE GOT TO GET GOING?!
I DON'T BELIEVE THIS! ARE YOU SERIOUS?!
C'MON, KID-- JUST SPIT IT OUT.
?
WHAT'S SHE SHAKING LIKE THAT FOR?
YOU REALLY AREN'T HUMAN!
MANJI...
YEAH?

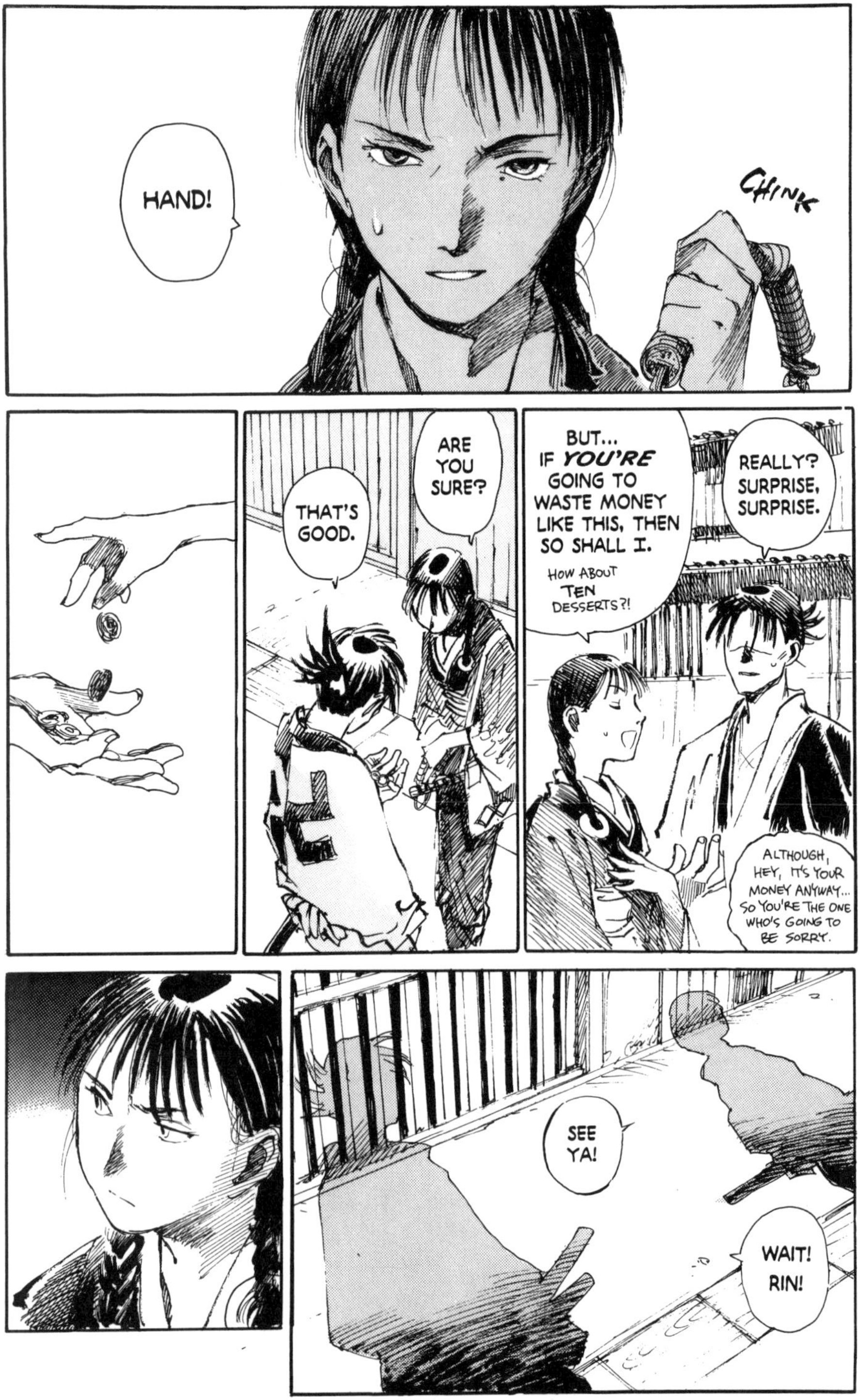
HAND!
CHINK
THAT'S GOOD.
ARE YOU SURE?
BUT... IF *YOU'RE* GOING TO WASTE MONEY LIKE THIS, THEN SO SHALL I.
HOW ABOUT TEN DESSERTS?!
REALLY? SURPRISE, SURPRISE.
ALTHOUGH, HEY, IT'S YOUR MONEY ANYWAY... SO YOU'RE THE ONE WHO'S GOING TO BE SORRY.
SEE YA!
WAIT! RIN!

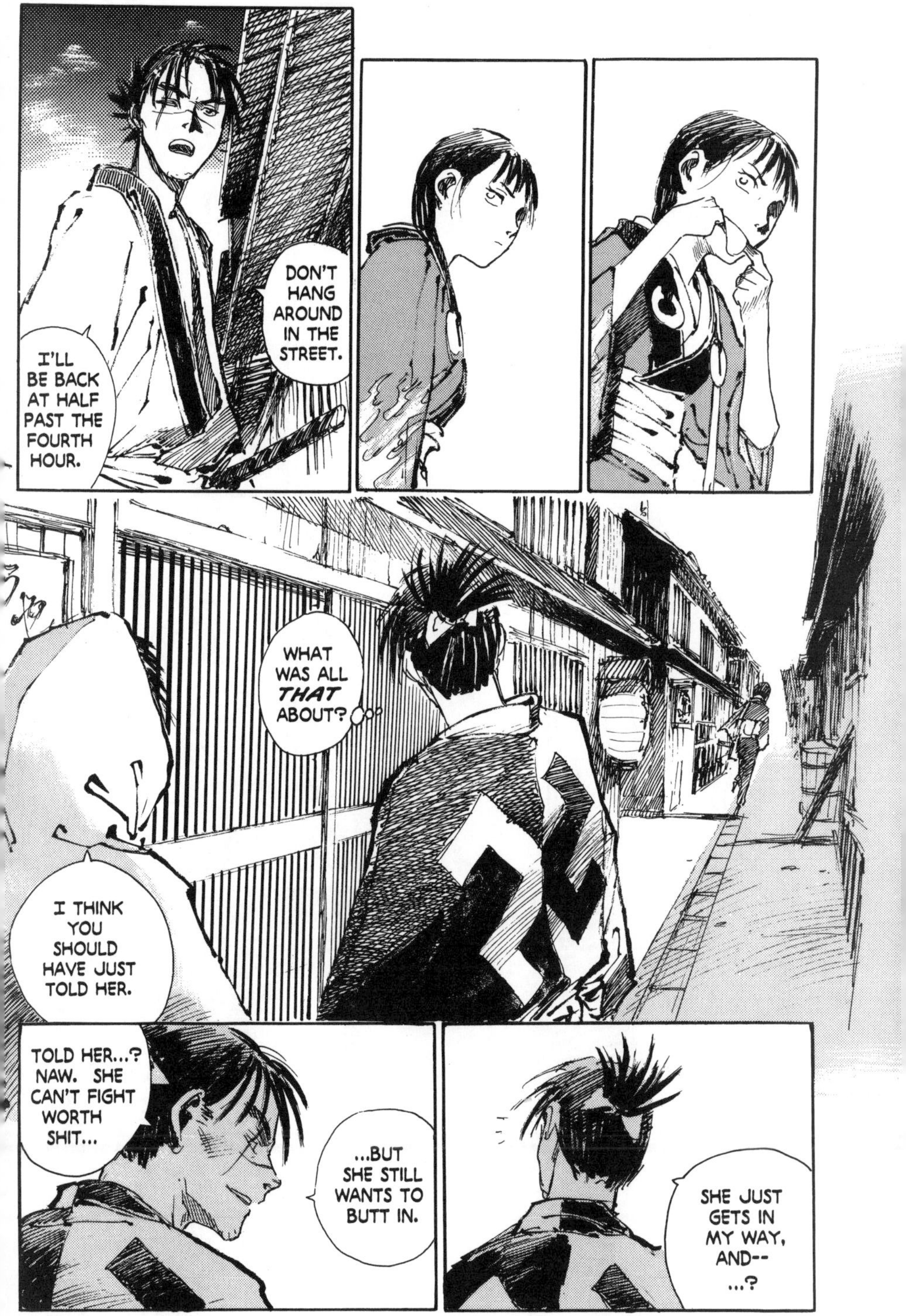
I'LL BE BACK AT HALF PAST THE FOURTH HOUR.
DON'T HANG AROUND IN THE STREET.
WHAT WAS ALL *THAT* ABOUT?
I THINK YOU SHOULD HAVE JUST TOLD HER.
TOLD HER...? NAW. SHE CAN'T FIGHT WORTH SHIT...
...BUT SHE STILL WANTS TO BUTT IN.
SHE JUST GETS IN MY WAY, AND--
...?

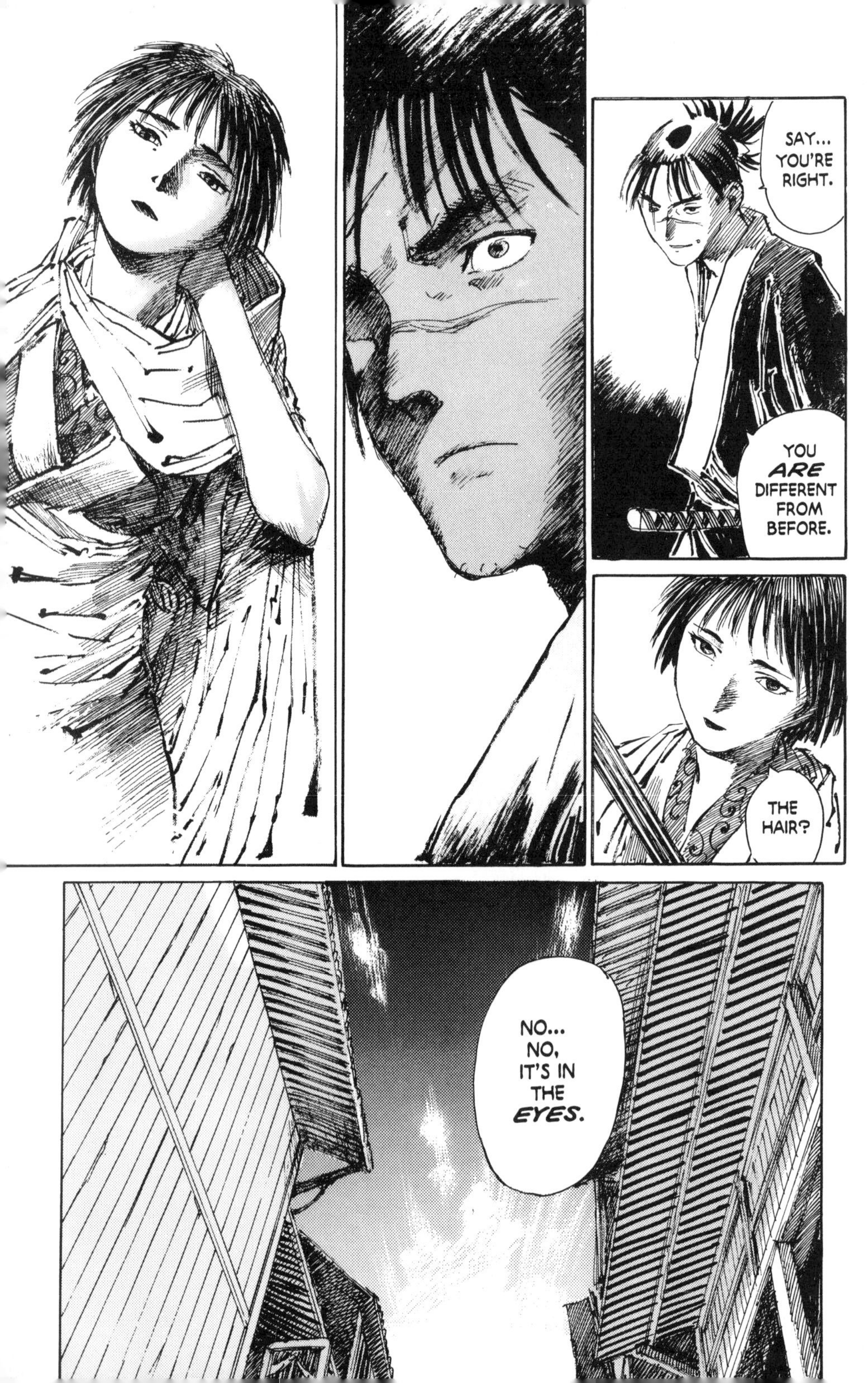
SAY... YOU'RE RIGHT.
YOU *ARE* DIFFERENT FROM BEFORE.
THE HAIR?
NO... NO, IT'S IN THE *EYES*.

DREAMSONG
Part 4

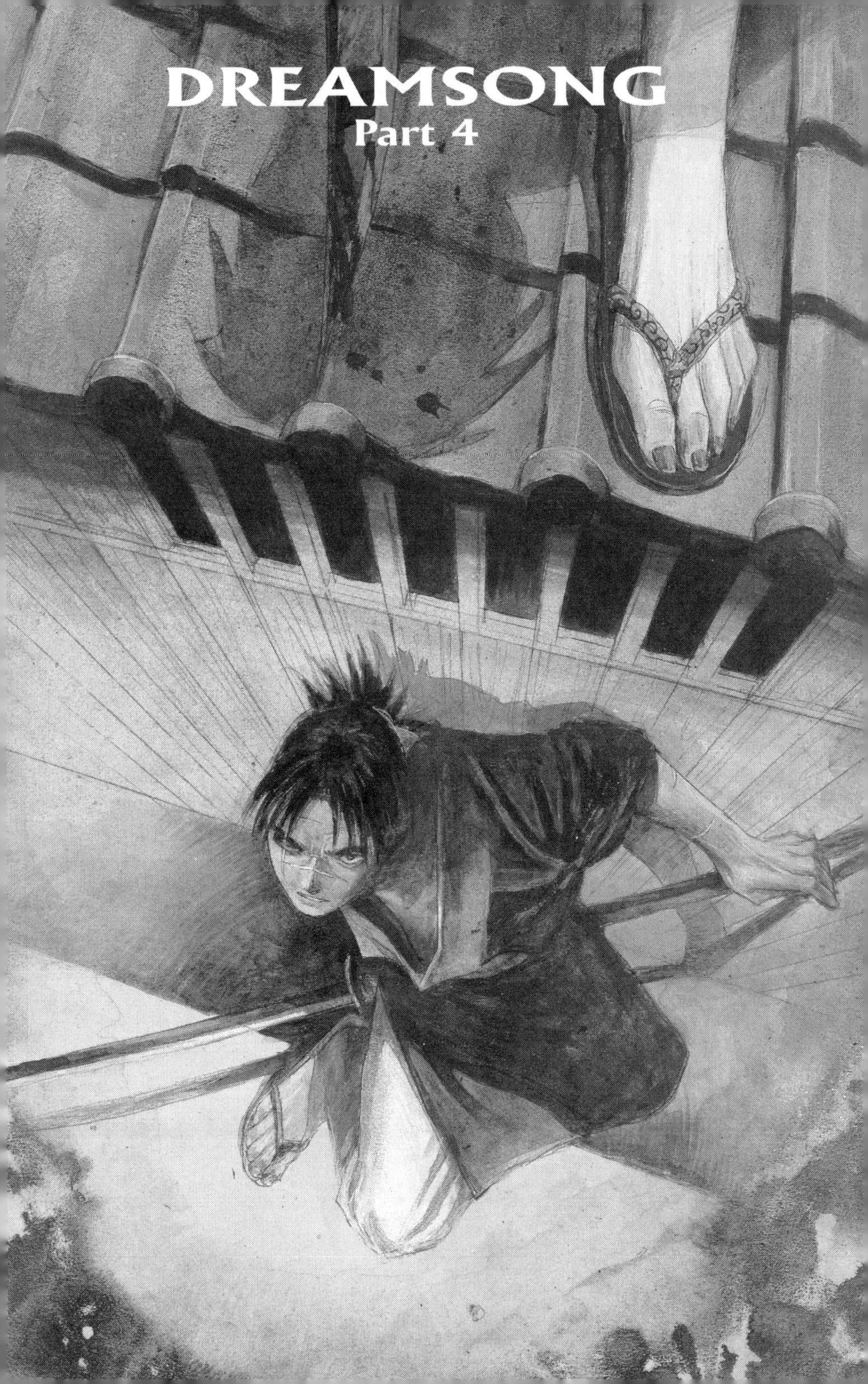

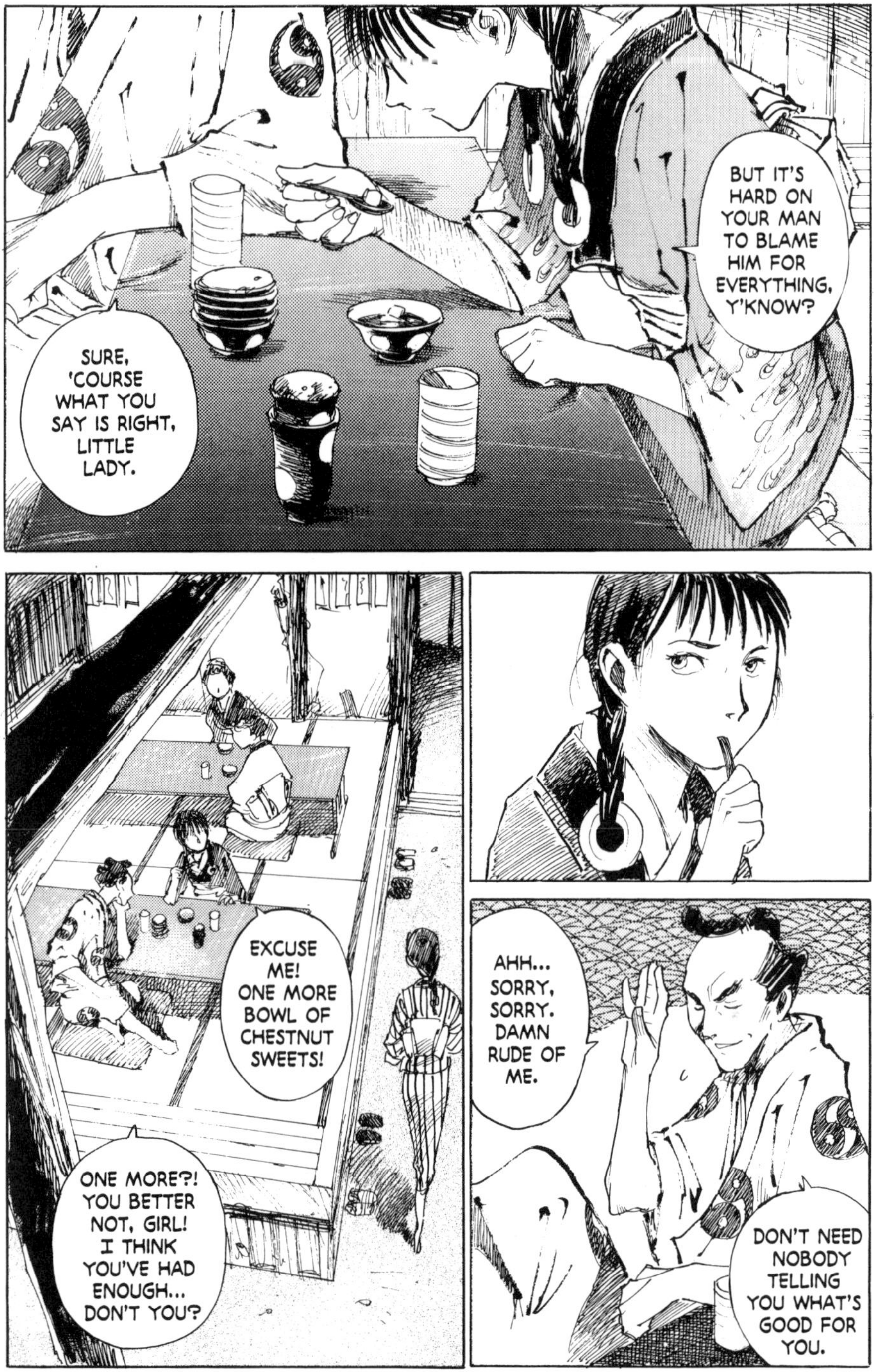
SURE, 'COURSE WHAT YOU SAY IS RIGHT, LITTLE LADY.
BUT IT'S HARD ON YOUR MAN TO BLAME HIM FOR EVERYTHING, Y'KNOW?
EXCUSE ME! ONE MORE BOWL OF CHESTNUT SWEETS!
ONE MORE?! YOU BETTER NOT, GIRL! I THINK YOU'VE HAD ENOUGH... DON'T YOU?
AHH... SORRY, SORRY. DAMN RUDE OF ME.
DON'T NEED NOBODY TELLING YOU WHAT'S GOOD FOR YOU.

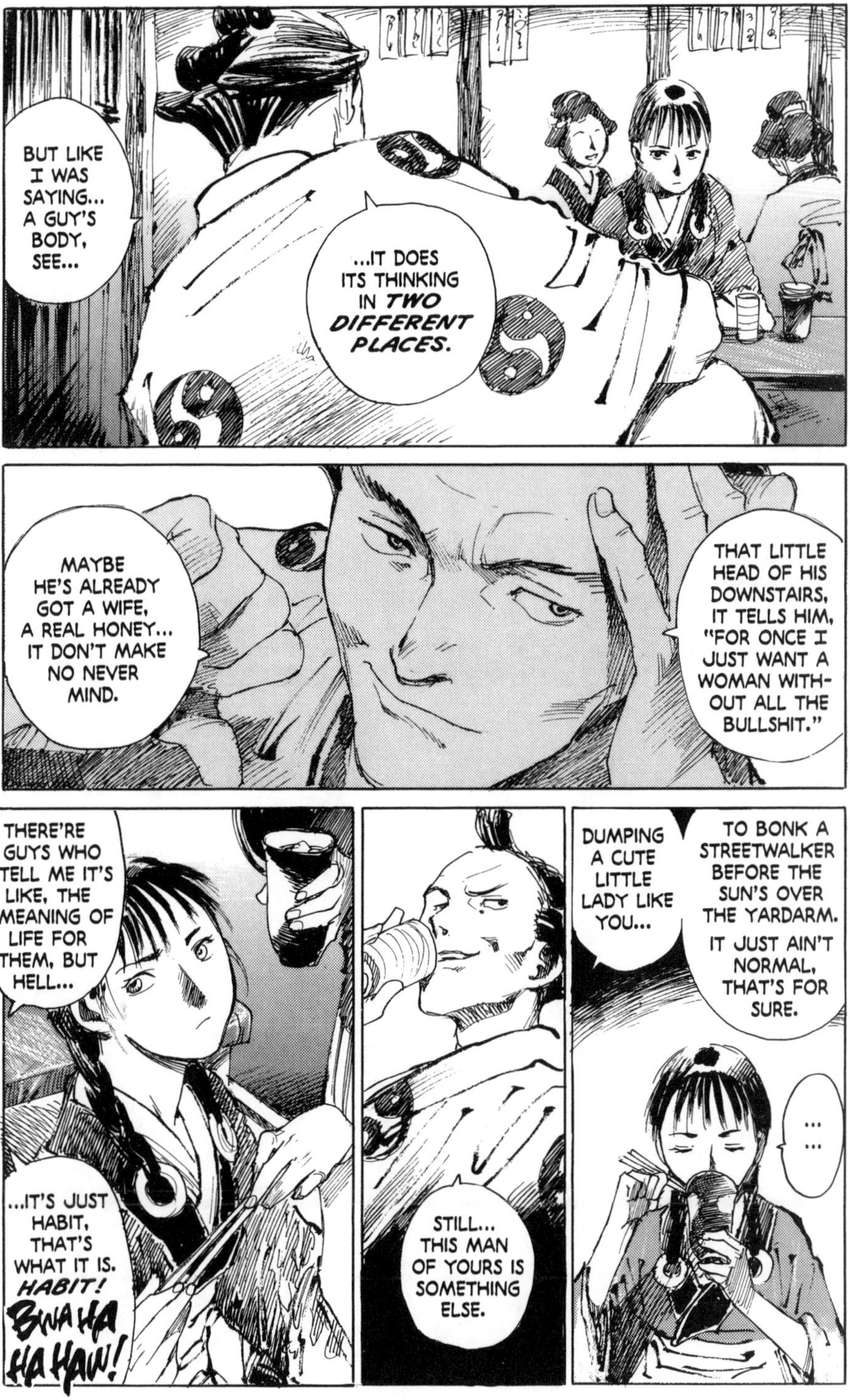
BUT LIKE I WAS SAYING... A GUY'S BODY, SEE...
...IT DOES ITS THINKING IN *TWO DIFFERENT PLACES.*
MAYBE HE'S ALREADY GOT A WIFE, A REAL HONEY... IT DON'T MAKE NO NEVER MIND.
THAT LITTLE HEAD OF HIS DOWNSTAIRS, IT TELLS HIM, "FOR ONCE I JUST WANT A WOMAN WITH-OUT ALL THE BULLSHIT."
THERE'RE GUYS WHO TELL ME IT'S LIKE, THE MEANING OF LIFE FOR THEM, BUT HELL...
...IT'S JUST HABIT, THAT'S WHAT IT IS. *HABIT!*
BWA HA HA HAW!
STILL... THIS MAN OF YOURS IS SOMETHING ELSE.
DUMPING A CUTE LITTLE LADY LIKE YOU...
TO BONK A STREETWALKER BEFORE THE SUN'S OVER THE YARDARM.
IT JUST AIN'T NORMAL, THAT'S FOR SURE.
... ...

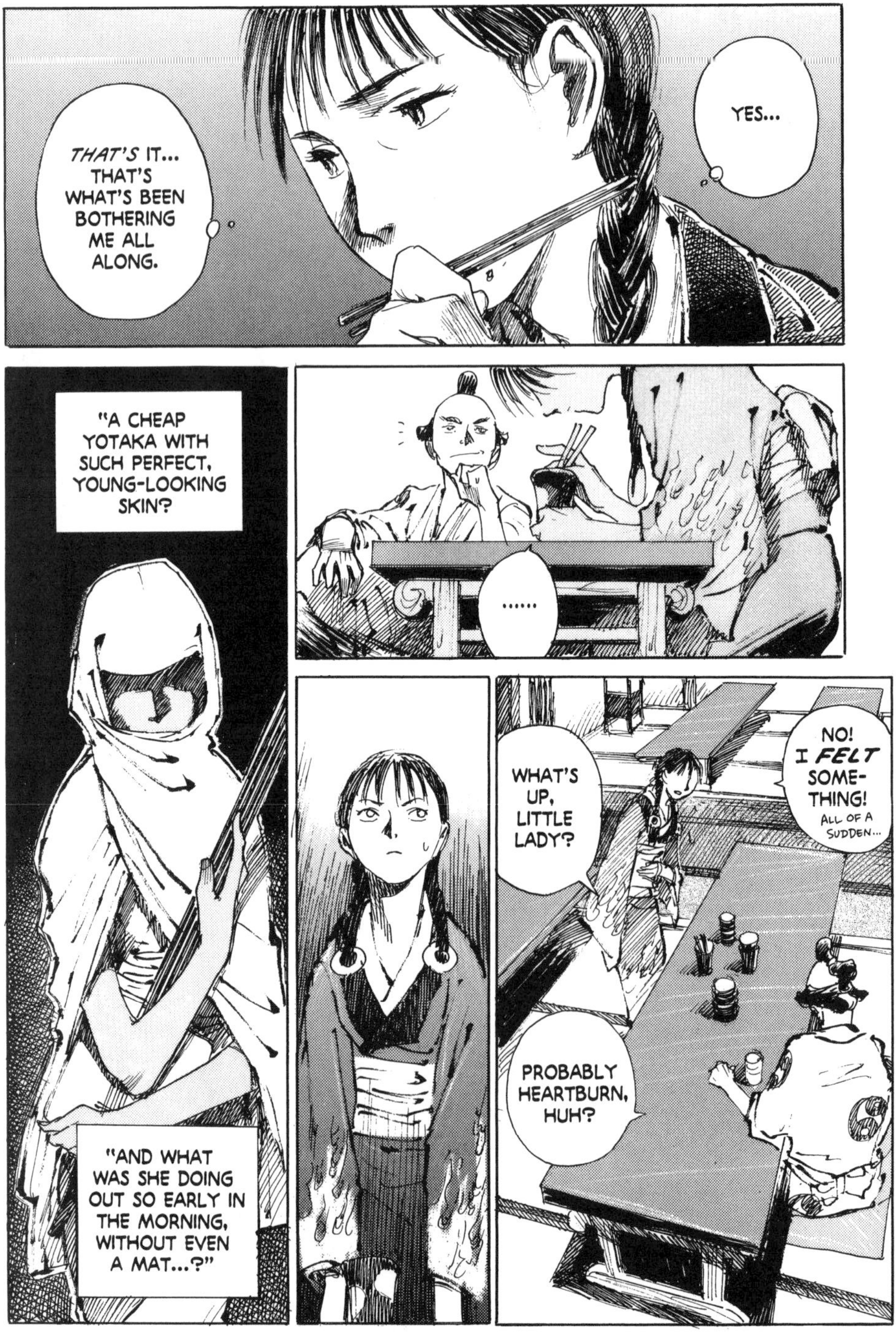
THAT'S IT... THAT'S WHAT'S BEEN BOTHERING ME ALL ALONG.
YES...
"A CHEAP YOTAKA WITH SUCH PERFECT, YOUNG-LOOKING SKIN?
"AND WHAT WAS SHE DOING OUT SO EARLY IN THE MORNING, WITHOUT EVEN A MAT...?"
......
WHAT'S UP, LITTLE LADY?
NO! I FELT SOMETHING! ALL OF A SUDDEN...
PROBABLY HEARTBURN, HUH?

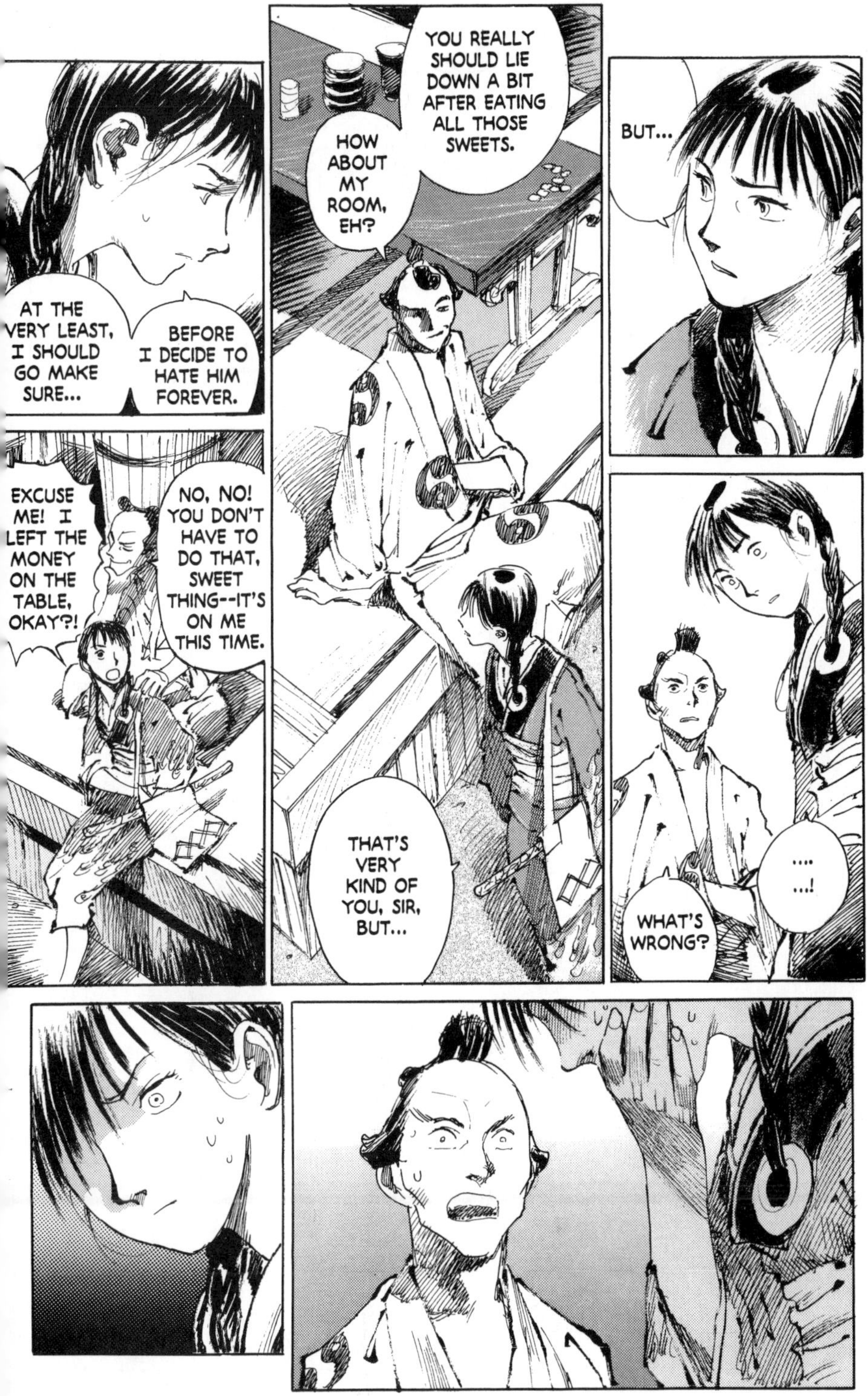
AT THE VERY LEAST, I SHOULD GO MAKE SURE...
BEFORE I DECIDE TO HATE HIM FOREVER.
EXCUSE ME! I LEFT THE MONEY ON THE TABLE, OKAY?!
NO, NO! YOU DON'T HAVE TO DO THAT, SWEET THING--IT'S ON ME THIS TIME.
YOU REALLY SHOULD LIE DOWN A BIT AFTER EATING ALL THOSE SWEETS.
HOW ABOUT MY ROOM, EH?
THAT'S VERY KIND OF YOU, SIR, BUT...
BUT...
....
...!
WHAT'S WRONG?

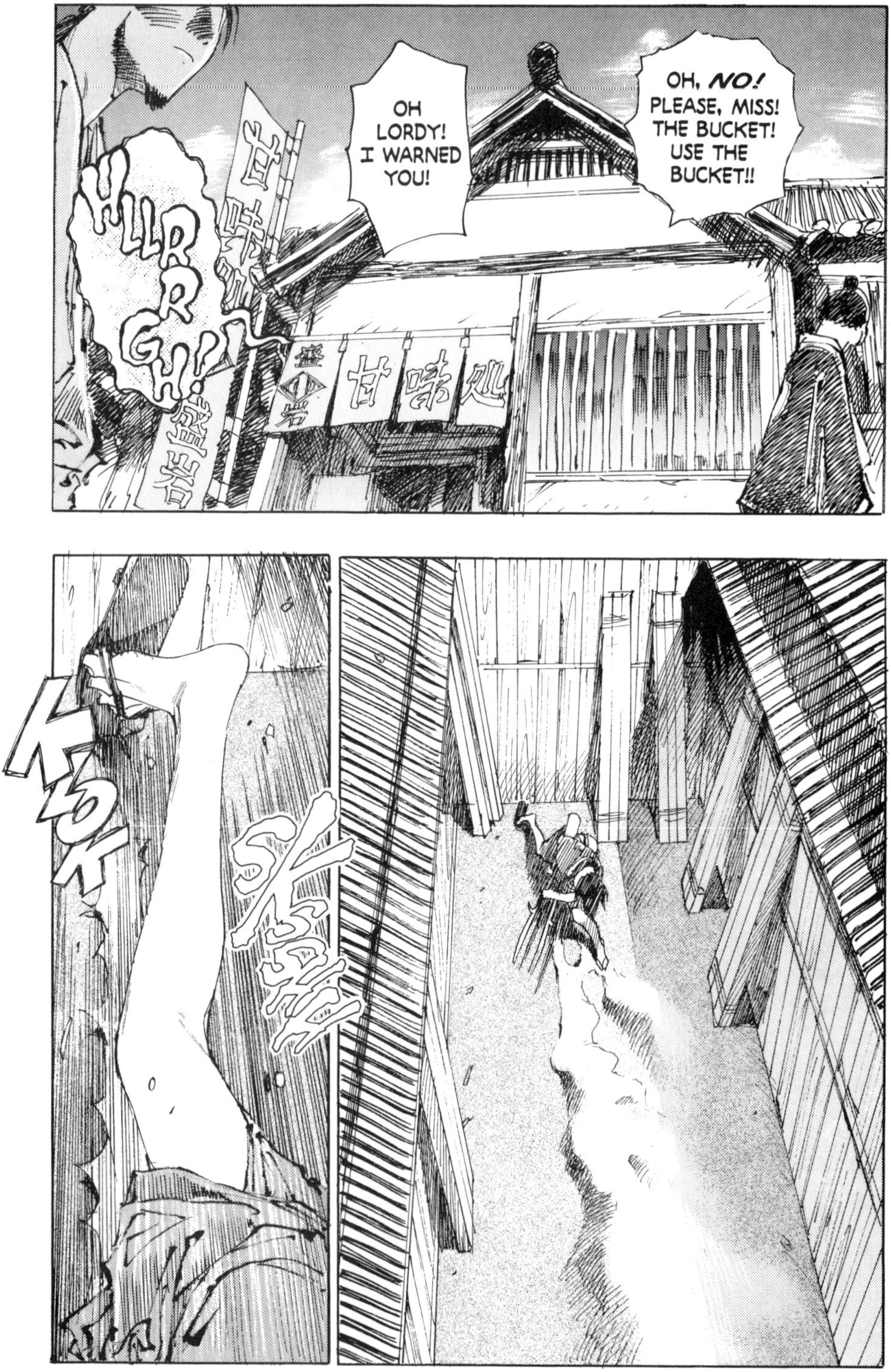
HLLRRGH!
OH LORDY! I WARNED YOU!
OH, ***NO!*** PLEASE, MISS! THE BUCKET! USE THE BUCKET!!
甘味処
KLOK

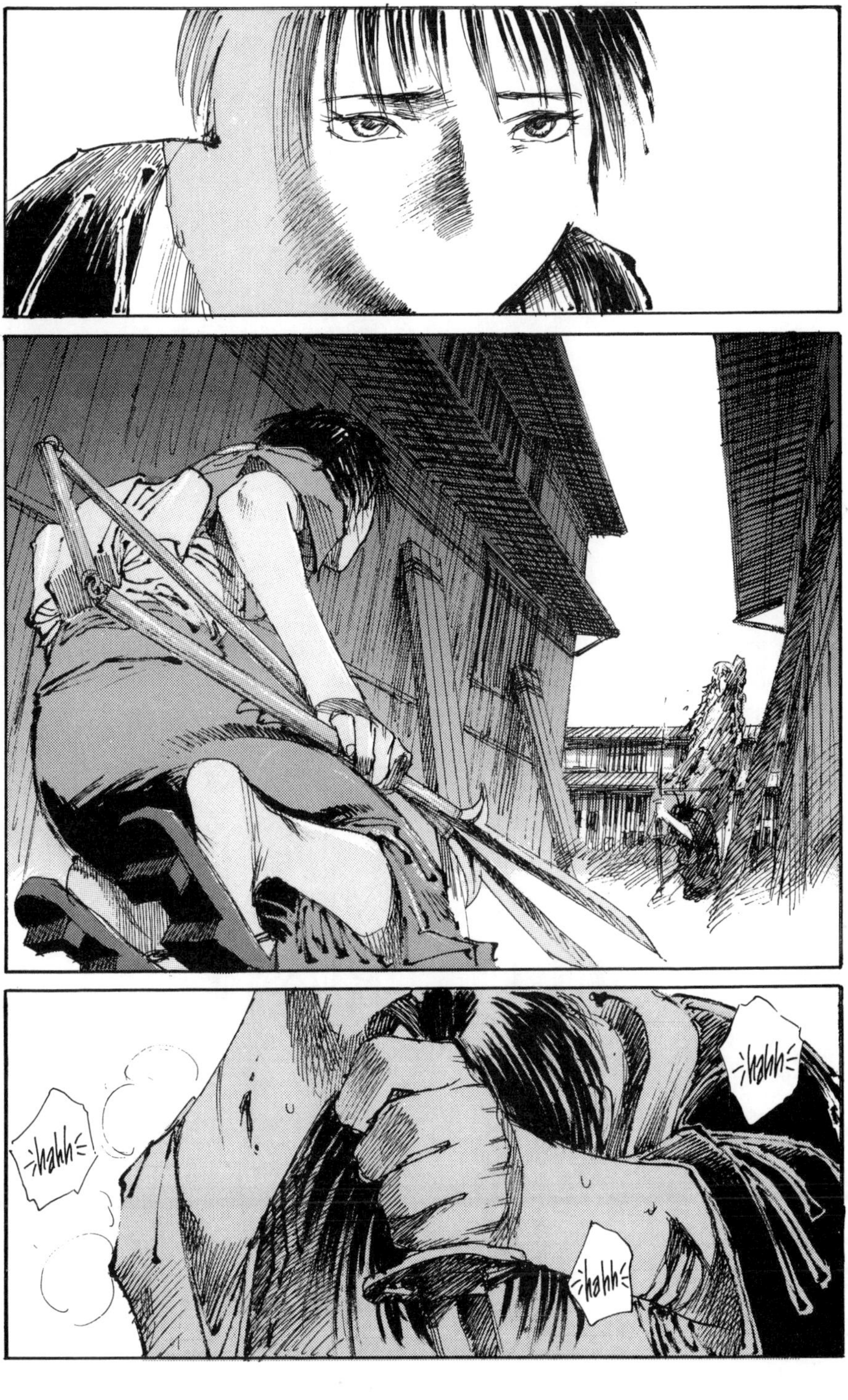
hahh
hahh
hahh

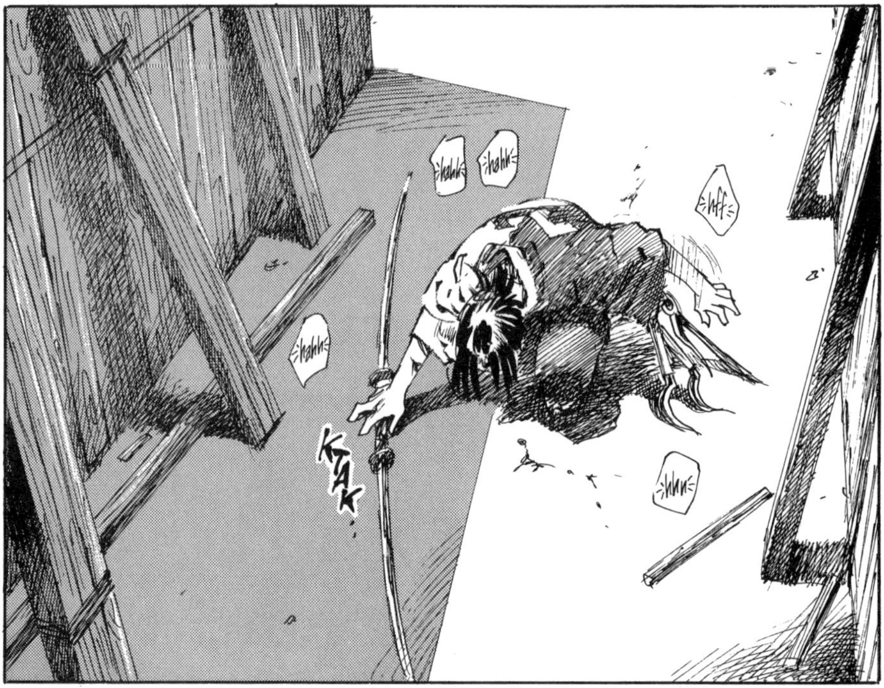
hahh
hahh
huff
hahh
KTAK
hhn
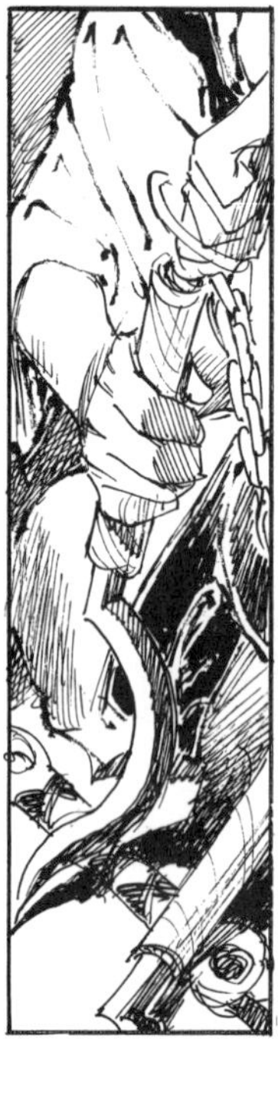
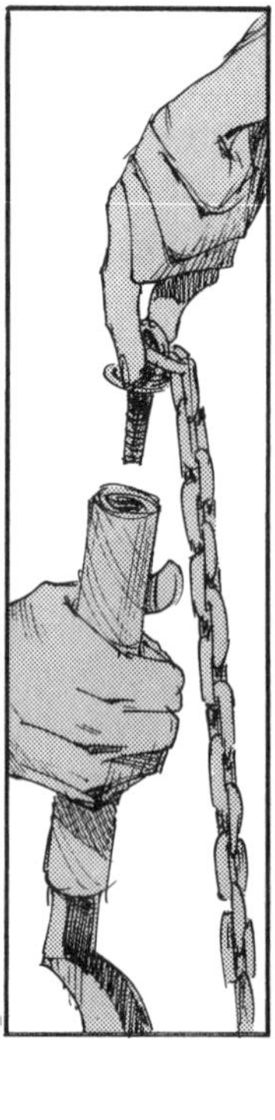
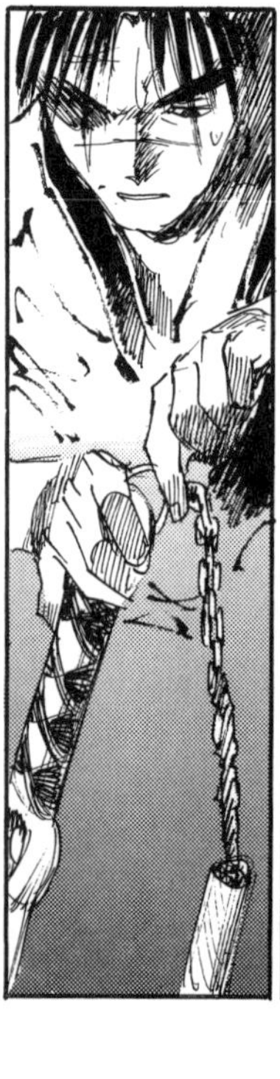
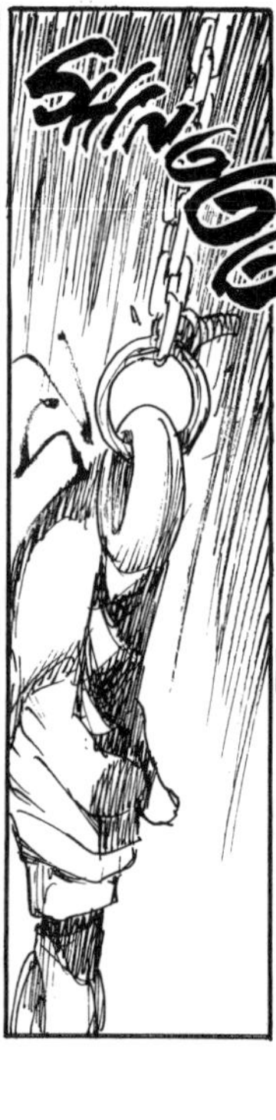
SHINGGG
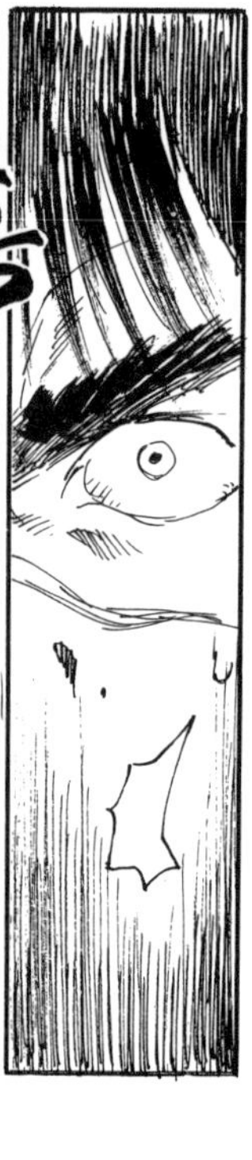

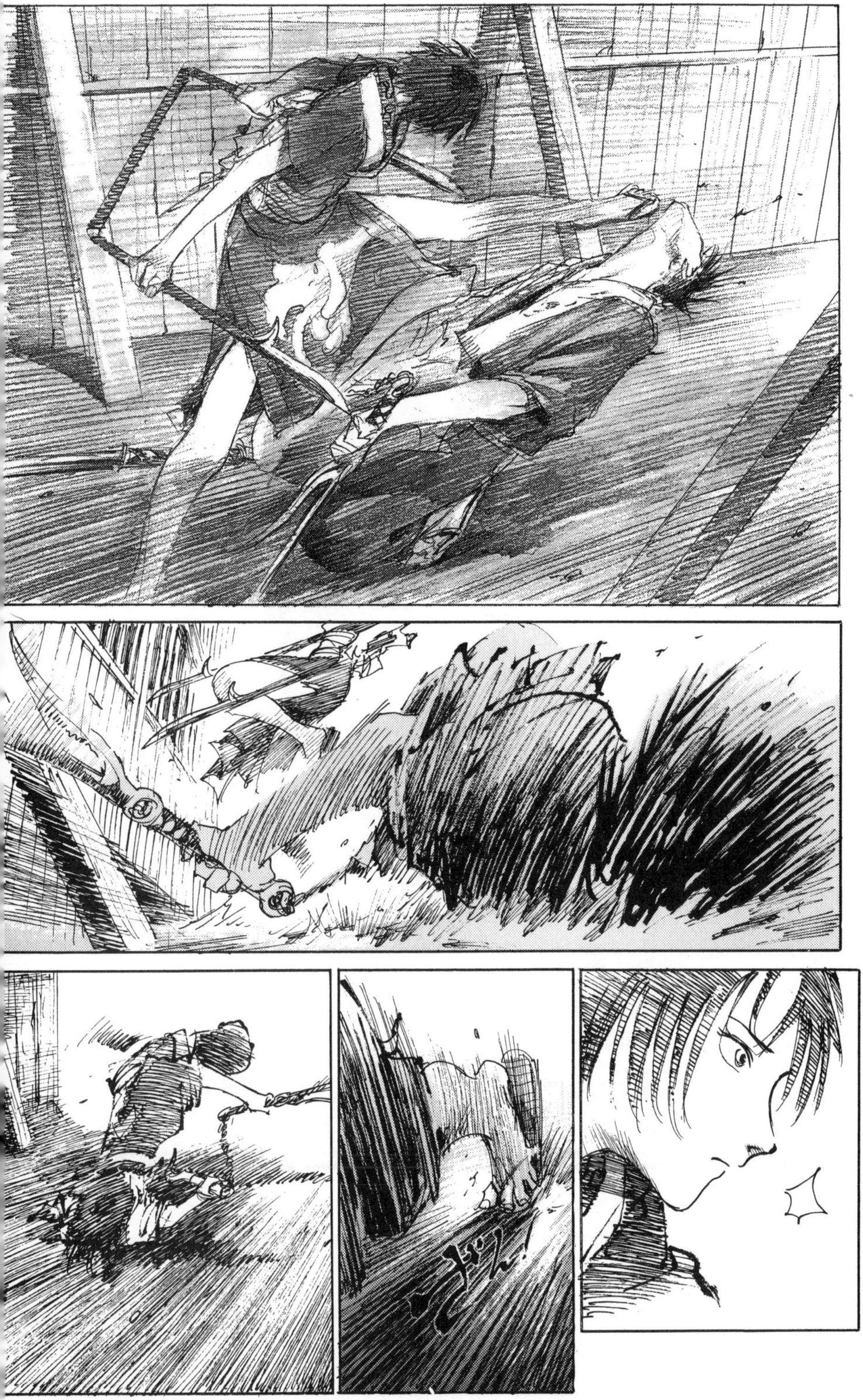

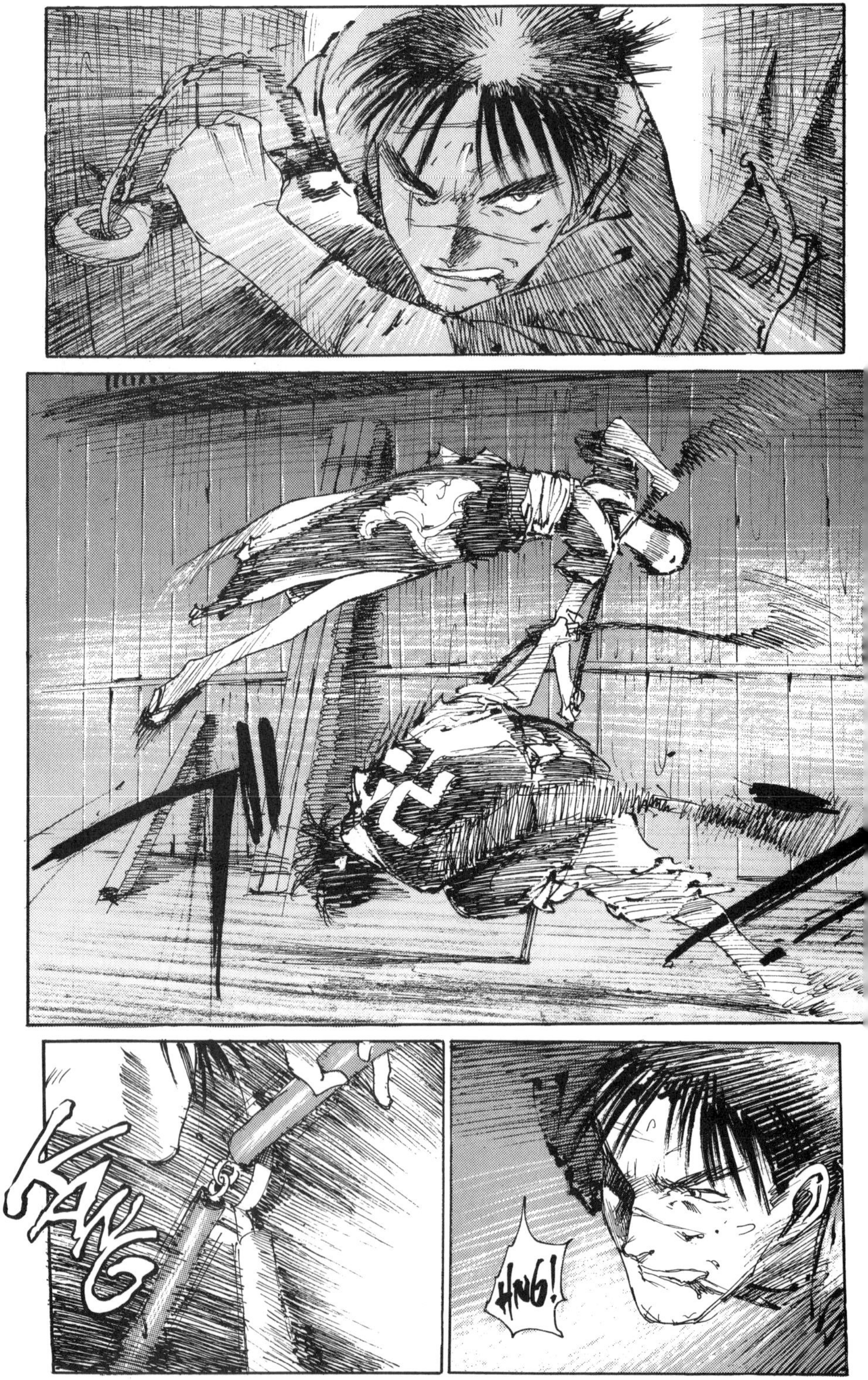
HNG!
KANG

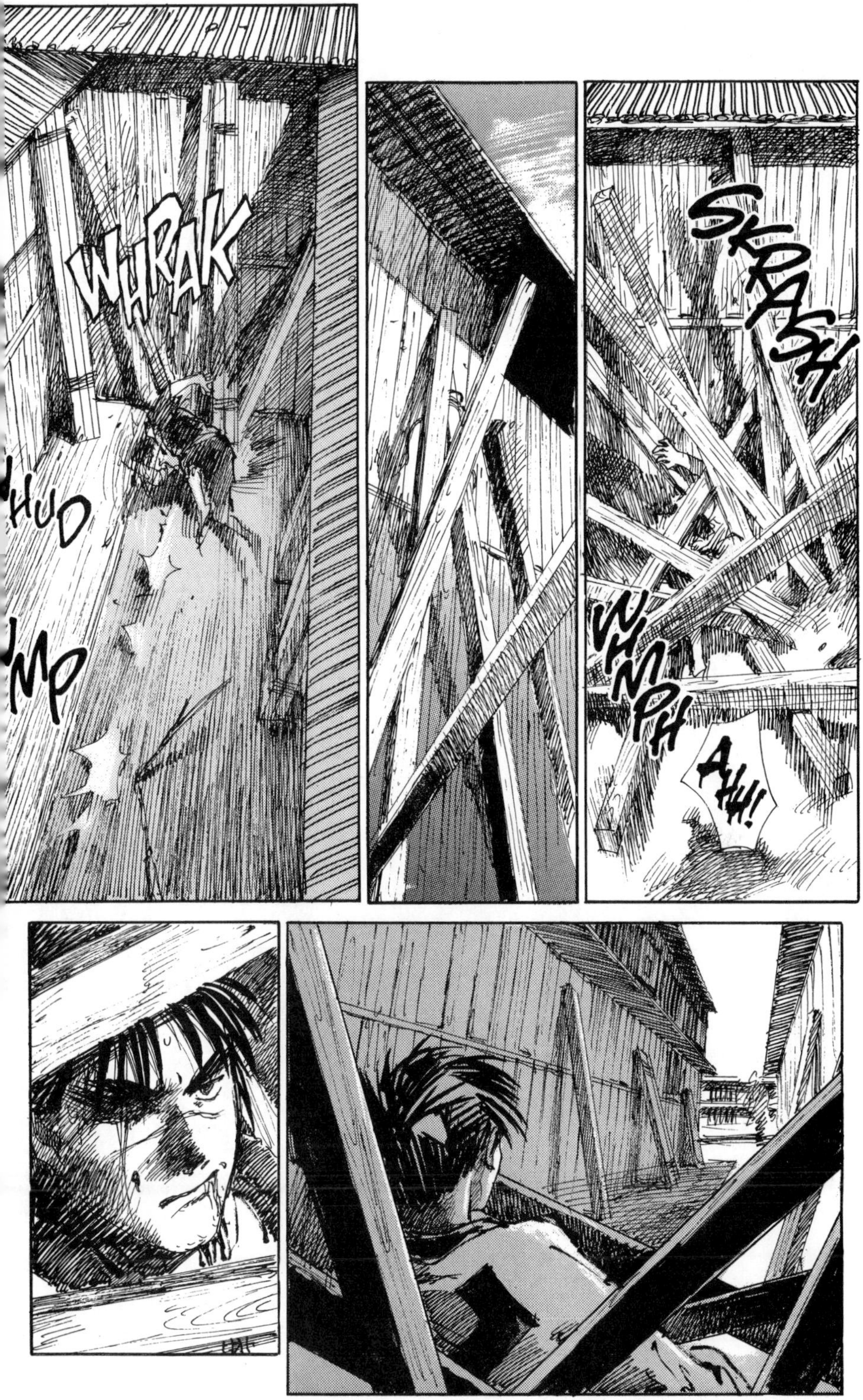
WHRAK
HUD
MP
SKRASH
WHMPH
AHH!

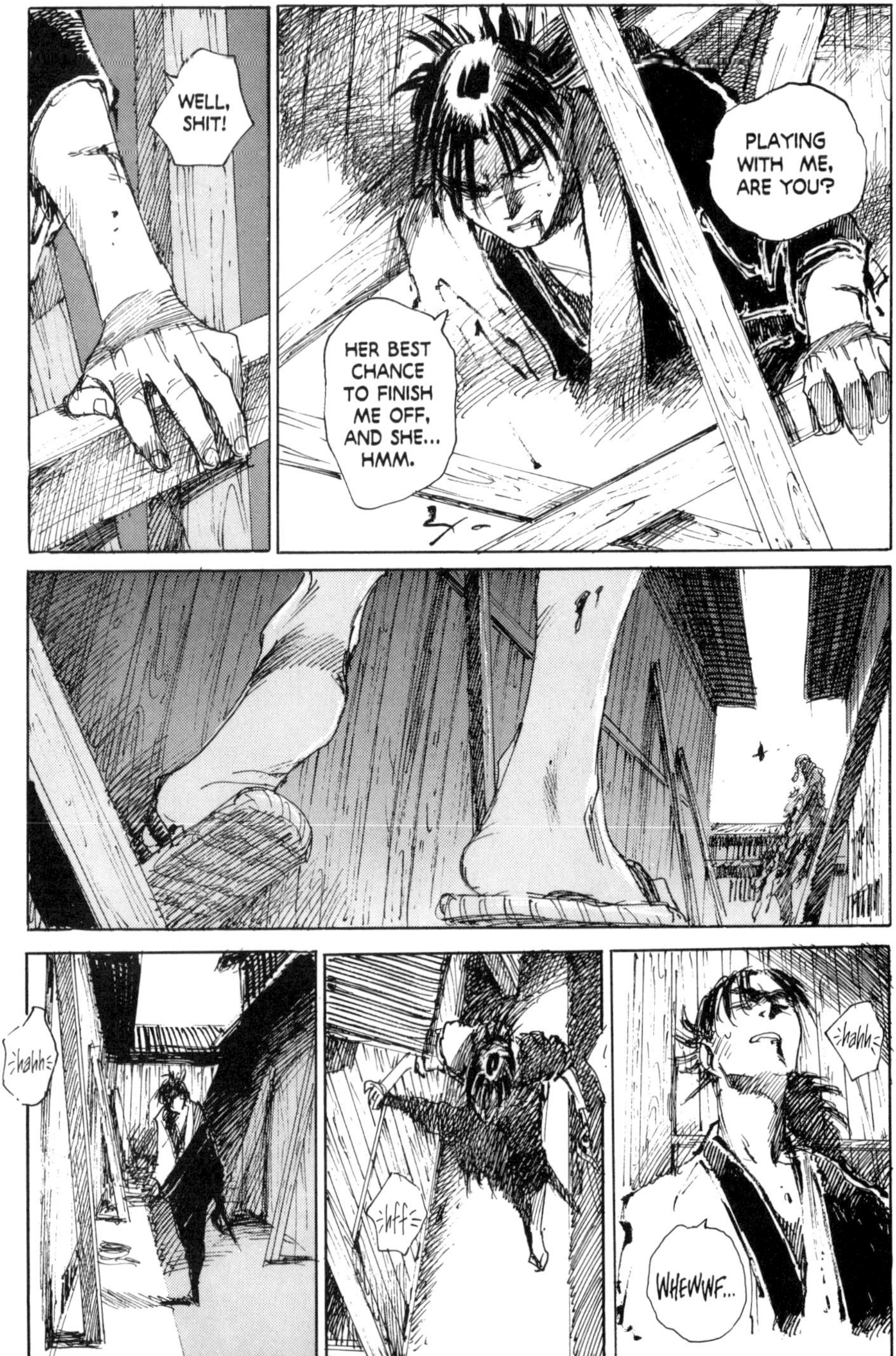
WELL, SHIT!
PLAYING WITH ME, ARE YOU?
HER BEST CHANCE TO FINISH ME OFF, AND SHE... HMM.
hahh
hff
hahh
WHEWWF...

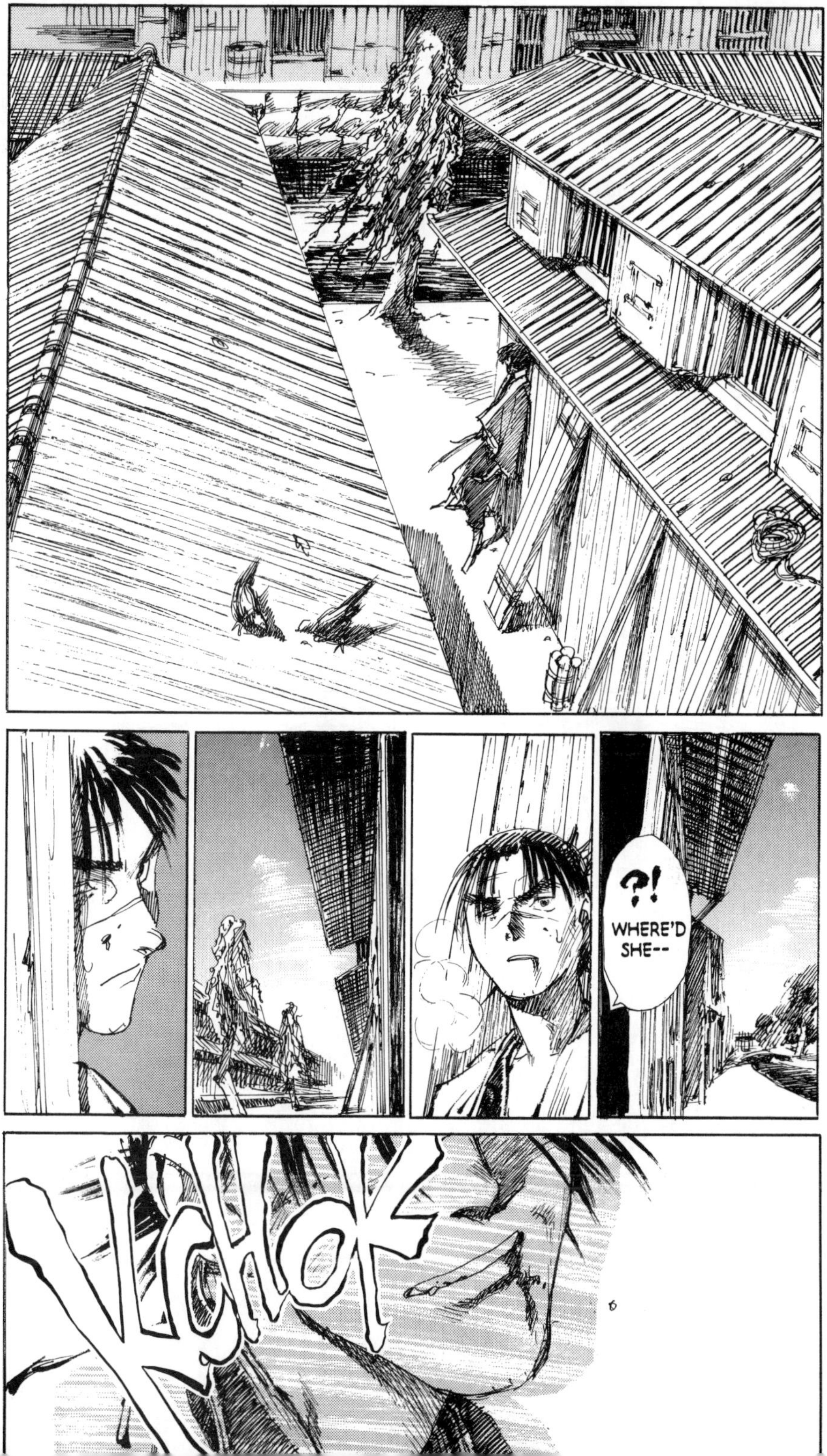
?!
WHERE'D SHE--
KCHOK

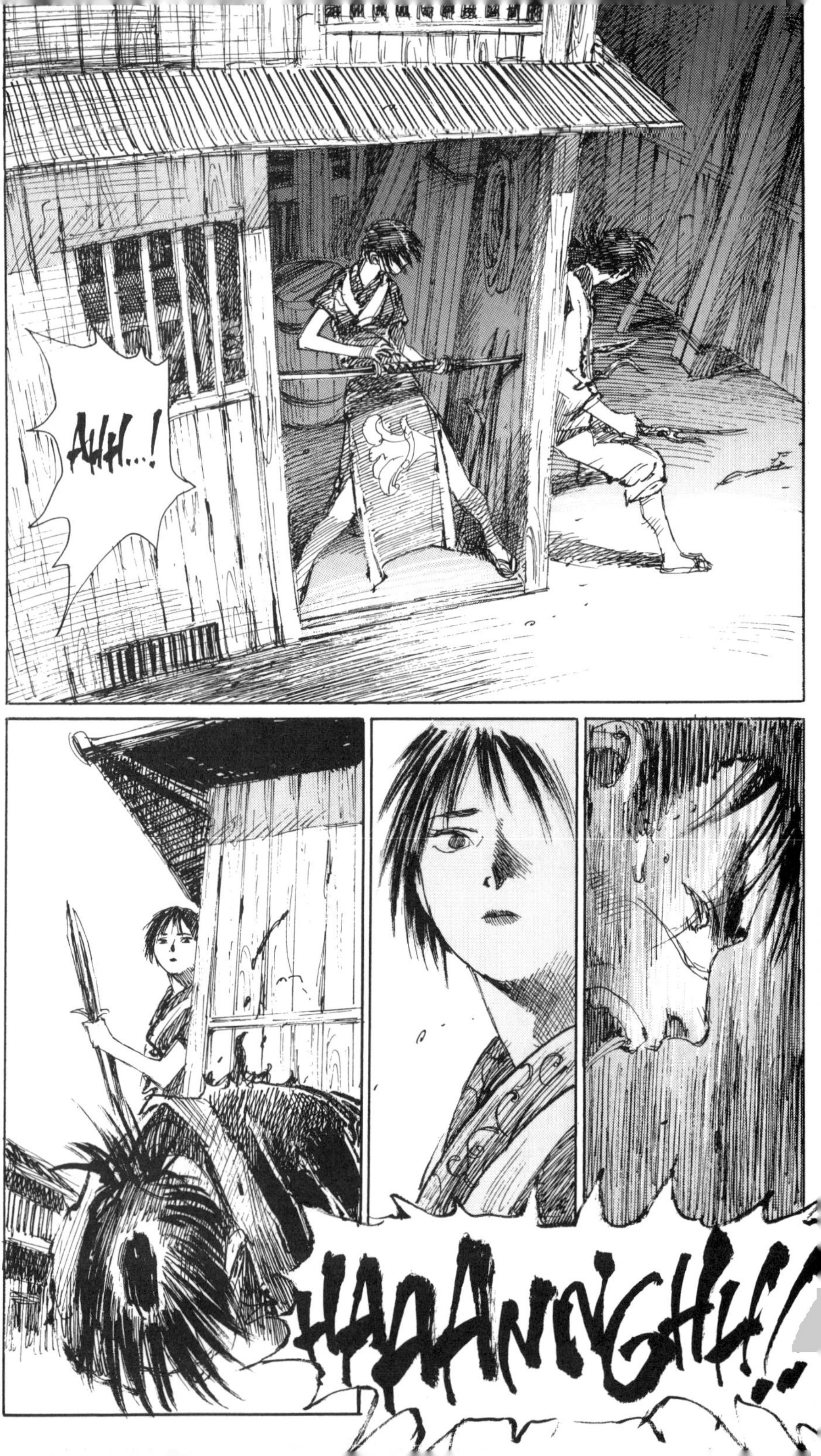
AHH...!
HAAANNGHH!!

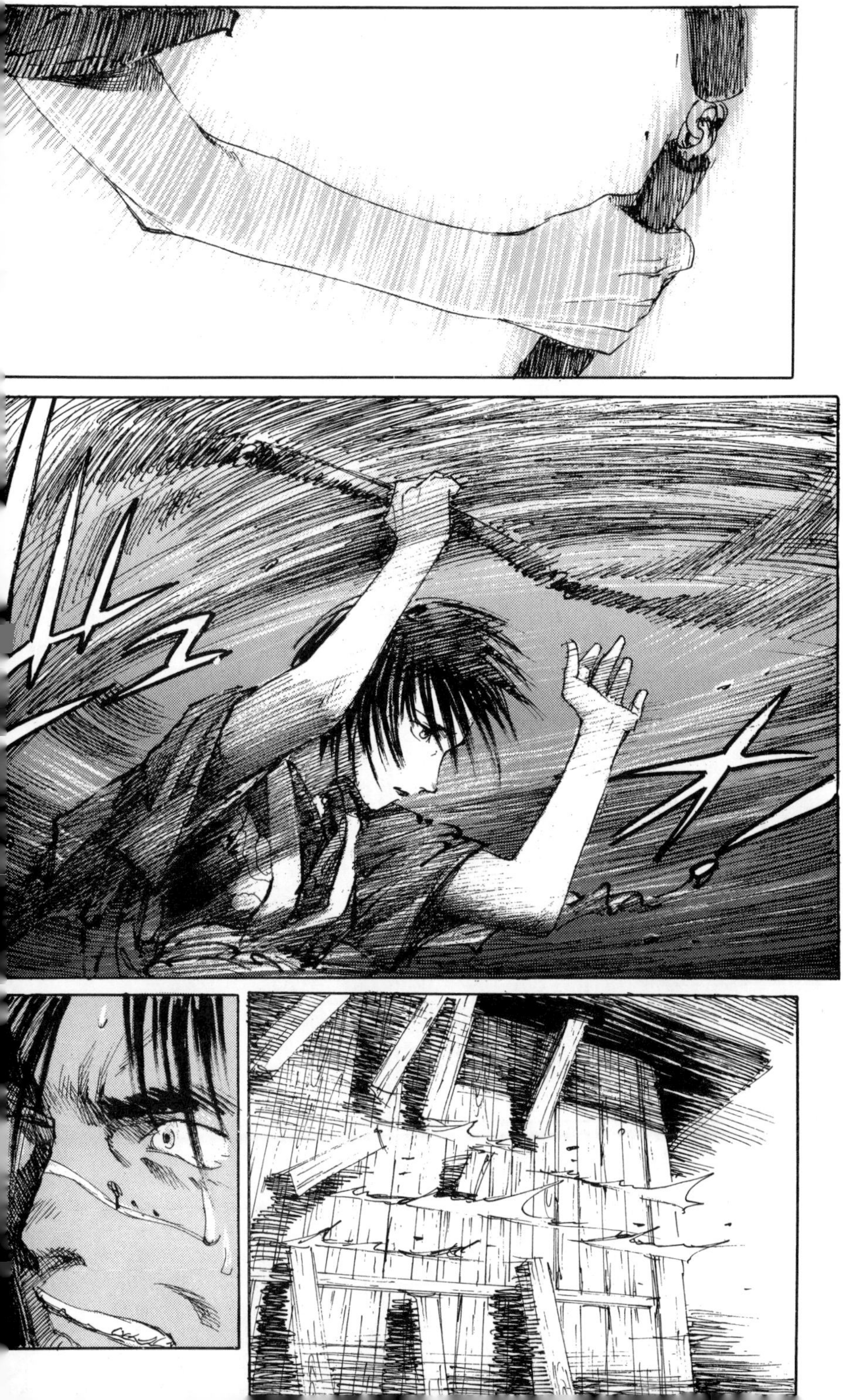

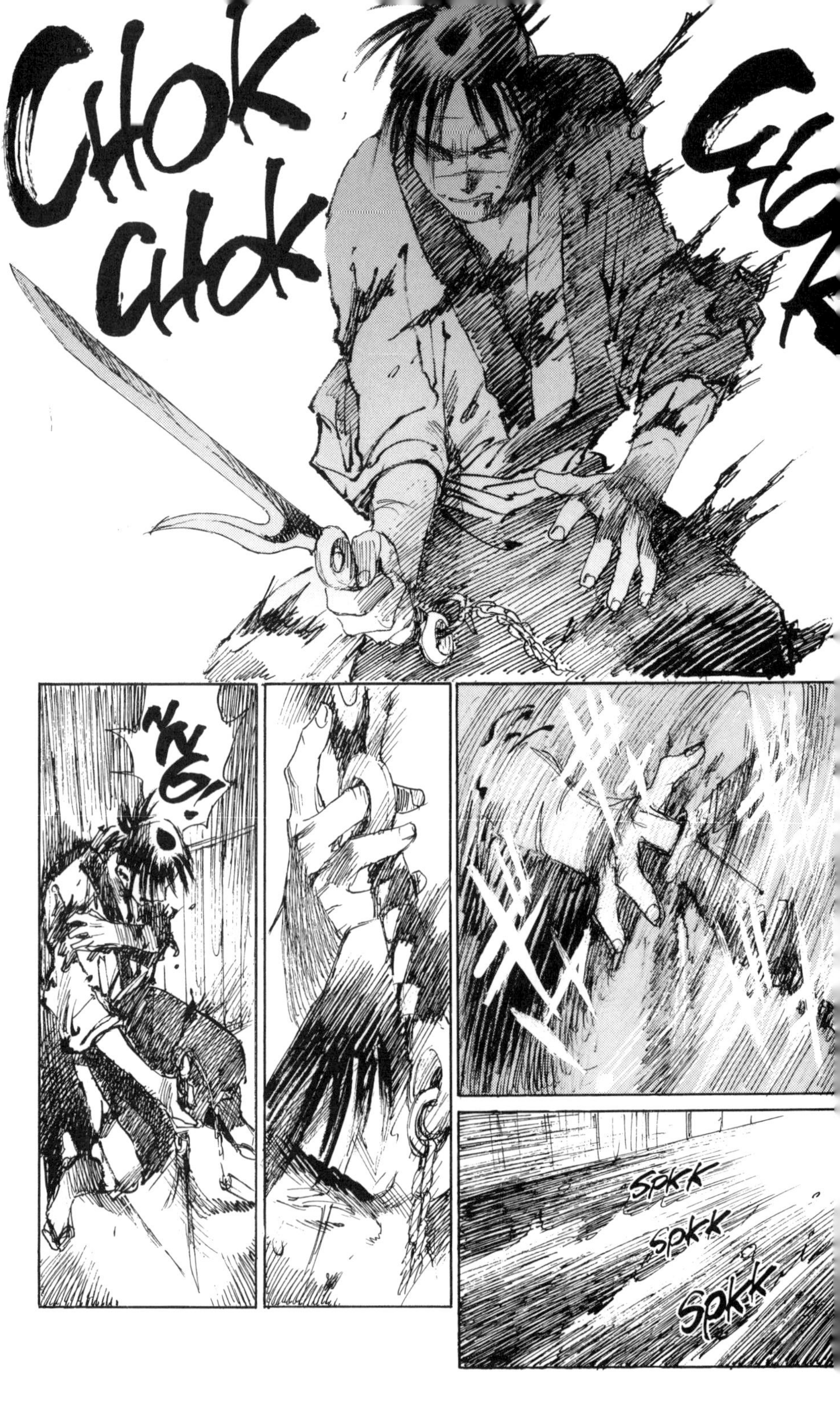

CHOK
CHOK
CHOK
NNG!
SPKK
SPKK
SPKK

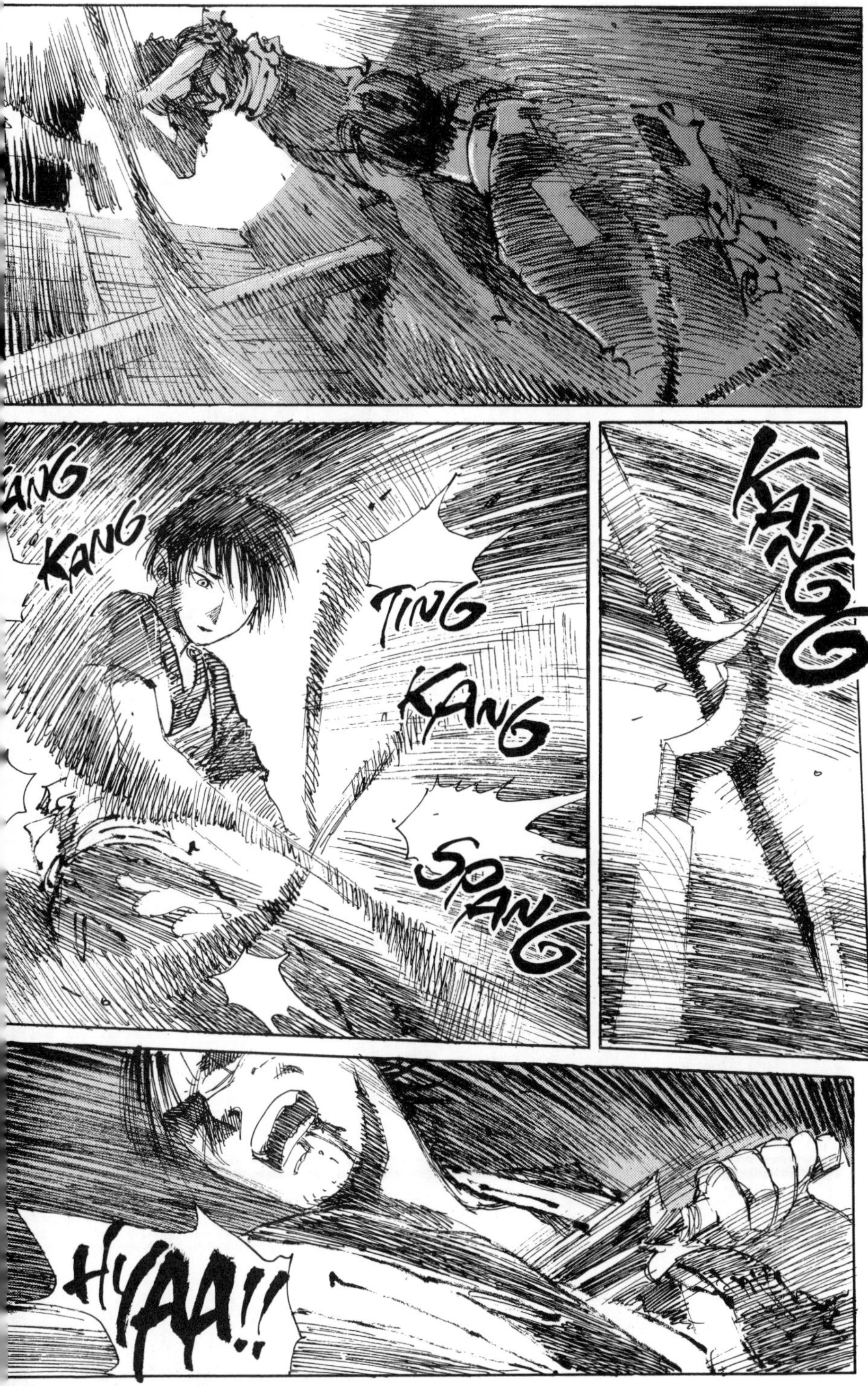
KANGG
TING
KANG
SPANG
ANG
KANG
HYAA!!

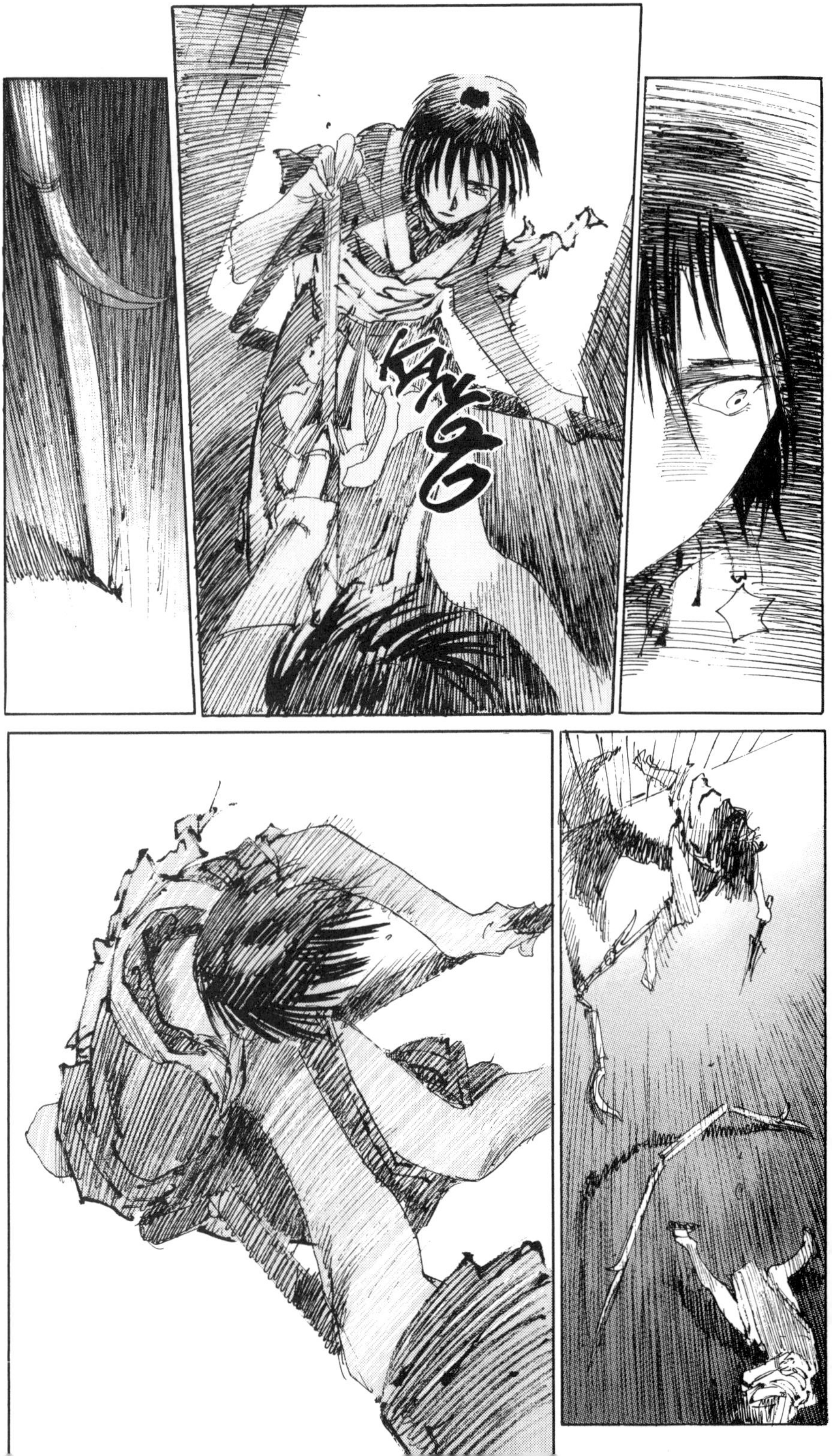
KANGG

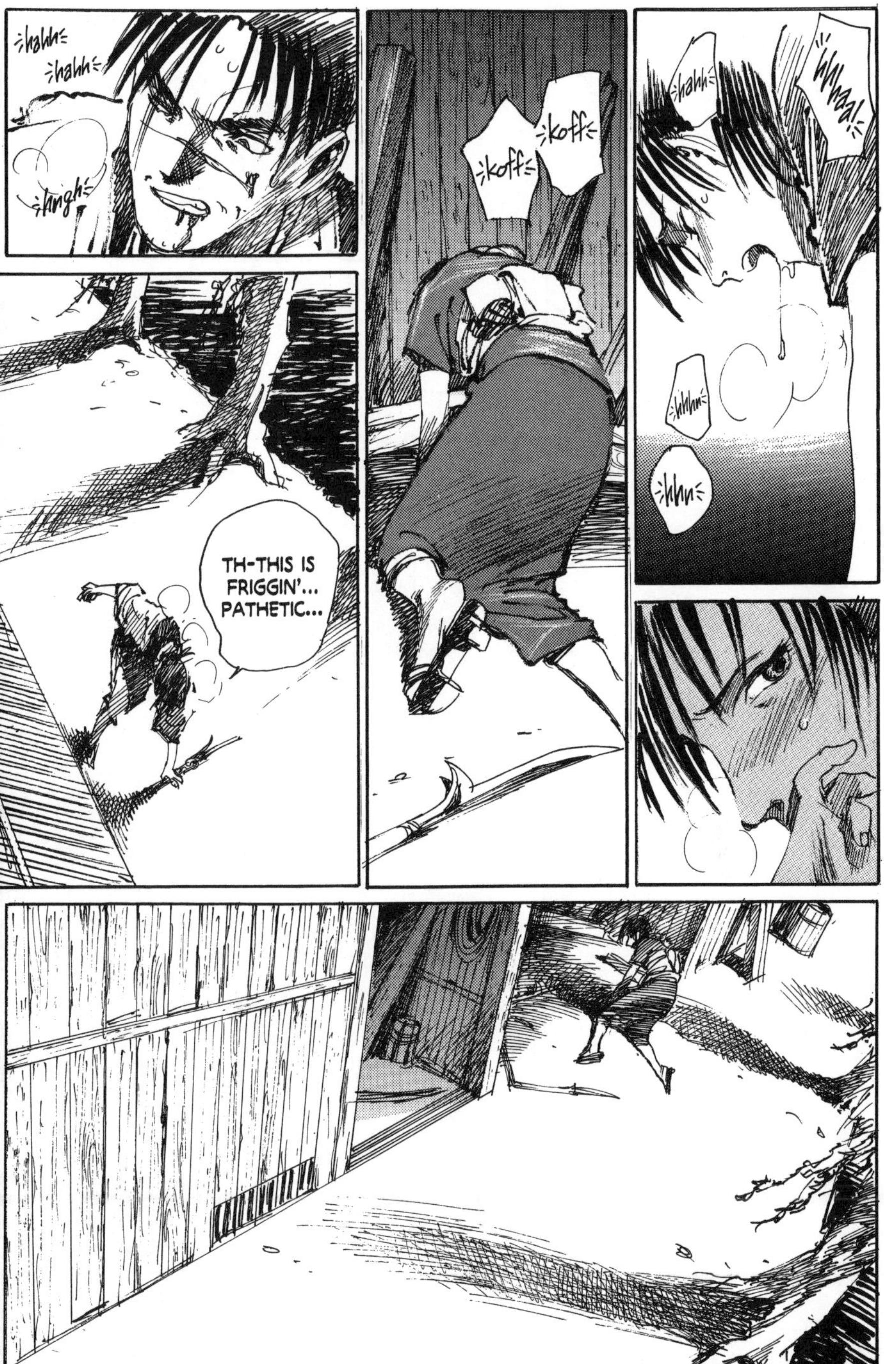
hahh
hahh
hngh
TH-THIS IS FRIGGIN'... PATHETIC...
koff
koff
hahh
hhhaa!
hhhn
hhn

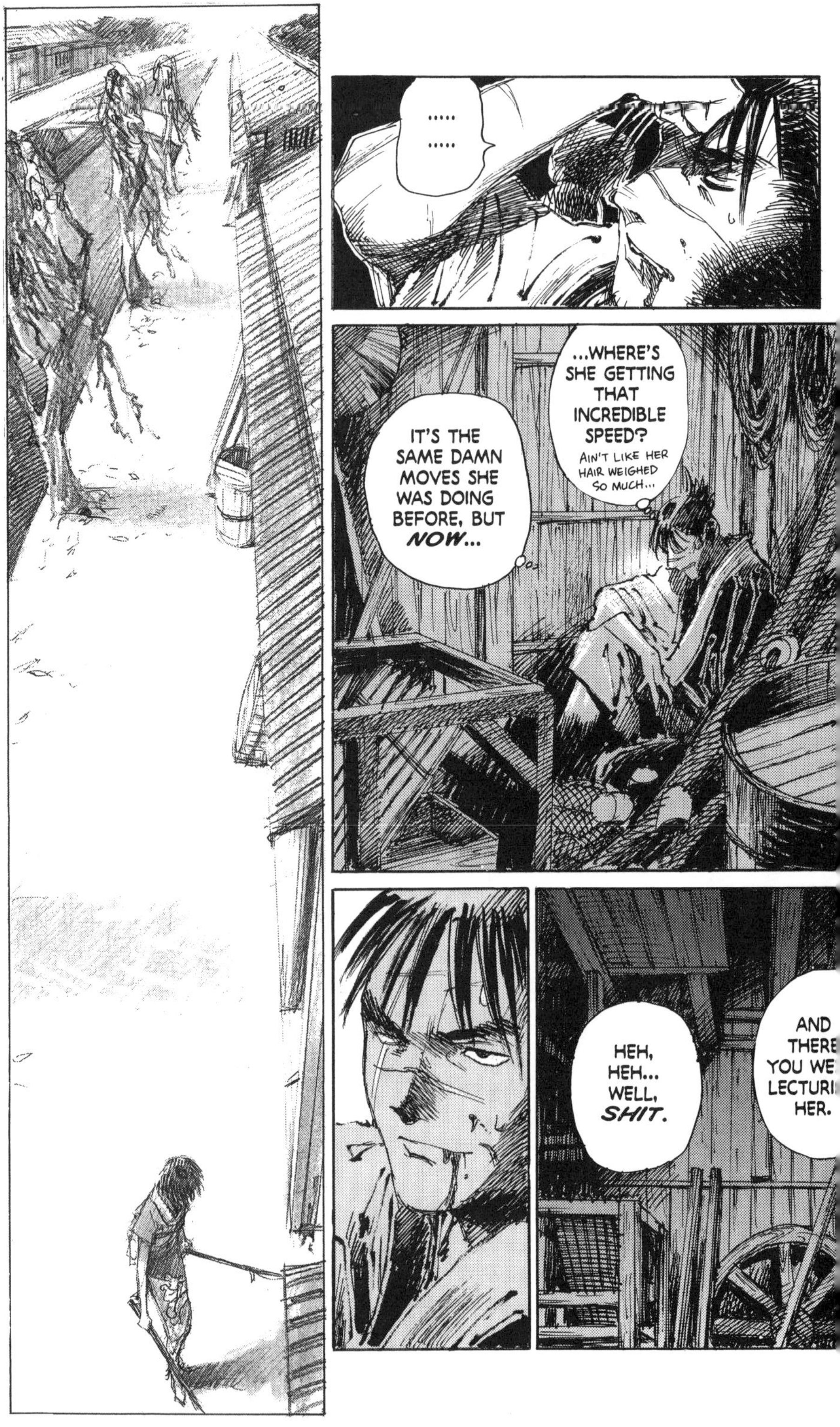

.....
.....
IT'S THE SAME DAMN MOVES SHE WAS DOING BEFORE, BUT NOW...
...WHERE'S SHE GETTING THAT INCREDIBLE SPEED? AIN'T LIKE HER HAIR WEIGHED SO MUCH...
HEH, HEH... WELL, SHIT.
AND THERE YOU WE LECTURI HER.

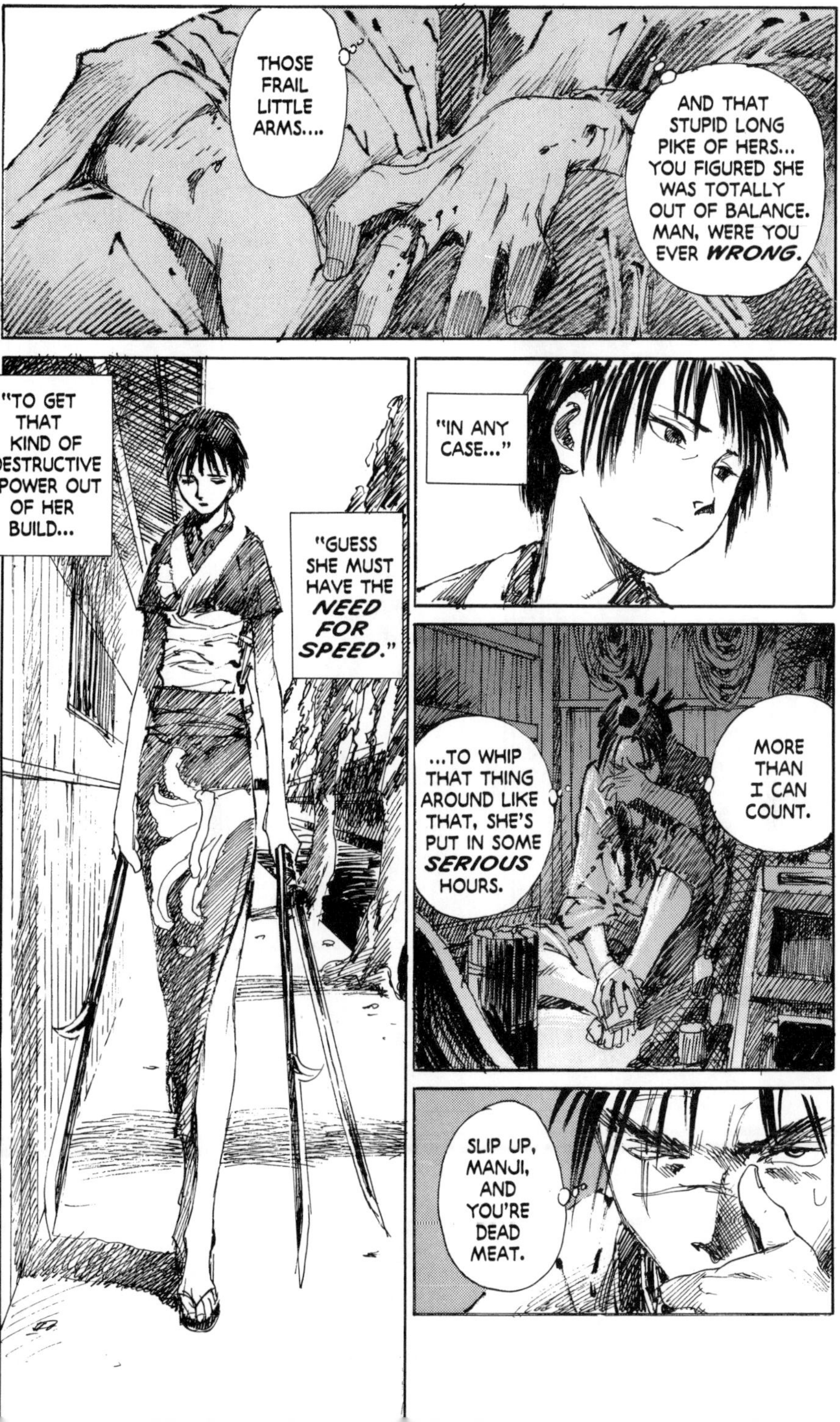
THOSE FRAIL LITTLE ARMS....
AND THAT STUPID LONG PIKE OF HERS... YOU FIGURED SHE WAS TOTALLY OUT OF BALANCE. MAN, WERE YOU EVER *WRONG*.
"TO GET THAT KIND OF DESTRUCTIVE POWER OUT OF HER BUILD...
"GUESS SHE MUST HAVE THE *NEED FOR SPEED*."
"IN ANY CASE..."
...TO WHIP THAT THING AROUND LIKE THAT, SHE'S PUT IN SOME *SERIOUS* HOURS.
MORE THAN I CAN COUNT.
SLIP UP, MANJI, AND YOU'RE DEAD MEAT.

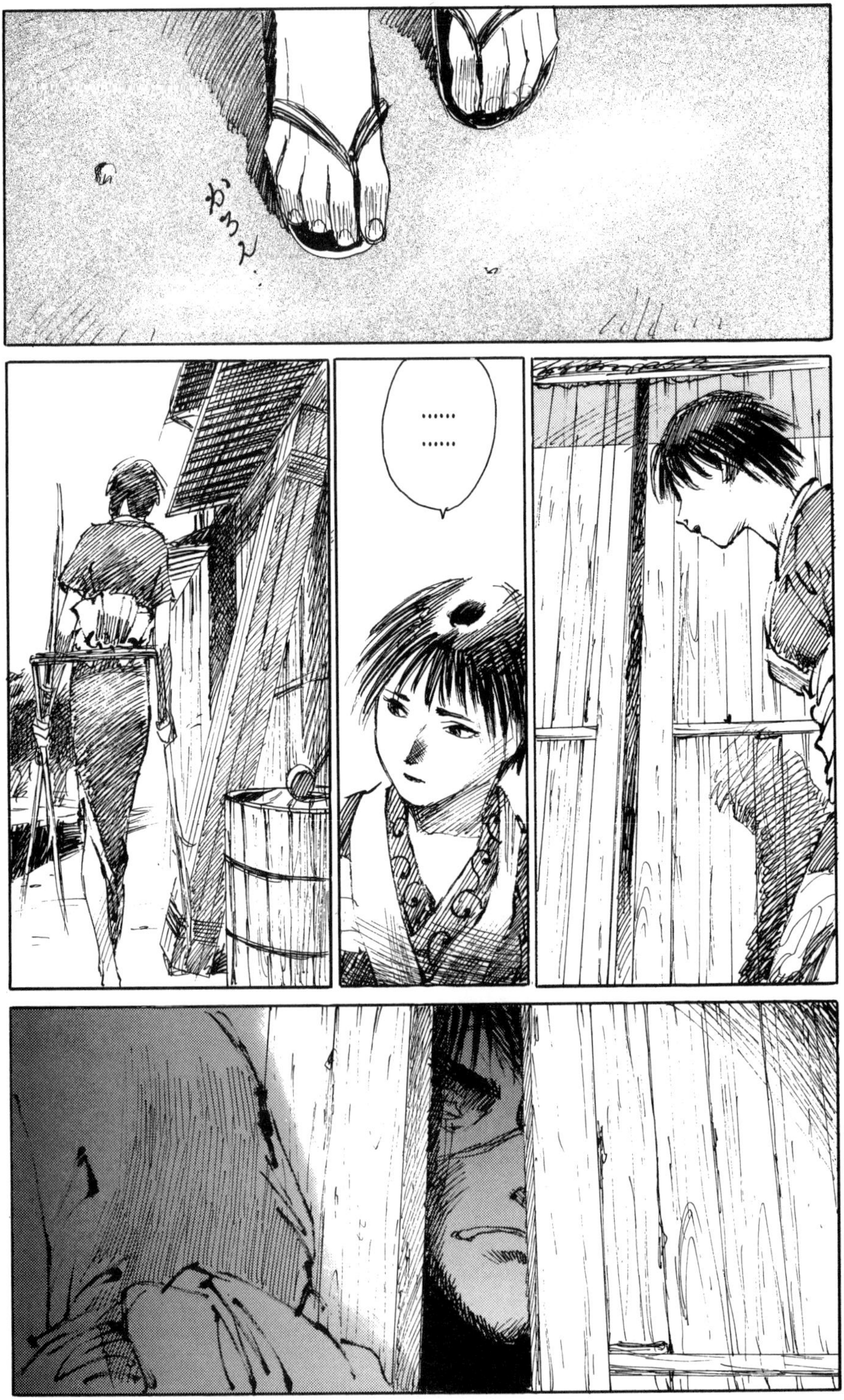

おろん..
…… ……

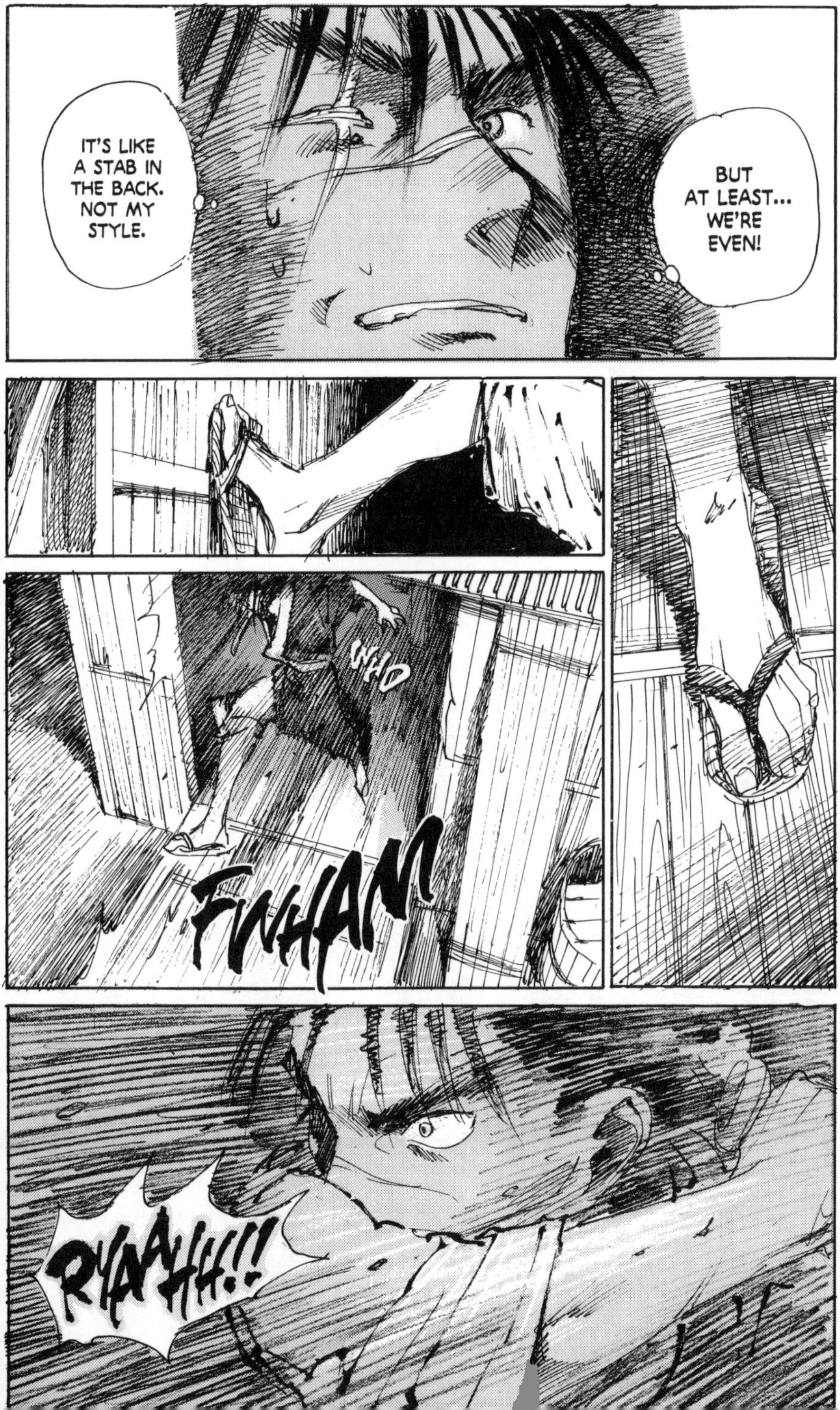
IT'S LIKE A STAB IN THE BACK. NOT MY STYLE.
BUT AT LEAST... WE'RE EVEN!
WHO
FWHAM
RYAAHH!!

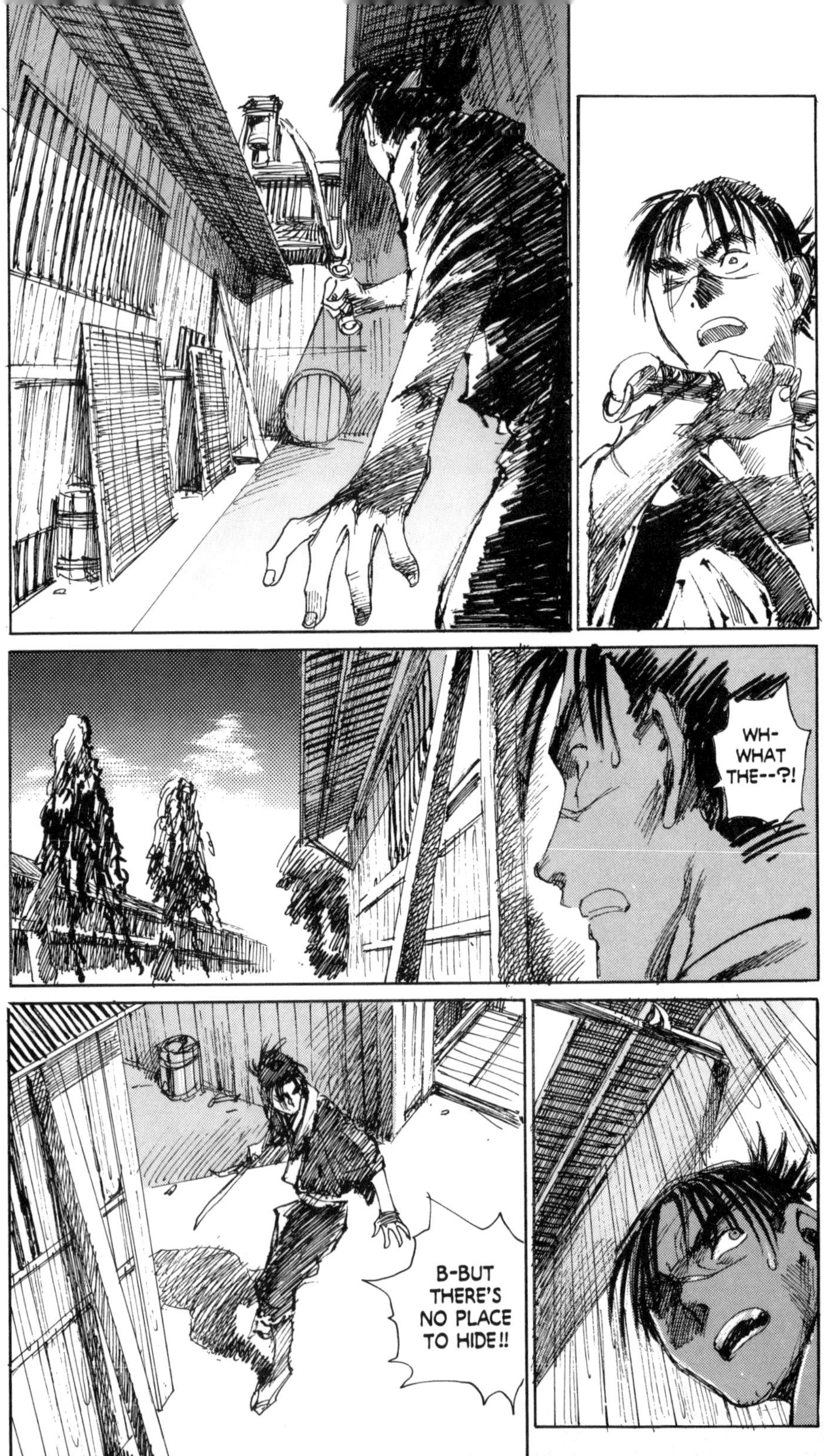
WH-
WHAT
THE--?!
B-BUT
THERE'S
NO PLACE
TO HIDE!!

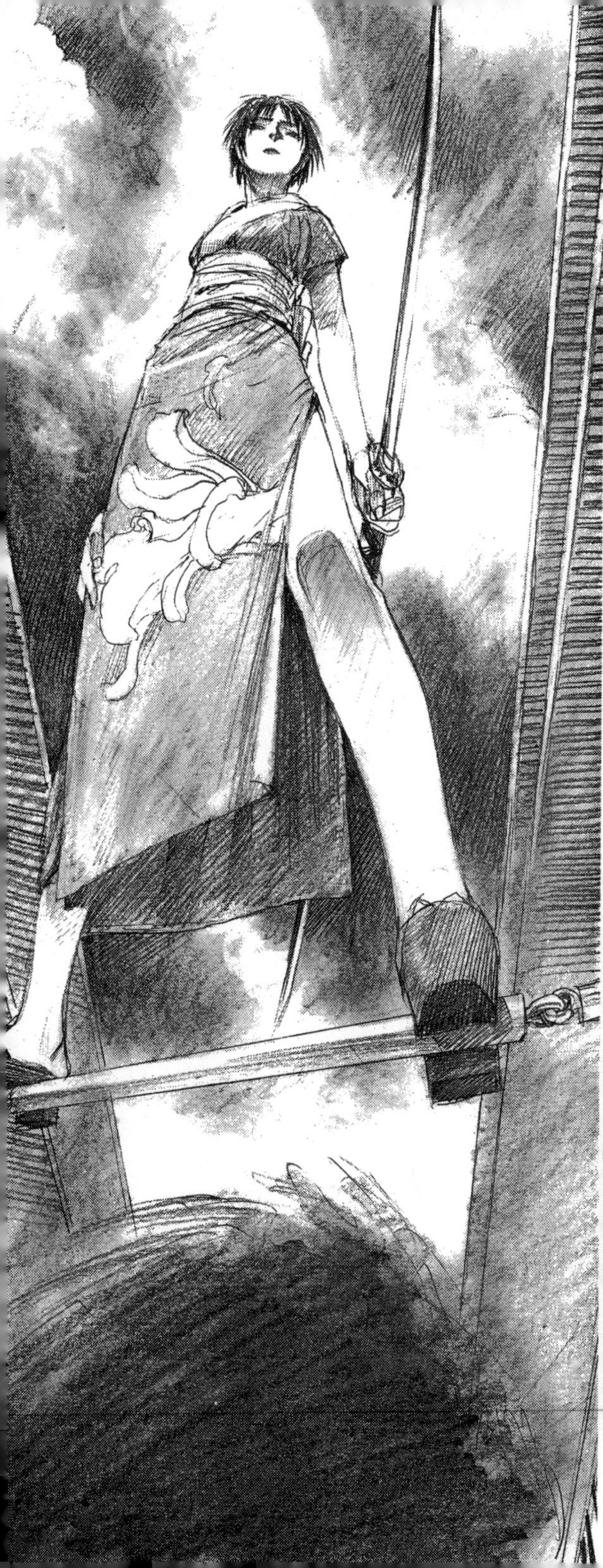
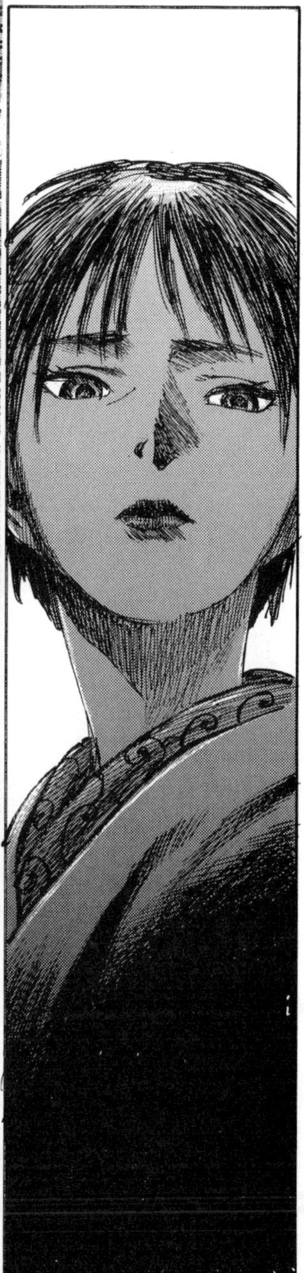

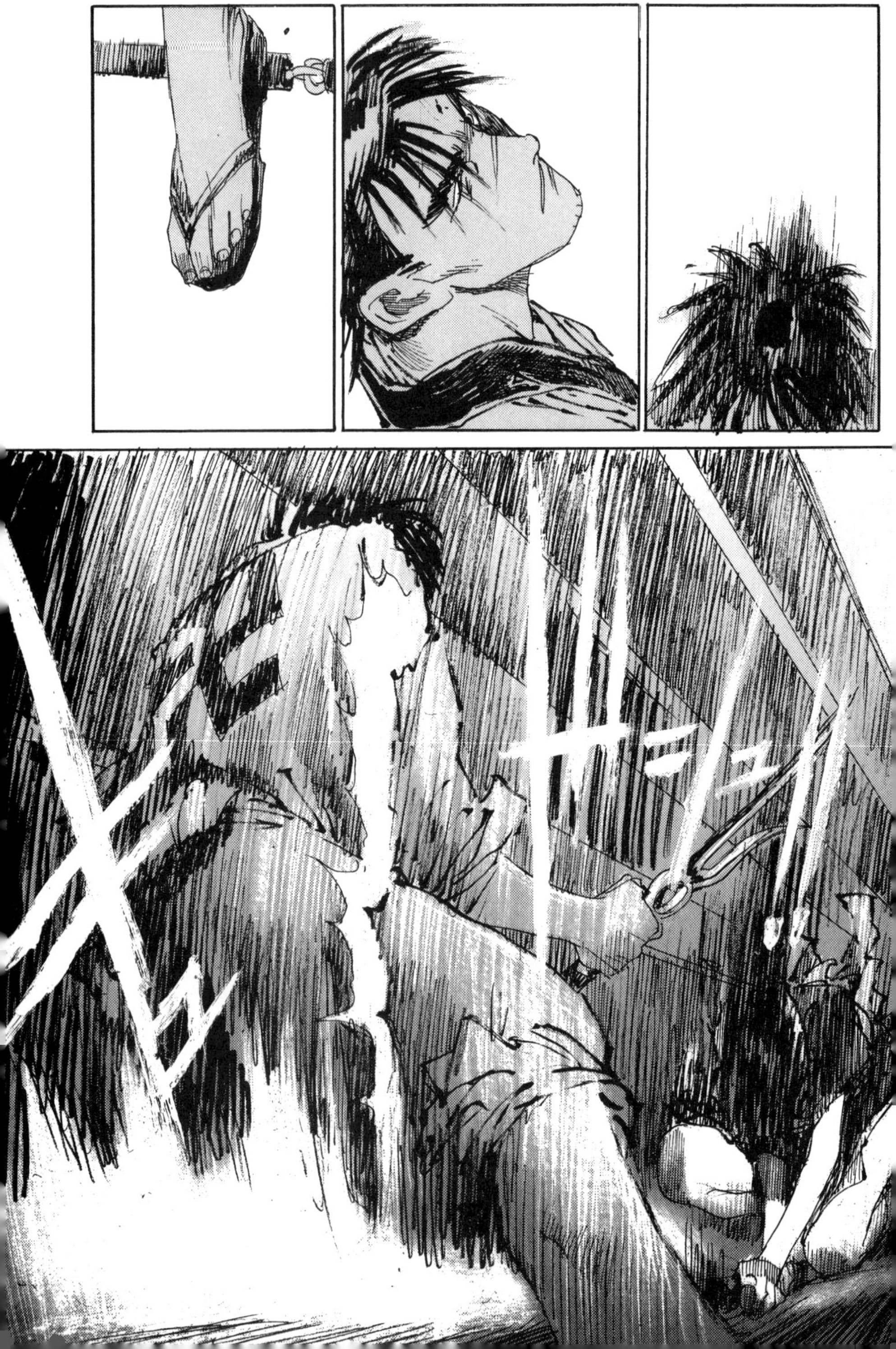

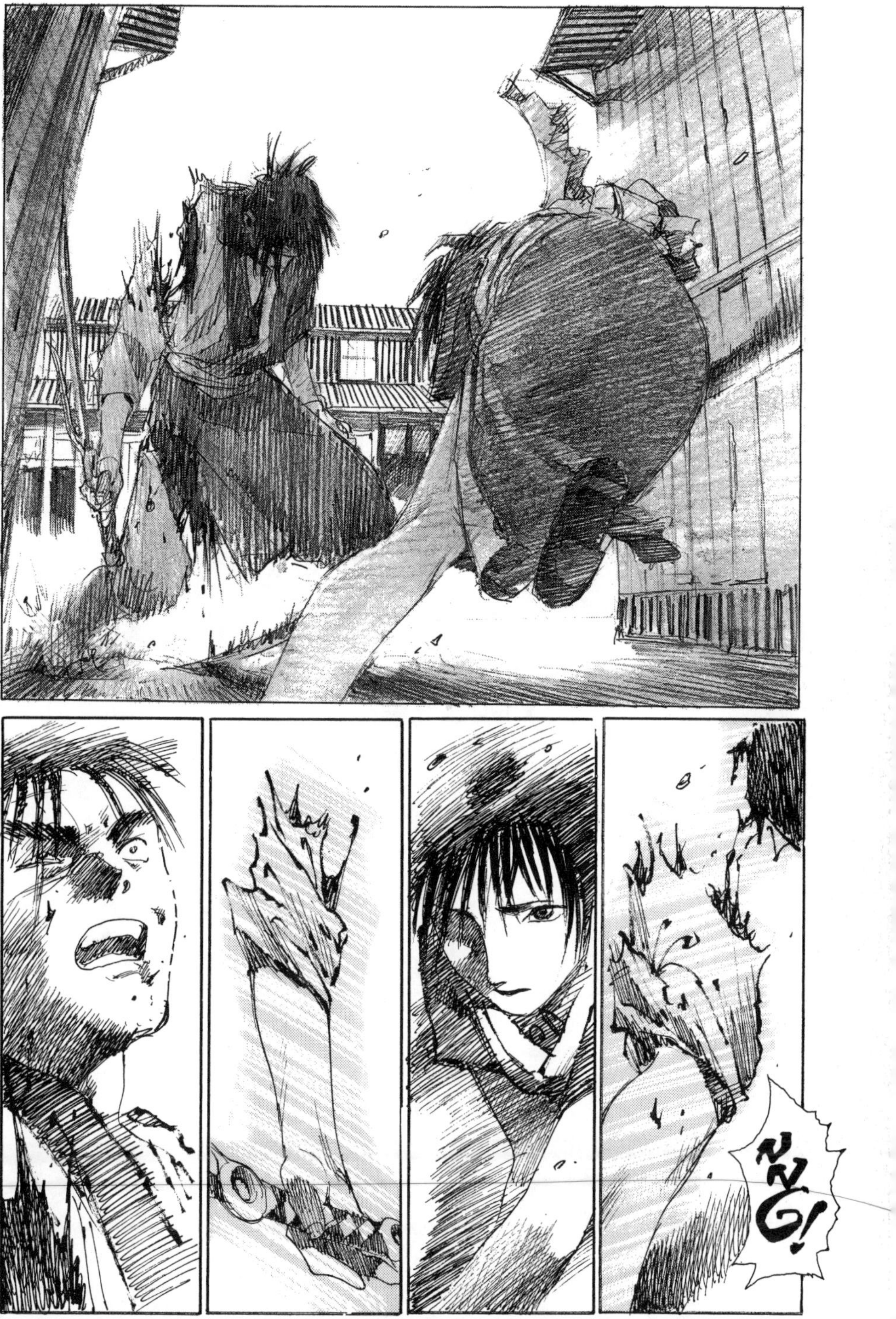
NNG!

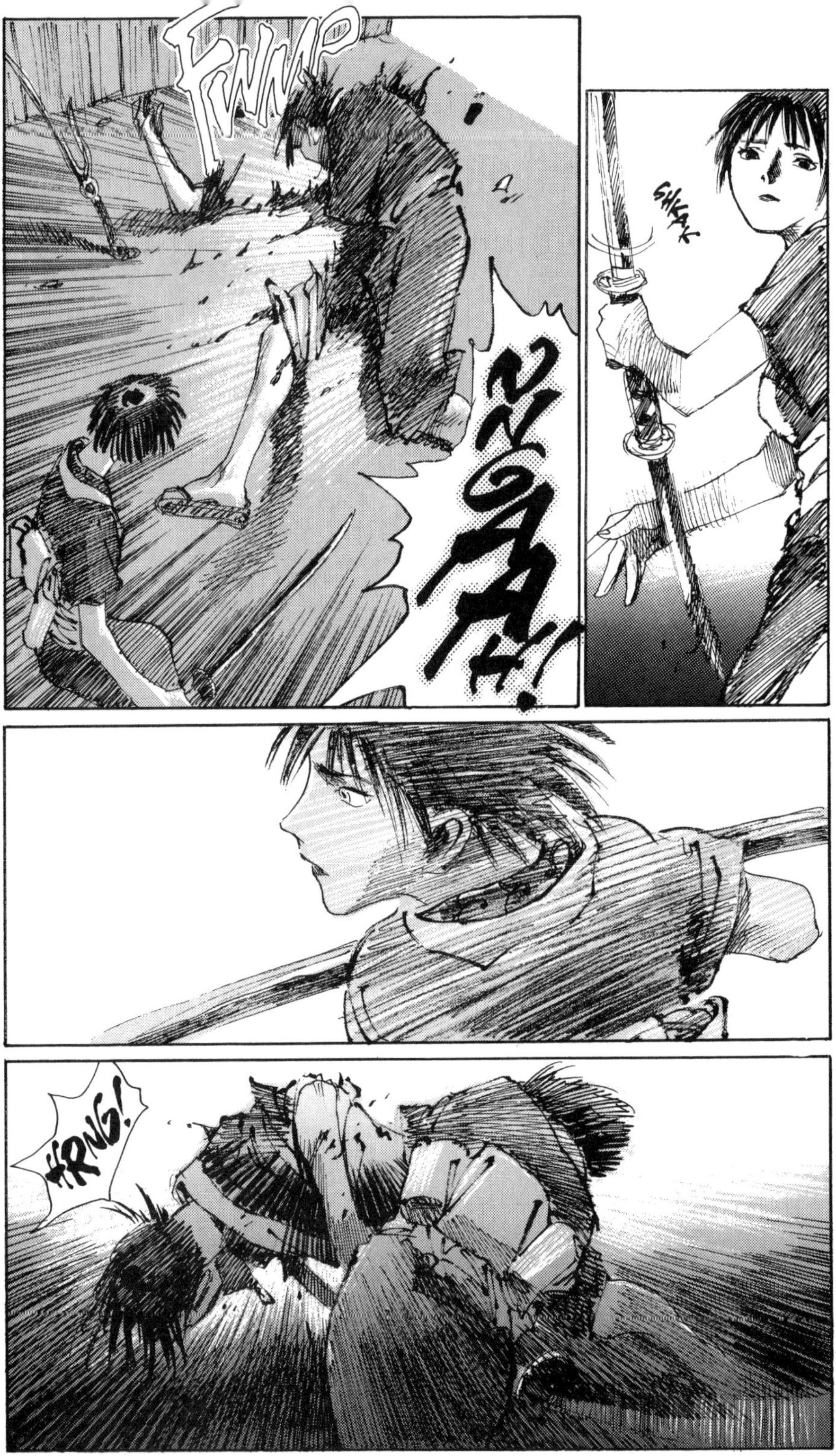
FWMP
NNGAAH!
SHKAK
HRNG!

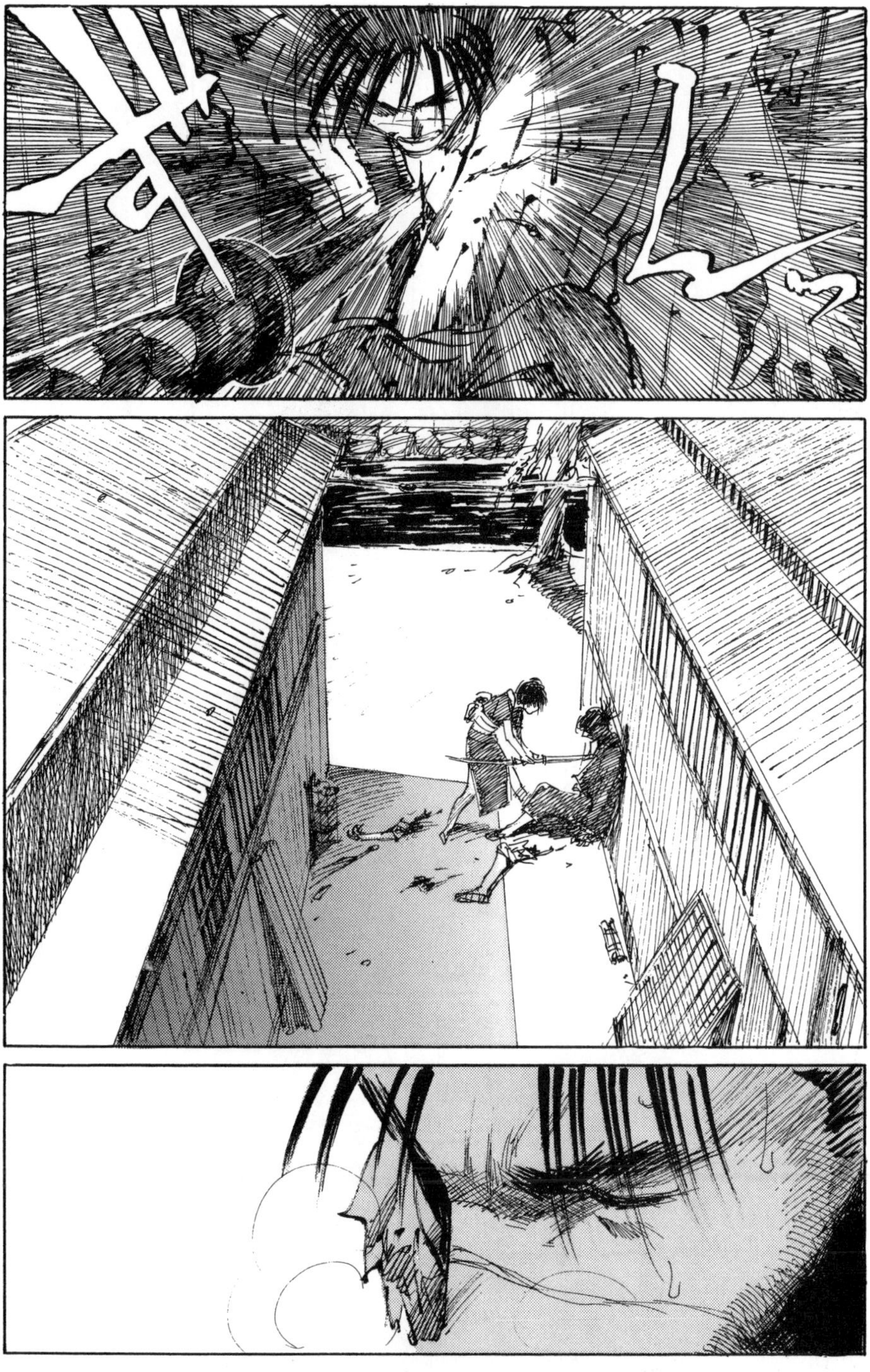

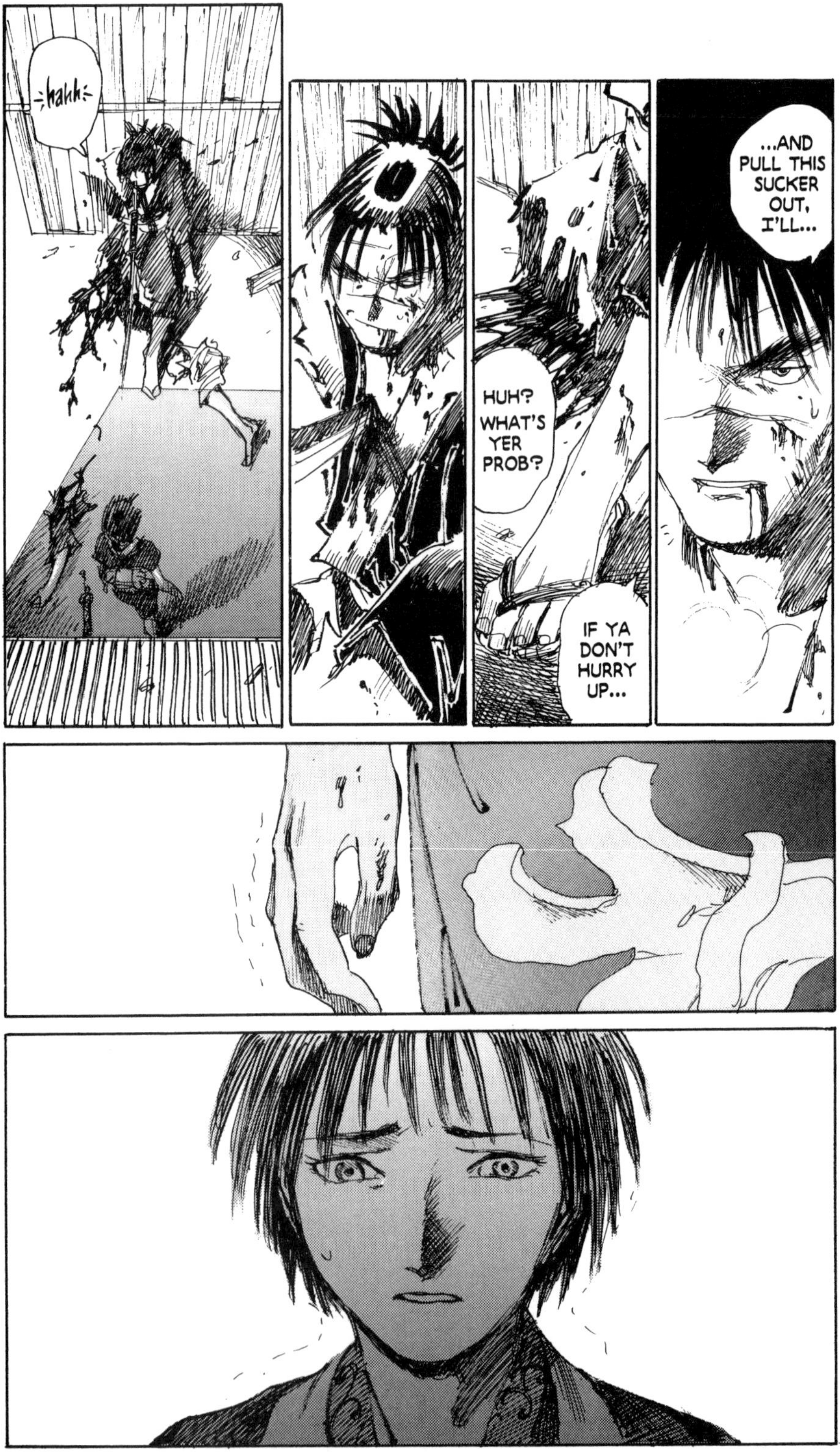
hahh
HUH? WHAT'S YER PROB?
IF YA DON'T HURRY UP...
...AND PULL THIS SUCKER OUT, I'LL...

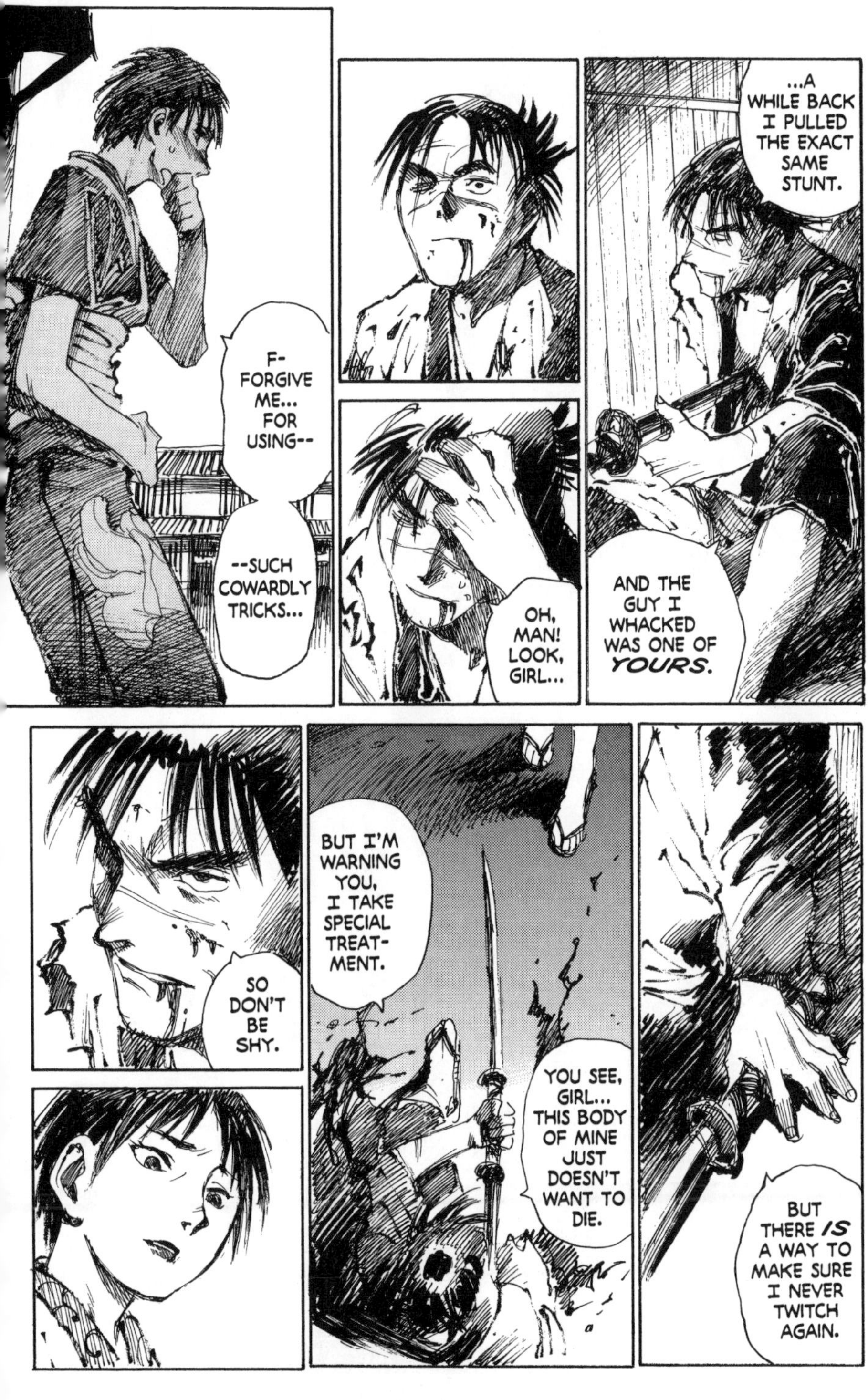
F-FORGIVE ME... FOR USING--
--SUCH COWARDLY TRICKS...
OH, MAN! LOOK, GIRL...
...A WHILE BACK I PULLED THE EXACT SAME STUNT.
AND THE GUY I WHACKED WAS ONE OF *YOURS*.
SO DON'T BE SHY.
BUT I'M WARNING YOU, I TAKE SPECIAL TREATMENT.
YOU SEE, GIRL... THIS BODY OF MINE JUST DOESN'T WANT TO DIE.
BUT THERE *IS* A WAY TO MAKE SURE I NEVER TWITCH AGAIN.

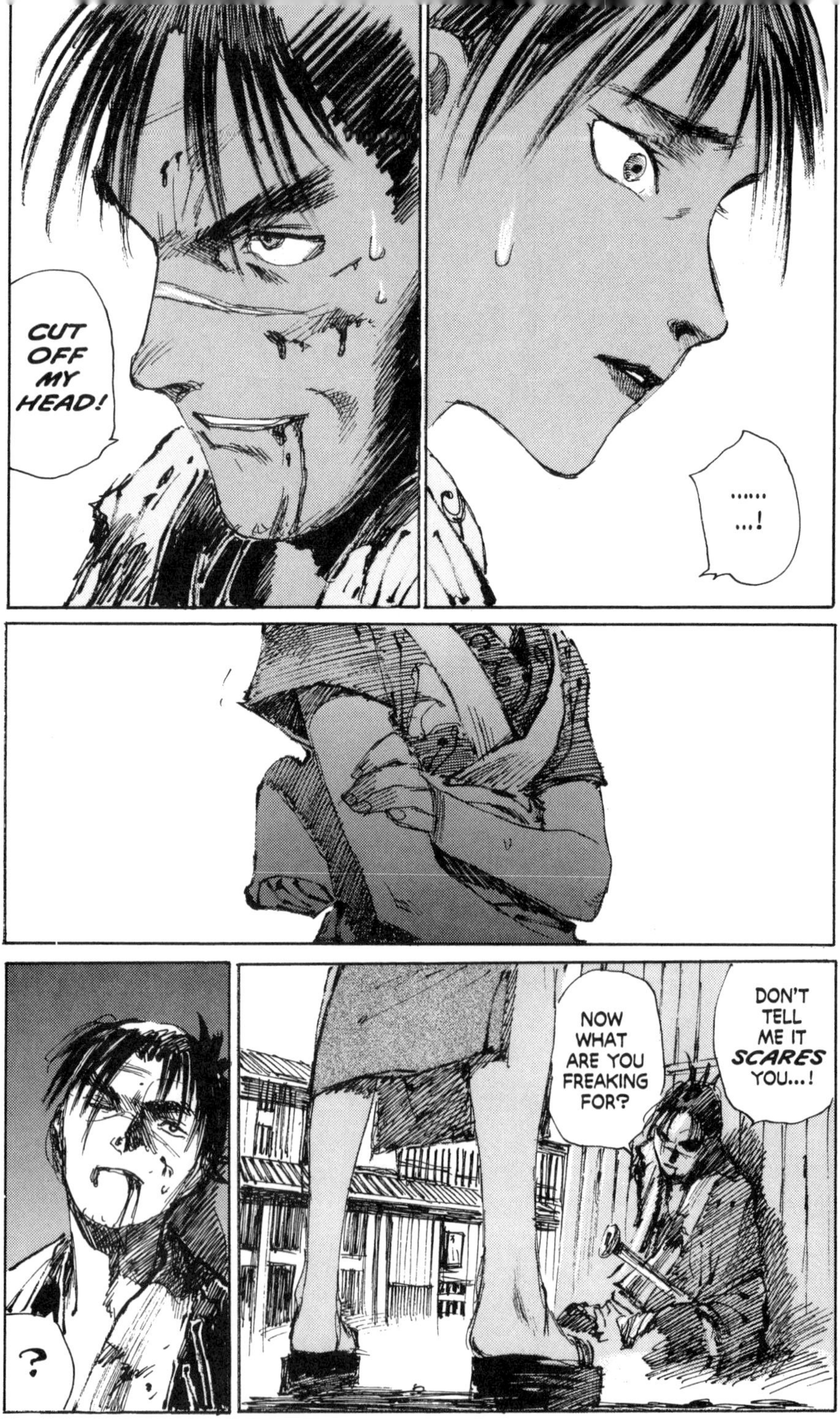
CUT OFF MY HEAD!
......
...!
?
NOW WHAT ARE YOU FREAKING FOR?
DON'T TELL ME IT *SCARES* YOU...!

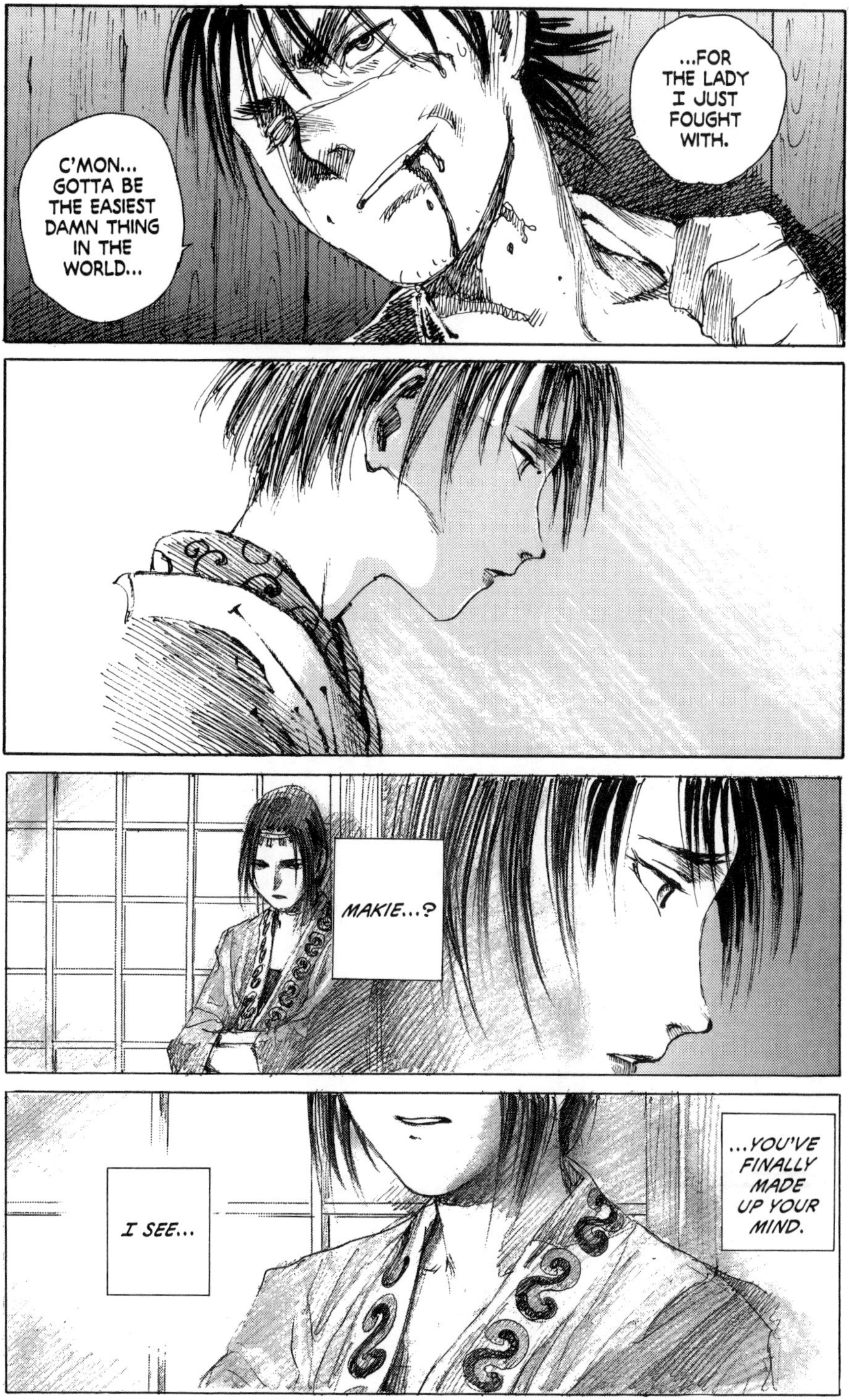
C'MON... GOTTA BE THE EASIEST DAMN THING IN THE WORLD...
...FOR THE LADY I JUST FOUGHT WITH.
MAKIE...?
I SEE...
...YOU'VE FINALLY MADE UP YOUR MIND.

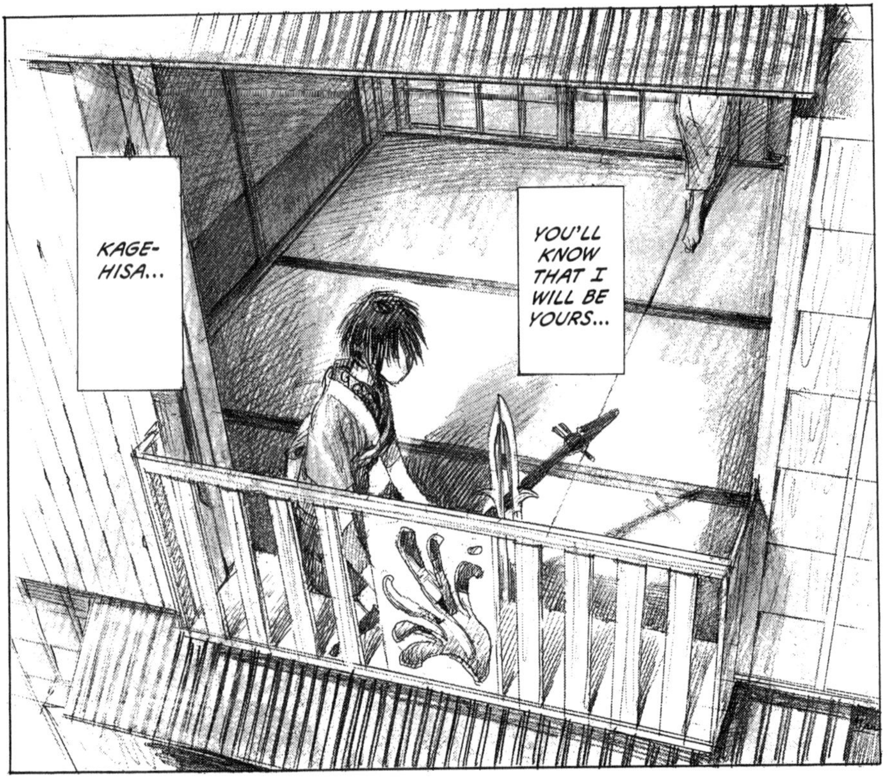
KAGE-HISA...
YOU'LL KNOW THAT I WILL BE YOURS...

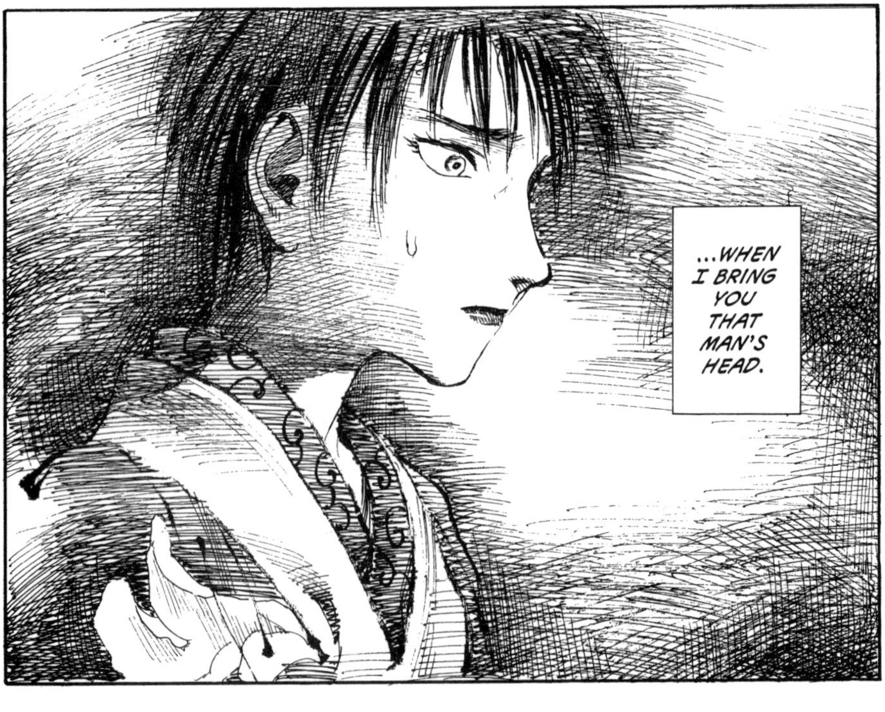
...WHEN I BRING YOU THAT MAN'S HEAD.

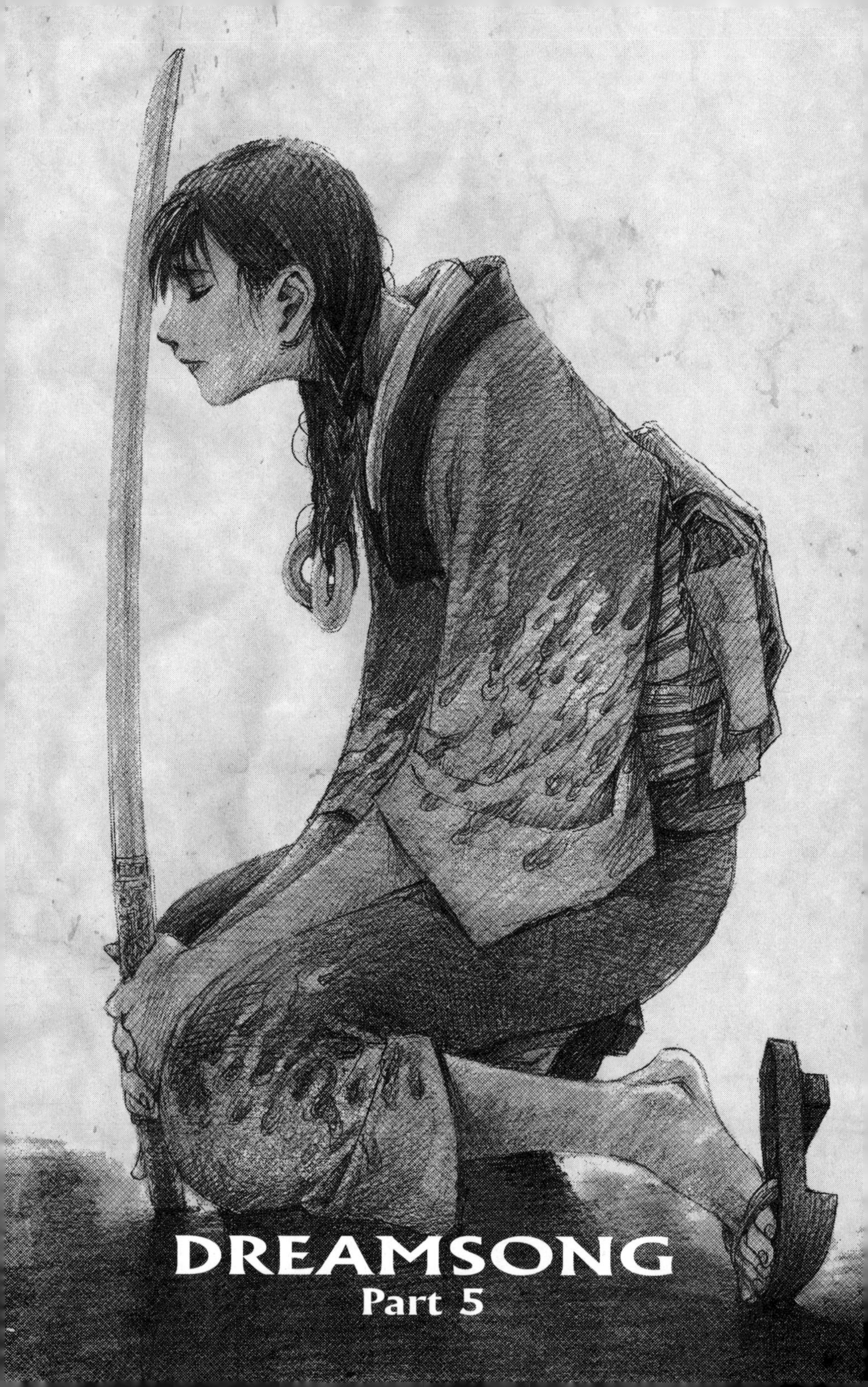
DREAMSONG
Part 5

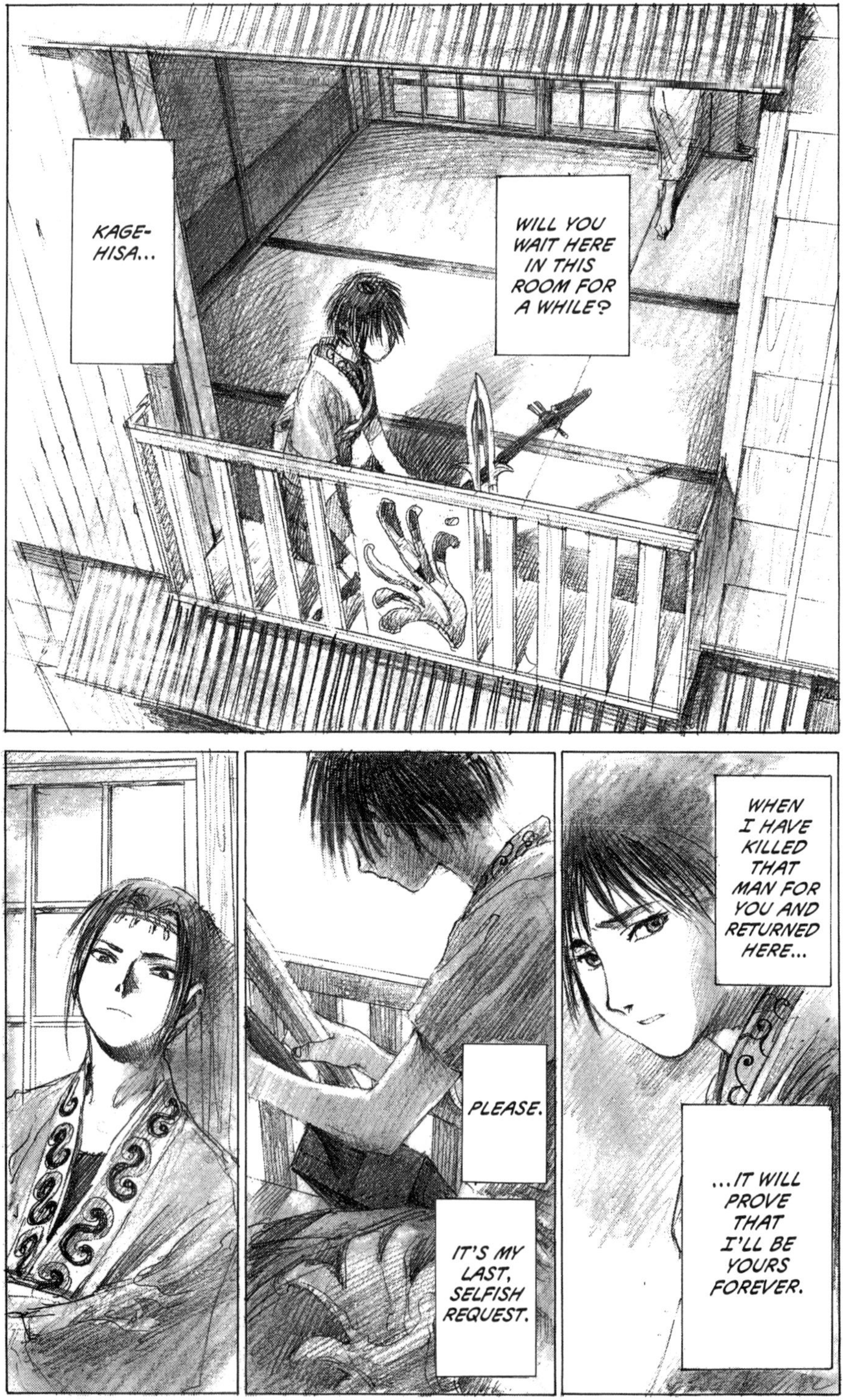
KAGE-HISA...
WILL YOU WAIT HERE IN THIS ROOM FOR A WHILE?
PLEASE.
IT'S MY LAST, SELFISH REQUEST.
WHEN I HAVE KILLED THAT MAN FOR YOU AND RETURNED HERE...
...IT WILL PROVE THAT I'LL BE YOURS FOREVER.

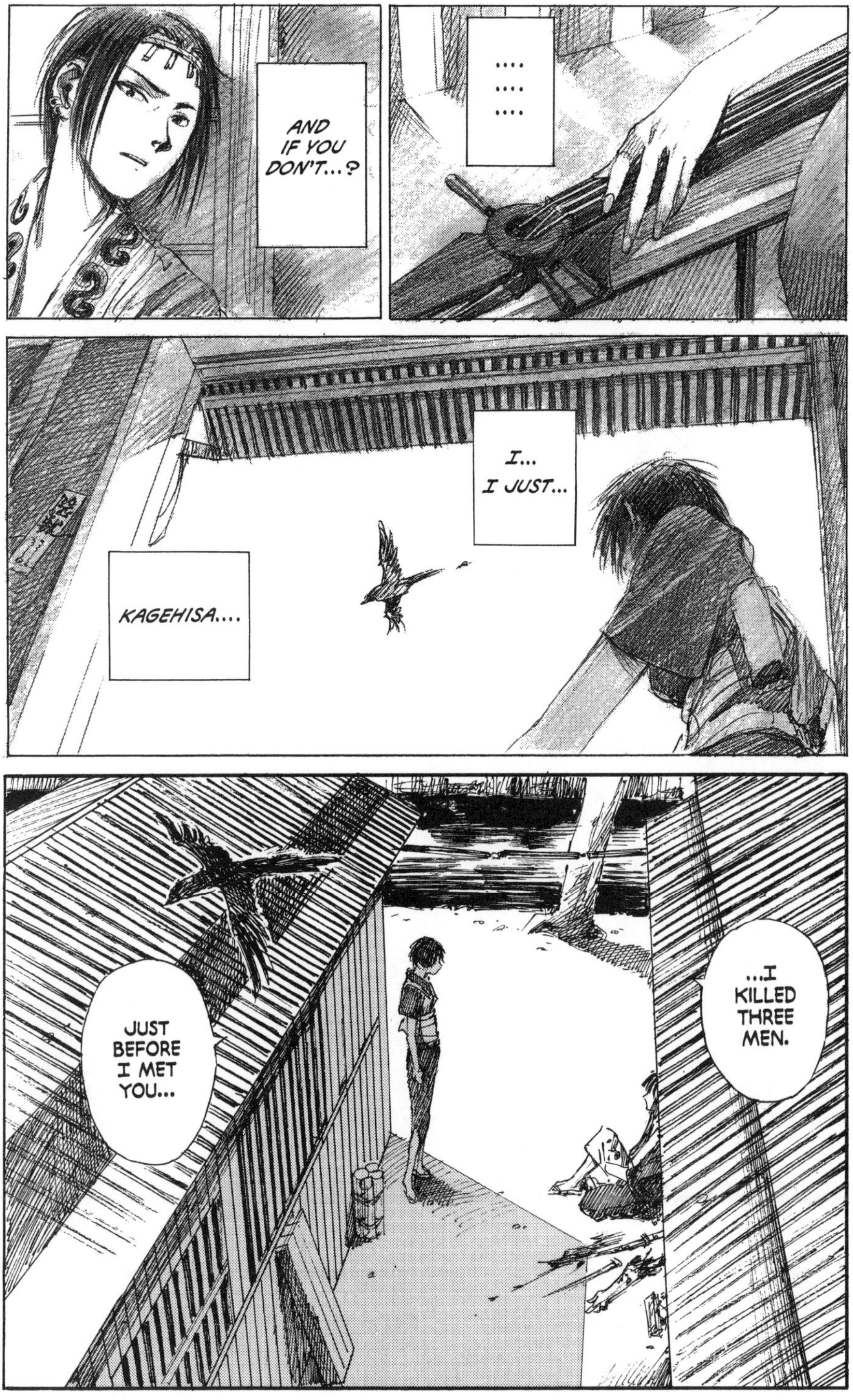
AND IF YOU DON'T...?
....
....
....
KAGEHISA....
I...
I JUST...
JUST BEFORE I MET YOU...
...I KILLED THREE MEN.

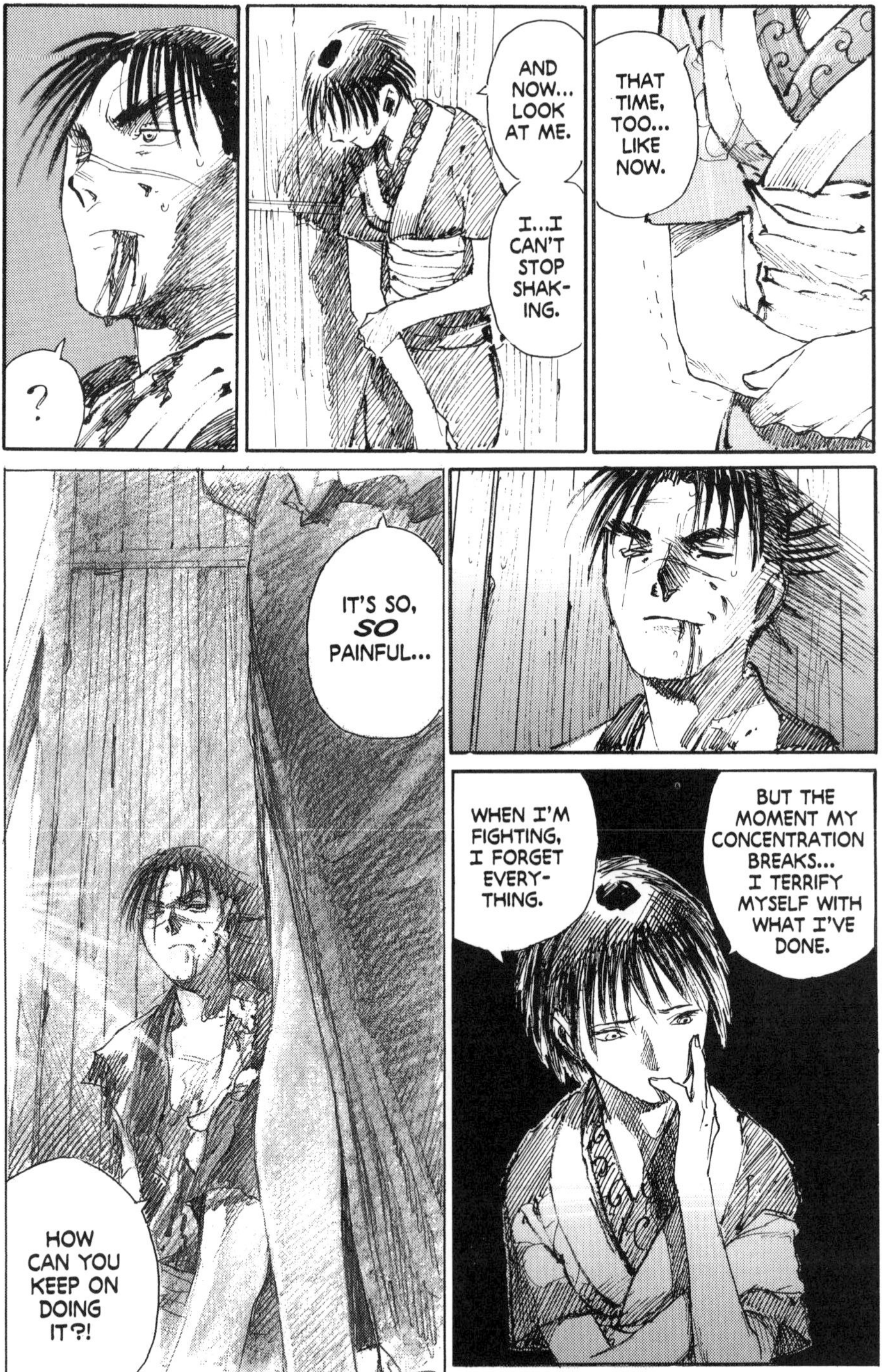
?
AND NOW... LOOK AT ME.
I...I CAN'T STOP SHAK-ING.
THAT TIME, TOO... LIKE NOW.
IT'S SO, *SO* PAINFUL...
HOW CAN YOU KEEP ON DOING IT?!
WHEN I'M FIGHTING, I FORGET EVERY-THING.
BUT THE MOMENT MY CONCENTRATION BREAKS... I TERRIFY MYSELF WITH WHAT I'VE DONE.

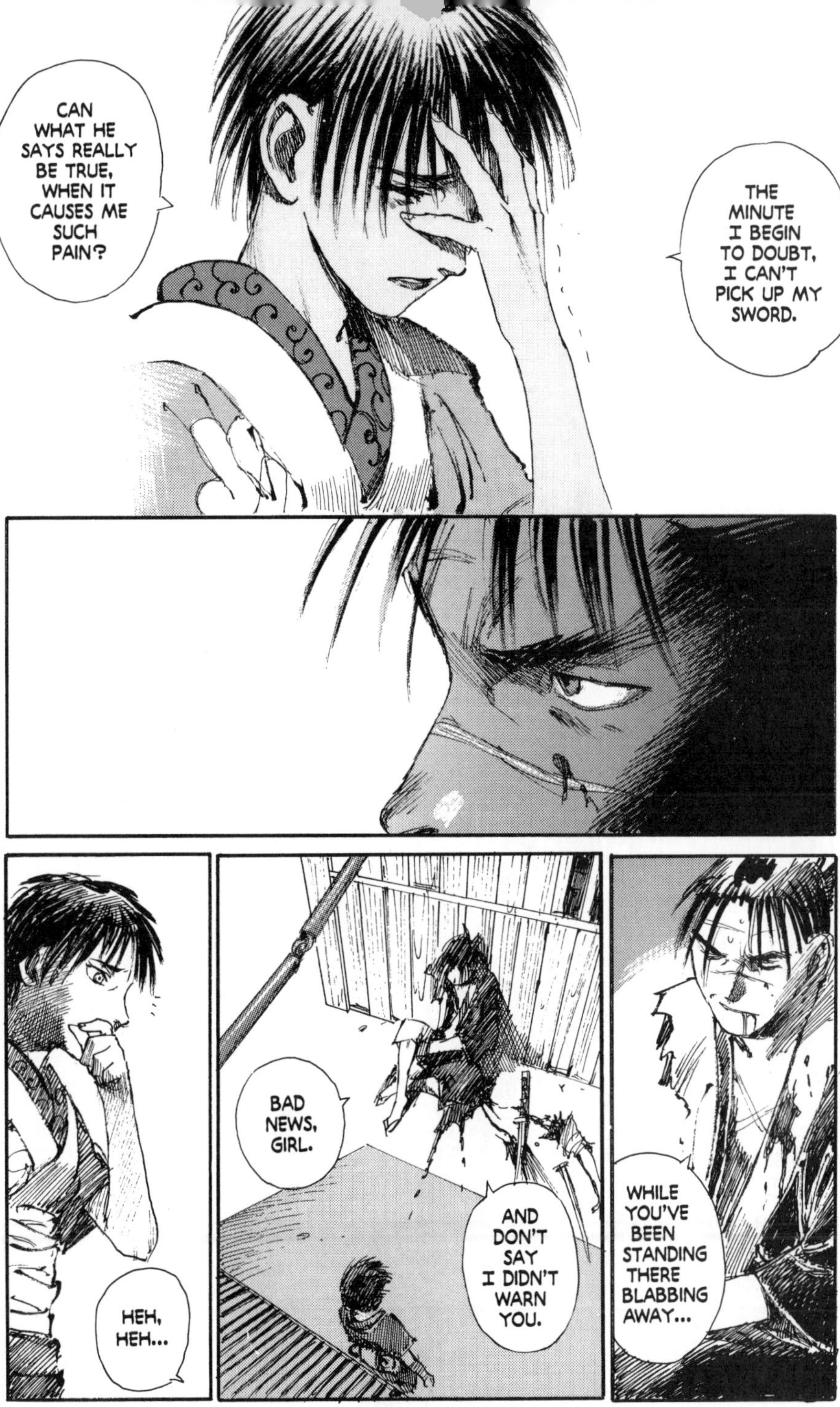
CAN WHAT HE SAYS REALLY BE TRUE, WHEN IT CAUSES ME SUCH PAIN?
THE MINUTE I BEGIN TO DOUBT, I CAN'T PICK UP MY SWORD.
HEH, HEH...
BAD NEWS, GIRL.
AND DON'T SAY I DIDN'T WARN YOU.
WHILE YOU'VE BEEN STANDING THERE BLABBING AWAY...

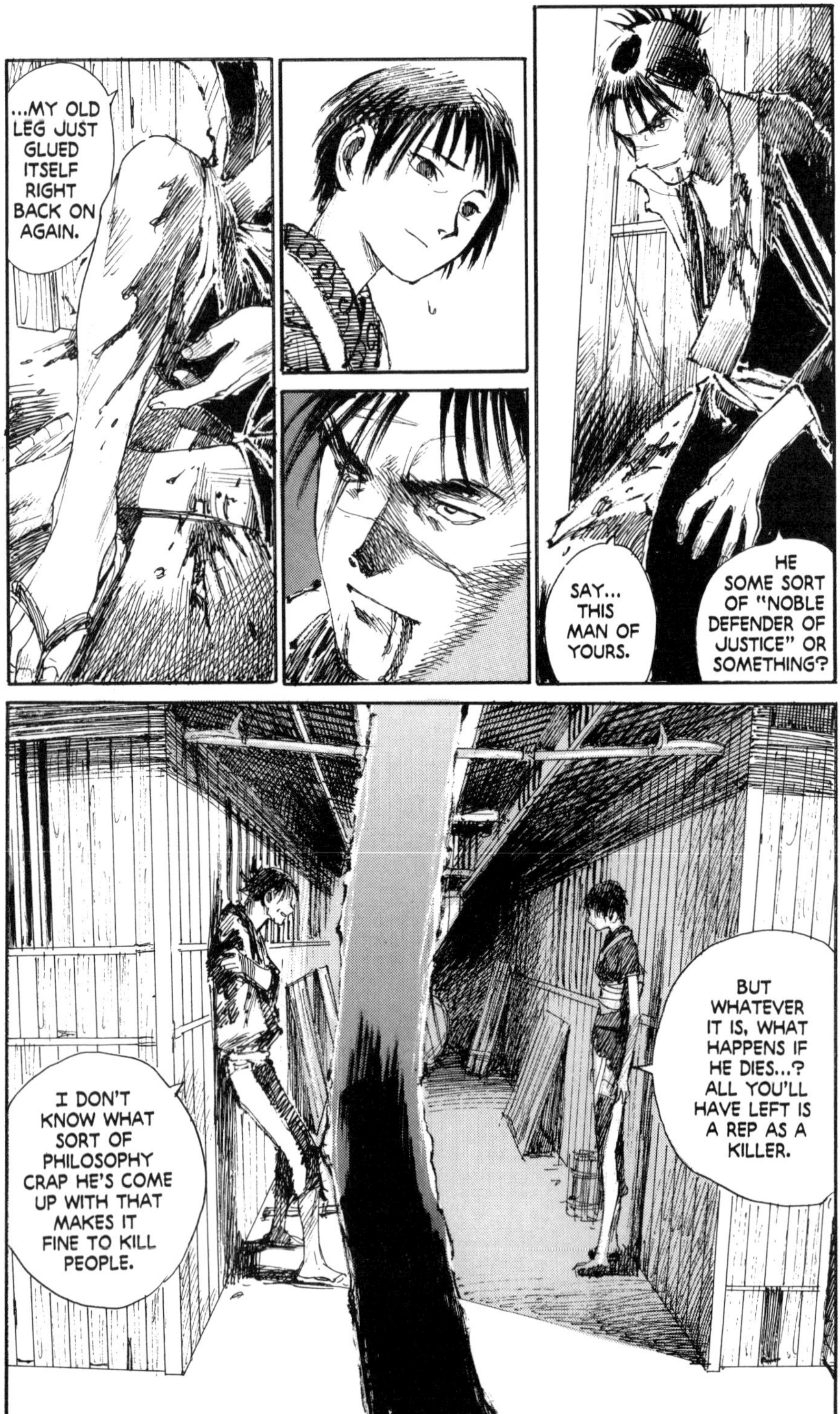
...MY OLD LEG JUST GLUED ITSELF RIGHT BACK ON AGAIN.
SAY... THIS MAN OF YOURS.
HE SOME SORT OF "NOBLE DEFENDER OF JUSTICE" OR SOMETHING?
I DON'T KNOW WHAT SORT OF PHILOSOPHY CRAP HE'S COME UP WITH THAT MAKES IT FINE TO KILL PEOPLE.
BUT WHATEVER IT IS, WHAT HAPPENS IF HE DIES...? ALL YOU'LL HAVE LEFT IS A REP AS A KILLER.

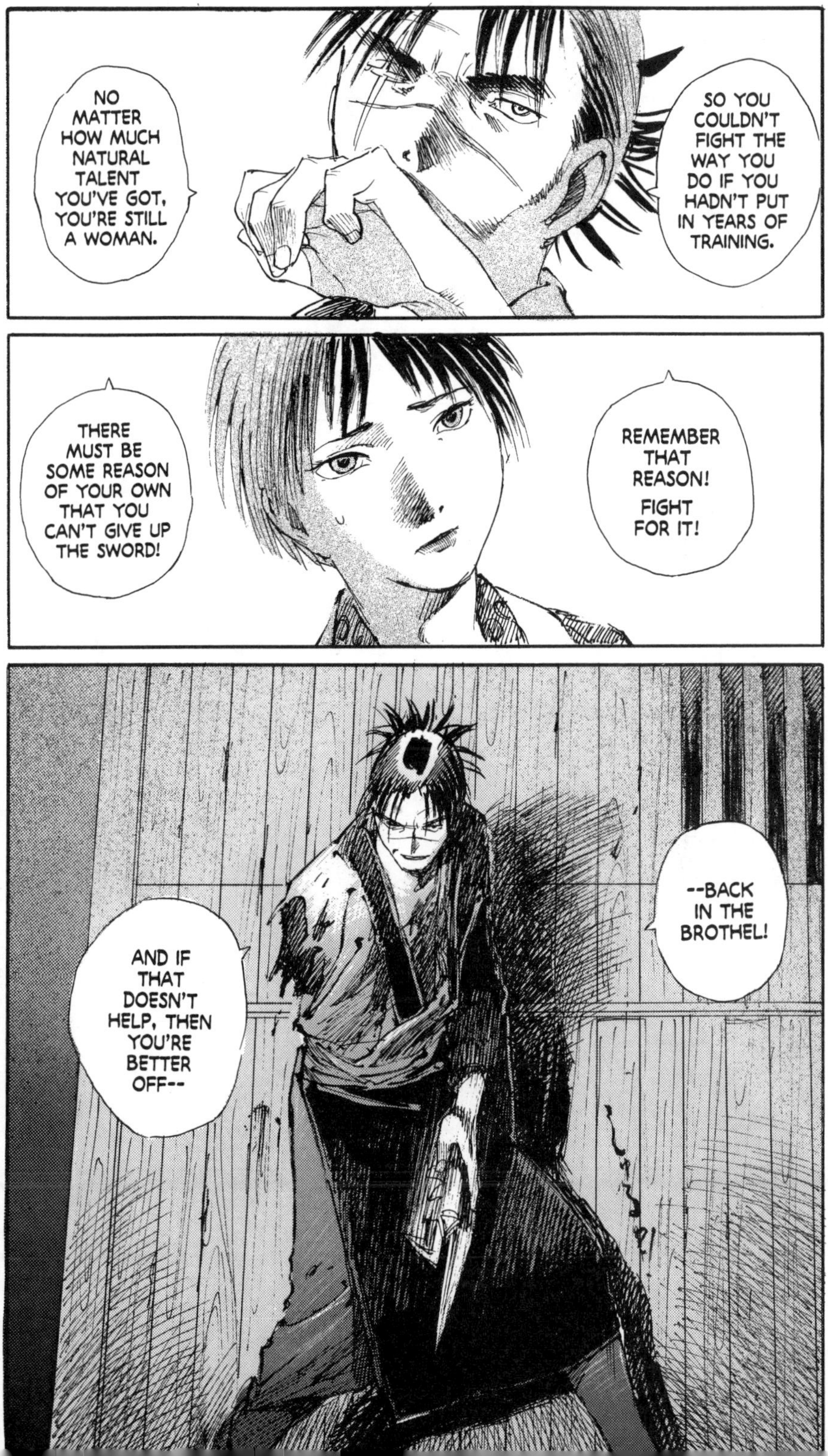
NO MATTER HOW MUCH NATURAL TALENT YOU'VE GOT, YOU'RE STILL A WOMAN.
SO YOU COULDN'T FIGHT THE WAY YOU DO IF YOU HADN'T PUT IN YEARS OF TRAINING.
THERE MUST BE SOME REASON OF YOUR OWN THAT YOU CAN'T GIVE UP THE SWORD!
REMEMBER THAT REASON!
FIGHT FOR IT!
AND IF THAT DOESN'T HELP, THEN YOU'RE BETTER OFF--
--BACK IN THE BROTHEL!

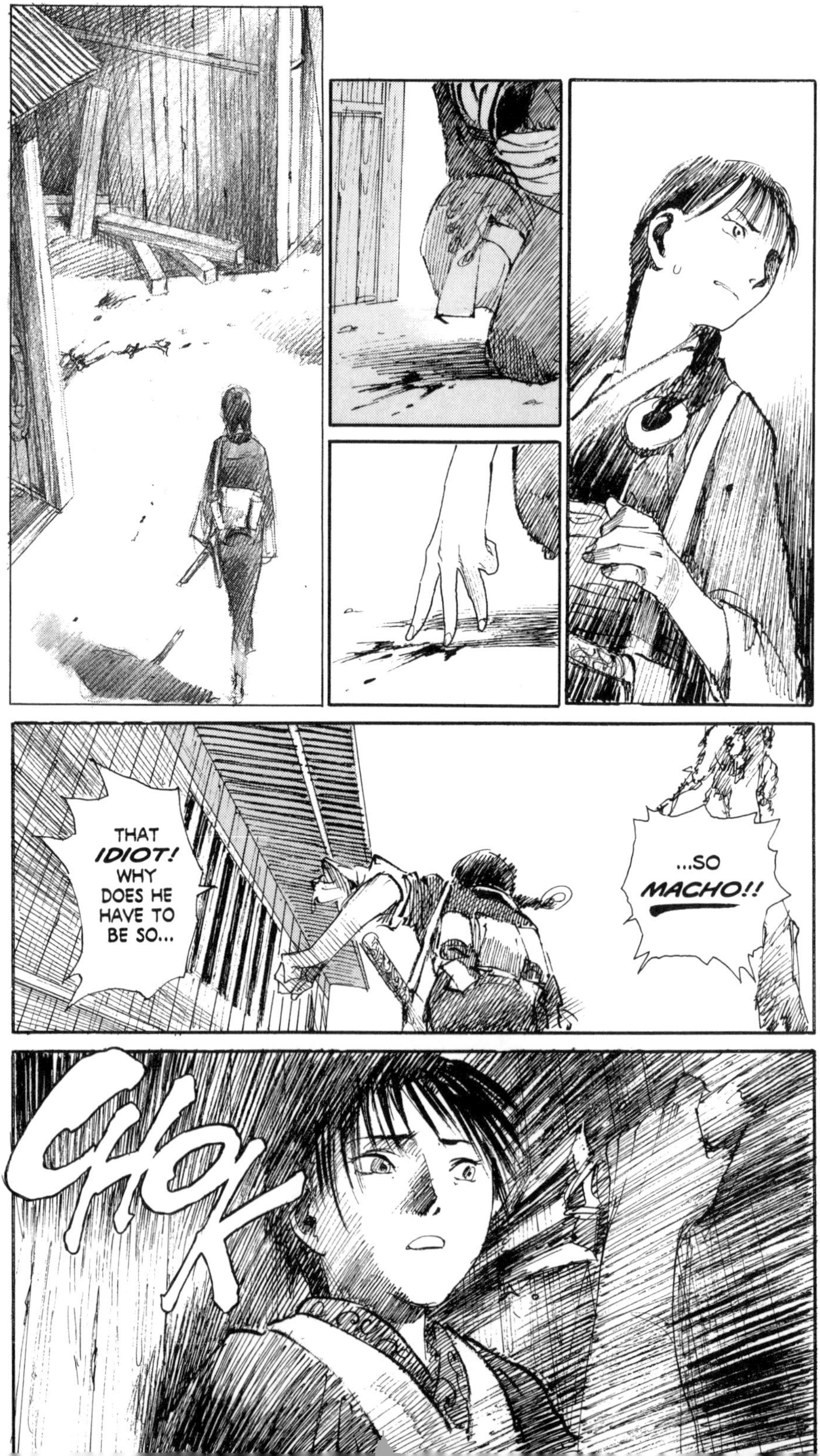
THAT IDIOT! WHY DOES HE HAVE TO BE SO...
...SO MACHO!!
CHAK

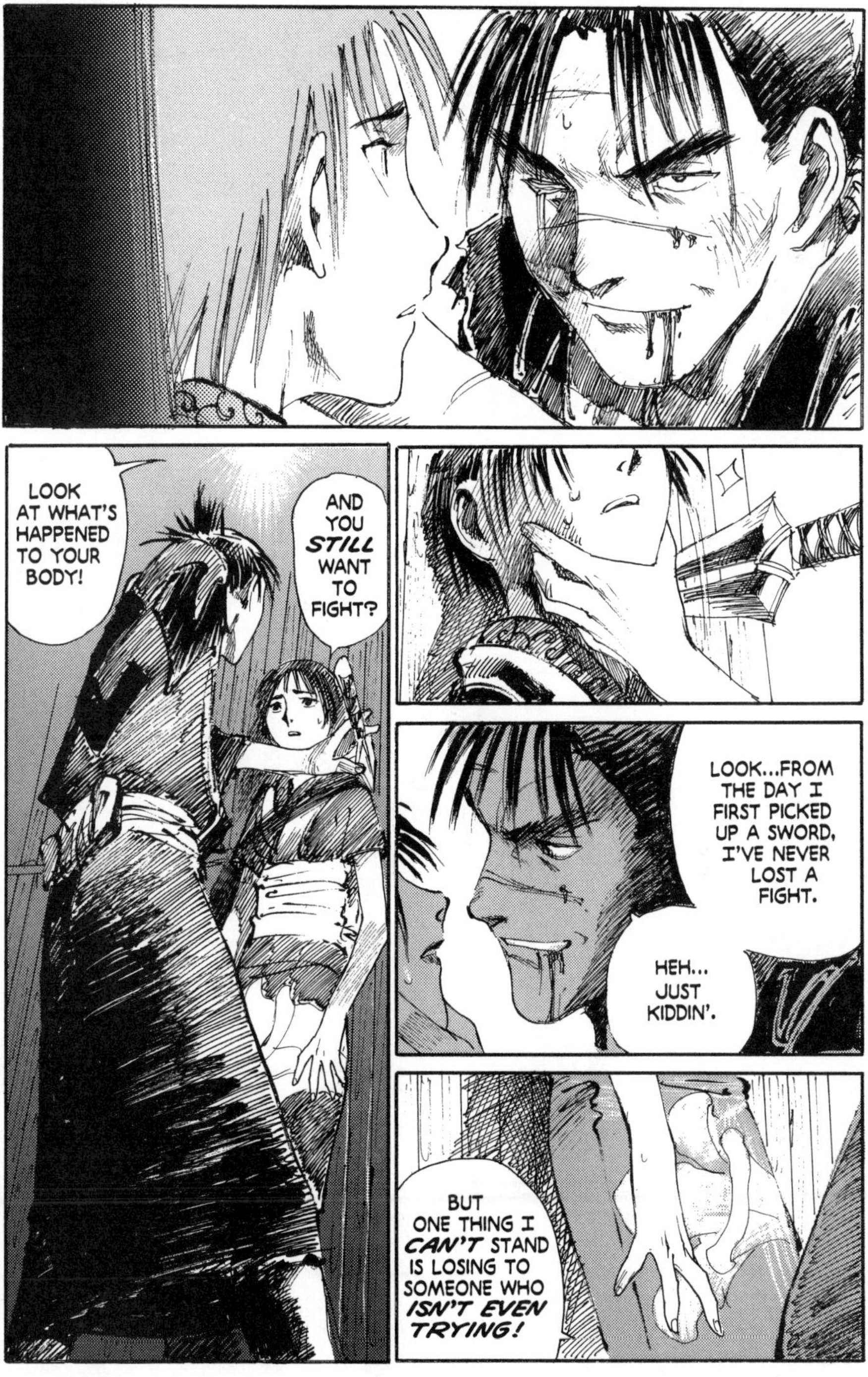
LOOK AT WHAT'S HAPPENED TO YOUR BODY!
AND YOU *STILL* WANT TO FIGHT?
LOOK...FROM THE DAY I FIRST PICKED UP A SWORD, I'VE NEVER LOST A FIGHT.
HEH... JUST KIDDIN'.
BUT ONE THING I *CAN'T* STAND IS LOSING TO SOMEONE WHO *ISN'T EVEN TRYING!*

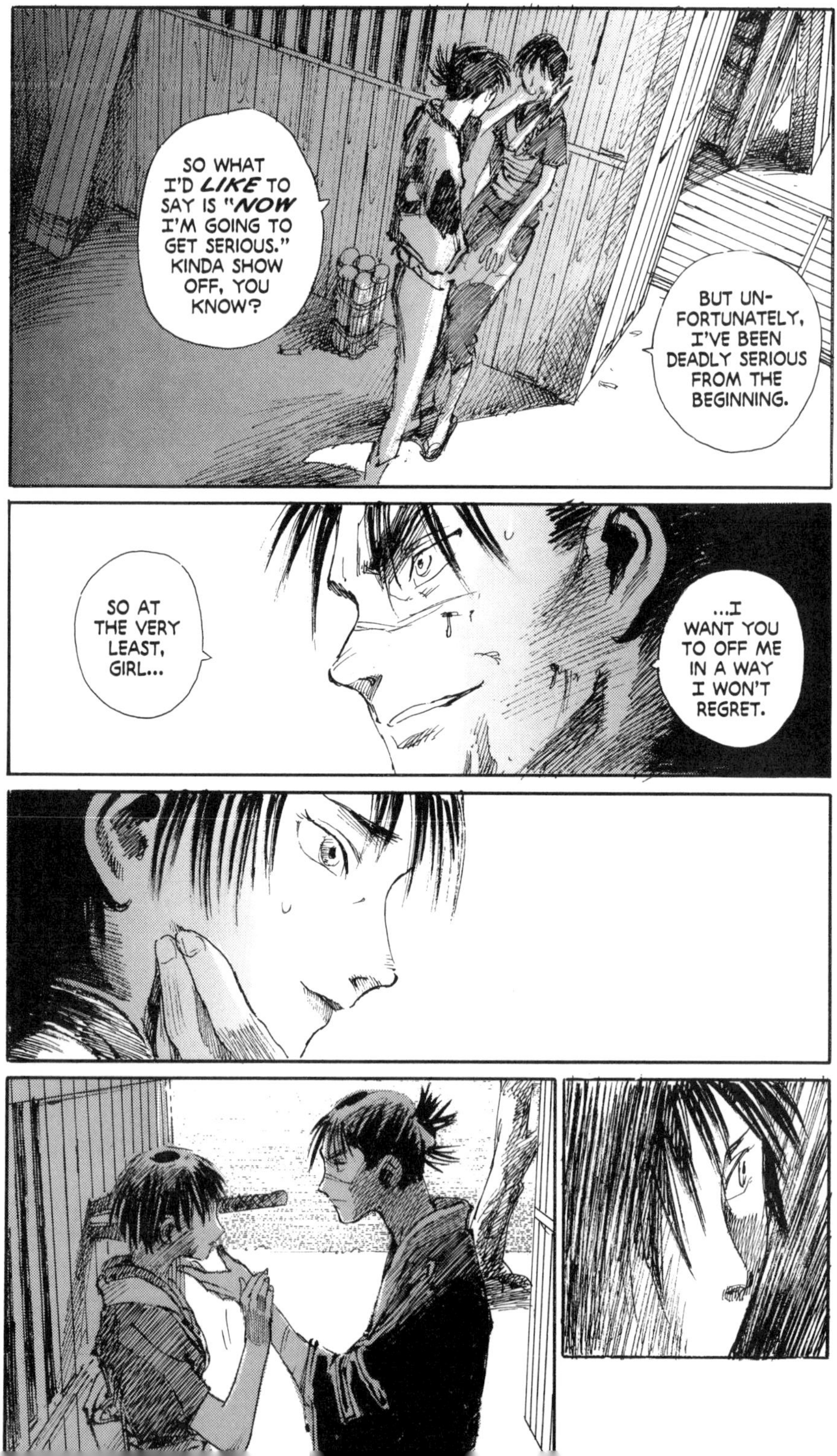
SO WHAT I'D *LIKE* TO SAY IS "*NOW* I'M GOING TO GET SERIOUS." KINDA SHOW OFF, YOU KNOW?
BUT UN-FORTUNATELY, I'VE BEEN DEADLY SERIOUS FROM THE BEGINNING.
SO AT THE VERY LEAST, GIRL...
...I WANT YOU TO OFF ME IN A WAY I WON'T REGRET.

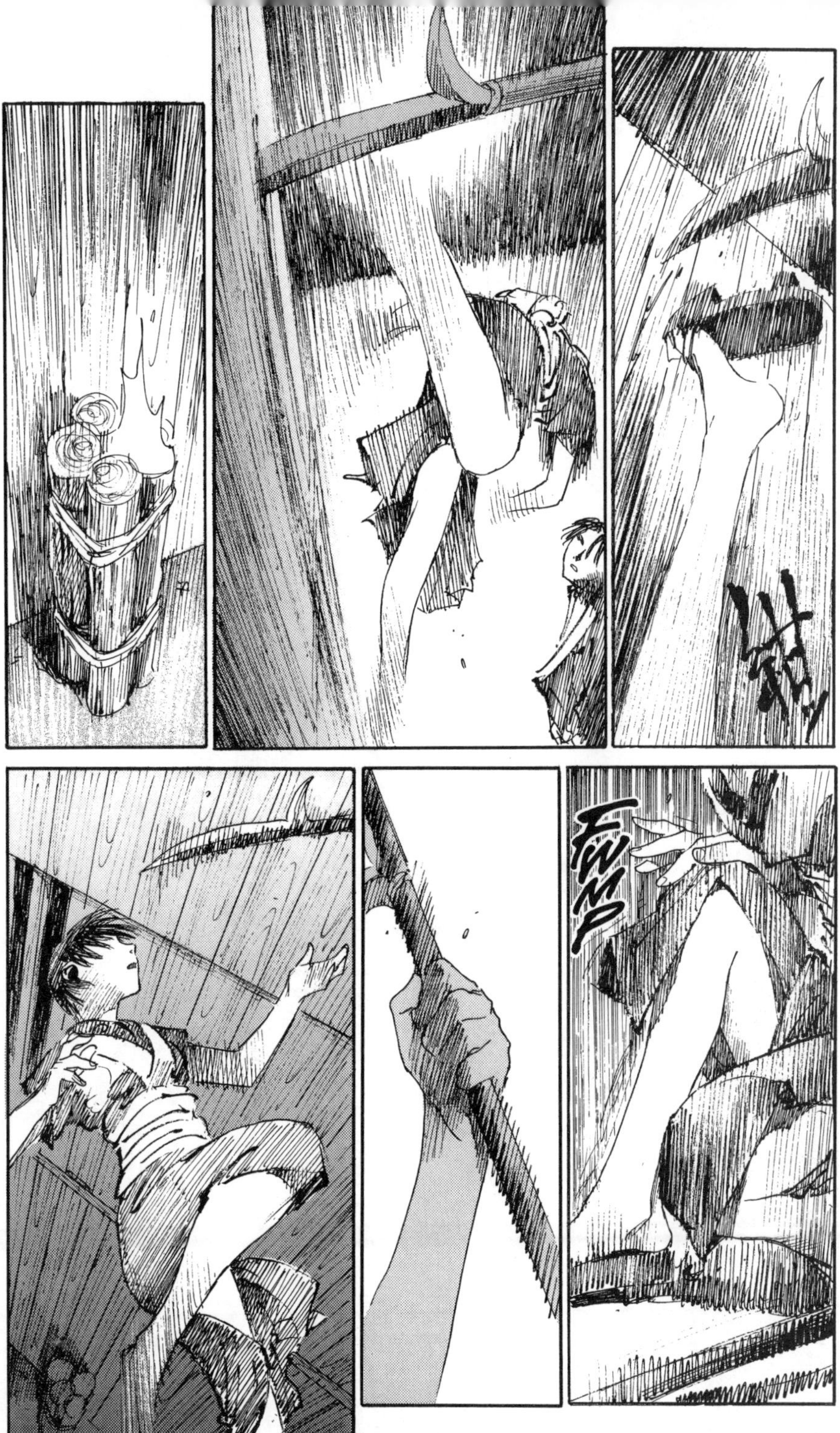
FWMP

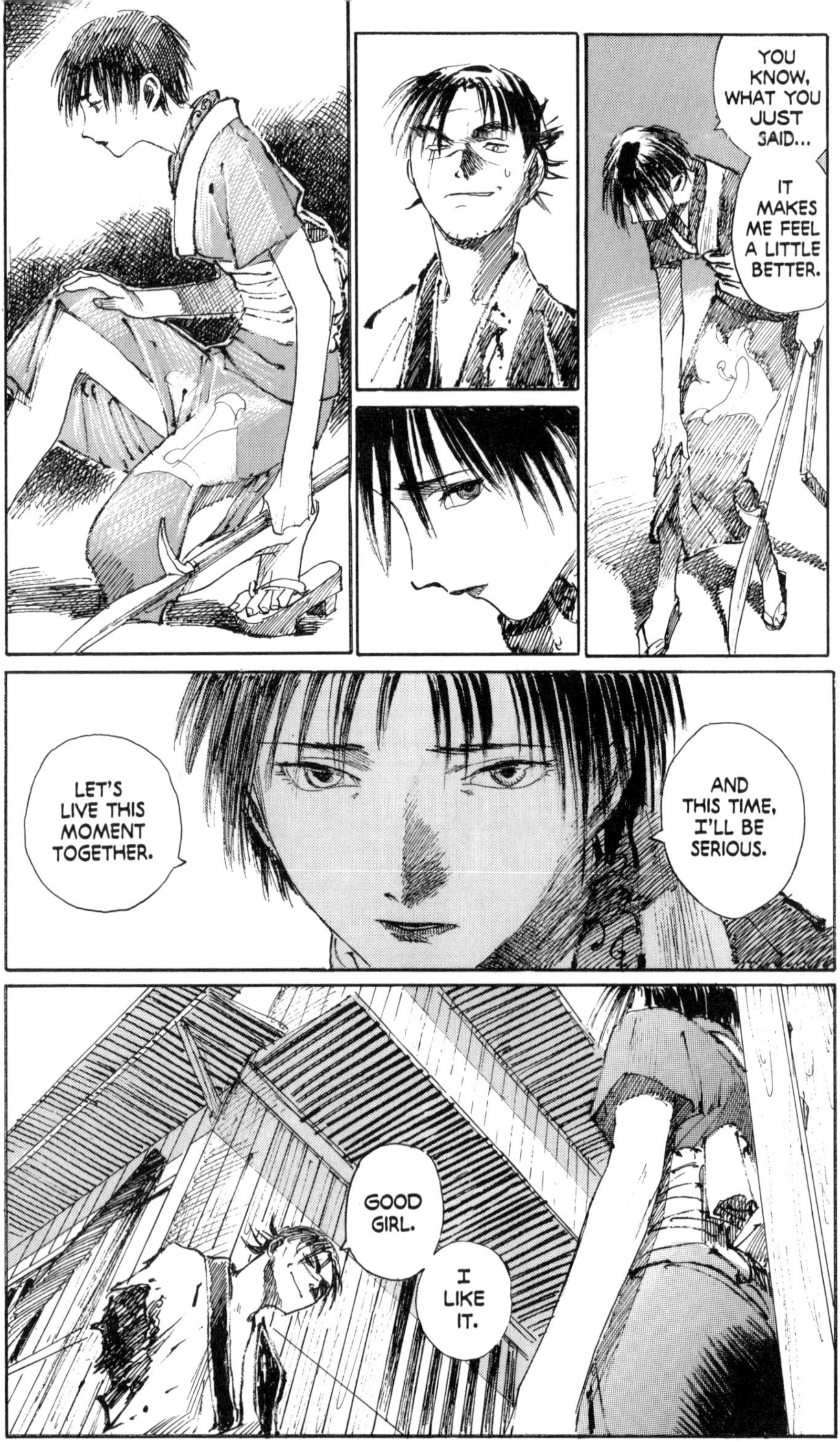
YOU KNOW, WHAT YOU JUST SAID...
IT MAKES ME FEEL A LITTLE BETTER.
LET'S LIVE THIS MOMENT TOGETHER.
AND THIS TIME, I'LL BE SERIOUS.
GOOD GIRL.
I LIKE IT.

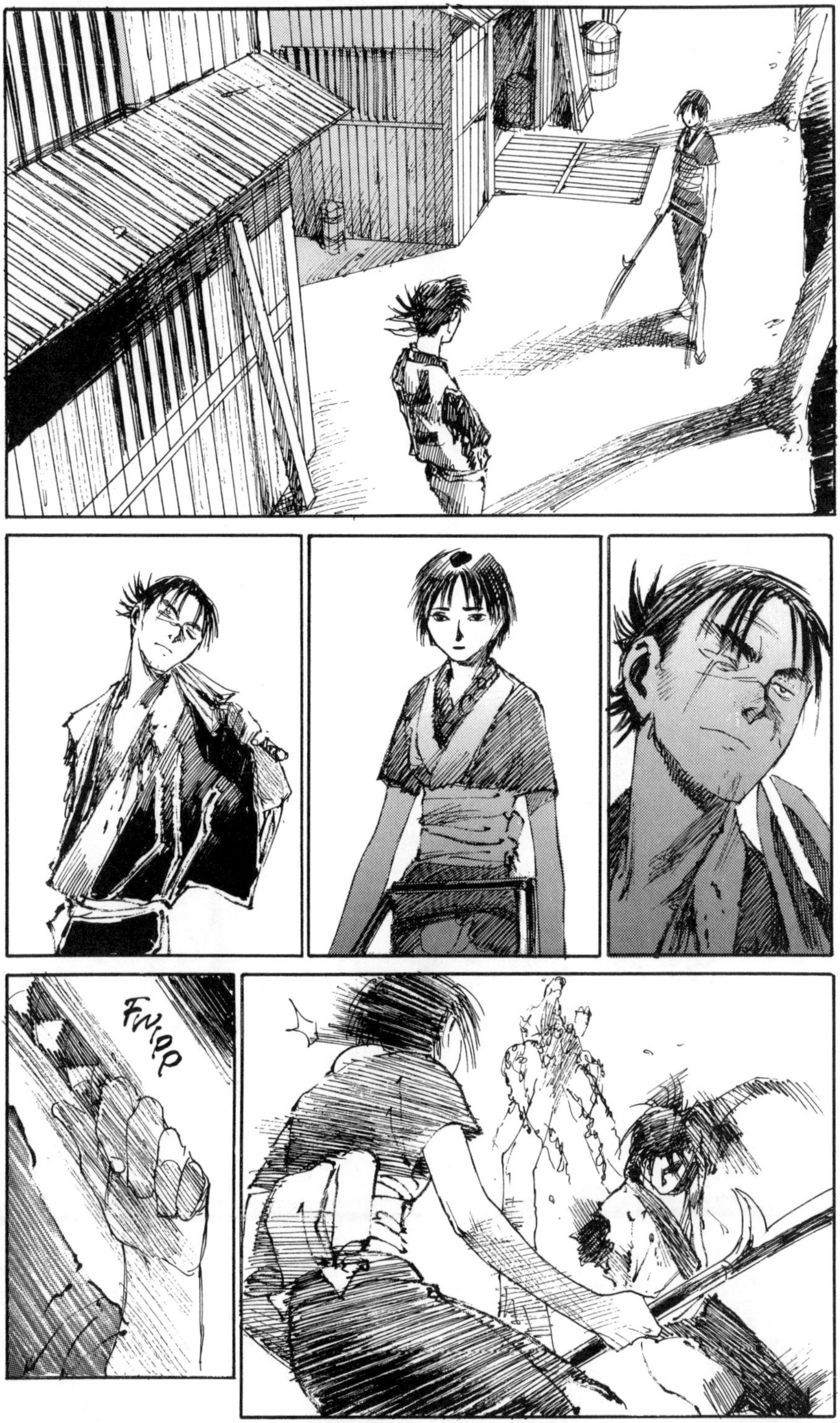
FWIPP

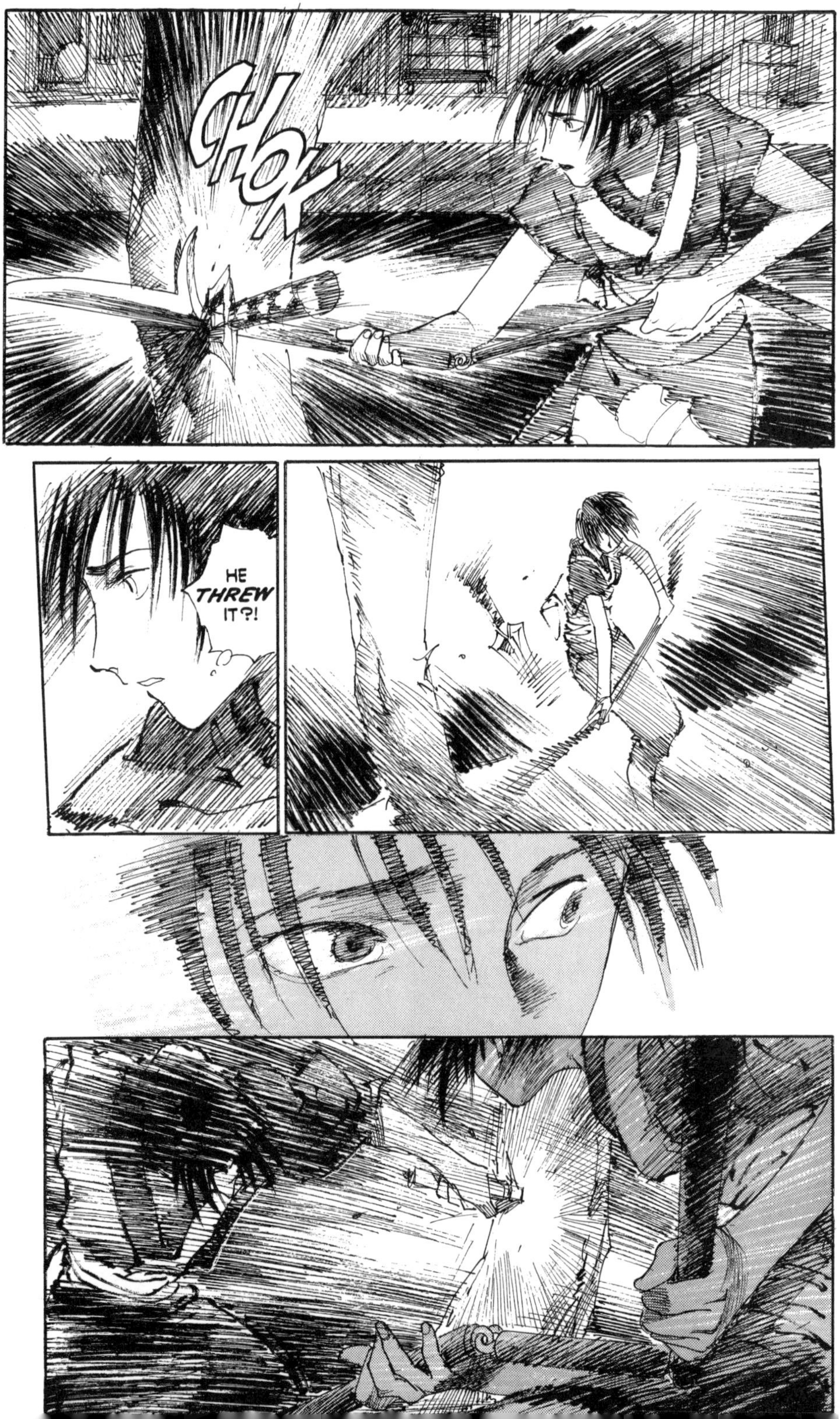
CHOK
HE THREW IT?!

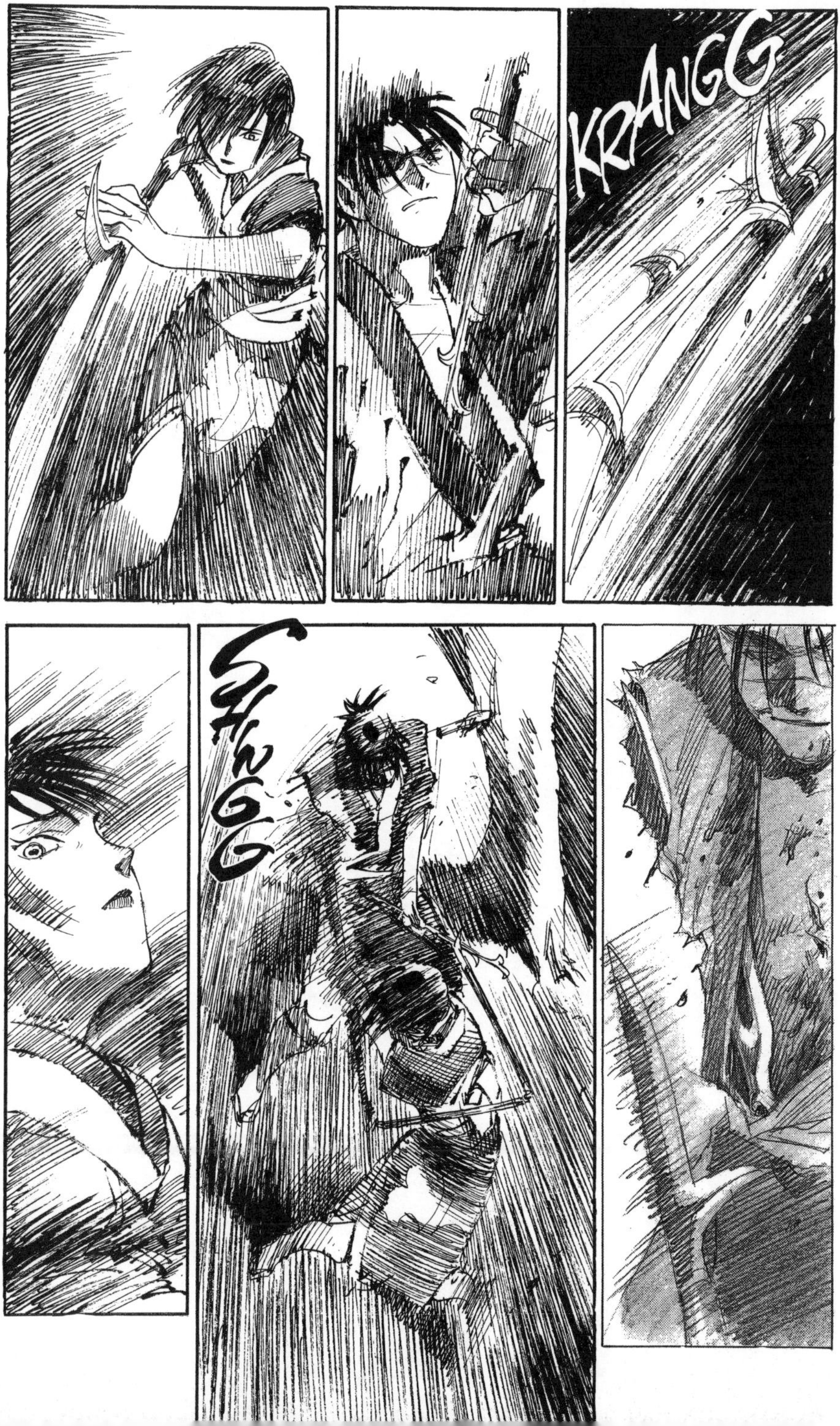
KRANGG
SHINGG

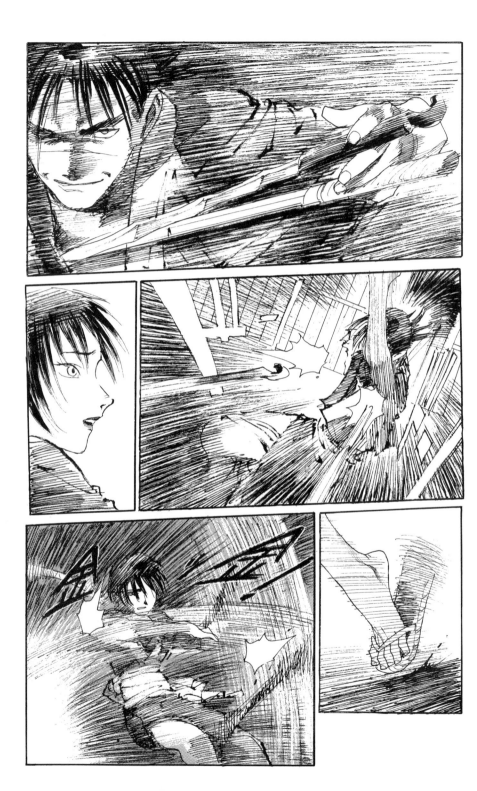

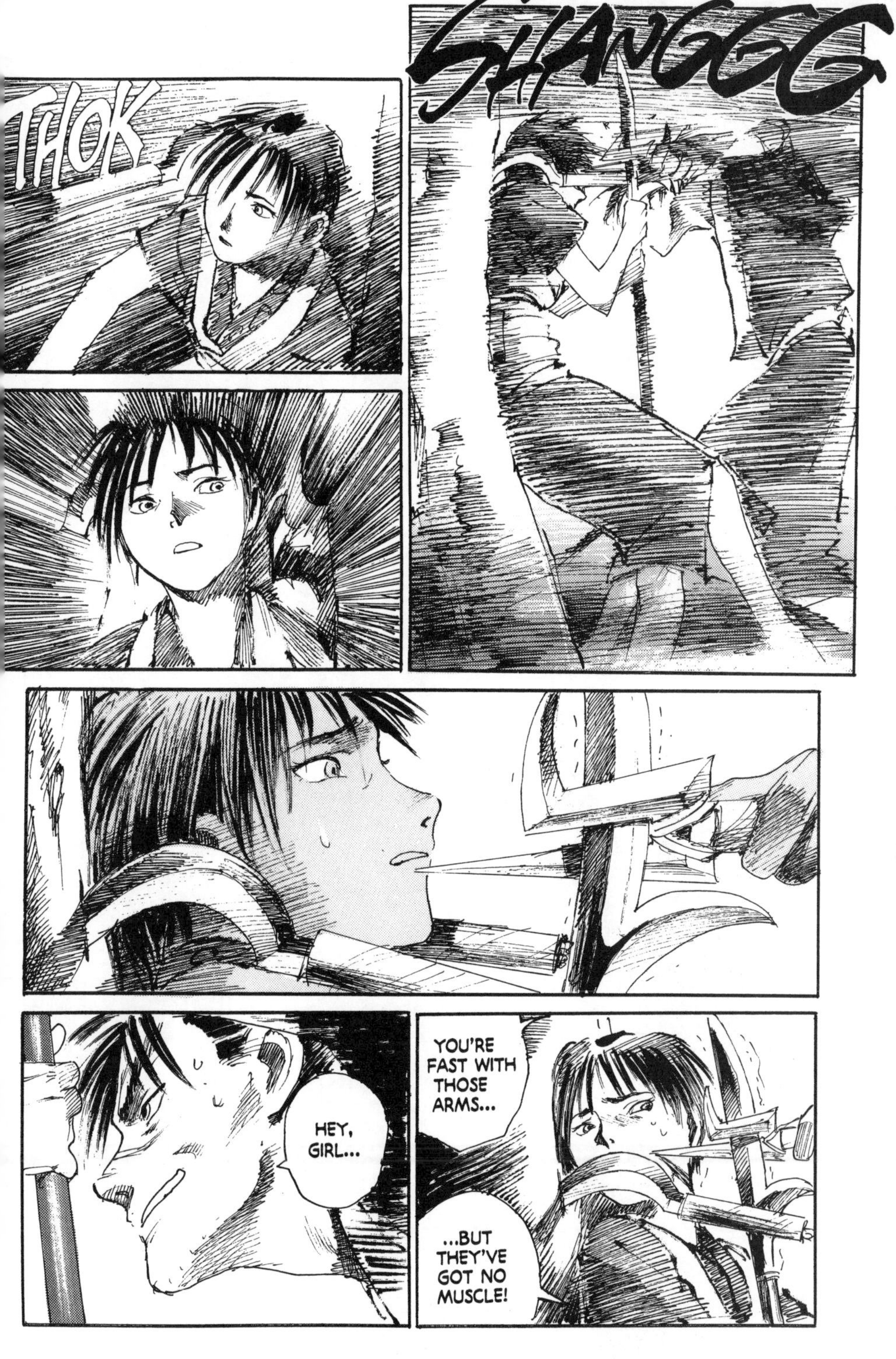
THOK
SHANGGG
HEY, GIRL...
YOU'RE FAST WITH THOSE ARMS...
...BUT THEY'VE GOT NO MUSCLE!

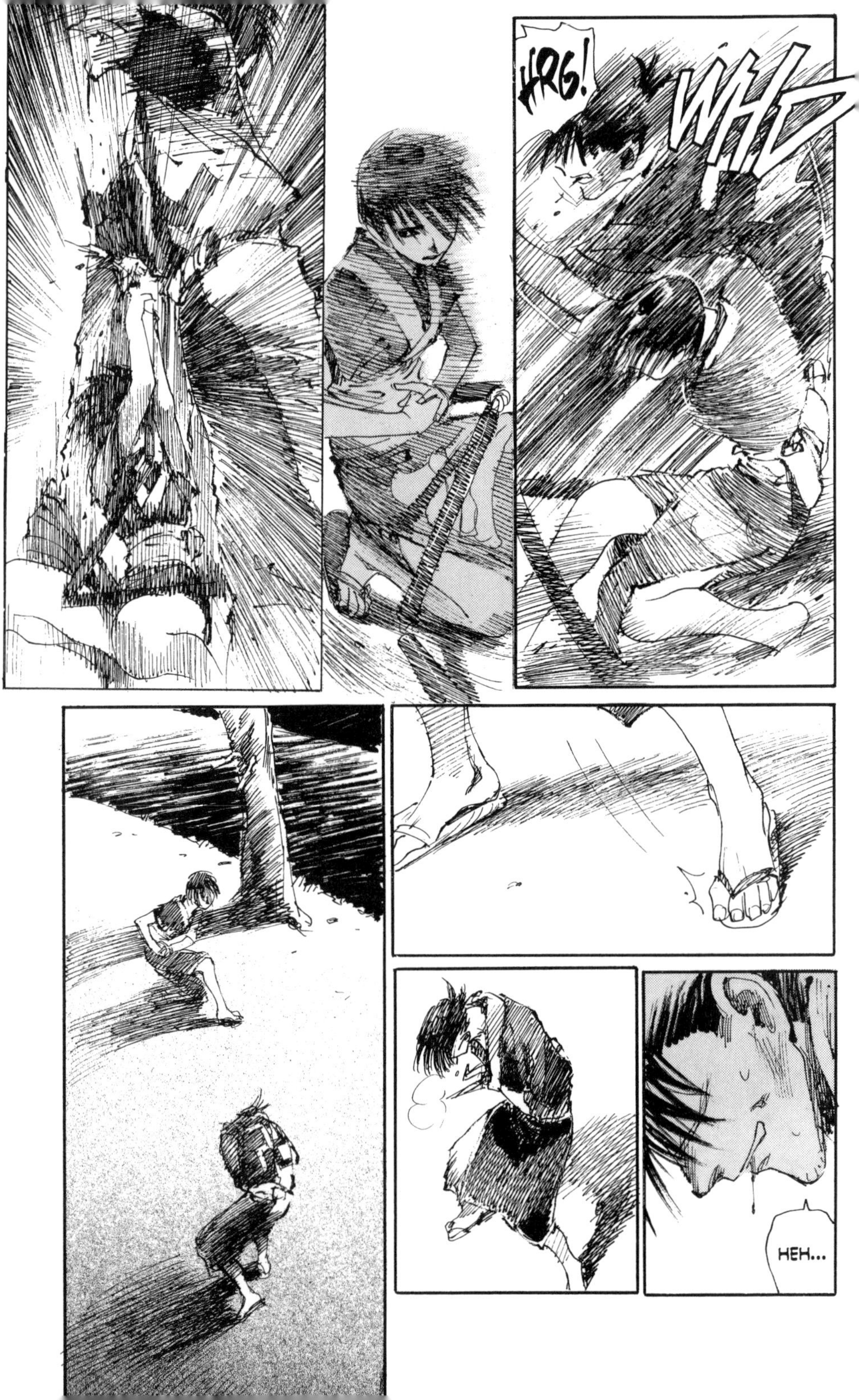
HRG!
WHD
HEH...

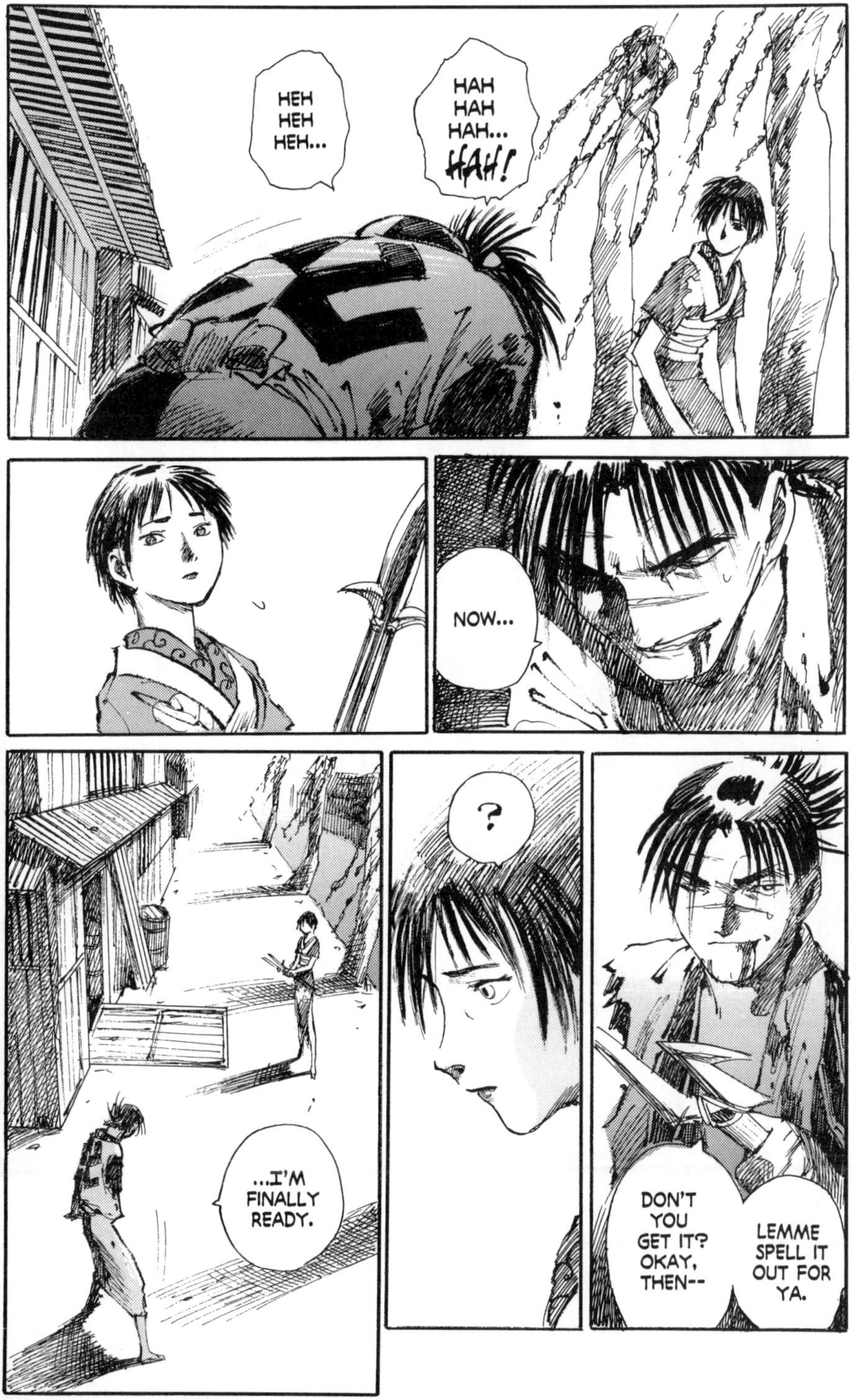
HEH HEH HEH...
HAH HAH HAH... HAH!
NOW...
...I'M FINALLY READY.
?
DON'T YOU GET IT? OKAY, THEN--
LEMME SPELL IT OUT FOR YA.

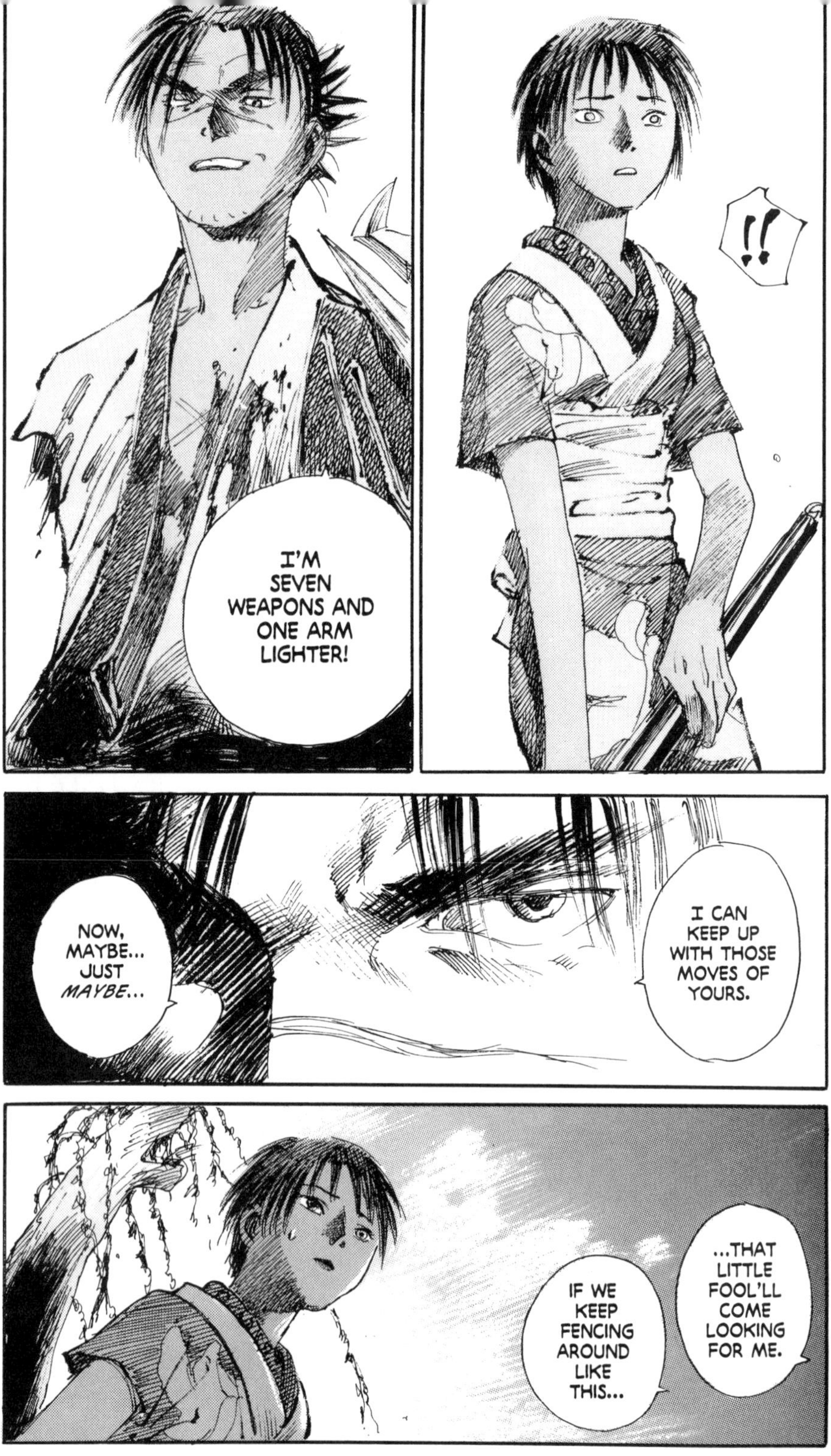
I'M SEVEN WEAPONS AND ONE ARM LIGHTER!
!!
NOW, MAYBE... JUST *MAYBE*...
I CAN KEEP UP WITH THOSE MOVES OF YOURS.
IF WE KEEP FENCING AROUND LIKE THIS...
...THAT LITTLE FOOL'LL COME LOOKING FOR ME.

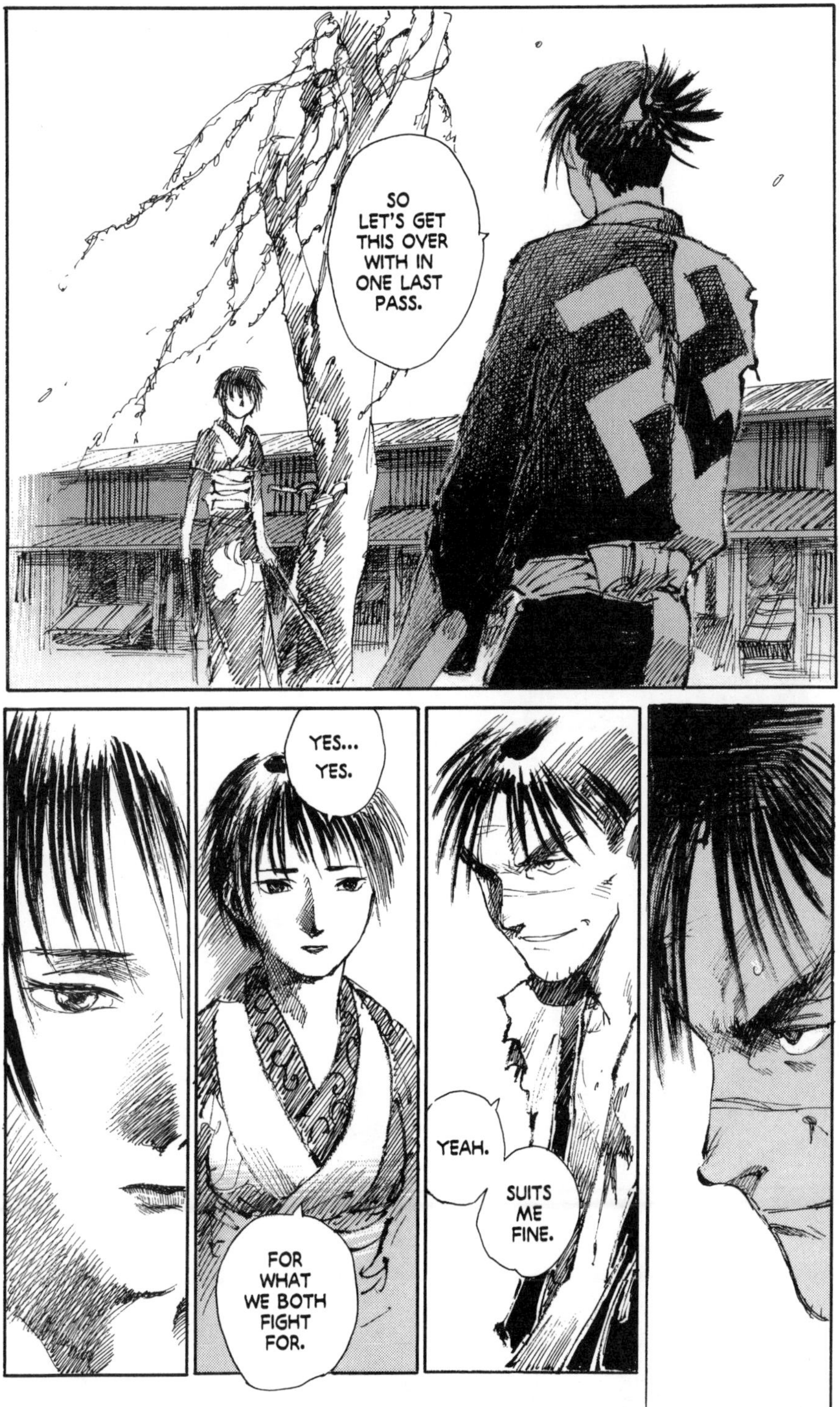
SO LET'S GET THIS OVER WITH IN ONE LAST PASS.
YES... YES.
FOR WHAT WE BOTH FIGHT FOR.
YEAH.
SUITS ME FINE.

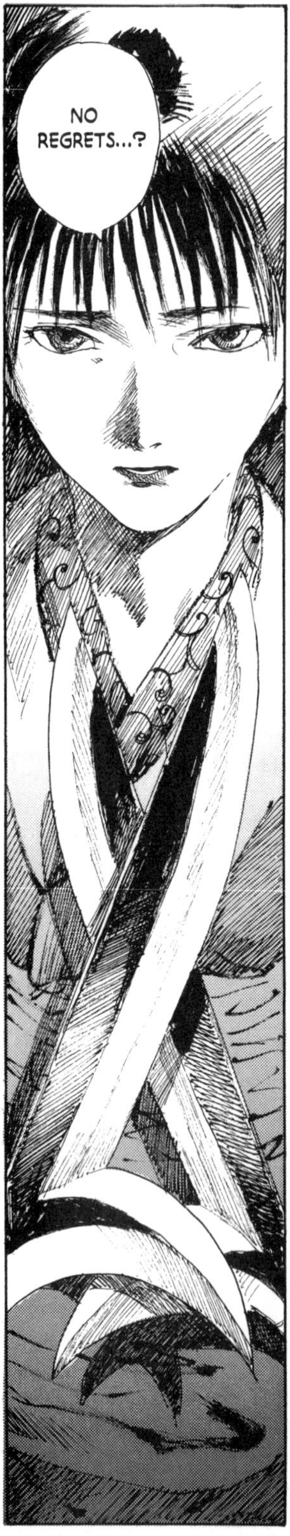
NO REGRETS...?
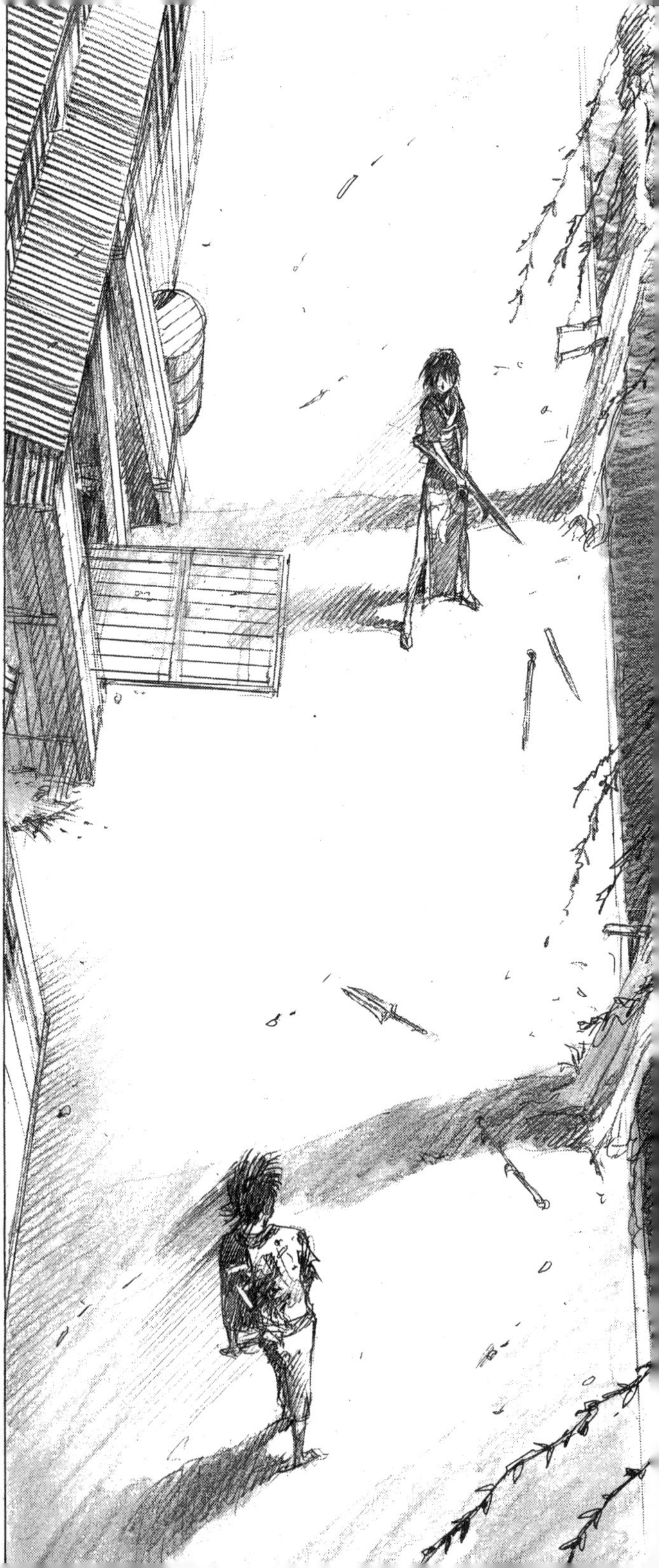

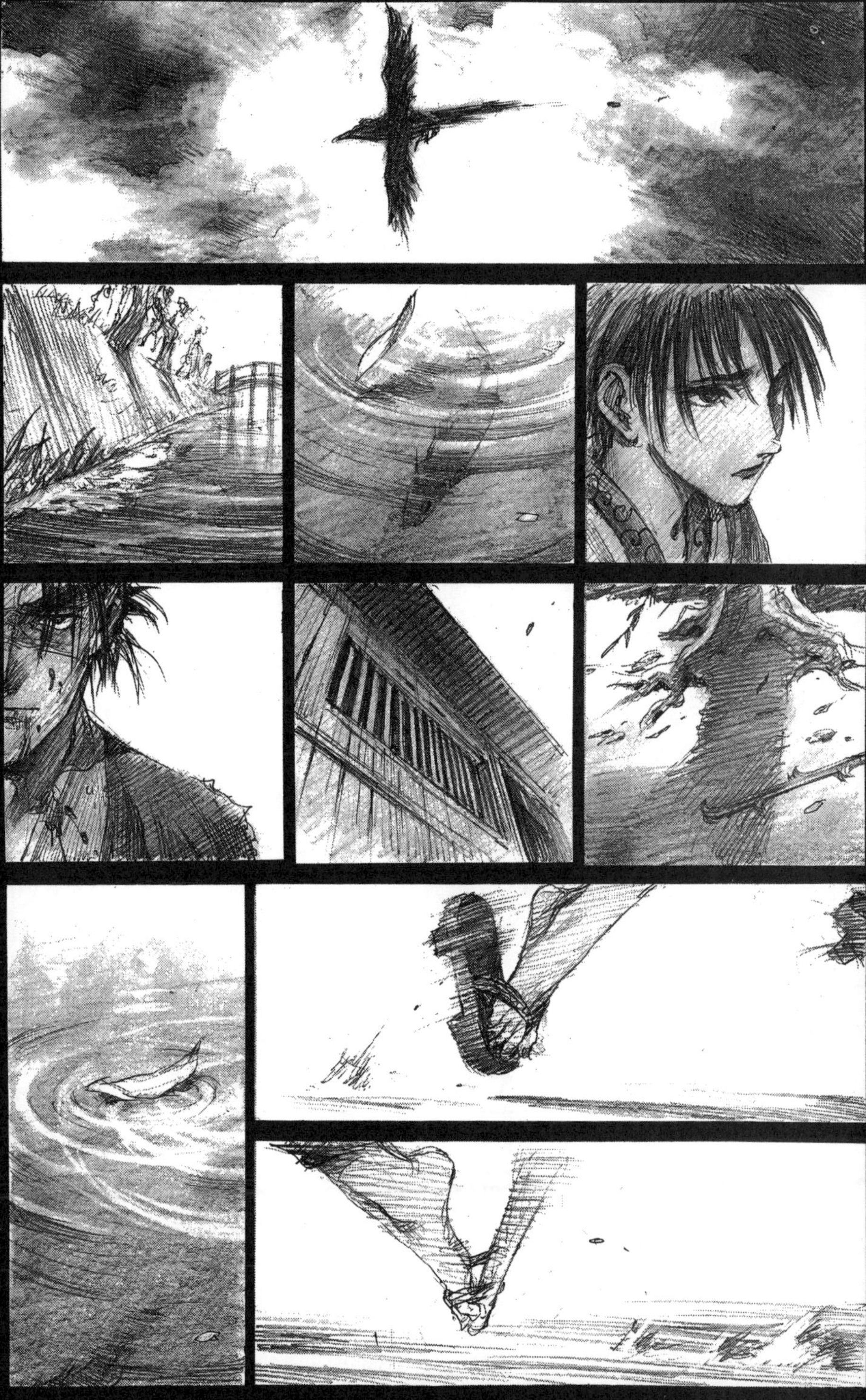

SHINNG

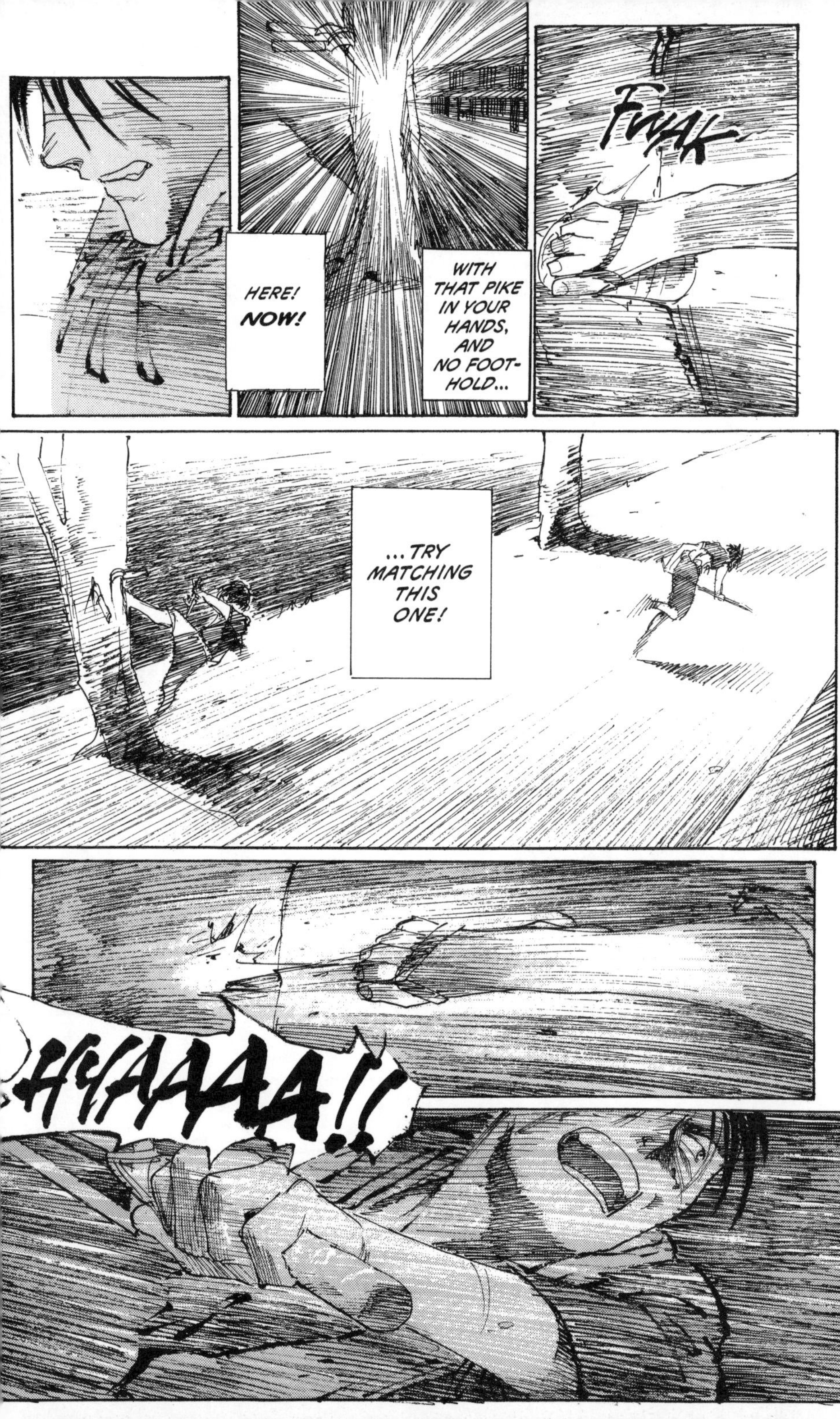
HERE! NOW!
WITH THAT PIKE IN YOUR HANDS, AND NO FOOT-HOLD...
FWAK
...TRY MATCHING THIS ONE!
HYAAAAA!!

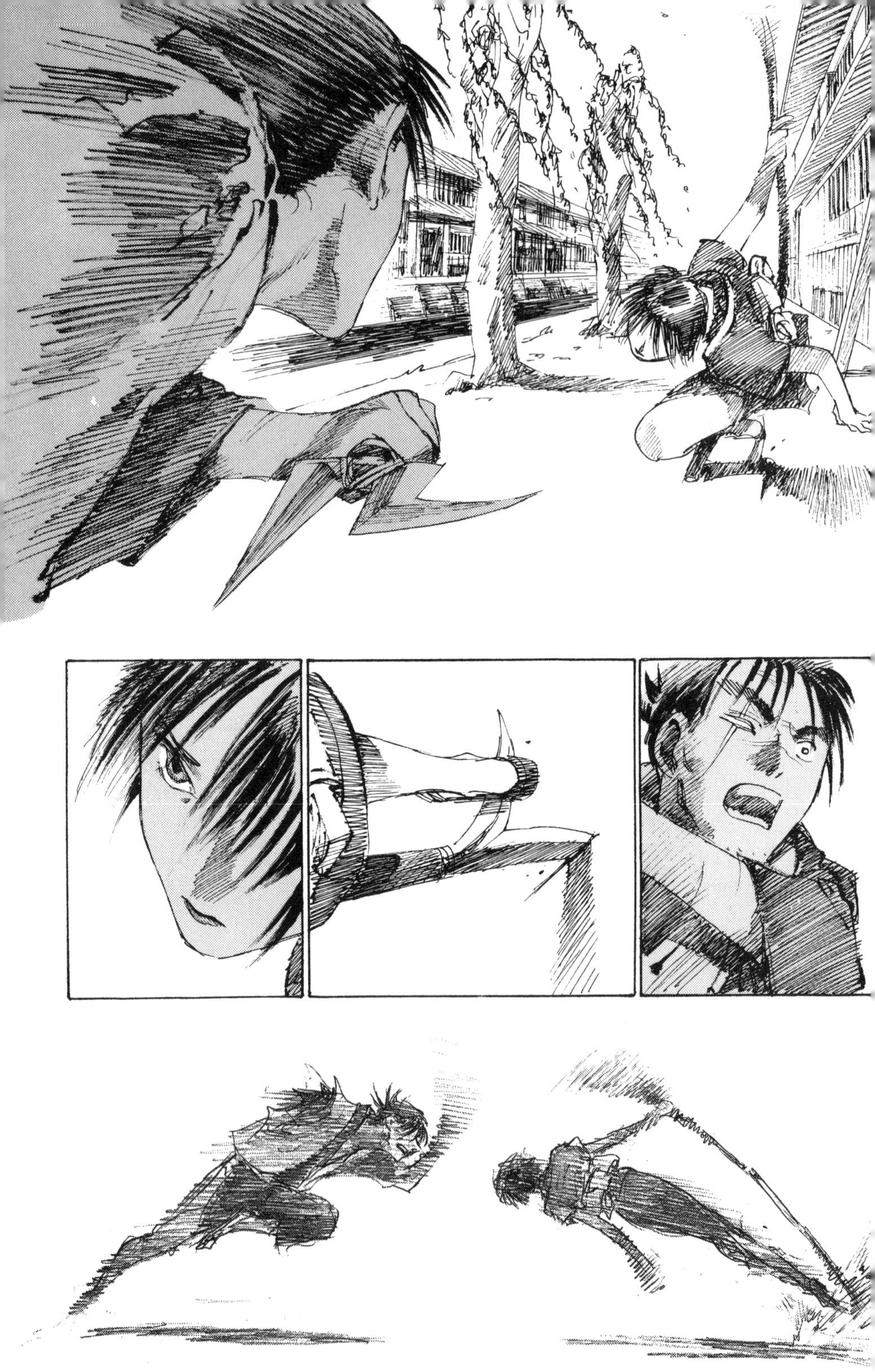

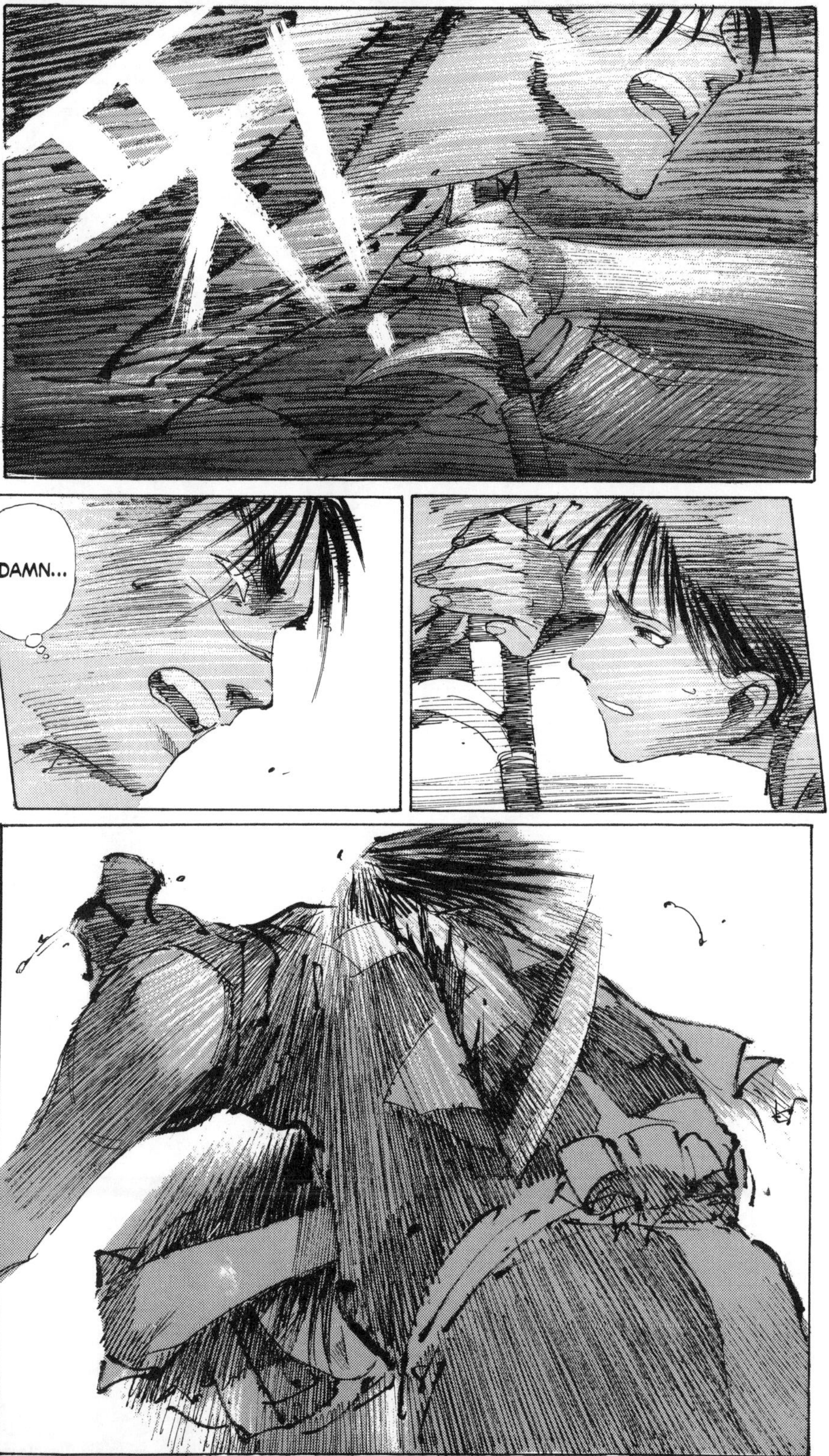
DAMN...

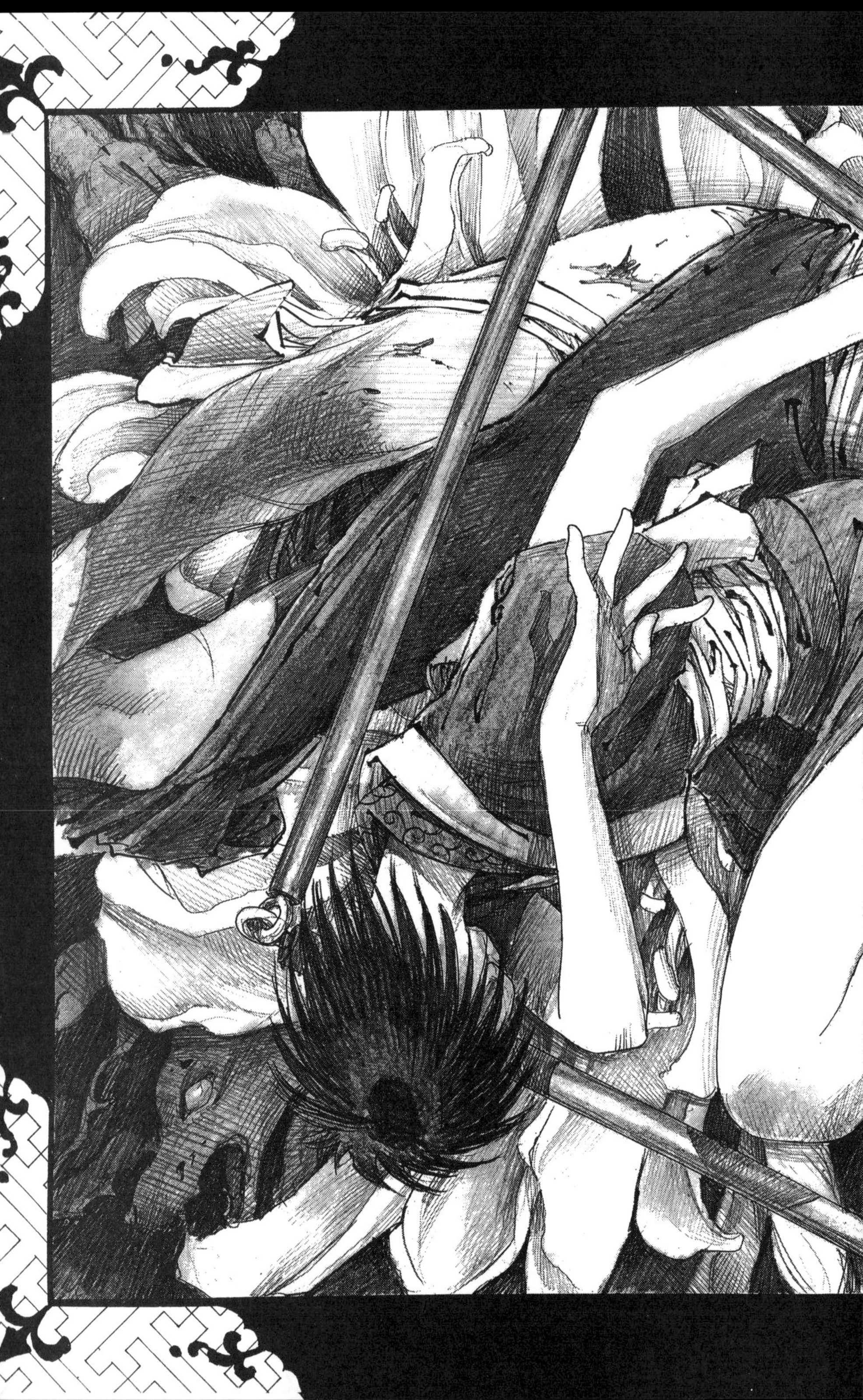

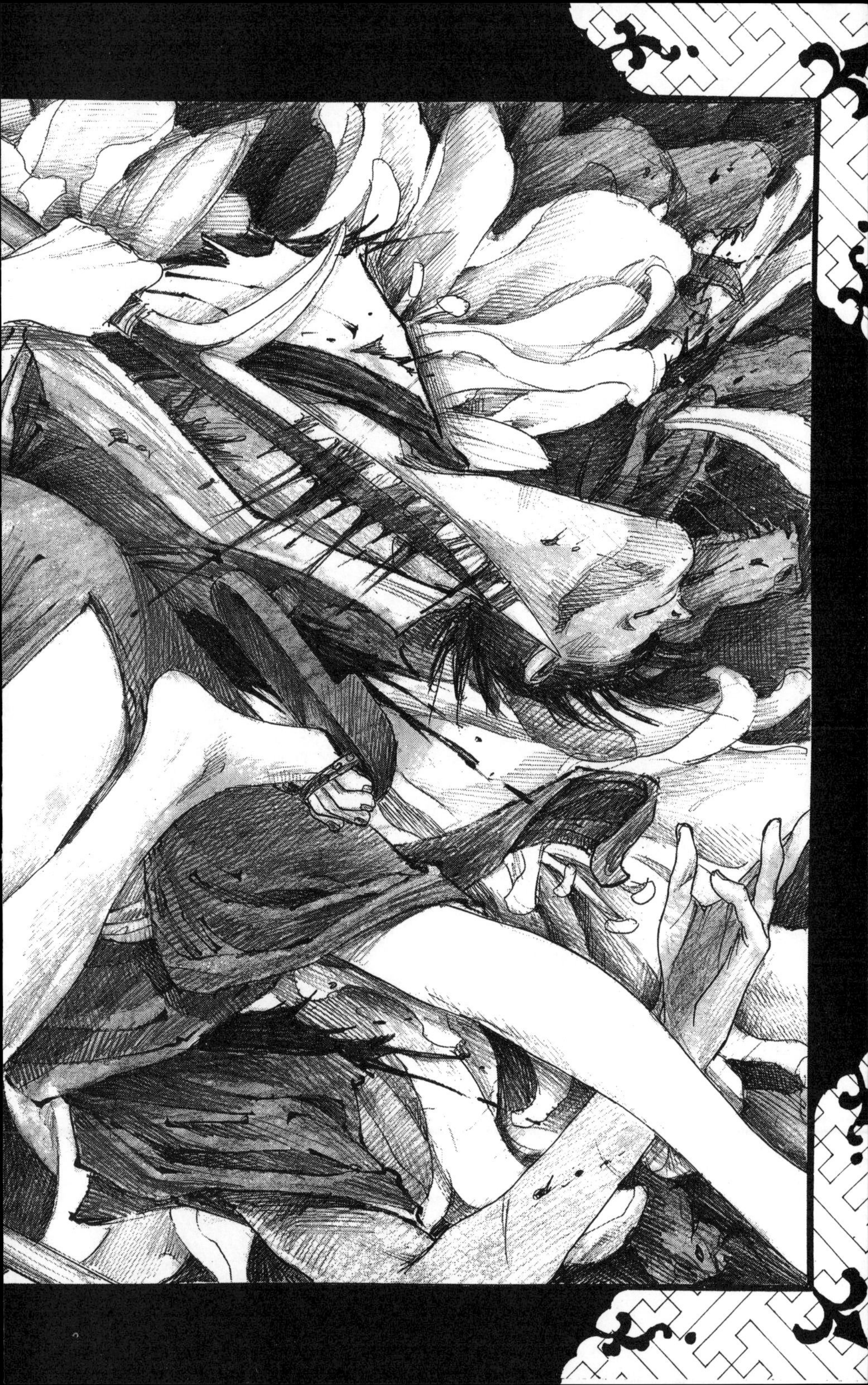

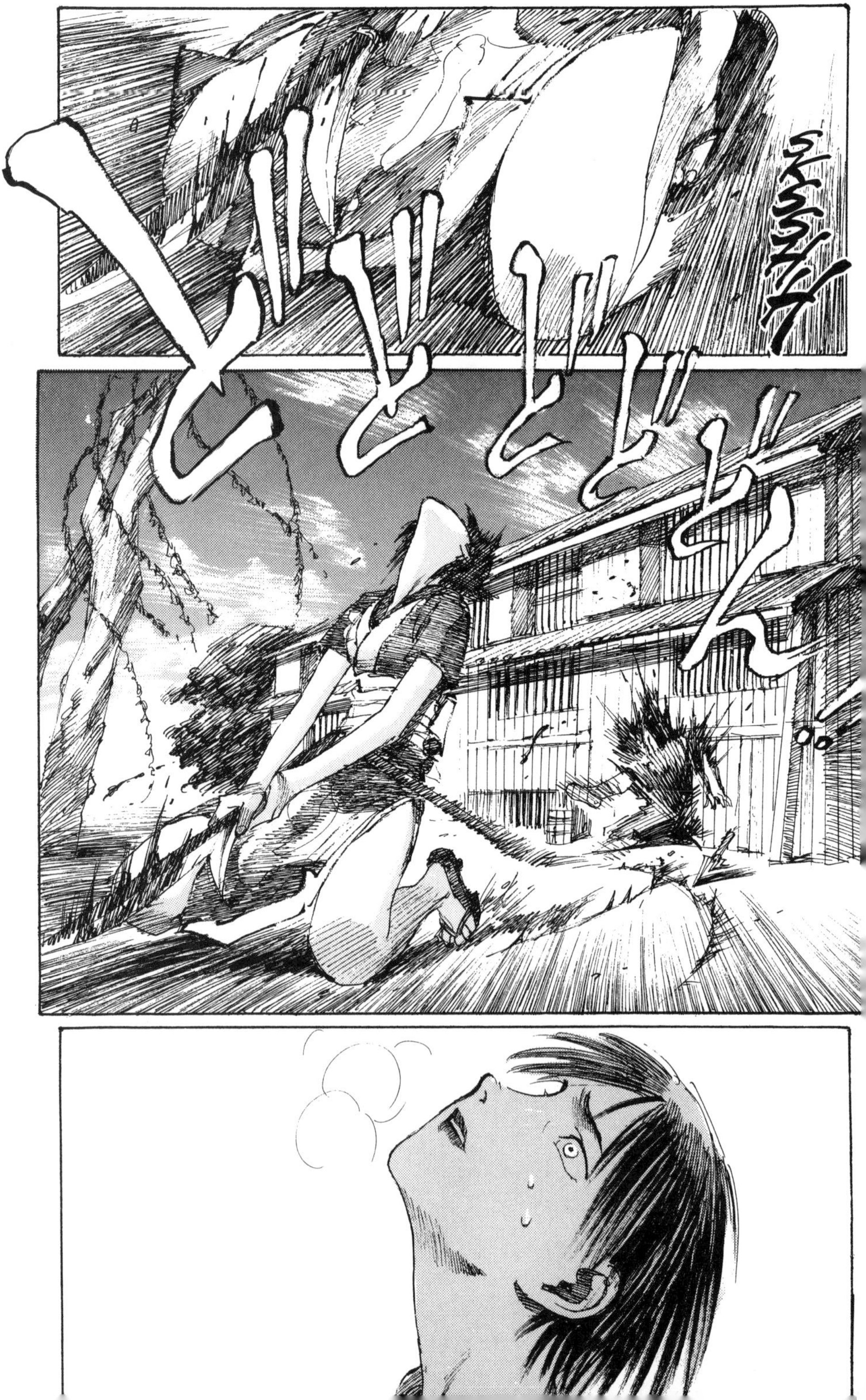
どどどどどん

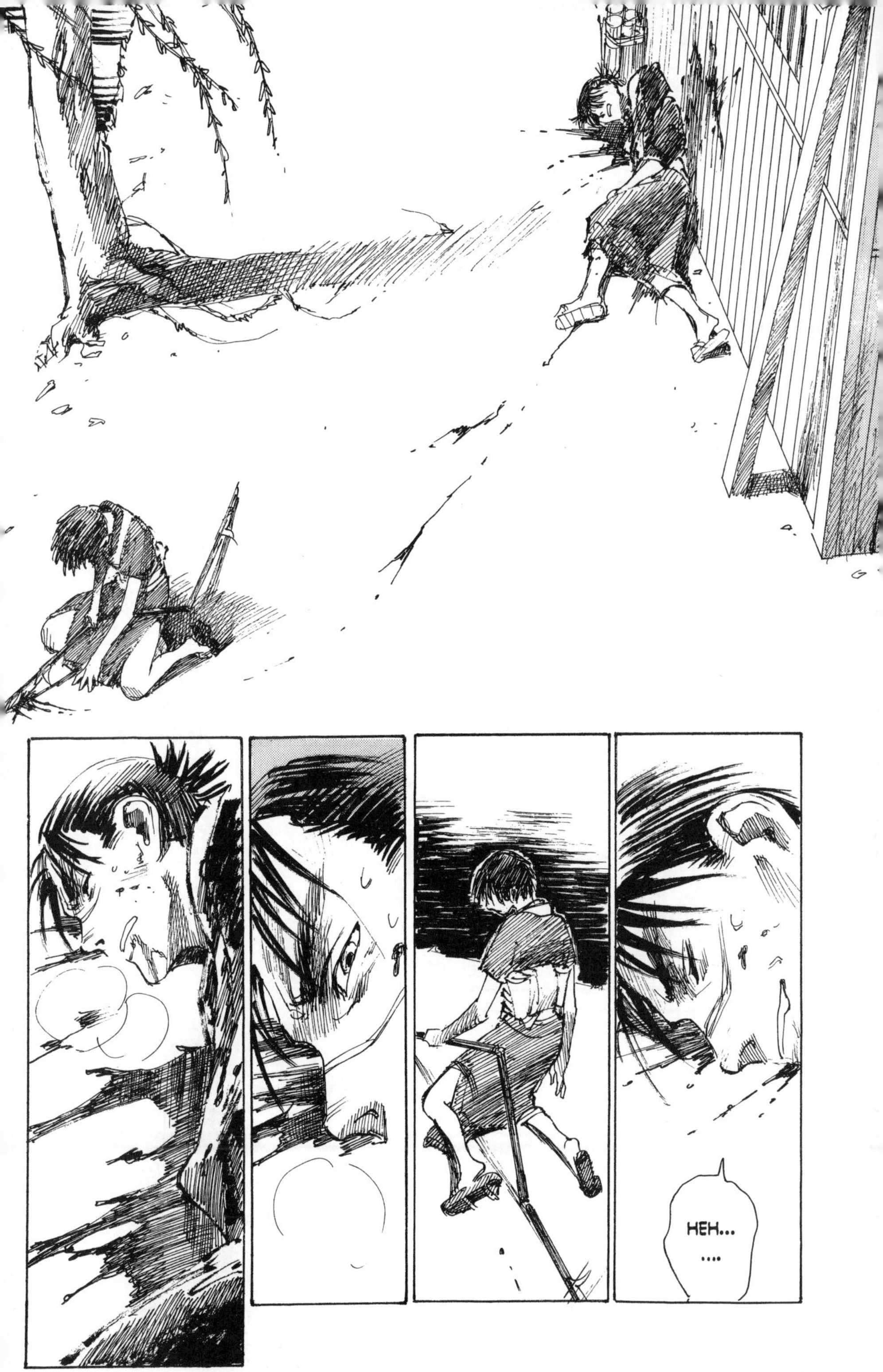
HEH...
....

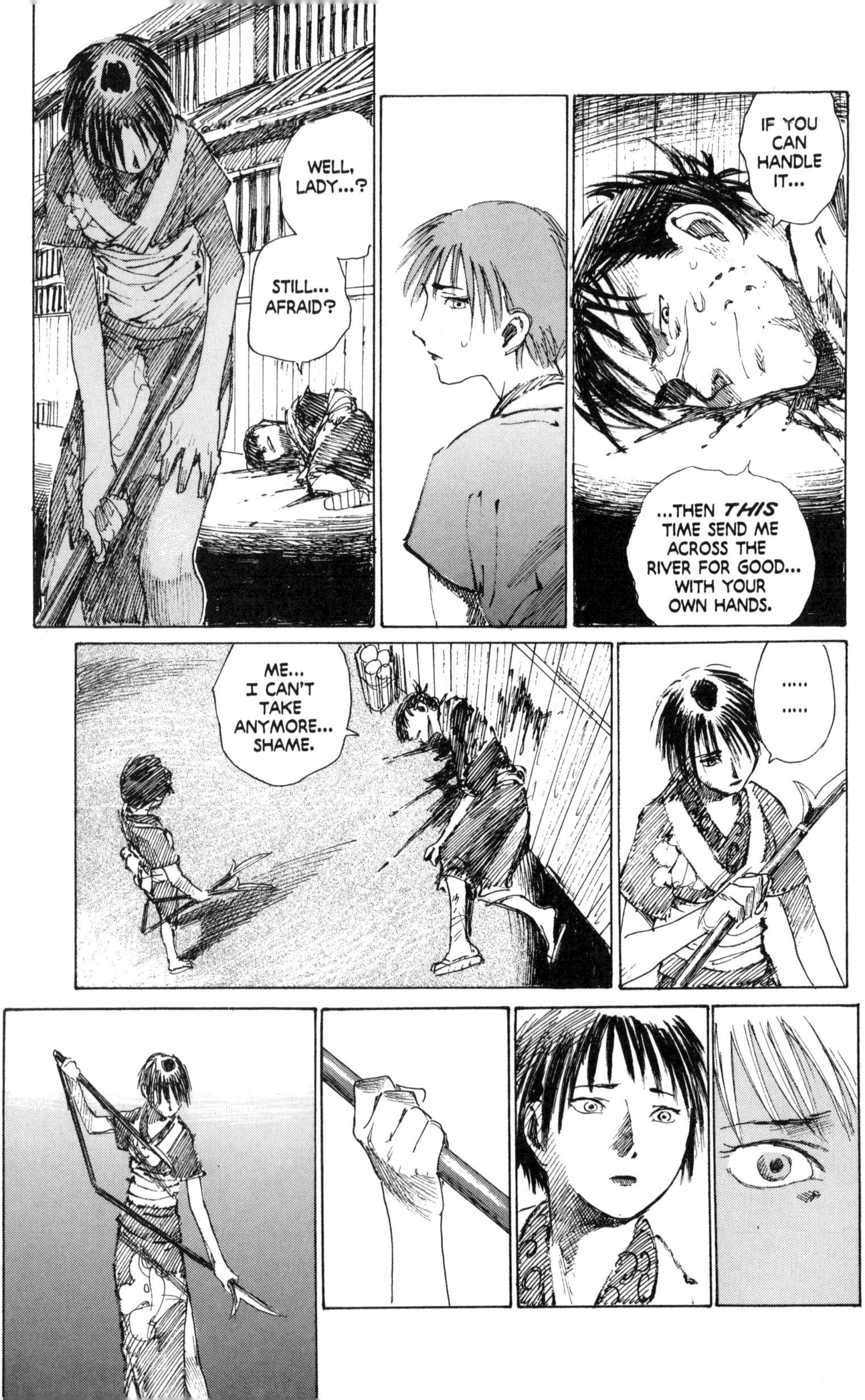
WELL, LADY...?
STILL... AFRAID?
IF YOU CAN HANDLE IT...
...THEN *THIS* TIME SEND ME ACROSS THE RIVER FOR GOOD... WITH YOUR OWN HANDS.
ME... I CAN'T TAKE ANYMORE... SHAME.
.....
.....

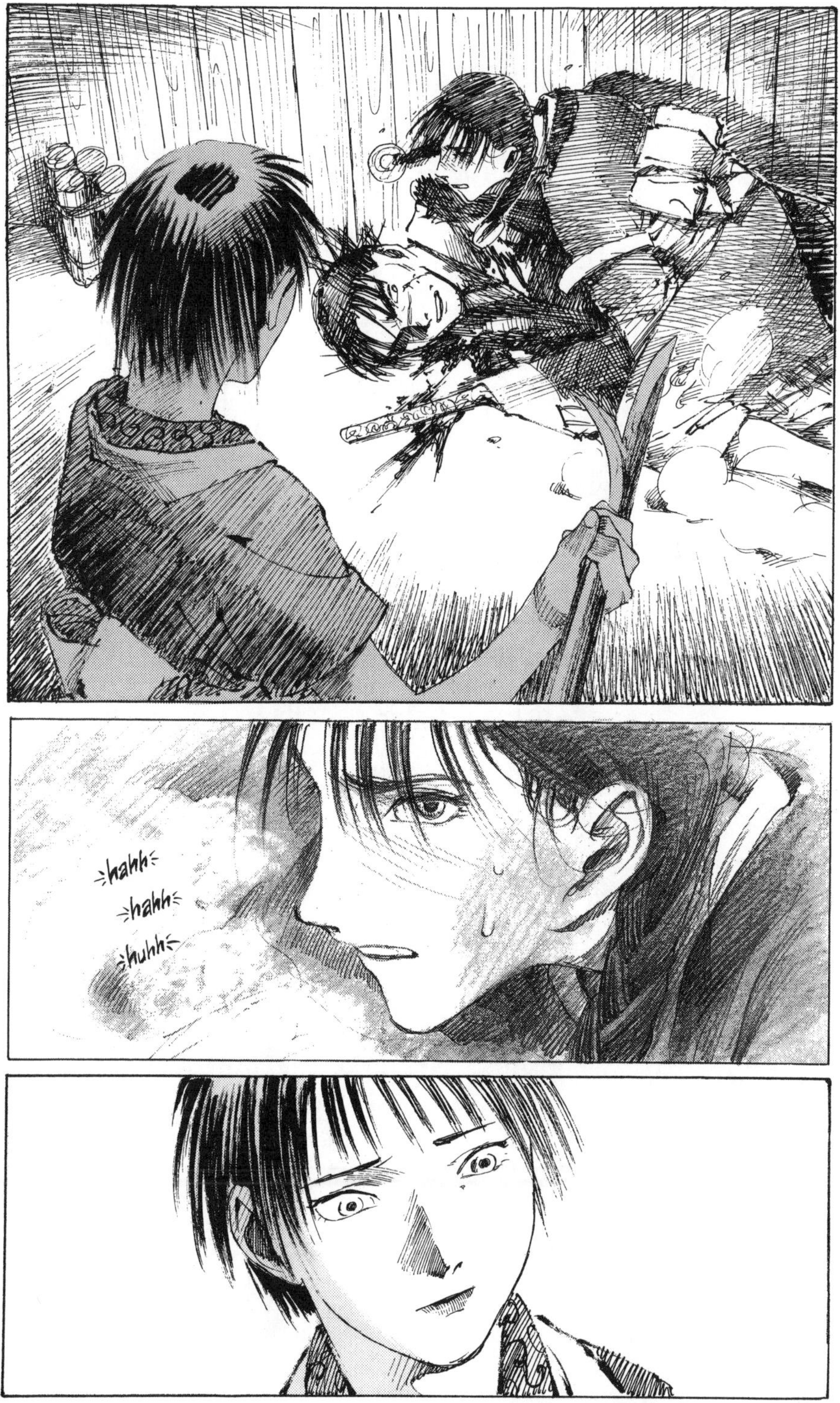
hahh
hahh
huhh

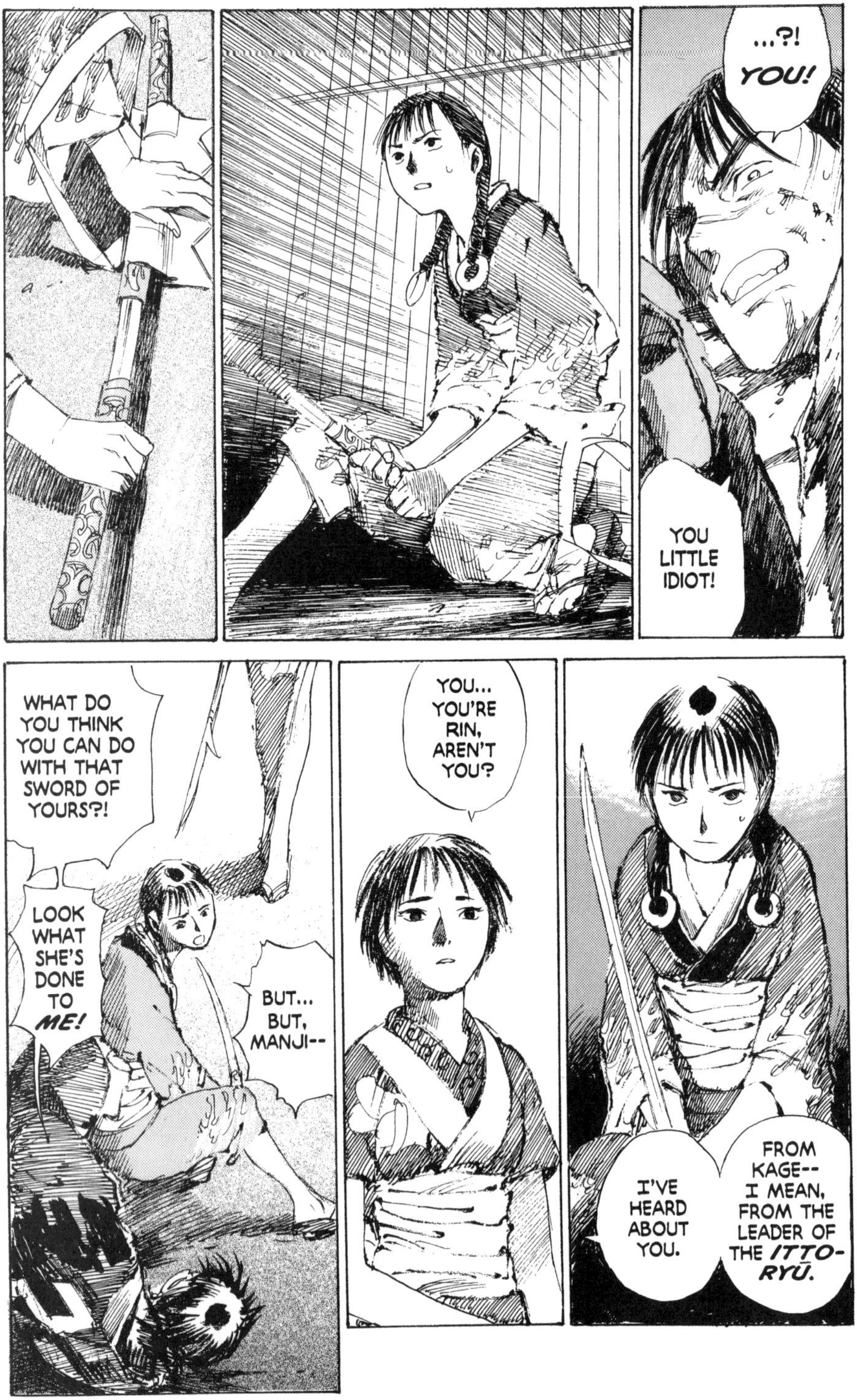
...?!
YOU!
YOU LITTLE IDIOT!
WHAT DO YOU THINK YOU CAN DO WITH THAT SWORD OF YOURS?!
LOOK WHAT SHE'S DONE TO ME!
BUT... BUT, MANJI--
YOU... YOU'RE RIN, AREN'T YOU?
I'VE HEARD ABOUT YOU.
FROM KAGE-- I MEAN, FROM THE LEADER OF THE ITTO-RYŪ.

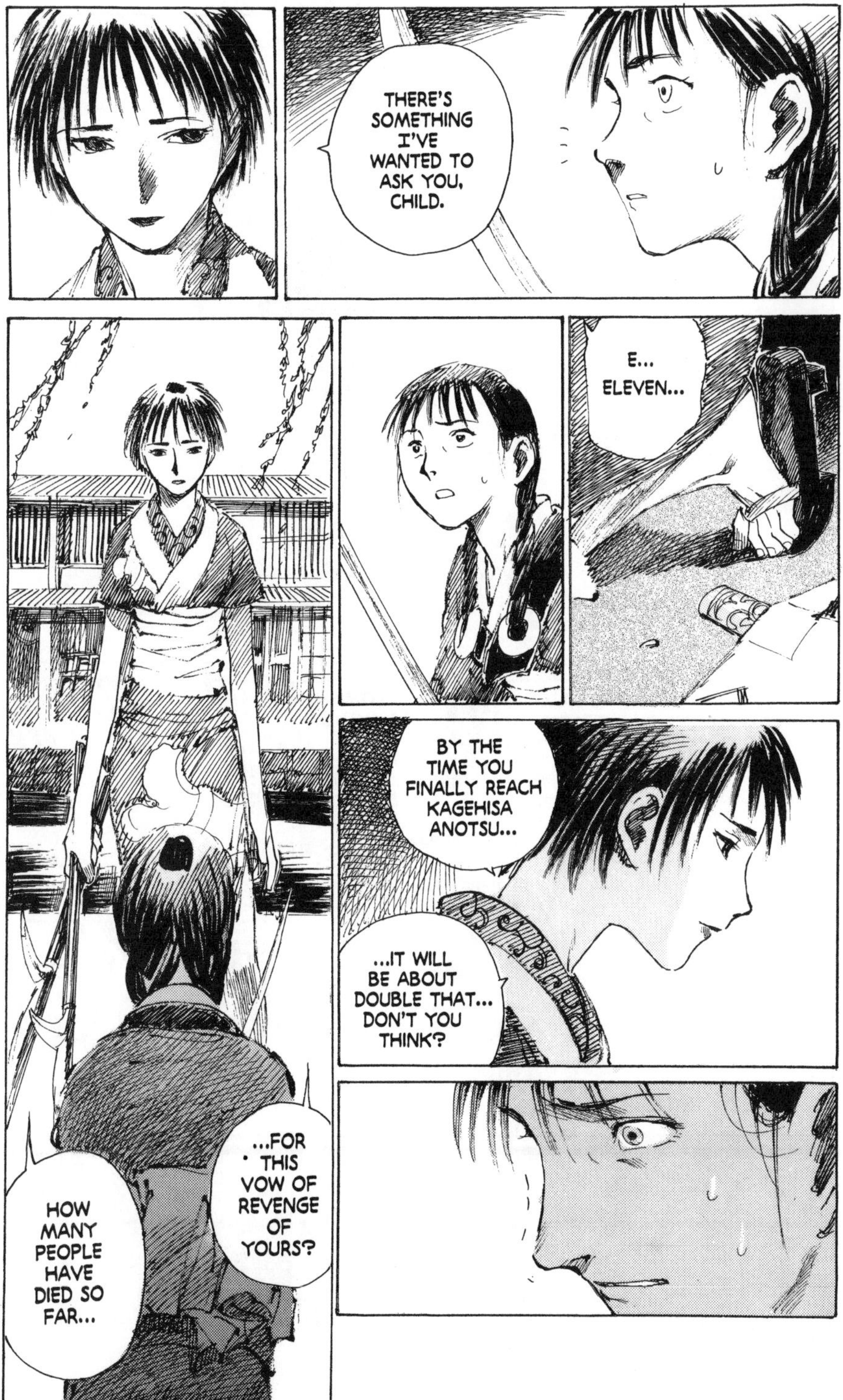
THERE'S SOMETHING I'VE WANTED TO ASK YOU, CHILD.
HOW MANY PEOPLE HAVE DIED SO FAR...
...FOR THIS VOW OF REVENGE OF YOURS?
E... ELEVEN...
BY THE TIME YOU FINALLY REACH KAGEHISA ANOTSU...
...IT WILL BE ABOUT DOUBLE THAT... DON'T YOU THINK?

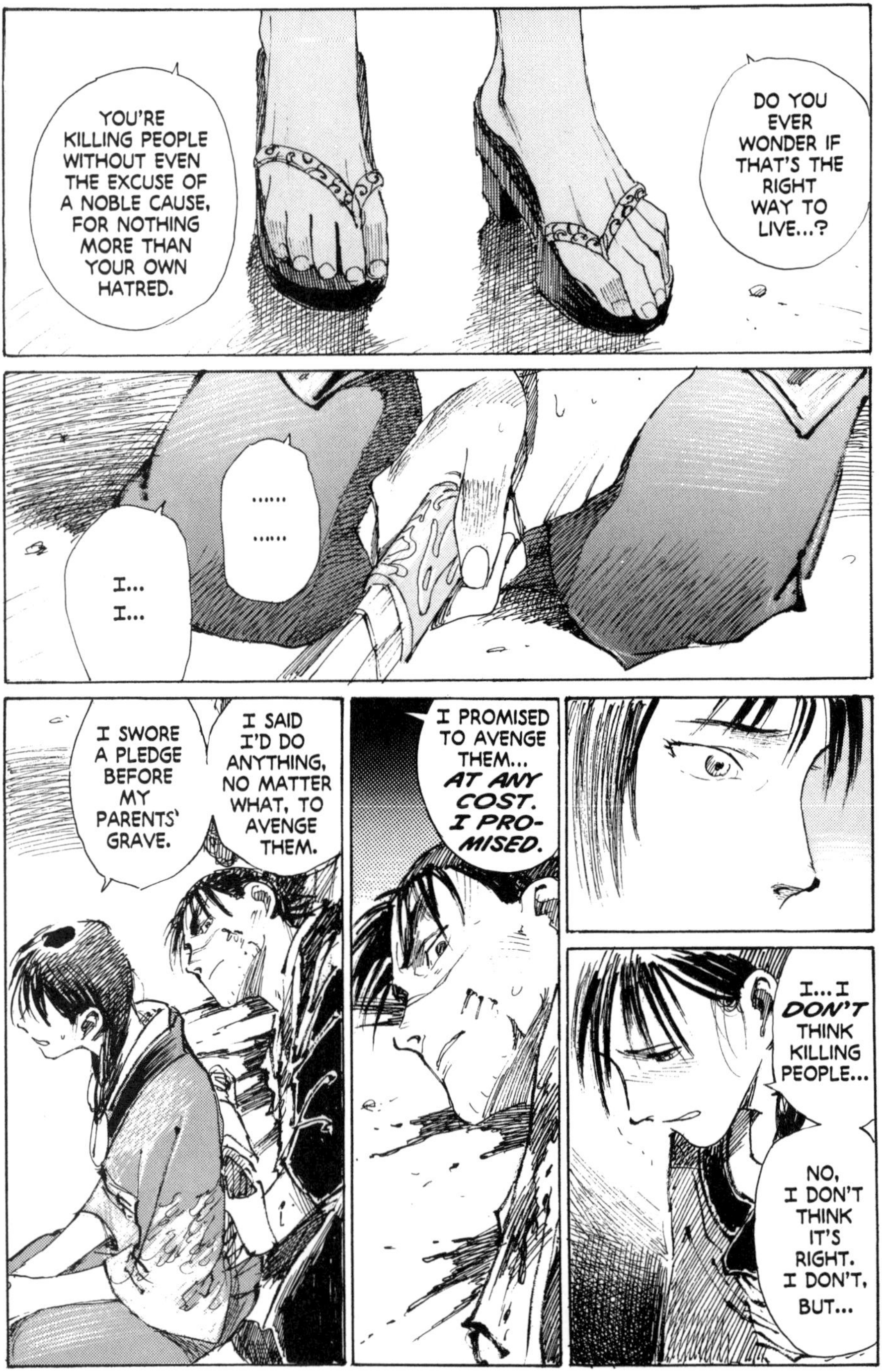
YOU'RE KILLING PEOPLE WITHOUT EVEN THE EXCUSE OF A NOBLE CAUSE, FOR NOTHING MORE THAN YOUR OWN HATRED.
DO YOU EVER WONDER IF THAT'S THE RIGHT WAY TO LIVE...?
I... I...
....
I SWORE A PLEDGE BEFORE MY PARENTS' GRAVE.
I SAID I'D DO ANYTHING, NO MATTER WHAT, TO AVENGE THEM.
I PROMISED TO AVENGE THEM... *AT ANY COST. I PROMISED.*
I...I *DON'T* THINK KILLING PEOPLE...
NO, I DON'T THINK IT'S RIGHT. I DON'T, BUT...

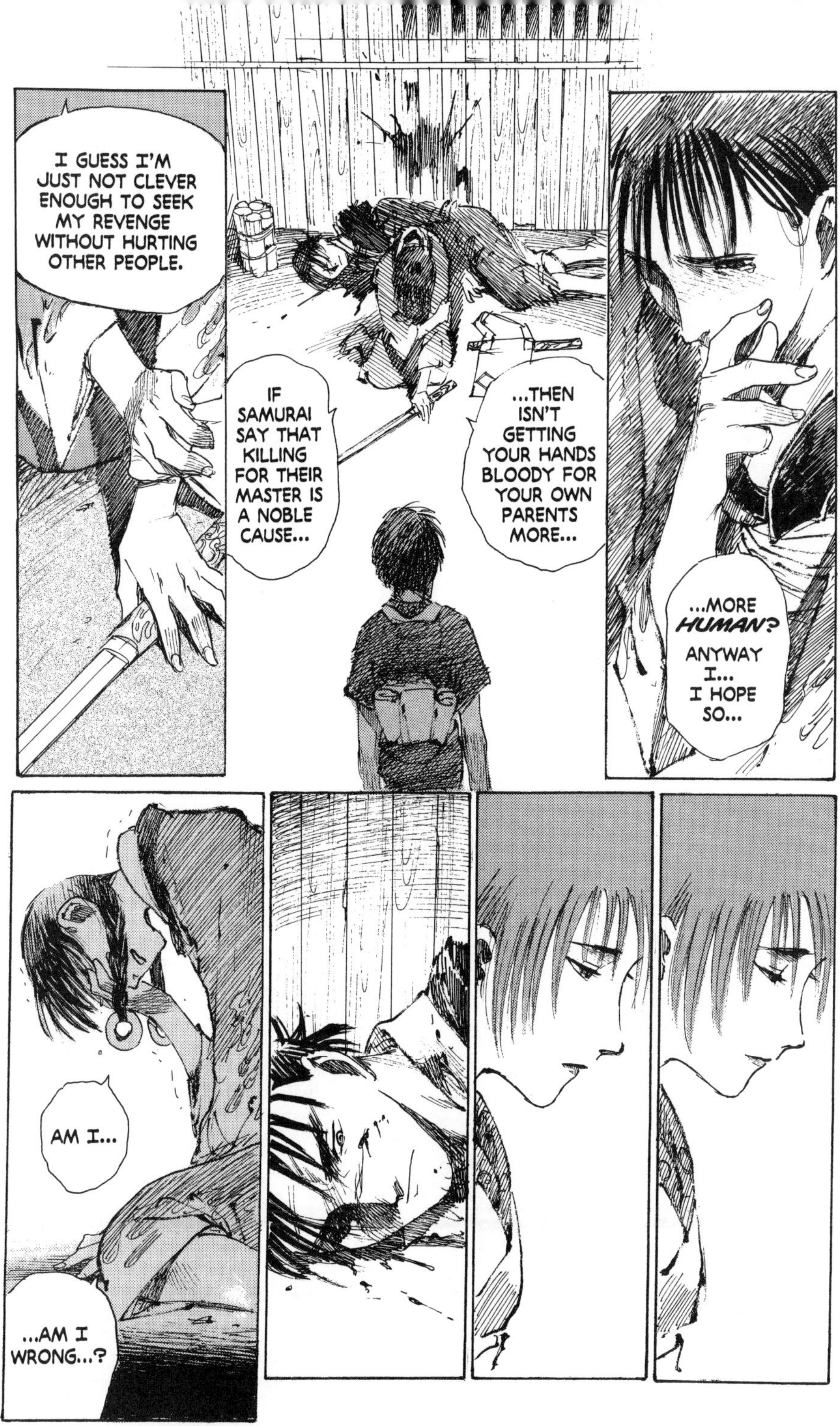
I GUESS I'M JUST NOT CLEVER ENOUGH TO SEEK MY REVENGE WITHOUT HURTING OTHER PEOPLE.
IF SAMURAI SAY THAT KILLING FOR THEIR MASTER IS A NOBLE CAUSE...
...THEN ISN'T GETTING YOUR HANDS BLOODY FOR YOUR OWN PARENTS MORE...
...MORE *HUMAN?* ANYWAY I... I HOPE SO...
AM I...
...AM I WRONG...?

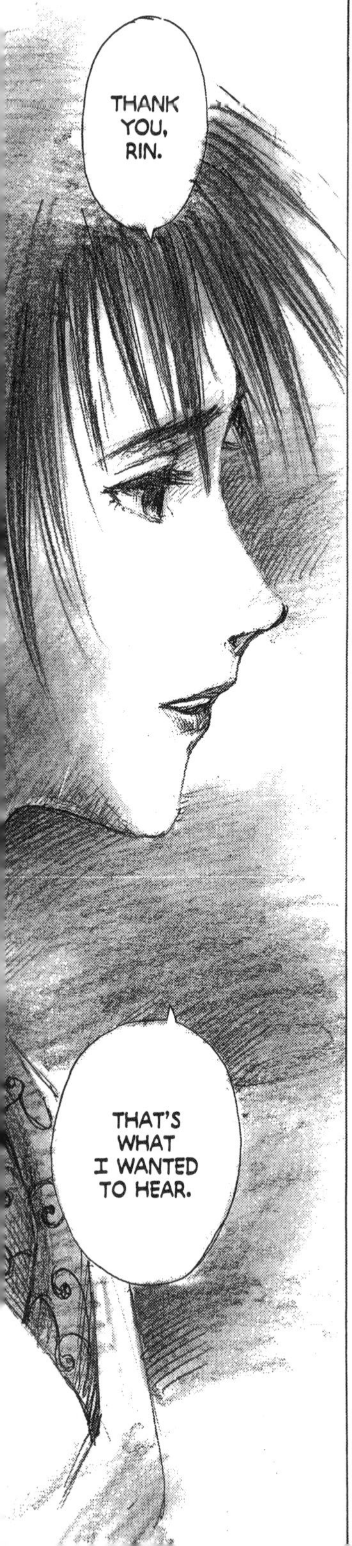
THANK YOU, RIN.
THAT'S WHAT I WANTED TO HEAR.
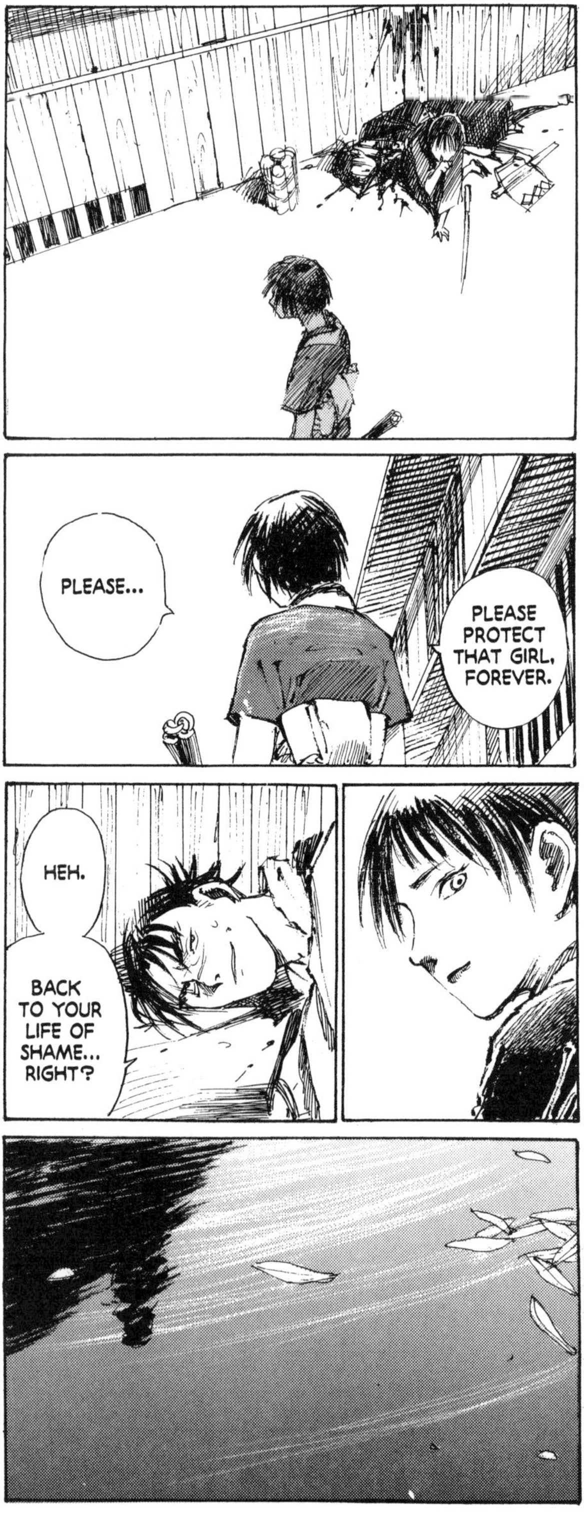
PLEASE...
PLEASE PROTECT THAT GIRL, FOREVER.
HEH.
BACK TO YOUR LIFE OF SHAME... RIGHT?

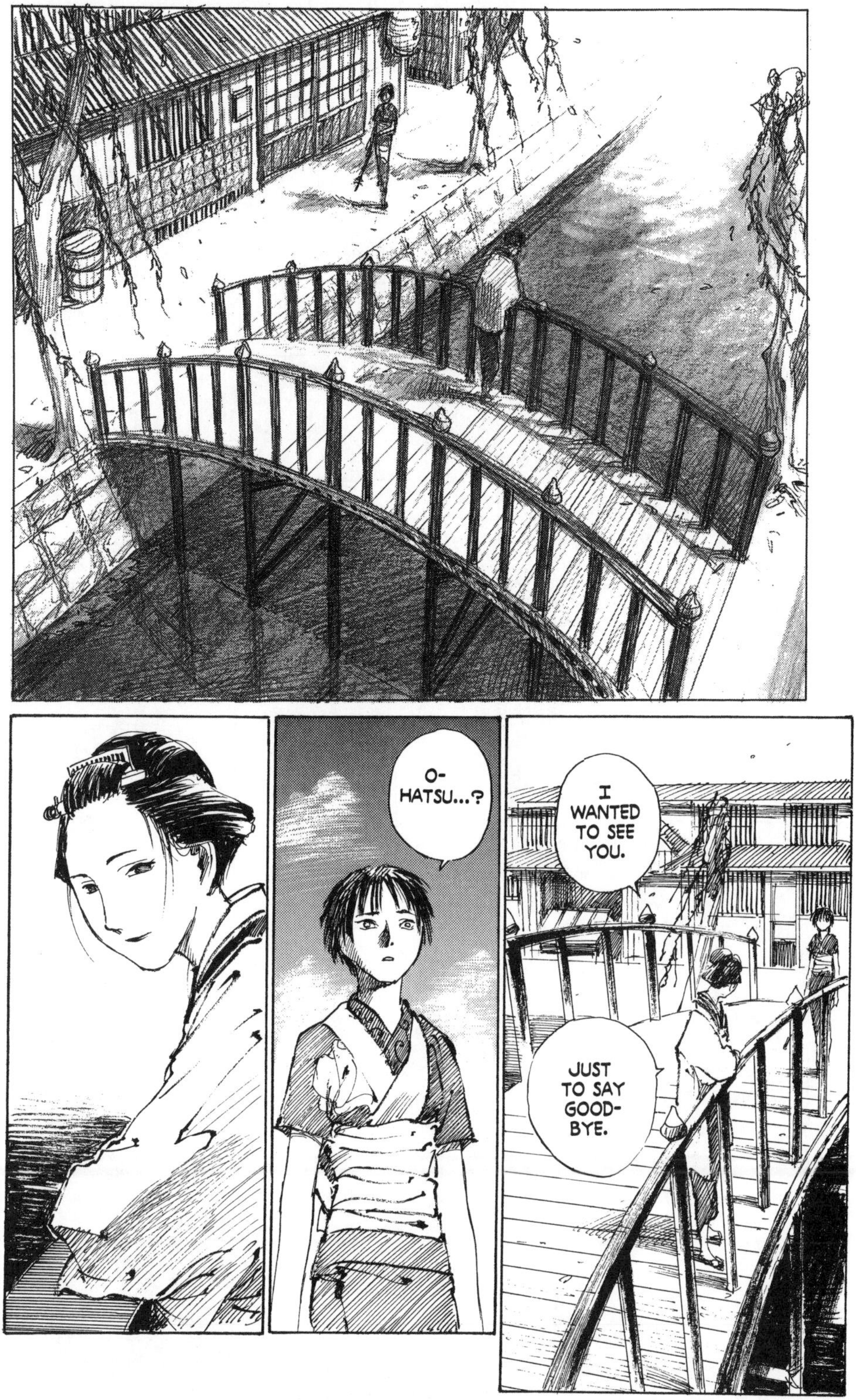
O-HATSU...?
I WANTED TO SEE YOU.
JUST TO SAY GOOD-BYE.

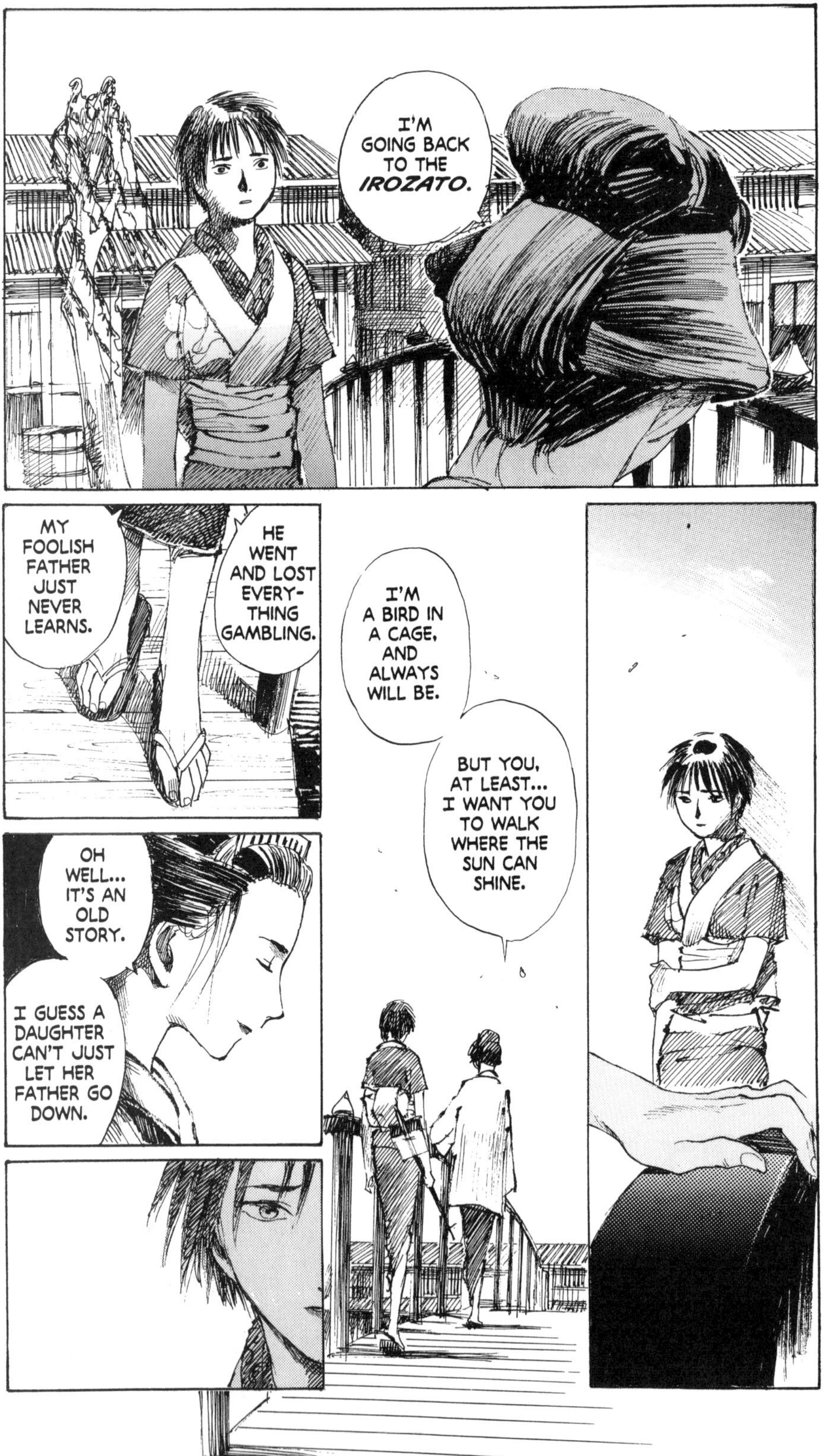
I'M GOING BACK TO THE *IROZATO*.
MY FOOLISH FATHER JUST NEVER LEARNS.
HE WENT AND LOST EVERY-THING GAMBLING.
OH WELL... IT'S AN OLD STORY.
I GUESS A DAUGHTER CAN'T JUST LET HER FATHER GO DOWN.
I'M A BIRD IN A CAGE, AND ALWAYS WILL BE.
BUT YOU, AT LEAST... I WANT YOU TO WALK WHERE THE SUN CAN SHINE.

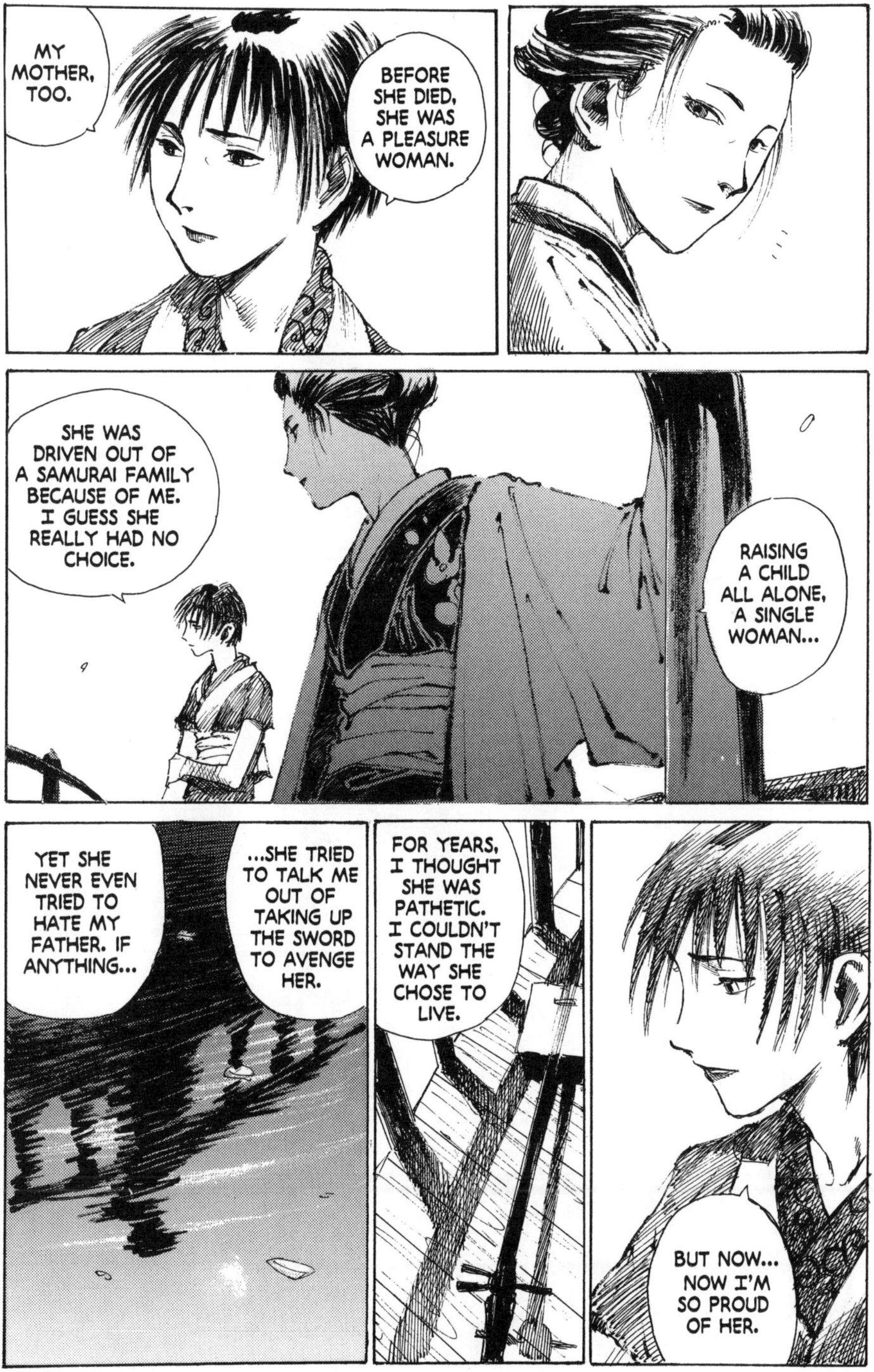
MY MOTHER, TOO.
BEFORE SHE DIED, SHE WAS A PLEASURE WOMAN.
SHE WAS DRIVEN OUT OF A SAMURAI FAMILY BECAUSE OF ME. I GUESS SHE REALLY HAD NO CHOICE.
RAISING A CHILD ALL ALONE, A SINGLE WOMAN...
YET SHE NEVER EVEN TRIED TO HATE MY FATHER. IF ANYTHING...
...SHE TRIED TO TALK ME OUT OF TAKING UP THE SWORD TO AVENGE HER.
FOR YEARS, I THOUGHT SHE WAS PATHETIC. I COULDN'T STAND THE WAY SHE CHOSE TO LIVE.
BUT NOW... NOW I'M SO PROUD OF HER.

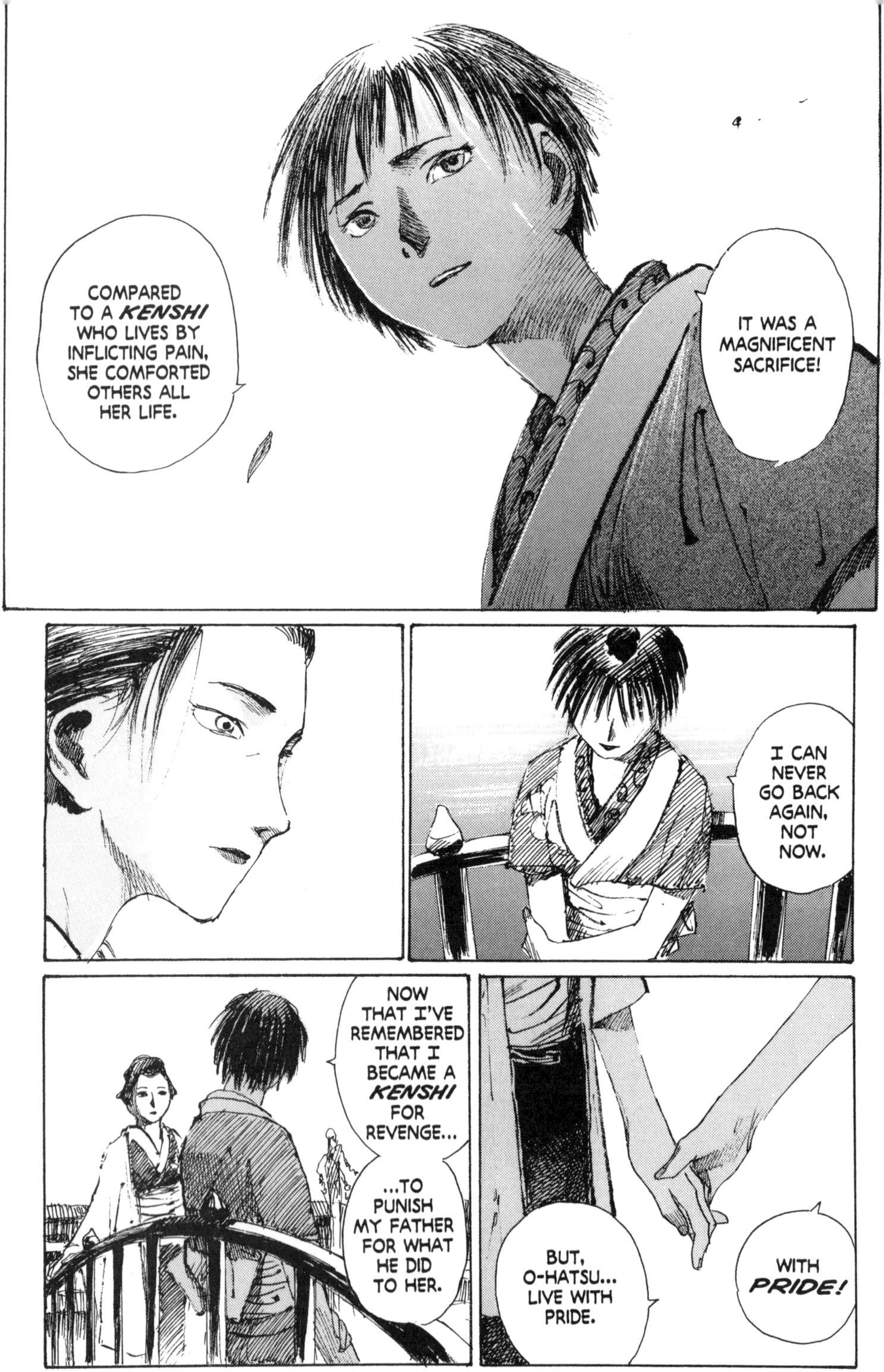
COMPARED TO A *KENSHI* WHO LIVES BY INFLICTING PAIN, SHE COMFORTED OTHERS ALL HER LIFE.
IT WAS A MAGNIFICENT SACRIFICE!
I CAN NEVER GO BACK AGAIN, NOT NOW.
NOW THAT I'VE REMEMBERED THAT I BECAME A *KENSHI* FOR REVENGE...
...TO PUNISH MY FATHER FOR WHAT HE DID TO HER.
BUT, O-HATSU... LIVE WITH PRIDE.
WITH *PRIDE!*

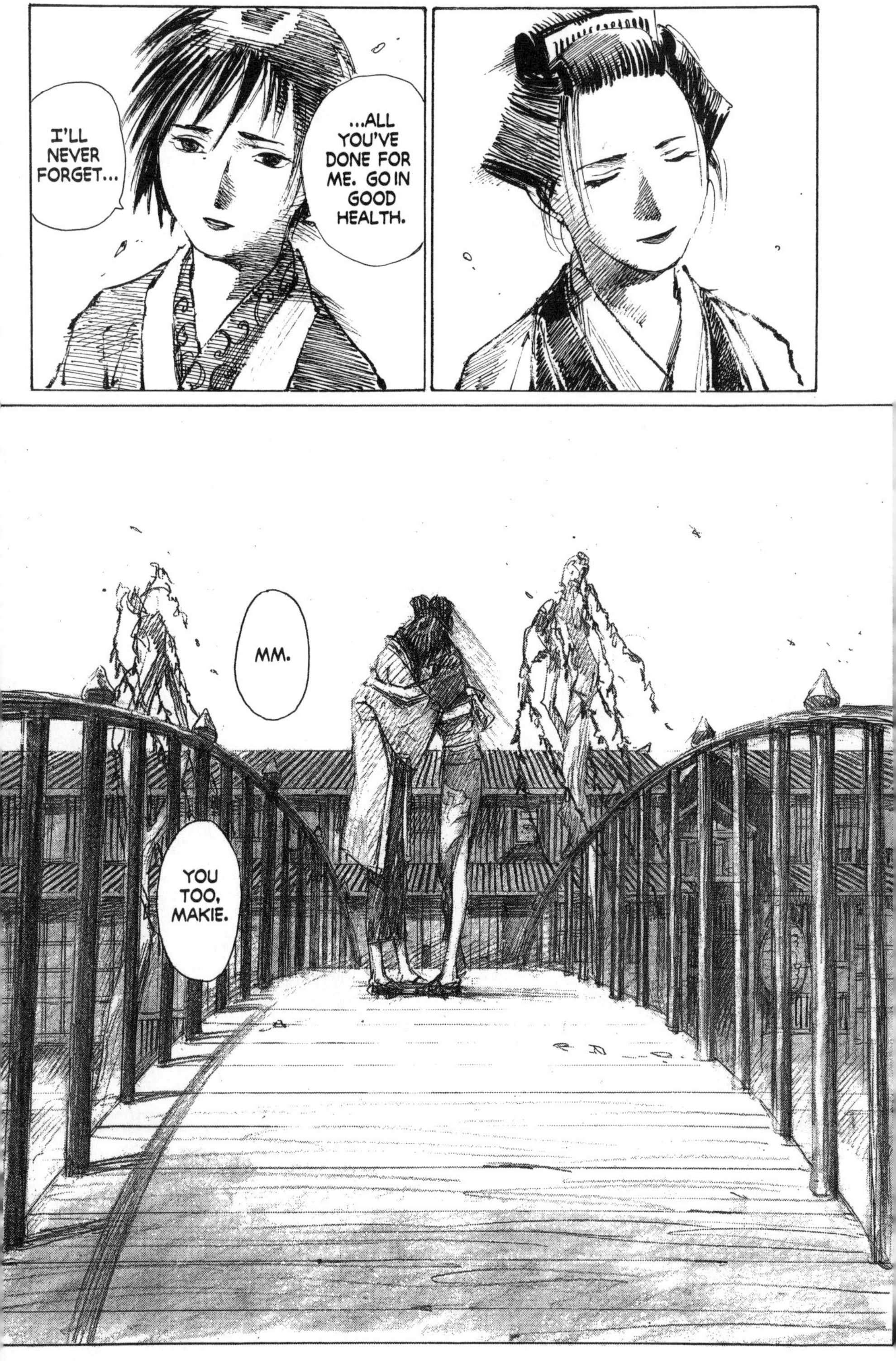
I'LL NEVER FORGET...
...ALL YOU'VE DONE FOR ME. GO IN GOOD HEALTH.
MM.
YOU TOO, MAKIE.

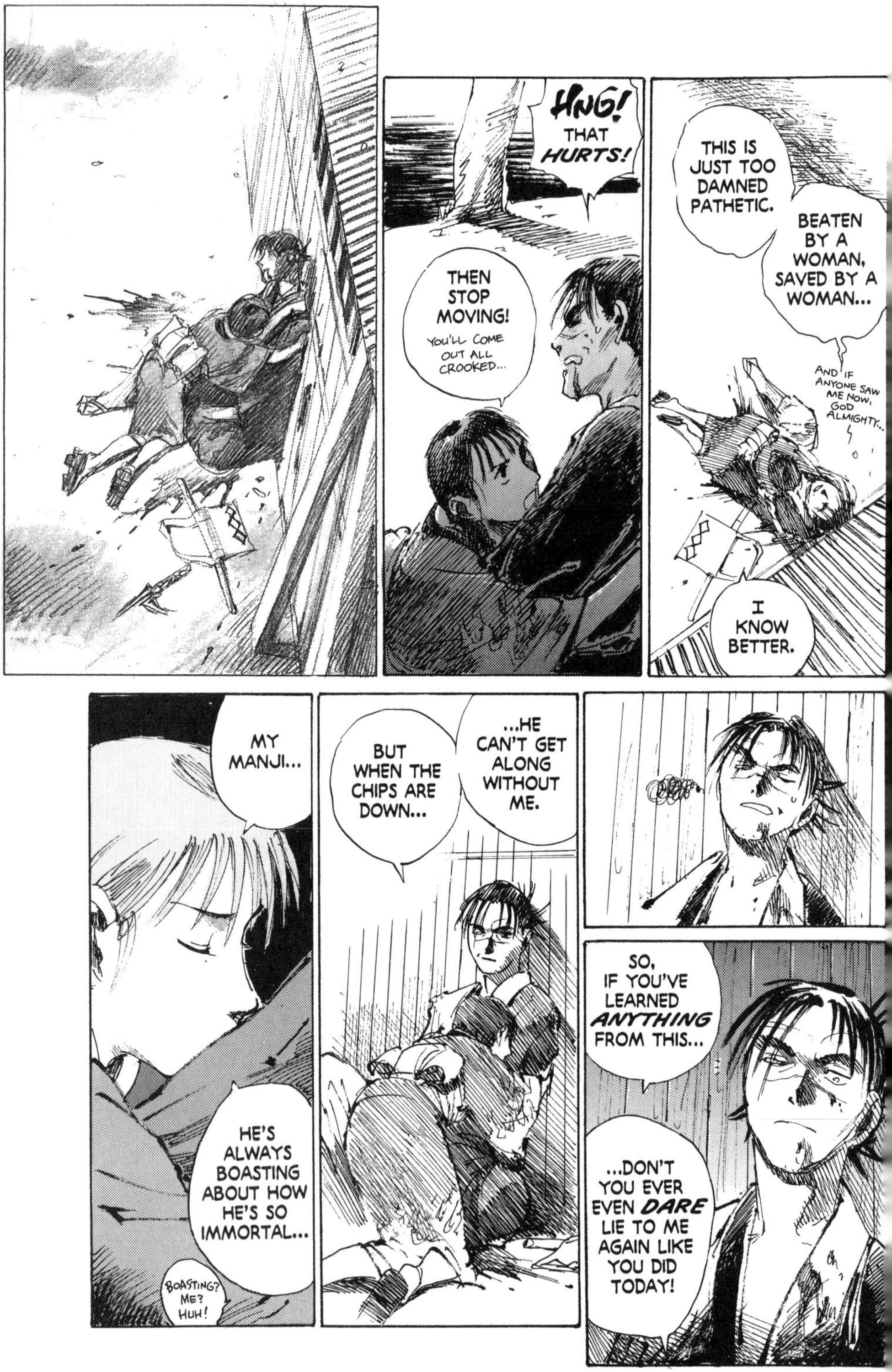
HNG! THAT HURTS!
THEN STOP MOVING!
YOU'LL COME OUT ALL CROOKED...
THIS IS JUST TOO DAMNED PATHETIC.
BEATEN BY A WOMAN, SAVED BY A WOMAN...
AND IF ANYONE SAW ME NOW, GOD ALMIGHTY...
I KNOW BETTER.
MY MANJI...
HE'S ALWAYS BOASTING ABOUT HOW HE'S SO IMMORTAL...
BOASTING? ME? HUH!
BUT WHEN THE CHIPS ARE DOWN...
...HE CAN'T GET ALONG WITHOUT ME.
SO, IF YOU'VE LEARNED ANYTHING FROM THIS...
...DON'T YOU EVER EVEN DARE LIE TO ME AGAIN LIKE YOU DID TODAY!

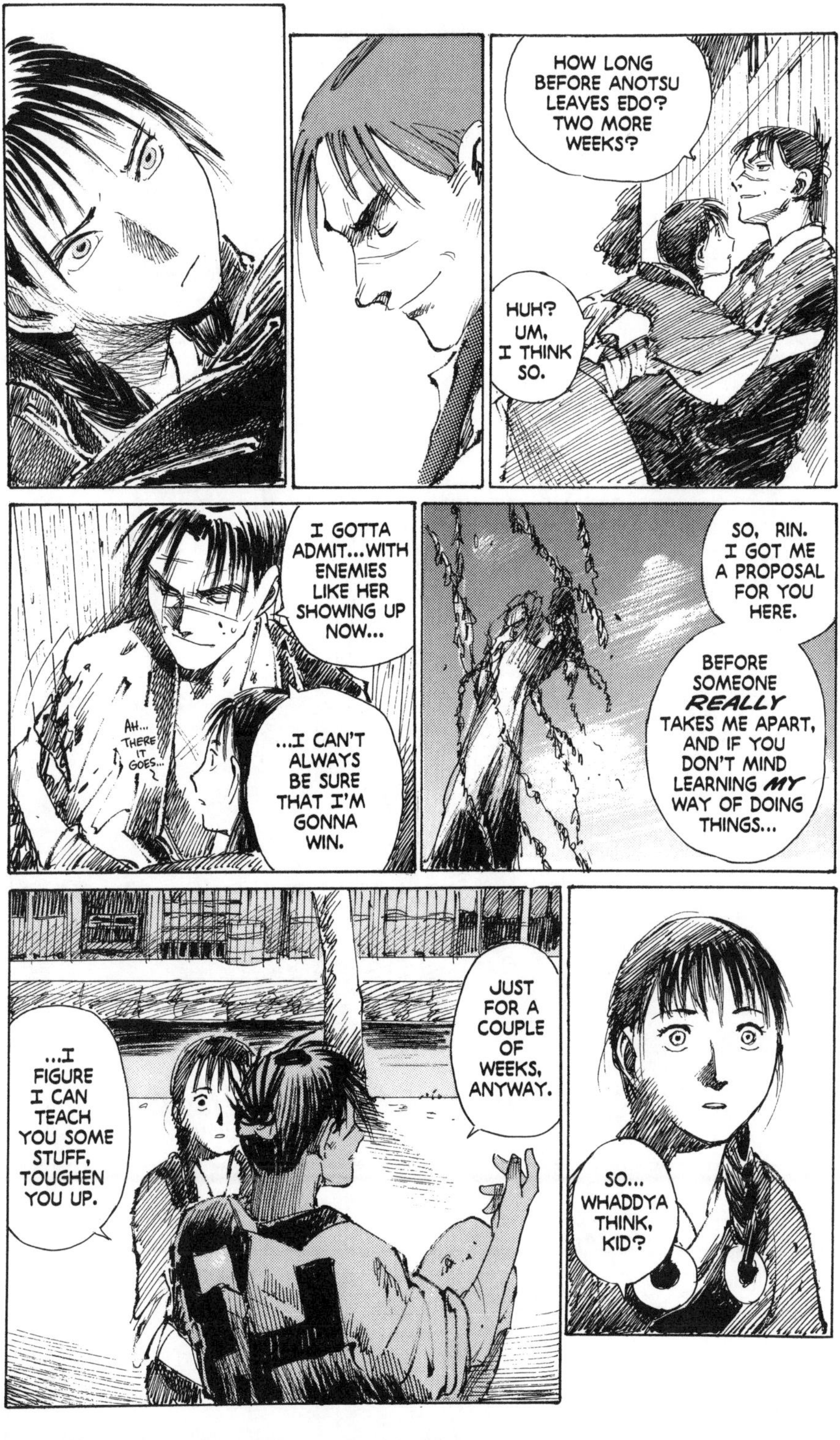
HOW LONG BEFORE ANOTSU LEAVES EDO? TWO MORE WEEKS?
HUH? UM, I THINK SO.
I GOTTA ADMIT...WITH ENEMIES LIKE HER SHOWING UP NOW...
AH... THERE IT GOES...
...I CAN'T ALWAYS BE SURE THAT I'M GONNA WIN.
SO, RIN. I GOT ME A PROPOSAL FOR YOU HERE.
BEFORE SOMEONE *REALLY* TAKES ME APART, AND IF YOU DON'T MIND LEARNING *MY* WAY OF DOING THINGS...
...I FIGURE I CAN TEACH YOU SOME STUFF, TOUGHEN YOU UP.
JUST FOR A COUPLE OF WEEKS, ANYWAY.
SO... WHADDYA THINK, KID?

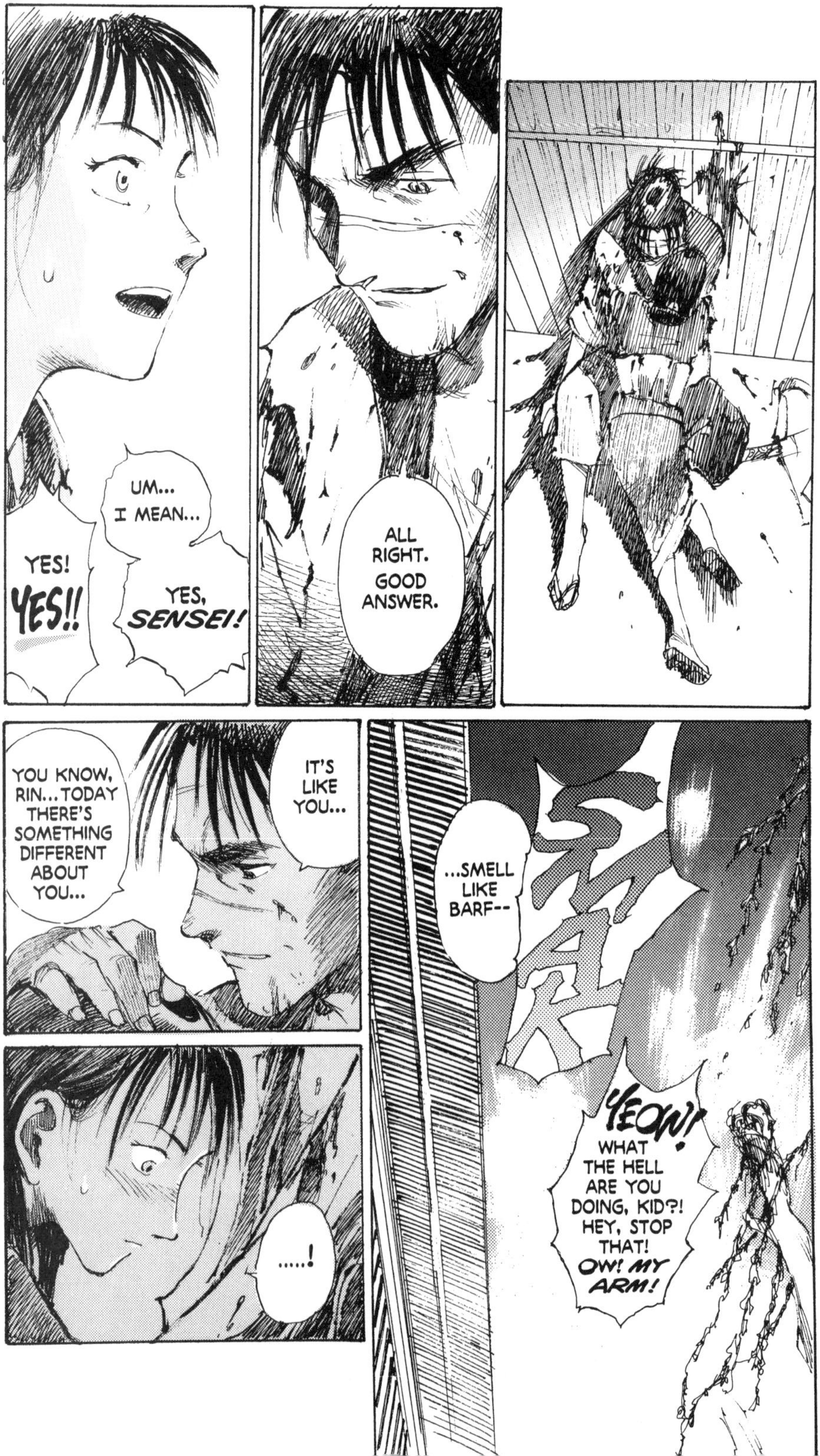
UM... I MEAN...
YES! YES!!
YES, SENSEI!
ALL RIGHT. GOOD ANSWER.
YOU KNOW, RIN... TODAY THERE'S SOMETHING DIFFERENT ABOUT YOU...
IT'S LIKE YOU...
.....!
...SMELL LIKE BARF--
YEOW!
WHAT THE HELL ARE YOU DOING, KID?! HEY, STOP THAT! OW! MY ARM!

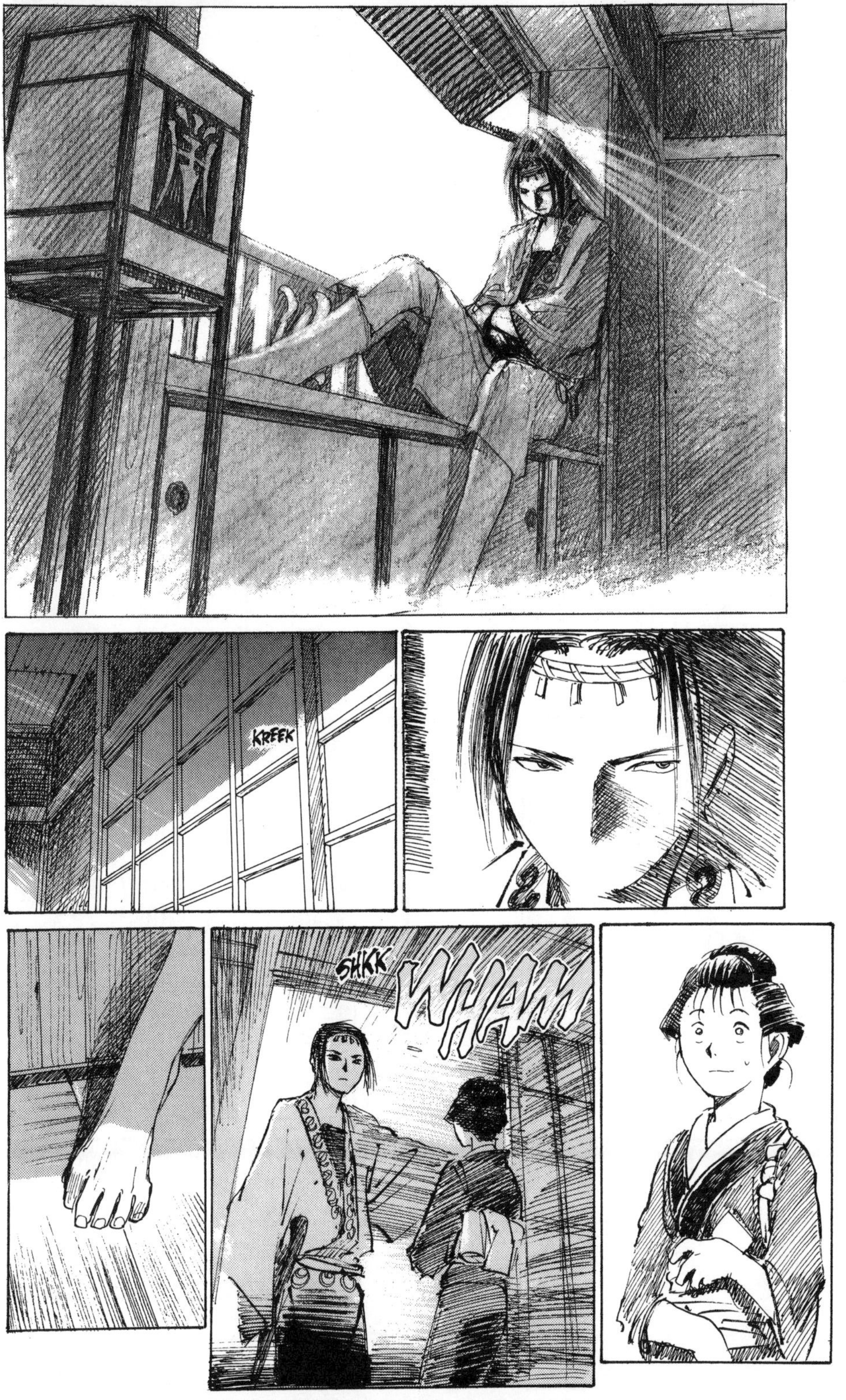
KREEK
SHKK
WHAM

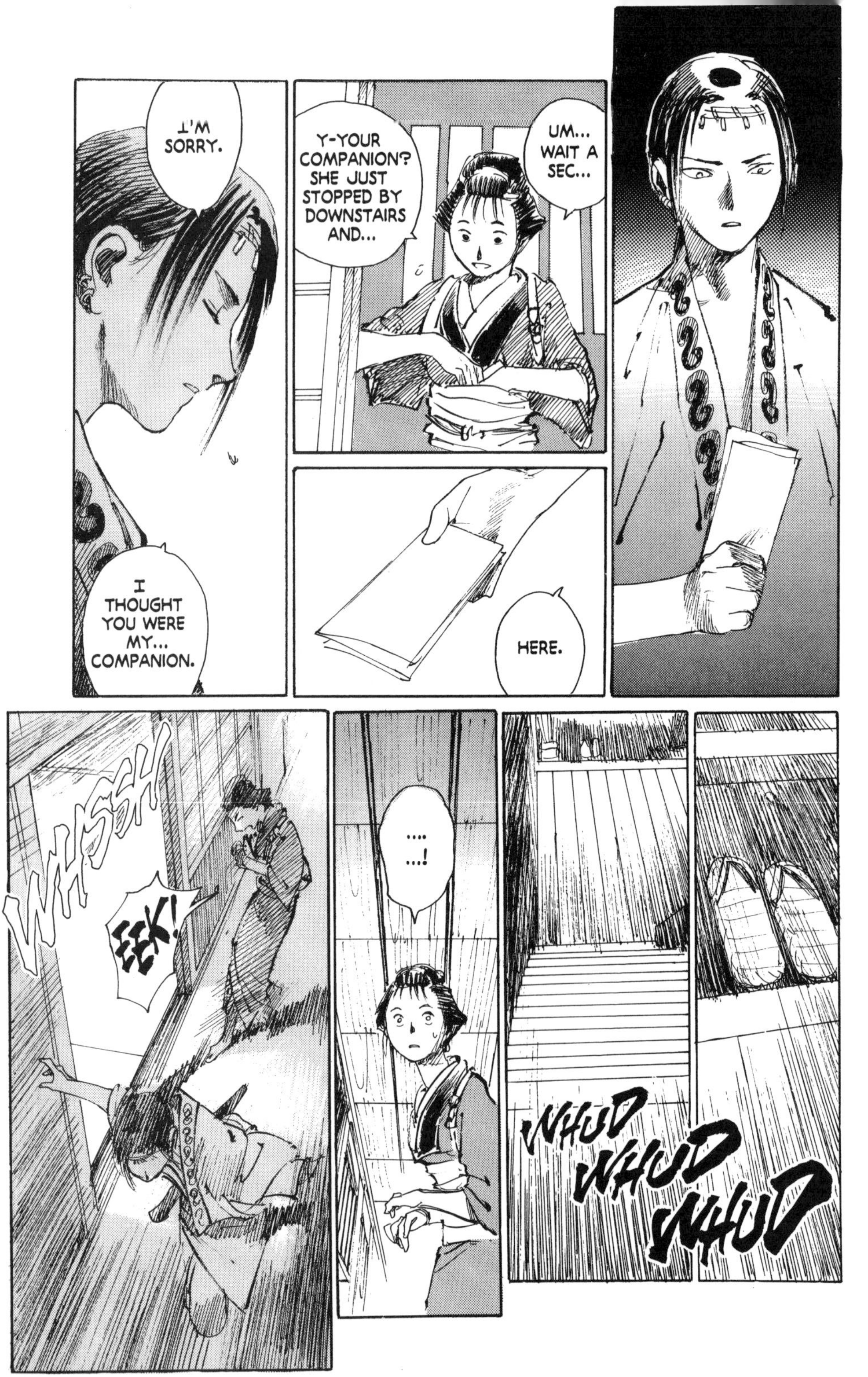
I'M SORRY.
I THOUGHT YOU WERE MY... COMPANION.
Y-YOUR COMPANION? SHE JUST STOPPED BY DOWNSTAIRS AND...
UM... WAIT A SEC...
HERE.
WHSSH
EEK!
....!
WHUD WHUD WHUD

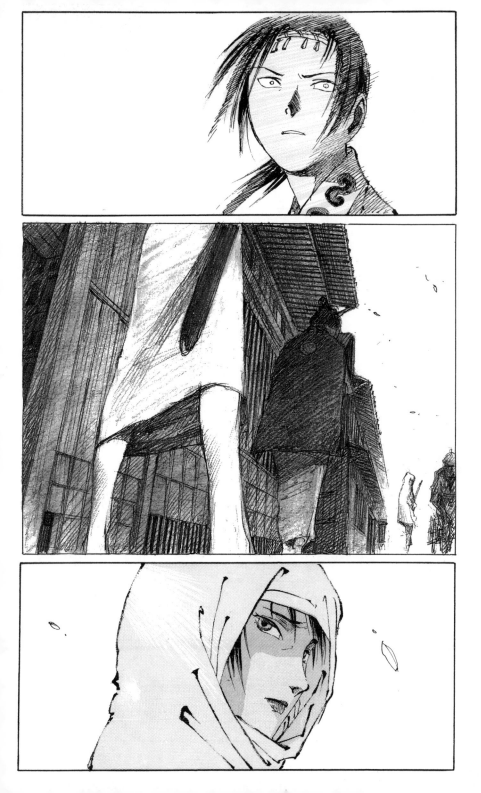

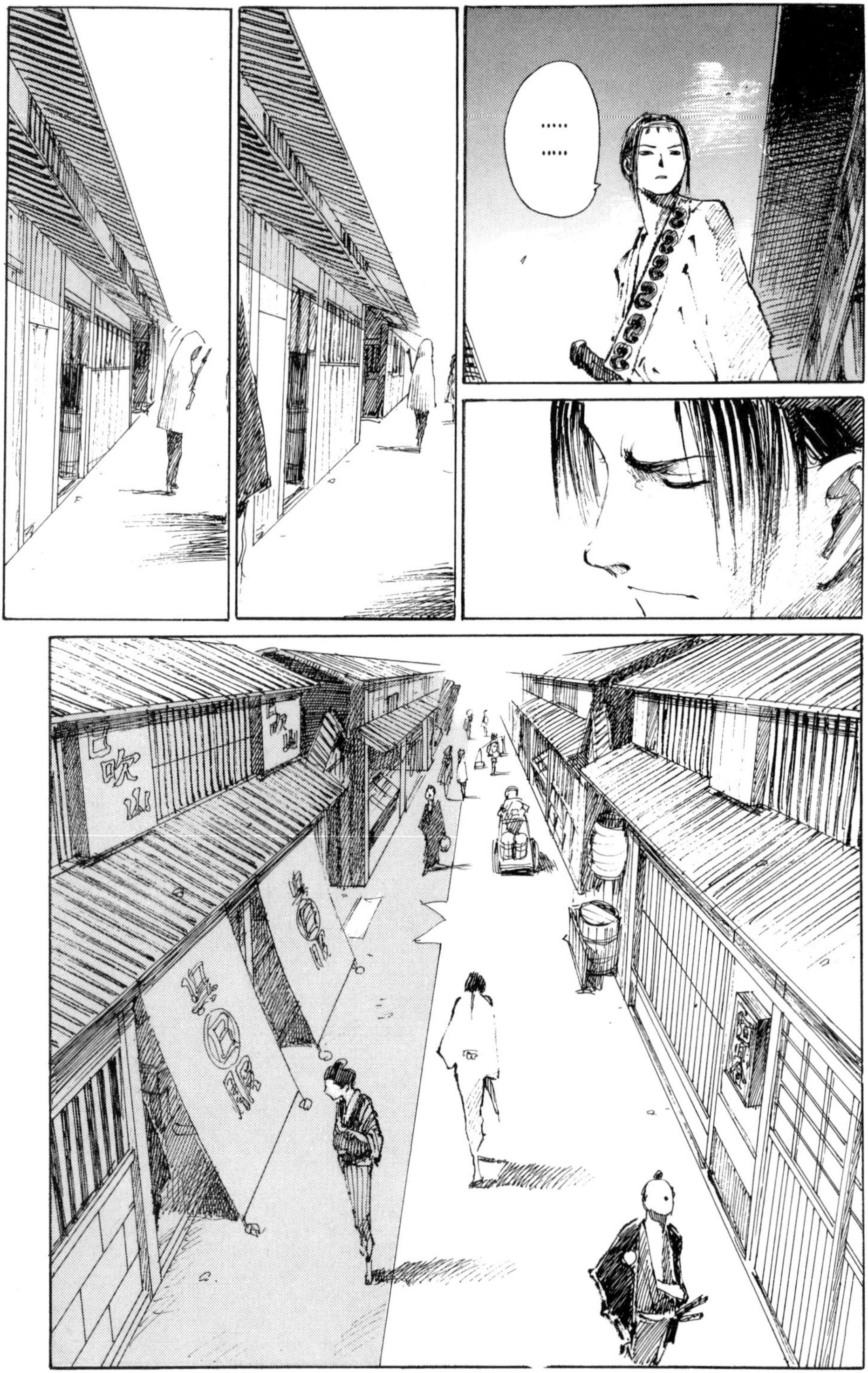
……
……